D0339189

Medieval Europe:
a short history

about the author...

Warren Hollister is Professor of History at the University of California, Santa Barbara. He is a Fellow of the Royal Historical Society, past president of the Pacific Coast Conference on British Studies, and former Visiting Research Fellow of Merton College, Oxford. The author of many books and scholarly articles on medieval history, he has been honored with Guggenheim and Fulbright Fellowships and has lectured at such universities as Cambridge, Oxford, Ghent, Leyden, Utrecht, London, and Bologna. In 1970 he was the American Historical Association's representative in medieval history to the Thirteenth International Congress of Historical Sciences, Moscow, USSR. Among his other honors are the Triennial Book Prize of the Conference on British Studies and the E. Harris Harbison Award for Distinguished Teaching.

C. Warren Hollister

Medieval Europe

a short history

3rd edition

John Wiley & Sons, Inc.
new york, london, sydney, toronto

Copyright © 1964, 1968, 1974, by John Wiley & Sons, Inc.

All rights reserved. Published simultaneously in Canada.

No part of this book may be reproduced by any means, nor transmitted, nor translated into a machine language without the written permission of the publisher.

Library of Congress Cataloging in Publication Data:

Hollister, Charles Warren.
    Medieval Europe: a short history.

    Includes bibliographies.
      1. Europe—History—476-1492. I. Title.
D117.H6   1974   940.1   73-13622
ISBN 0-471-40697-X
ISBN 0-471-40698-8 (pbk.)

Printed in the United States of America

10 9 8 7 6 5 4 3 2 1

to my parents

preface

This edition retains the basic goals of the two earlier editions. It is designed to be used as a core book; it aspires to be lively, unified, trustworthy, and brief. The text has been reexamined word by word and revised when necessary to incorporate new research and to achieve greater clarity. Major changes have been made in the treatment of Byzantium and Islam in order to describe more comprehensively the basic contributions and contours of these civilizations and their impact on Europe.

A number of instructors have been using this book in sequence with my *Roots of the Western Tradition: A Short History of the Ancient World.* The two books were conceived as a pair that together would cover the ancient and medieval worlds. But each of the two was designed to stand on its own as a survey of its respective era. Since courses in ancient history often conclude with A.D. 500, and since medieval courses often begin about A.D. 300, a certain amount of overlapping between the two books has been unavoidable. To compensate, instructors using both books should omit Chapters 1 and 2 of *Medieval Europe* from their reading assignments.

I am indebted to Professors Brian Tierney, Richard Dales, Robert Brentano, and Norman Cantor for their perceptive suggestions on various portions of the original edition, and to the more recent suggestions of instructors and students who have been using the book in their classes.

C. Warren Hollister

Santa Barbara, California, 1973

contents

List of Maps   xi
List of Illustrations   xiii
Introduction   1

Part I:
The Early Middle Ages

1. The Christian Empire   5
2. The Decline of Rome and
   the Germanic Invasions   14
3. Byzantium Endures   29
4. The Barbarian West   45
5. The Explosion of Islam   59
6. Carolingian Europe   74
7. The New Invasions   101
8. Europe Survives the Siege   112

Part II:
The High Middle Ages

9. Economic Revolution and
   New Frontiers   145
10. New Dimensions in
    Medieval Christianity   174
11. Empire and Papacy   196
12. England and France   225
13. Literature and Art   260
14. The World of Intellect   288

Part III:
The Late Middle Ages

15. *Church State in
    the 14th and 15th Centuries*   325
16. *Economic and Cultural Change*   350

Illustration Credits   377
Index   379

list of maps

The Germanic Invasions   22

Europe at Clovis's Death, A.D. 511   26

The Conquests of Justinian   39

Europe around 600   50

The Islamic Empire   66

The Carolingian Empire   89

Partition of the Empire: Treaty of Verdun, 843   103

The Viking, Hungarian and Muslim Invasions   109

England about 885   114

The Holy Roman Empire in 962   126

The Reconquest of Spain   155

The Crusader States   165

The German Eastward Penetration   172

The Holy Roman Empire in 1190   211

The Angevin Empire, 1154   233

The Expansion of the French Royal Domain   255

English Possessions in France, 1328–1453   335

Spain at the Time of Ferdinand and Isabella   341

Italy, c. 1490   344

The Empire and Central Europe, c. 1490   346

The Ottoman Advance   349

Maps by Russell H. Lenz and John V. Morris

list of
illustrations

San Vitale, Ravenna	34, 35
Female Martyrs, S. Apollinare Nuovo	36
St. Mark's, Venice	36
Sancta Sophia, Constantinople	37
Cross Page from the *Lindisfarne Gospels*	57
Capilla de Villaviciosa, Cordova	72
July and September from the Flemish *Hours of the Virgin*	78
Contemporary figure of Charlemagne	85
"Mary Church," Aachen	93
The Holy Roman Emperor from the Gospel Book of Otto	125
Abbey Church, Cluny	134
Capella Palatina, Palermo	158
Mosaic of Christ, Monreale	159
St. Francis, by Cimabue	189
Minstrels	267
Romanesque architecture	274-277
Romanesque capitals	278, 279
Notre Dame, Paris	281
Gothic architecture	282-284
Gothic sculpture	286, 287
Amiens Cathedral	360
Saint-Etienne at Beauvais	361
Saint-Maclou, Rouen	362
Chapel of Henry VII, Westminster Abbey, London	363
Le beau dieu, Amiens Cathedral	364
Three Mourners, by Claus Sluter and Claus de Werve	364

The Madonna of the Chancellor Rolin,
by Jan van Eyck   365

Sistine Madonna, by Raphael   367

The Golden Virgin, Amiens Cathedral   368

David, by Michelangelo   368

Venus, by Titian   368

S. Andrea at Mantua   369

Medieval Europe:
a short history

introduction

A few generations ago the medieval centuries of European history were widely regarded as "The Dark Ages." Western man was thought to have dropped into a deep slumber at the fall of the Western Roman Empire in A.D. 476, awakening at length, like Rip Van Winkle, in the bright dawn of the Italian Renaissance. Indeed, it was the humanists of fifteenth-century Renaissance Italy who first created this dismal image of their medieval forebears, and the condemnation was echoed by the sixteenth-century Protestant reformers and by the philosophers of the eighteenth-century French Enlightenment. The term "Middle Ages" was coined to denote a prolonged era of spiritual and cultural intermission separating classical antiquity from the Renaissance and unworthy of a name of its own. It was an age whose art was barbaric or "Gothic"—a millennium of darkness—a thousand years without a bath.

Today this ungenerous point of view stands discredited, although it persists among the half-educated. Several generations of rigorous historical scholarship have demonstrated that the medieval period was an epoch of immense vitality and profound creativity. The age that produced Thomas Aquinas and Dante, Notre Dame de Paris and Chartres, Parliament and the university, can hardly be described as "dark" or "barbaric."

Still, one is reminded endlessly in textbooks that life in medieval Europe was vastly different from life in modern America and that the medieval intellectual climate was far removed from our own. Countless students have been taught to contrast feudalism with democracy, the medieval mind with the modern mind, the "Age of Faith" with our own age of technology, or doubt, or cybernetics, or whatever it might be. These are truths that few would be inclined to doubt, and it seems unnecessary to belabor the point that the political

1

and cultural leaders of today are not very much like St. Bernard or Pope Gregory VII. The chief pitfall in understanding medieval Europe is not a failure to recognize its all too obvious contrasts with modern society. Rather, it is the danger that in dwelling too intently upon these alien qualities we may overlook the all-important fact that the Middle Ages constituted the earliest phase of our own civilization. One of the great benefits in the study of medieval history is the opportunity it affords to examine the birth, youth, and early maturity of Western European society. As we investigate the Middle Ages we are scrutinizing our own cultural origins. By the twelfth and thirteenth centuries Western Civilization had succeeded in attaining a cultural level comparable to that of the great civilizations of the past, but it also possessed an enormous potential for further development. It was destined, in later centuries, to transcend by far the achievements of the past and, for good or ill, transform the world.

part I The Early Middle Ages: the genesis of western civilization

1

the christian empire

The Mood of the Late Empire

During the three centuries following the end of the Roman imperial line in the West, in A.D. 476, the Mediterranean world underwent a profound transformation. Where once a single state had encompassed the far-flung lands of the Mediterranean basin, now three distinct civilizations were established on the ruins of the old Empire. These three—Byzantium, Western Europe, and Islam—differed sharply from the traditions of Old Rome. Yet each, to a different degree, was a product of the Greco-Roman past. Although no longer Roman, all were deeply indebted to the legacy of classical antiquity.

Each of Rome's three heirs was animated by a powerful transcendental faith based on the Hebrew religious tradition. Each, in its own way, was shaped by the intense religious experience of the late Empire itself. Accordingly, our examination of these three successor civiliations must begin with a study of the Roman Empire's Christian phase, that is, of the crucial decades between Constantine's conversion and the fall of the Western Empire. In these decades Church and Caesar worked together toward the Christianization of the ancient world.

As Rome grew old, the allegiance of her people gradually shifted from the traditional gods of hearth, field, and city to potent transcendental deities of the Orient—deities such as the Egyptian Isis, the Persian Mithras, and the Great Mother from Asia Minor—who promised the priceless gifts of personal redemption and eternal life. Even in the buoyant years of the second century A.D., imperial culture and prosperity had failed to affect a vast, wretched substratum of the population. And as the peace of the second century gave way to the turbulence and disintegration of the third, an ever-increasing portion of the Empire's inhabitants was reduced to a state of grinding poverty and futility. To men such as these the shining dreams of classical humanism—an ordered universe, an ideal republic, a good life—were cruel illusions. For them, the world was not enough, and the salvation cults became their one hope.

The older pagan cults of Jupiter, Minerva, and the other deities of the classical pantheon survived the turmoil of the third century but only in profoundly altered form. They, too, were transformed by the great transcendental upsurge of the age, for during the third century all that was vital in the traditional pagan cults was incorporated into a vast philosophical scheme known as Neoplatonism. One of the most influential philosophers of the Roman era, Plotinus, taught this doctrine of one god, infinite, unknowable, and unapproachable except through a mystical experience. Plontinus' god was the ultimate source of all things, physical and spiritual. All existence was conceived as a vast hierarchy radiating outward from God, like concentric ripples in a pond, diminishing in excellence and significance in proportion to its distance from the divine source. Human reason, which the Greeks had earlier exalted, was now reduced to impotence, for the nexus of reality was an unknowable god that lay beyond reason's scope.

Despite their mystical doctrine of monotheism, the Neoplatonists allowed a place in their system for the manifold deities of paganism. The pagan gods were interpreted as symbols of the Neoplatonic god—crude symbols, but useful nevertheless. The pagan pantheon, so radically unsuited to the deepening mood of otherworldliness, was now galvanized and given new relevance by the overarching structure of Neoplatonic philosophy. So it was that the deities of Old Rome came to participate increasingly in the new trend toward mysticism and monotheism. The distinction between Jupiter and Mithras was steadily fading.

Christianity and the Empire

It was in this atmosphere of mysticism and the supernatural that Christianity won its final victories. By Constantine's reign (A.D.

306–337) the age of questing rationalism and fallible, anthropomorphic gods had long passed, and with Constantine's conversion and his subsequent victory at the Milvian Bridge (312), the triumph of Christianity over its mystical rivals was all but assured.

The Christians were deeply grateful to Constantine, their first imperial convert. But had they possessed the retrospective view available to the modern historian they might have expressed a kind of gratitude also toward Diocletian (284–305), their last imperial persecutor. For the ruthless, authoritarian measures by which Diocletian and Constantine revived the faltering Empire had the effect of postponing imperial collapse in the West for nearly two centuries, and the Christians put this borrowed time to good use. Indeed, Constantine's new capital at Constantinople provided the foundation for the Christian Byzantine Empire that endured for a millennium. Had Rome collapsed at the end of the third century—had there been no experience of a Christian Roman Empire—the subsequent history of Europe, North Africa, and Western Asia would have been substantially altered.

The fourth-century Empire witnessed mass conversions to Christianity under the benevolent support of Christian emperors. From a vigorous, dedicated minority sect, Christianity expanded during the fourth century to become the dominant religion of the Mediterranean world. No longer persecuted and disreputable, Christianity became official, conventional, respectable. And of course it lost much of its former spiritual élan in the process. Moreover, total victory was accompanied by a new surge of internal dissension. The fourth century was an age of bitter doctrinal struggle, and here, too, the Christian emperors played a commanding role. It was only through imperial suppression that Arianism, the most powerful of the fourth-century heresies, lost its hold on the inhabitants of the Empire. The Arians, who followed Christ's teachings but denied his full divinity, constituted a potent force in the Church until Emperor Theodosius I (378–395) condemned them and broke their power, making orthodox Christianity the official religion of the Roman state. Indeed, Theodosius proscribed paganism itself, and the old gods of Rome, deprived of imperial sanction, gradually passed into memory.

Orthodox Christianity now dominated the Empire; yet old heresies lingered on and vigorous new ones arose. And although Arianism was dying in the Empire by the late fourth century, it survived among the Germanic peoples along the frontiers. These barbarians had been converted by Arian missionaries around the middle of the century, at a time when Arianism was still strong in the Empire, and the persecutions of the orthodox Emperor Theodosius had no effect on the faith of Germanic tribes. Consequently, when in time the barbarians built their successor states on the debris of the Western Empire they were divided from their Roman subjects not only by culture but also by bitter religious antagonisms.

Christianity gained much from Constantine's conversion but it also lost much. The post-Constantine Church was less fervent, less dedicated than before; it was also less independent. For the gratitude of Christians toward Constantine almost reached the point of adulation. He was regarded as a thirteenth Apostle, as the master of all churches, as a monarch whose office was commissioned by God. His regal presence dominated the great Ecumenical Council of Nicaea in 325, and it was at his bidding that the Council denounced Arianism. In the decades that followed, the Arian-orthodox struggle swayed back and forth according to the inclinations of the emperors. First the Arian leaders were condemned to exile, then the orthodox, until finally, late in the fourth century, Arianism subsided under the pressure of the sternly orthodox Theodosius. Good Catholics rejoiced when Theodosius banned Arianism, but they might well have been apprehensive of a situation in which such crucial matters of faith depended upon imperial fiat.

A situation of this sort is traditionally called "Caesaropapism." It arises from a political structure in which Church and state are both controlled by a single individual—a "Caesar-pope." Caesaropapism was a significant characteristic of the Christian Empire, and in the East it became a fundamental ingredient in the organization of the Byzantine state throughout its age-long history. For a thousand years Church and state tended to merge under the encompassing authority of the emperor at Constantinople. His subjects regarded him not merely as a Caesar but as the supreme ruler of a Christian state (or rather, in the eyes of the East Romans, *the* Christian state). As such, he was usually able to depend on the fervent support of his Christian subjects, and their allegiance gave the Eastern Empire the strength to endure. On the other hand, the Eastern emperor's orthodoxy evoked a spirit of uncompromising hostility in districts where heterodox views held sway. The religious disaffection of these districts—most notably Egypt and Syria—

facilitated their absorption into the Arab world during the opening stages of the seventh-century Islamic conquests.

Dominant in the East, caesaropapism failed in the West, for the fifth century brought renewed turbulence and, ultimately, political catastrophe to the Western Empire; Western Christians began to doubt the wisdom of placing all their hope in the imperium. Gradually they came to realize that the disintegration of the Empire did not mean the end of the world or the collapse of the Church. Eastern Christians might indeed regard their Empire as the Ark of Christ, but those in the West wisely refused to bind themselves to a sinking ship. Accordingly, the Western Church slowly began to assert its independence of imperial authority, thereby laying the foundation for the Church-state tension that became such a dominant theme in the evolution of European civilization.

The Latin Doctors

The conversion of Constantine was merely one event in the long and significant process of fusion between Christianity and Greco-Roman civilization. This process had been at work among the early Christian apologists who sought to present their faith in the intellectually respectable context of Greek philosophy. The classical-Christian synthesis was carried still further by great third-century theologians such as Origen of Alexandria, who produced a masterful fusion of Christian doctrine and Platonic philosophy. The process reached its climax in the Western Empire during the later fourth and early fifth centuries with the work of three Christian intellectuals, St. Ambrose, St. Jerome, and St. Augustine, who came to be regarded as "Doctors of the Latin Church." Working at a time when the Christianization of the Empire was proceeding apace, yet before the intellectual vigor of classical antiquity had faded, these three scholar-saints applied all the sophisticated wisdom of their fine classical educations to the elucidation of the Christian faith. Nearly seven centuries were to pass before Western Europe regained the intellectual level of late antiquity, and the writings of these three Latin Doctors therefore exerted a powerful influence on the thought of the succeeding ages.

Although Ambrose, Jerome, and Augustine made their chief impact on the realm of intellectual history, all three were deeply involved in the political and ecclesiastical affairs of their day. Saint Ambrose (*c.* 340–397) was bishop of Milan, a great city of northern Italy that in the later fourth century replaced Rome as the imperial capital in the West. Ambrose was a superb administrator, a powerful orator, and a vigorous opponent of Arianism. Thoroughly grounded in the literary and philosophical traditions of Greco-Roman Civilization, he enriched his Christian writings by drawing heavily from Plato, Cicero, Virgil, and other giants of the pagan past. And as one of the first champions of ecclesiastical independence from the authority of the Christian Empire he stood at the source of the Church-state controversy that was to affect Western Europe for more than a millennium. When Theodosius I massacred the rebellious inhabitants of Thessalonica, St. Ambrose excommunicated him from the Church of Milan, forcing Theodosius to humble himself and beg forgiveness. The Emperor's public repentance set a momentous precedent for the principle of ecclesiastical supremacy in matters of faith and morals—a precedent that would not be forgotten by churchmen of later centuries.

Saint Jerome (*c.* 340–420) was the most scholarly of the three Latin Doctors. A restless, troubled man, he roamed widely through the Empire, living in Rome for a time, then fleeing the worldly city to found a monastery in Bethlehem. Jerome's monks in Bethlehem devoted themselves to the copying of manuscripts, a task that was to be taken up by countless monks in centuries to come and which, in the long run, resulted in the preservation of important works of Greco-Roman antiquity that would otherwise have vanished. The modern world owes a great debt to St. Jerome and his successors for performing this humble but essential labor.

St. Jerome himself was torn by doubts as to the propriety of a Christian immersing himself in pagan literature. On one occasion Jesus appeared to him in a dream and banished him from paradise with the words, "Thou art a Ciceronian, not a Christian." For a time Jerome renounced all pagan learning, but he was much too devoted to the charms of classical literature to persevere in this harsh resolve. In the end he concluded that Greco-Roman letters might properly be used in the service of the Christian faith.

Jerome's supreme achievement lay in the field of scriptural commentary and translation. It was he who produced the definitive Latin translation of the Bible from its original Hebrew and Greek—

the Latin Vulgate Bible, which Catholics have used ever since. By preparing a trustworthy Latin text of the fundamental Christian book he made an essential contribution to the civilization of Western Europe.

St. Augustine of Hippo (354–430) was the towering intellect of his age. His achievements exceeded those of St. Ambrose, the ecclesiastical statesman, and St. Jerome, the scholar. For St. Augustine too was a statesman and a scholar, and he was a great philosopher as well. As bishop in the important North African city of Hippo he was deeply immersed in the affairs of his day, and his writings were produced in response to vital contemporary issues. Augustine's thought combines profundity and immediacy—the abstract and the human. In his *Confessions* he describes his own intellectual and moral Odyssey through paganism and Manichaeism into Christian orthodoxy. He writes with the hope that others, lost as he once was, might be led by God to the spiritual haven of the Church.

Augustine wrote voluminously against the various pagan and heretical doctrines that threatened Christian orthodoxy in his age. Out of these diverse writings there emerged a lofty system of speculative thought that served as the intellectual foundation for medieval philosophy and theology. Like so many of his predecessors and contemporaries he worked toward the synthesis of classical and Christian thought, but more than any before him he succeeded in welding the two cultures into one. He was disturbed, as Jerome was, by the danger of pagan thought to the Christian soul. But, like Jerome, he concluded that although a good Christian ought not to *enjoy* pagan culture he might properly *use* it for Christian ends. Accordingly, Augustine used the philosophy of Plato and the Neoplatonists as a basis for a new and thoroughly Christian philosophical scheme. It has been said that Augustine baptized Plato. As the thirteenth-century philosopher St. Thomas Aquinas observed, "Whenever Augustine, who was imbued with the philosophy of the Platonists, found in their teaching anything consistent with faith, he adopted it; those things which he found contrary to faith, he amended."

Thus Augustine stressed the Platonic notion of ideas or archetypes* as the models of tangible things, but instead of placing his archetypes in some abstract "heaven," as Plato did, he placed them in the mind

---

* For a fuller discussion of the Platonic archetypes see below, p. 300.

of God. For Augustine, the Platonic archetypes were "divine ideas." These ideas constituted the highest form of reality—the only true knowledge—and the human mind had access to the archetypes through a form of God's grace that Augustine called "divine illumination." Augustine was much too good a Christian to fall into the old Persian notion that matter was worthless or that the human body was evil. But by emphasizing the superiority of ideas over particulars he was led to the conclusion that the material world was less important—less real—than the spiritual world. He concluded that man's body was a prison for his soul, and that the soul's escape from its material body was the chief goal of the Christian life. And he insisted that man, corrupted by the original sin of Adam's fall, was incapable of escaping the prison of his body except through God's grace. Hence man could not earn his own way into heaven; he was predestined to salvation or damnation by the will of God.

St. Augustine developed these and other doctrines in the course of his long struggle against the various heretical sects that flourished in his age. In the course of his arguments he examined many of the central problems that have occupied theologians ever since—the nature of the Trinity, the existence of evil in a world created and governed by an omnipotent God, the special power and authority of the priesthood, the compatibility of free will and predestination.

When pagan critics ascribed the Visigothic sack of Rome in 410 to Rome's desertion of her former gods, Augustine met the challenge by writing his profoundly influential *City of God* which set forth a complete Christian philosophy of history. Human development was interpreted not in economic or political terms but in moral terms. Kingdoms and empires rise, prosper, and decline according to a divine plan, ordained from the beginning, yet forever beyond human comprehension. But even though the pattern of history must always elude us, we do know this: God is not interested in the fate of cities and empires except insofar as they affect the destiny of individual men; the chief business of history is the salvation of human souls. And salvation depends not on the victories of Caesar but on the grace of God. Therefore true history has less to do with the struggles of states than with the war between good and evil that rages within each state and within each soul. The human race is divided into two distinct groups: not Romans and barbarians as the pagan writers would have it, but those who live in God's grace and those who do not. The former are members of the "City of God," the latter belong to the "Earthly City." The two cities are hopelessly intertwined in this life, but their members will be separated at death by eternal salvation or damnation. The divine plan for human history therefore has one fundamental purpose: the growth and welfare of the City of God. As for the city of Rome, perhaps in the long run its decline will be beneficial—perhaps even irrelevant!

The Romans had never excelled in the realm of speculative thought, but with the Christian Augustine, Latin philosophy came into its own at last. He was the Western Empire's greatest philosopher and, indeed, one of the two or three foremost minds in the history of Christianity. His theory of the two cities, although often simplified and reinterpreted in later generations, influenced Western thought and politics for a thousand years. His Christian Platonism dominated medieval philosophy until the mid-twelfth century and remains a significant theme in religious thought to this day. His distinction between the ordained priesthood and the laity has always been basic to Catholic theology. And his emphasis on divine grace and predestination was to be a crucial source of inspiration to the Protestant leaders of the sixteenth century.

As a consequence of Augustine's work, together with that of his great contemporaries, Ambrose and Jerome, Christian culture was firmly established on classical foundations. At Augustine's death in 430 the classical-Christian fusion was essentially complete. The strength of the Greco-Roman tradition that underlies medieval Christianity and Western Civilization owes much to the fact that these three Latin Doctors, and others like them, found it possible to be both Christians and Ciceronians.

2

the decline of rome and the germanic invasions

Decline and Fall

The catastrophe of Rome's decline and fall has always fascinated historians, for it involves not only the collapse of mankind's most impressive and enduring universal state but also the demise of Greco-Roman civilization itself. The reasons are far too complex to be explained satisfactorily by any single cause—Christianity, disease, slavery, soil exhaustion, lead poisoning, or any of the other master keys that have been proposed from time to time. We must always bear in mind that the Roman Empire "fell" only in the West. It endured in the East, although there, too, Greco-Roman civilization changed significantly. The civilization of the Eastern Empire during the medieval centuries is described not as "Roman" or even "Greco-Roman" but as "Byzantine,"* and the change in name betokens a profound alteration in mood. In other words, Greco-Roman culture was gradually transformed in both East and West, but its transformation in the West was accompanied by the dismemberment of the Roman state, whereas its transformation in

* After Byzantium, the name of the town on whose site Constantinople was established.

the East occurred despite an underlying political continuity in which emperor followed emperor in unbroken succession.

In the West, then, we are faced with two separate phenomena— political breakdown and cultural transformation. The political collapse culminated in the deposition of the last Western emperor in A.D. 476, but the real period of crisis was the chaotic third century. The recovery under Diocletian and Constantine was merely partial and temporary; the impending death of the body politic was delayed, but the disease remained uncured. The impoverished masses in town and countryside had never participated meaningfully in Roman civilization, and the third-century anarchy resulted in the spiritual disengagement of the middle classes as well. Initiative and commitment ebbed in the atmosphere of economic and political upheaval and were stifled by the autocracy that followed. Fourth-century Rome was a totalitarian police state that robbed its subjects of their independence and watched over them by means of a vast network of informers and secret agents. The collapse of such a state cannot be regarded as an unmitigated disaster. To many it must have seemed a blessing.

The West had always been poorer and less urbanized than the East, and its economy, badly shaken by the political chaos of the third century, began to break down under the growing burden of imperial government and the defense of hard-pressed frontiers. Perhaps the fatal flaw in the Western economy was its inability to compensate for the cessation of imperial expansion by more intensive internal development. There was no large-scale industry, no mass production; the majority of the population was far too poor to provide a mass market. Industrial production was inefficient and technology progressed at a snail's pace. The economy remained fundamentally agrarian, and farming techniques advanced very little during the centuries of the Empire. The Roman plow was rudimentary; windmills were unknown and water mills exceptional. The horse could not be used as a draught animal because the Roman harness crossed the horse's windpipe and tended to strangle him under a heavy load. Consequently, Roman agriculture was based on the ox and on the muscles of slaves and peasants.

Economic exhaustion brought with it the twin evils of population decline and creeping poverty. And at the very time that the manpower shortage was becoming acute and impoverishment was paralyzing the middle classes, the expenses of government were soaring. The army and bureaucracy steadily expanded until at length the state payroll contained more names than the tax rolls. One result of these processes was the deurbanization of the West. By the fifth century the once vigorous cities were becoming ghosts of their former selves, drained of their wealth and much of their population. Only the small class of great landowners managed to prosper in the economic atmosphere of the late Western Empire, and these men now abandoned their town houses, withdrew from civic affairs, and retired to their estates where they often assembled sizable private armies and defied the tax collector. The aristocracy, having now fled the city, would remain an agrarian class for the next thousand years. The rural nobility of the Middle Ages had come into being.

The decline of the city was fatal to the urbanized administrative structure of the Western Empire. More than that, it brought an end to the urban-oriented culture of Greco-Roman antiquity. The civilization of Athens, Alexandria, and Rome could not survive in the fields. It is in the decay of urban society that we find the crucial connecting link between political collapse and cultural transformation. In a very real sense Greco-Roman culture was dead long before the final demise of the Western Empire; the deposition of the last emperor in 476 was merely the faint postscript to a process that had been completed long before. By then the cities were moribund. The rational, humanist outlook had given way completely to transcendentalism and mysticism. The army and even the civil government had become barbarized as the desperate emperors, faced with a growing shortage of manpower and resources, turned more and more to Germanic peoples to defend their frontiers and keep order in their state. In the end, barbarians abounded in the army, entire tribes were hired to defend the frontiers, and Germanic military leaders came to hold positions of high authority in the Western Empire. Survival had actually come to depend on the success of Germanic defenders against Germanic invaders.

Despite the deurbanization, the mysticism, and the barbarism of the late Empire, in a certain sense Greco-Roman culture never died in the West. It exerted a profound influence, as we have seen, on the Doctors of the Latin Church and, through them, on the mind of the Middle Ages. It was the basis of repeated cultural revivals, great and small, down through the centuries—in the era of Charlemagne, in the High Middle Ages, in the Italian Renaissance, and in the neoclassical eighteenth century. And if in one sense the Roman state was dead long before the line of Western emperors ended in 476, in another it survived long thereafter—in the ecclesiastical organization of the Roman Catholic Church and in the medieval Holy Roman Empire. Roman law endured to inspire Western jurisprudence; the Latin tongue remained the language of educated Europeans for more than a millennium while evolving in the lower levels of society into the Romance languages, Italian, French, Spanish, Portuguese, and Roumanian. In countless forms the rich legacy of classical antiquity was passed on to the Middle Ages. Europeans for centuries to come would be nourished by Greek thought and haunted by the memory of Rome.

The Germanic Peoples

The civilization of medieval Europe built creatively upon a synthesis of three cultures: Classical, Christian, and Germanic. The age of Ambrose, Jerome, and Augustine witnessed the virtual completion of the Classical-Christian synthesis, but the impact of Germanic culture had only begun to be felt. It was not until the eighth century or thereabouts that a fusion of Classical-Christian culture and Germanic culture was achieved, and only then can it be said that Western Civilization was born. The intervening centuries, which are sometimes called the "Dark Ages," provide a fascinating view of a new civilization in the process of formation. Throughout these turbulent years the Classical-Christian tradition was preserved and fostered by the Church while the Germanic tradition governed the political and social organization of the barbarian successor states that rose on the carcass of the Western Empire. The Germanic invaders soon became at least nominal Christians, but for centuries a cultural gulf remained between the Church, with its Greco-Roman-Christian heritage, and the Germanic kingdoms with their primitive, war-oriented culture. The Church of the Early Middle Ages was able to preserve ancient culture only in a debased form, for as time went on ecclesiastical leaders and aristocratic laymen came more and more to be drawn from the same social milieu. Still, it remained the great task of the early medieval Church to civilize and Christianize the Germanic peoples.

Most of the tribes that invaded the Western Empire seem to have come originally from the Scandinavian area, the homeland of the later Vikings. Gradually they migrated into Eastern and South-eastern Europe and began to press against the Rhine and Danube frontiers. It is hazardous to make broad generalizations regarding their culture and institutions, for customs varied considerably from tribe to tribe. The Franks, the Angles, and the Saxons, for example, were agrarian peoples whose movements were slow, but who, once settled, were difficult to displace. Little influenced by Roman civilization they came into the empire as heathens. The Visigoths, Ostrogoths, and Vandals, on the other hand, were far more mobile. All three had absorbed Roman culture to some degree before they crossed the frontiers, and all had been converted in the fourth century to Arian Christianity. But whether agrarian or nomadic, the Germanic tribes had certain characteristics in common; their political and social structures disclose significant similarities and parallels.

A good contemporary account of early Germanic institutions is to be found in a short book entitled *Germania*, written by the Roman historian Tacitus in A.D. 98. This work is not entirely trustworthy; it is a morality piece written with the intention of criticizing the "degeneracy" of the Romans by comparing them unfavorably with the simple and upright barbarians. Nevertheless, it is an invaluable source of information on early Germanic customs and institutions. We can certainly accept Tacitus' description of the Germans as large men with reddish-blond hair and blue eyes, living in simple villages, but his eulogy of their virtue and chastity is a gross exaggeration. On the whole they appear to have been drunks, liars, and lechers, whose vices were certainly no less numerous than those of the Romans, only cruder. Their standards of personal hygiene are suggested by the observation of a fifth-century Roman gentleman: "Happy the nose that cannot smell a barbarian."*

Although the Germans used iron tools and weapons, their social and economic organization was in many ways reminiscent of late-stone-age cultures. Their chief activities were tending crops or herds and fighting wars. The key social unit within the tribe had tradi-tionally been the kindred group or clan, which protected the welfare

---

* The author, some of whose best friends are Anglo-Saxons, disclaims any ethnic bias. The crudeness of the barbarians was due to their lack of social and educational opportunities.

of its members by means of the blood feud. When a man was killed, his clan was bound to avenge his death by conducting a feud—declaring war, as it were—against the killer and his clan. In the boisterous atmosphere of the tribe, killings were only too common, and in order to keep the social fabric from being torn asunder by blood feuds it became customary for the tribe to establish a _wergeld,_ a sum of money that the killer might pay to the relatives of his victim to appease their vengeance. Wergeld schedules became quite elaborate, the amount of money to be paid by the killer varying in accordance with the social status of his victim. Smaller wergelds were established for lesser injuries such as the cutting off of a victim's arm, leg, thumb, or finger until in time the wergeld schedules came to cover every imaginable injury down to the little toe. There was no guarantee, however, that the man who did the killing or maiming would agree to pay the wergeld, or that the victim or his clan would agree to accept it. In spite of the wergeld system, blood feuds continued far into the Middle Ages.

The ties of kinship were strong among the early Germans, but they were rivaled by those of another social unit, the war band or _comitatus_. Kinship played no part in this institution; it consisted rather of a group of warriors bound together by their loyalty to a chief or king. The comitatus was a kind of military brotherhood based on honor, fidelity, courage, and mutual respect between the leader and his men. In warfare the leader was expected to excel his men in courage and prowess, and should the leader be killed, his men were honor-bound to fight to the death even if their cause should appear hopeless. The heroic virtues of the comitatus persisted throughout the Early Middle Ages as the characteristic ideology of the European warrior nobility.

The comitatus and the clan were subdivisions of a larger unit, the tribe, whose members were bound together by their allegiance to a chieftain or king and by their recognition of a common body of customary law. The laws of the barbarian tribes were childish and irrational compared with those of the Roman Empire. Legal decisions often depended on whether the parties were able to adhere precisely to complex procedural formalities. An accused man was presumed guilty unless he could prove his innocence, and in many cases innocence could be established only by the accused submitting to an "ordeal." He might, for example, be required to grasp a bar of red-hot iron and carry it some specified distance, or take a stone from a boiling cauldron. If, after several days, his hand was healing properly, he was judged innocent. If his hand was infected, he was guilty. Similarly, he might be required to leap into a lake or pond. If he sank he was innocent; if he floated he was guilty; the pure waters would not "accept" a guilty man. Throughout the Early Middle Ages it was chiefly these Germanic customs rather than the sophisticated concepts of Roman law that governed jurisprudence in Western Europe. Roman law persisted in fragmentary or bastardized form, but not until the twelfth century did it undergo a fundamental revival in the West. And even then its victory over Germanic law was gradual and incomplete.

Germanic law, crude though it was, made one crucial contribution to Western thought: implicit in the Germanic system was the concept that law arose from the immemorial customs of the people rather than from the will of the ruler. Since law transcended the royal authority, no king could be absolute. The rulers of the Early Middle Ages often put the customs of their people into writing, but changed them only with great caution and in consultation with a council of nobles. The constitutional principle of government under the law did not emerge clearly for centuries to come, but when it did appear at last, in the High Middle Ages, it was rooted in the traditions of Europe's Germanic past.

The centuries just preceding the invasions witnessed the development of relatively stable royal dynasties among many of the Germanic tribes. Perhaps an unusually gifted warrior with a particularly large comitatus might start such a dynasty, but before many generations had gone by the kings were claiming descent from some divine ancestor. When a king died, the assembly of the tribe chose as his successor the ablest member of his family. This might or might not be his eldest son, for the tribal assembly was given considerable latitude in its power to elect. The custom of election persisted in most Germanic kingdoms far into the Middle Ages. Its chief consequence during the fifth-century invasions was to insure that the barbarian tribes were normally led by clever, battle-worthy kings or chieftains at a time when the Western Empire was ruled by weaklings and nincompoops.

Nineteenth-century historians made much of the fact that certain Germanic institutions seemed to contain the seeds of constitutionalism and popular sovereignty. Democracy, so it was said, had its genesis in the forests of Germany. It should be obvious, however, that the veneration of a customary "law of the folk" or the political prominence of a tribal assembly is not uniquely Germanic but is common to many primitive peoples. The significant fact is not that early Germanic kings were limited by customary law, but that the institution of limited monarchy endured and developed over the centuries of the Middle Ages.

The Barbarian Invasions

The Germanic peoples had long been a threat to the Empire. They had defeated a Roman army in the reign of Augustus; they had probed deeply into the Empire in the second century and again in the mid-third. But until the late fourth century the Romans had always managed eventually to drive the invaders out. Beginning in the mid-370s, however, an exhausted Empire was confronted by renewed barbarian pressures of an unprecedented magnitude. Lured by the relative wealth, the good soil, and the sunny climate of the Mediterranean world, the barbarians tended to regard the Empire not as something to destroy but as something to enjoy. Their age-long yearning for the fair lands across the Roman frontier was suddenly transformed into an urgent need by the westward thrust of a tribe of Asiatic nomads known as the Huns. These fierce horsemen conquered one Germanic tribe after another and turned them into satellites. The Ostrogoths fell before their might and became a subject people. The other Gothic tribe, the Visigoths, sought to avoid a similar fate by appealing for sanctuary behind the Roman Danube frontier. The Eastern emperor Valens, a fervent Arian, sympathized with the Arian Visigoths, and in 376 the entire tribe crossed peacefully into the Empire.

There was trouble almost immediately. Corrupt imperial officials cheated and abused the Visigoths, and the hot-tempered tribesmen retaliated by going on a rampage. At length Emperor Valens himself took the field against them, but the emperor's military incapacity cost him his army and his life at the battle of Adrianople in 378. Adrianople was a military debacle of the first order. Valens' successor, Theodosius I, managed to pacify the Visigoths, but he could not expel them. When Theodosius died in 395 the Roman Empire was split among his two incompetent sons, and, as it happened, the Eastern and Western halves were never again rejoined. A vigorous new

THE GERMANIC INVASIONS

Visigothic leader named Alaric now led his people on a second campaign of pillage and destruction that threatened Italy itself. In 406 the desperate Western Empire recalled most of its troops from the Rhine frontier to block Alaric's advance, with the disastrous consequence that the Vandals and a number of other tribes swept across the unguarded Rhine into Gaul. Shortly thereafter the Roman legions abandoned distant Britain, and the defenseless island was gradually overrun by Angles, Saxons, and other barbarian war bands. In 408 the only able general in the West was executed by the frantic, incompetent Emperor Honorius, who then abandoned Rome and took refuge behind the marshes of Ravenna. The Visigoths entered Rome unopposed in 410 and Alaric permitted them to plunder the city for three days.

The sack of Rome had a devastating impact on imperial morale, but in historical perspective it appears as a mere incident in the disintegration of the Western Empire. The Visigoths soon left the city to its feeble emperor and turned northward into Southern Gaul and Spain. There they established a kingdom that endured until the Moslem conquests of the eighth century. Meanwhile other tribes were carving out kingdoms of their own. The Vandals swept through Gaul and Spain and across the Straits of Gibraltar into Africa. In 430, the very year of St. Augustine's death, they took his city of Hippo. A new Vandal kingdom arose in North Africa, centering on ancient Carthage. Almost immediately the Vandals began taking to the sea as buccaneers, devastating Mediterranean shipping and sacking one coastal city after another. Vandal piracy shattered the long peace of the Mediterranean and dealt a crippling blow to the waning commerce of the Western Empire.

Midway through the fifth century the Huns themselves moved against the West, led by their brilliant pitiless leader Attila, the "Scourge of God." Defeated by a Roman-Visigothic army in Gaul in 451, they returned the following year, hurling themselves toward Rome and leaving a path of devastation behind them. The Western emperor abandoned Rome to Attila's mercies, but the Roman bishop, Pope Leo I, traveled northward from the city to negotiate with the Huns on the wild chance that they might be persuaded to turn back. Oddly enough, Pope Leo succeeded in his mission. Perhaps because the health of the Hunnish army was adversely affected by the Italian climate, perhaps because the majestic Pope Leo was able to overawe the superstitious Attila, the Huns retired from Italy. Shortly afterward Attila died, the Hunnish empire collapsed, and the Huns themselves vanished from history. They were not mourned.

In its final years the Western Empire, whose jurisdiction now scarcely extended beyond Italy, fell under the control of hard-bitten military adventurers of Germanic birth. The emperors continued to reign for a time, but their Germanic generals were the powers behind the throne. In 476 the barbarian general Odovacar, who saw no point in perpetuating the farce, deposed the last emperor, sent the imperial trappings to Constantinople, and asserted his sovereignty over Italy by confiscating farmlands for the use of his Germanic troops. Odovacar claimed to rule as an agent of the Eastern Empire, but in fact he was on his own. A few years later the Ostrogoths, now free of Hunnish control and led by a brilliant king named Theodoric, advanced into Italy, conquered Odovacar, and established a strong state of their own.

Theodoric ruled Italy from 493 to 526. More than any other barbarian king he appreciated and respected Roman culture, and in his kingdom the Arian Ostrogoths and the orthodox Romans lived and worked together in relative harmony, repairing aqueducts, erecting impressive new buildings, and bringing a degree of prosperity to the long-troubled peninsula. The improving political and economic climate gave rise to a minor intellectual revival that contributed to the transmission of Greco-Roman culture into the Middle Ages. The philosopher Boethius, a high official in Theodoric's regime, produced philosophical works and translations which served as fundamental texts in Western schools for the next five hundred years. His masterpiece, *The Consolation of Philosophy*, was written at the end of his life, when he had fallen from official favor and been placed in prison. This important work draws from Platonism and Stoicism without so much as mentioning Christianity, yet it remained immensely popular throughout the Middle Ages. Theodoric's own secretary, Cassiodorus, was another scholar of considerable distinction. Cassiodorus spent his later years as abbot of a monastery and set his monks to the invaluable task of copying and preserving the great literary works of antiquity, both Christian and pagan. His example was not lost on a younger contemporary, St. Benedict of Nursia, who stressed manuscript copying in the Benedictine monastic rule, thus prompting countless generations of Western monks to carry on the good work.*

During the years of Theodoric's rule in Ostrogothic Italy, another famous barbarian king, Clovis (481-511), was creating a Frankish kingdom in Gaul. Clovis was far less Romanized, far less enlightened, far crueler than Theodoric, but his kingdom proved to be the most

* See pp. 52–53.

enduring of all the barbarian successor states. The Franks were good farmers as well as good soldiers, and they established deep roots in the soil of Gaul. Moreover, the Frankish regime was buttressed by the enthusiastic support of the Catholic Church, for Clovis, who had been untouched by Arianism, was converted directly from heathenism to Catholic Christianity. The conversion of Clovis doomed Arianism and foreshadowed the rise of Catholic France. Clovis himself remained a savage to the end, yet the Church came to regard him as another Constantine, a defender of orthodoxy in a sea of Arianism. As the centuries went by the royal name "Clovis" was softened to "Louis" and the "Franks" became the "French." And the friendship between the Frankish monarchy and the Church developed into one of the great determining elements in European politics.

Europe in A.D. 500

As the sixth century dawned, the Western Empire was only a memory. In its place was a group of barbarian successor states that prefigured in certain respects the nations of modern Western Europe. Theodoric headed a tolerant and relatively enlightened Ostrogothic-Arian regime in Italy. The barbaric but orthodox Clovis was completing the Frankish conquest of Gaul. The Vandal monarchy, Arian in religion and increasingly corrupt and intolerant, lorded it over the restive population of North Africa. The Arian Visigoths were being driven out of southern Gaul by the Franks, but their regime continued to dominate Spain for the next two centuries. And the Angles and Saxons were in the process of establishing a group of small heathen kingdoms in Britain that would one day coalesce into "Angle-land" or England.

At the very time that the Germanic kingdoms were establishing themselves in the West, the Roman papacy was beginning to play an important independent role in European society. We have seen how the mid-fifth-century pope, Leo I (440–461), assumed the task of protecting the city of Rome from the Huns, thereby winning for himself the moral leadership of Italy. Leo and his successors declared that the papacy was the highest authority in the Church, and, following the example of St. Ambrose, they insisted on the supremacy of Church over state in spiritual matters. In proclaiming its doctrines of papal supremacy in the Church and ecclesiastical independence from

EUROPE AT CLOVIS'S DEATH A.D. 511

state control, the papacy was hurling a direct challenge at Byzantine caesaropapism. In the fifth century these papal doctrines remained little more than words, but they were to result in an ever-widening gulf between the Eastern and Western Church. More than that, they constituted the opening phase of the prolonged medieval struggle between the rival claims of Church and state. The mighty papacy of the High Middle Ages was yet many centuries away, but it was already foreshadowed in the bold independence of Leo I. The Western Empire was dead, but eternal Rome still claimed the allegiance of the world.

CHRONOLOGY OF THE LATER EMPIRE

All Dates A.D.

  96–180: The age of the great second-century emperors
185–254: Origen
205–270: Plotinus
235–284: Height of the anarchy
284–305: Reign of Diocletian
306–337: Reign of Constantine
     325: Council of Nicaea
     330: Founding of Constantinople
354–430: St. Augustine of Hippo
     376: Visigoths cross Danube
     378: Battle of Adrianople
378–395: Reign of Theodosius I
     395: Final division of Eastern and Western Empires
     410: Alaric sacks Rome
     430: Vandals capture Hippo
451–452: Huns invade Western Europe
440–461: Pontificate of Leo I
     476: Last Western emperor deposed by Odovacar
481–511: Clovis rules Franks, conquers Gaul
493–526: Theodoric the Ostrogoth rules Italy.

3

byzantium endures

The Survival of the East Roman Empire

By the opening of the sixth century the Western Empire had dissolved into a group of barbarian successor states. But the Eastern emperors, with their capital at Constantinople, retained control of an immense, crescent-shaped realm girdling the eastern Mediterranean from the Balkans through Asia Minor, Syria, and Palestine, to Egypt. Many of the same forces that had weakened and demoralized the West had operated in the East as well, yet imperial authority collapsed in the West and survived in the East. Why was this so?

For one thing, the East had always been more populous than the West. Its civilization was far older and more deeply rooted; its cities were larger and more numerous. The East had remained the commercial and industrial center of the Empire even in the great days of Rome, and when disaster struck it proved to be far more resilient than the West.

Moreover, the Eastern Empire enjoyed important strategic and geopolitical advantages. The province of Asia Minor, protected from the barbarian incursions by invulnerable Constantinople, was the Eastern Empire's great reservoir of manpower and revenues. For centuries it was to remain the chief recruiting ground for the Byzantine army and the most dependable source of imperial taxes. During the cataclysmic fifth century, while barbarians were conquering the Western provinces, Asia Minor was a bulwark of the empire. Its tough, loyal troops provided the Eastern emperors with an invaluable alternative to the hazardous policy of complete dependence on hired Germanic armies.

With the rich material and human resources of Asia Minor behind it, the Eastern capital at Constantinople held fast against the barbarian onslaught. This great city, the New Rome, dominated the passage between the Black Sea and the Mediterranean. Secure behind its massive landward and seaward walls, it became the economic and political heart of the Eastern Empire, and so long as Constantinople remained inviolate, the Empire endured. Over the centuries Constantinople's walls repelled the attacks of barbarians, Persians, and Muslims. Under the circumstances, it is understandable that the Germanic tribes should have preferred to carve out their states in the feebler, more vulnerable West.

The Eastern Empire had the further advantage during the crucial fifth century of being much better governed than the Western Empire. A series of able Eastern emperors carefully husbanded their resources, fattened their treasury, and strengthened the fortifications of Constantinople while the Western Empire was collapsing. Superior leadership undoubtedly helped the East weather the storm, but its emperors could have accomplished little had it not been for the superb strategic location of their capital and the enduring commercial and human resources of the lands they ruled. The cradle of ancient civilizations had the strength to survive the barbarian flood that submerged the more recently civilized West.

Byzantine Government

The civilization of the Byzantine Empire was a synthesis of three elements: Roman government, Christian religion, and Greco-Oriental culture. From Rome the Eastern Empire drew its legal system, its bureaucracy, and its principles of administration. Indeed, Byzantine government was a direct offspring of the third- and fourth-century Roman political system. Byzantine autocracy had its roots in Diocletian's glorification of the emperor; Byzantine Caesaropapism evolved out of the Christian Empire of Constantine and Theodosius I. The heavy taxation of the late Roman emperors continued, and life in the Byzantine Empire remained burdensome and insecure.

The prevailing Byzantine mood, like the mood of the late Roman Empire, was one of defense, of self-preservation. To the Byzantines, their state was the ark of civilization in an ocean of barbarism—the political embodiment of the Christian faith—and as such it had to be preserved at all costs. The appropriate virtues in such a state were entrenchment, not expansion; caution, not daring.

This defensive, conservative mood is evident in both the Byzantine bureaucracy and the Byzantine army. The bureaucracy, huge and precedent-bound, abhorred change and seldom took risks. Resisting the policies of Byzantium's few vigorous and imaginative emperors, it gave cohesion to the state during the reigns of incompetents, thereby contributing to the endurance of the Empire. The army, small and highly trained, also clung to a policy of few risks. Its generals, often men of remarkable skill, usually pursued policies of cunning and caution. They knew only too well that the preservation of their Empire might depend on the survival of their armies.

Byzantine Christianity

The Byzantine emperors drew invaluable strength from the loyalty of their tax-ridden but fervent Christian subjects. The orthodox Christians within the Empire regarded their ruler as more than a mere secular sovereign: he was God's vice-regent, the protector of the Holy Church, and as such he merited their unquestioned allegiance. Thus, Byzantine armies fought not merely for the Empire but for God. The Byzantine warrior was no mere soldier, he was a crusader. Christianity was a potent stimulus to patriotism, and the Byzantine emperors enjoyed popular support to a degree unknown in the pagan Rome of old.

But the emperor's central position in Byzantine Christianity was a source of weakness as well as of strength. Religious controversy was a matter of imperial concern, and heresy became a grave threat to the state. The fifth and sixth centuries were singularly rich in doctrinal disputes, and in the end these religious conflicts cost the Empire dearly. The most widespread heresy of the age was Monophysitism, a doctrine that arose in Egypt and spread quickly into Syria and Palestine, creating a mood of hostility toward the orthodox emperors. The controversy between the orthodox and the Monophysites turned on the question of whether Christ's humanity and divinity constituted two separate natures (as the orthodox said) or were fused together into one nature (Monophysitism). The Monophysite Christ possessed a single nature in which divinity tended to supersede humanity. Monophysitism has thus been seen as a return to the spiritualism of the ancient Near East, which tended to regard the physical world as evil. The dualism of evil-matter versus good-spirit conflicted with the orthodox Christian doctrine of God-made-flesh.

Monophysitism can also be viewed as a protest doctrine, upheld in districts that had been civilized long before the days of Roman rule, by peoples whose commitment to Greco-Roman culture was compromised by their own far older cultures. Even without Monophysitism, the inhabitants of Egypt and Syria might well have been expected to show separatist tendencies against embattled Byzantium, and Monophysitism, although far more than a mere excuse for rebellion, was nevertheless an appropriate vehicle for the antagonisms of Near Eastern peoples against a millennium of Greco-Roman domination.

The orthodox-Monophysite quarrel raged long and bitterly and constituted a dangerous threat to the unity of the Byzantine Empire. The emperors, convinced that doctrinal unity was essential to the preservation of their state, followed first one policy, then another, sometimes persecuting the Monophysites, sometimes favoring them, sometimes proposing compromise doctrinal formulas intended to satisfy everyone but in fact satisfying no one. Whatever policy the emperors might follow, the controversy remained an open wound in the body politic until the seventh century when the rich but disaffected Monophysite provinces were swallowed by the expanding Islamic world. Only then, at the Ecumenical Council of Constantinople in 680, did Byzantine orthodoxy win its definitive victory within the Empire.

Byzantine Culture

Roman government, Christian religion, Greco-Oriental culture—these were the three pillars of Byzantine civilization. And all three were shaped—and to a degree transformed—by the experience of the fourth-century Christian Empire. As a consequence of that experience, Byzantium inherited Roman government in its late, authoritarian form. Byzantine Christianity was a direct outgrowth of the Christianity of the later Roman Empire—its theology tightened and defined by the reaction to Arianism, its priestly hierarchy overshadowed by the caesaropapism of the emperors. Just as Constantine had dominated the clergy at the Council of Nicaea in 325, so likewise did the Byzantine emperors, over the centuries, tend to dominate the patriarchs of Constantinople.

Byzantium's Greco-Oriental culture, too, was molded by the intellectual and cultural currents of the third, fourth, and fifth centuries. The Greek culture that Byzantium inherited was by no means the culture of Periclean Athens—with its sturdy, straightforward, superbly proportioned architecture, its deeply human drama, its bold flights into uncharted regions of speculative thought, and its controlled, tensely muscular sculpture. That tradition had undergone successive modifications in the Hellenistic age, during the Principate, and above all during the third- and fourth-century Empire. The mood of otherworldliness that gradually seized Roman culture resulted in a momentous transformation of the classical spirit. There had always been a potent spiritual-mystical element in Greco-Roman culture, coexisting with the traditional classical concern with the earthly and the concrete. Now the mystical element grew far stronger. More and more of the better minds turned to religious symbolism, spiritual fulfillment, and individual salvation. Artists were less interested in portraying physical perfection and more interested in portraying sanctity. The new Christian art depicted slender, heavily robed figures with solemn faces and deep eyes. Techniques of perspective, which the artists of antiquity had developed to a fine degree, mattered less to the artists of the new age. Deemphasizing physical realism, the artists of the late Empire adorned their works with rich, dazzling colors that stimulated in the beholder a sense of heavenly radiance and deep religious solemnity.

Such was the artistic tradition which Byzantium inherited. It conformed so perfectly to the Byzantine spirit that the artists of the Eastern Empire were able to produce enduring masterpieces without ever departing far from its basic aesthetic canons. Majestic churches arose in the Byzantine style—churches such as Sancta Sophia in Constantinople, St. Vitale in Ravenna, and St. Mark's in Venice—whose interiors shone with glistening mosaics portraying saints and statesmen, Christ and the Virgin, on backgrounds of gold. Here was an art vastly different from that of Greek antiquity, with different techniques and different goals, yet in its own way just as valid, just as successful, as the art of the Athenian golden age.

In this new, transcendental environment, Greek culture was significantly altered, yet Byzantine civilization remained Greek none the less. Greek was the language of most of its inhabitants, and, despite their deep commitment to the Christian faith, they never forgot their Greek heritage. Indeed, the transition from late Roman to Byzantine civilization is marked by an increasing dissociation from the Latin-Roman past and a heightened emphasis on the legacy of Hellenism. As time went on, Byzantine scholars forgot their Latin; Greek became the language of the imperial court. The Byzantine Church all but lost contact with the Roman pope. Greek philosophy and letters were studied with undying diligence by educated men who cherished their ties with the Hellenic past.

The Age of Justinian

The first great creative surge of Byzantine civilization occurred during the reign of Justinian (527–565). In many respects Justinian stands as the last of the Roman emperors; in others, he was a Byzantine through and through. He spoke in the Latin tongue, and was haunted by the dream of re-conquering the West and reviving the Roman Empire of old. It was under his direction that the vast heritage of Roman law was assembled into one coherent body. In all these respects he was a ruler in the great Roman tradition. On the other hand, his reign witnessed a golden age of Byzantine art and the climax of imperial autocracy and caesaropapism which typified Byzantine culture over the centuries that followed.

The spectacular achievements of Justinian's reign were a product not only of the genius of the emperor but also of the wise and cautious rule of his predecessors who endured the worst of the barbarian invasions, nurtured the financial resources of the Empire, and gradually accumulated a sizable surplus in the treasury. Justinian was also fortunate in the fact that the Germanic kingdoms of the West, which he had determined to conquer, were losing much of their early vigor. Theodoric, the great Ostrogothic king, died in 526, a year before Justinian ascended the Byzantine throne, and the Vandal monarchy of North Africa, once a cruel oppressor of its subject people, was now merely corrupt.

The opportunities were present, and Justinian was the man to seize them. He was a ruler of iron determination and boundless ambition, a prodigious administrator and organizer, and an able theologian. His tireless energy and daring represented a radical departure from Byzantine conservatism, but his vast plans, although largely successful in a limited sense, left the Empire bankrupt and exhausted. He applied his theological knowledge to the difficult problem of reconciling the orthodox and the Monophysites, but his compromise formula was satisfactory to neither side. When a series of riots early in his reign resulted in the burning of much of Constantinople, he lavished imperial funds on rebuilding the capital on an unprecedented scale. One

San Vitale, Ravenna (526–547): Exterior (below), Interior (opposite).

product of his rebuilding program was the church of Sancta Sophia—Byzantium's greatest work of art. Gold, silver, ivory, and dazzling mosaics adorned its interior, and a vast dome seemed almost to float on air above it. The total effect was such as to stun even Justinian: he is said to have exclaimed on its completion, "Glory to God who has judged me worthy of accomplishing such a work as this! O Solomon, I have outdone thee!"

Female Martyrs, mosaic from S. Apollinare Nuovo, Ravenna (493–525).

St. Mark's in Venice (begun in 1063).

It was at Justinian's bidding that a talented group of lawyers set about to assemble the immense mass of legal precedents, juridical opinions, and imperial edicts that constituted the legacy of Roman law. These materials were arranged into a vast, systematic collection known as the *Corpus Juris Civilis*—the "body of civil law." Justinian's *Corpus* not only became the keystone of future Byzantine jurisprudence but also served as the vehicle in which Roman law returned to Western Europe in the twelfth century to challenge the age-long domination of Germanic legal custom. The appearance of the *Corpus Juris Civilis* in the twelfth-century West was of incalculable importance to the development of sophisticated and rational legal systems in the European states. Indeed, its effect is still very much appar-

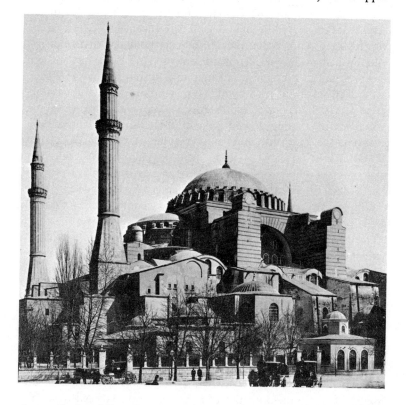

Sancta Sophia (The Church of Holy Wisdom) in Constantinople (532–537). The minarets are from a much later period.

ent in the legal codes of modern nations. But the importance of the *Corpus Juris Civilis* extended even beyond this. Roman law had formerly contained strong elements of popular sovereignty, but in Justinian's hand it acquired some of the autocratic flavor of the Byzantine state. Thus, in the late-medieval and early-modern West it tended to support the rise of royal absolutism, acting as a counterpoise to the limited-monarchy notions of Germanic legal tradition. The monarchs of late medieval and early modern Europe found much to admire in Justinian's precept that the highest law was the ruler's will.

Historians are prone to criticize Justinian for lavishing the limited resources of his empire on the chimerical policy of reconquering the West. In one sense they are correct: the reconquest did drain the treasury and prostrate the Empire, and the victories of Justinian's western armies proved in time to be largely ephemeral. Yet Justinian, with his keen sense of the Roman imperial tradition, could not rest until he had made one all-out attempt to recover the lost western provinces and to re-establish imperial authority in the city of Rome. His armies, small but led by brilliant generals, conquered the worm-eaten Vandal kingdom of North Africa with ease in 533–554, and succeeded in wresting a long strip of the Spanish Mediterranean coast from the Visigoths. For twenty years his troops struggled against the Ostrogoths in Italy, crushing them at length in 555 but only after enormous effort and expense. The campaigns in Italy, known as the "Gothic Wars," devastated the Italian peninsula and left Rome itself in ruins. The Visigothic sack of 410 was nothing compared with the havoc wrought by Justinian's armies.

During the final decade of his reign Justinian ruled almost the entire Mediterranean coastline, but his vastly expanded empire was impoverished and bankrupt. A devastating outbreak of bubonic plague struck in 541–543 and recurred sporadically over the succeeding decades, taking a fearful toll of human lives and crippling the Byzantine economy. But even without the plague Byzantium would have found it exceedingly difficult to hold its newly conquered territories. With his military attention focused westward, Justinian was powerless to prevent a great flood of Slavic peoples and Bulgars from ravaging the Balkans. In 561, the Avars, warlike nomads from the Asiatic steppes, settled on the Danube shore and proceeded to subjugate the Slavs and Bulgars. Byzantium now found itself living in

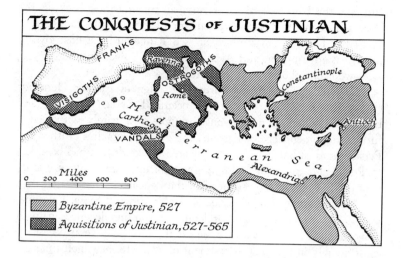

THE CONQUESTS OF JUSTINIAN

FRANKS

Ravenna

OSTROGOTHS

Rome

Constantinople

VISIGOTHS

M e d i

Carthage

VANDALS

t e r r a n e a n   S e a

Antioch

Miles
0   200   400   600   800

Alexandria

Byzantine Empire, 527
Aquisitions of Justinian, 527-565

the shadow of a hostile barbarian state, far more threatening than
Vandal North Africa or Ostrogothic Italy. This new danger pointed
up Justinian's great shortcomings—his inability to match ambitions to
resources. The huge empire that he bequeathed to his successors was
exhausted and dangerously vulnerable.

Retrenchment and Revival

The Byzantine Empire aspired to be Roman yet was destined by the
realities of geopolitics to be Balkan and Near-Eastern. Justinian's
western conquests were not enduring. In 568, three years after his
death, a savage Germanic tribe known as the Lombards (Langobards
or Long Beards) burst into Italy, further devastating that troubled
land and carving out an extensive kingdom in northern Italy centering on the Po Valley. Byzantium retained much of southern Italy and
clung to Ravenna and other cities along the Adriatic coast, but its
hold on Italy was badly shaken. Shortly afterward, the Visigoths
reconquered the Byzantine territories in southern Spain, and eventually, in the 690s, Byzantine North Africa—the former Vandal state—
fell to the Muslims. In 751 the Lombards took Ravenna, and Byzantine power in Italy was reduced still further.

Justinian's successors were forced to abandon his ambitious policies and face the hard necessities of survival, turning their back on the West to face more immediate threats from hostile peoples to the north and east. The Persian Empire pressed dangerously against Byzantium's eastern frontier, and Avars, with their Bulgar and Slavic subjects, won control of most of the Balkans.

The great crisis occurred during the reign of Empror Heraclius (640–641), when Persian armies occupied Syria, Palestine, and Egypt and when, in 626, Constantinople just barely withstood a furious combined siege of Persians and Avars. Heraclius crushed the Persian army at last in 628 and recovered the lands that had been lost to Persia. He succeeded also in reestablishing imperial suzerainty over the Balkans. But no sooner had the Persians been defeated than the Muslim armies exploded out of Arabia to wrest Syria, Palestine, and Egypt from the Empire and put Constantinople once again in grave danger. The Muslims besieged the city on several occasions, most notably in the great investment of 717–718, at which time the dogged Byzantine defense may have prevented not only the Empire but much of Eastern and Central Europe from being absorbed into the Arab world. The Empire withstood the powerful northwestward thrust of Islam, retaining Constantinople, Anatolia, and an unsteady overlordship in the Balkan peninsula, thereby preserving the division of medieval western Eurasia into the three great cultures of Byzantium, Islam, and Western Christendom. The Christian kingdoms of the West were able to develop behind the shield of Constantinople's walls.

The Macedonian Emperors and the Conversion of the Slavs

Byzantium had won the time necessary for the gradual conquest and conversion of southeastern Europe. In the course of the seventh century, it had lost such great urban cultural centers as Damascus, Alexandria, Antioch, and Carthage, with the result that the empire became far smaller and poorer, yet more homogeneous, more unified culturally, more completely centered on the one great city remaining: Constantinople.

After several generations of retrenchment and consolidation, Byzantium began to expand once again under the dynasty of "Macedonian" emperors (867–1056). A rich literary and artistic revival was accomplished by a series of important territorial conquests and by an evangelical surge that resulted in the conversion of countless Slavic peoples to Eastern Orthodox Christianity. Byzantium's political and religious expansion under the Macedonian emperors shaped the cultural development of Eastern Europe for the next millennium.

The Macedonians reconquered northern Syria for a time and pushed their frontiers in Asia Minor northeastward. But their most significant military accomplishment, in the long run, was the establishment of firm Byzantine rule over the Balkan Slavs and Bulgars. The greatest ruler of the dynasty, Basil II, "The Bulgar-slayer" (976–1025) campaigned year after year in the Balkans, demolishing a Bulgarian army in 1014 and eventually crushing all resistance to Byzantine imperial authority.

In the meantime, beginning in the middle years of the ninth century, the process of Byzantine religious conversion and acculturation among the peoples of southeastern Europe began in earnest. Missionaries such as Cyril and Methodius, "the Apostles to the Slavs," evangelized tirelessly among the south Slavs and Russians, drawing them into the orbit of Byzantine Christianity and culture. Cyril and Methodius, in the second half of the ninth century, invented the first Slavonic alphabet and employed it in the creation of a Slavic vernacular Bible and liturgy. Thus the Slavonic written language and the Slavonic Christian Church came into being side by side. Ultimately, the evangelism of the Macedonian age brought the Balkans and Russia into the Orthodox Church and into the sphere of Byzantine culture.

The Conversion of Russia

The age of the Macedonian emperors was concurrent with the rise of Russia—far beyond the political boundaries of the Empire. Byzantium had always had economic and political interests on the northern shore of the Black Sea. In the ninth and tenth centuries, trade flourished between the Black Sea and the Baltic and linked the Byzantine Empire with the vigorous commerce of the Viking world. Numerous Byzantine coin hoards dating from this era have been unearthed in Scandinavia, and Norsemen were widely employed as

Byzantine mercenaries. Swedish Vikings probed deep into Russia in the ninth century and established a dynasty in the Russian trading center of Novgorod, ruling over the native Slavic population and later intermarrying with it. In the tenth century a ruler of Novgorod captured the strategic Russian commercial town of Kiev, which became the nucleus of the first important Russian state.

The Macedonian emperors at Constantinople took great pains to maintain warm diplomatic relations with Kievan Russia. Basil II, the Bulgar-Slayer, received crucial military aid from Prince Vladimir of Kiev and promised in return to give his own sister to Vladimir in marriage. The result of this marriage was nothing less than the conversion of Kievan Russia. For Vladimir, on marrying his Byzantine princess, agreed to adopt Christianity. Kiev never submitted politically to the Byzantine emperors, but its people became spiritual subjects of the patriarch of Constantinople.

In the course of the eleventh century, Kievan Russia distintegrated politically, and in the thirteenth century it was brought under the yoke of Mongol invaders, but its Christian-Byzantine culture survived these political disasters. In the fifteenth century, when the Byzantine Empire itself was demolished, the Christian princes of Moscow assumed the imperial title (Caesar—Czar). As Constantinople had been the "Second Rome," they intended Moscow to become the "Third Rome," and they asserted their dominion over both church and state much as their imperial "predecessors" at Constantinople had done. Some scholars have even suggested that the present rulers of Russia, with their control of both the state and the Communist ideological apparatus, are carrying on the tradition of Byzantine caesaropapism in secularized form.

Military Disaster and Cultural Survival

The dynamism and grandeur of the Macedonian age came to an end in the eleventh century with the passing of the Macedonian dynasty (1056) and the coming of a powerful new Asian tribe, the Seljuk Turks, into the Middle East. Only recently converted to Islam, the Seljuks had made a puppet of the Islamic caliph at Baghdad. In 1065 they wrested Armenia from the Byzantines, and when an imperial army attempted to drive them from Asia Minor, it was annihilated at the epochal Battle of Manzikert in 1071.

Manzikert is one of the great turning points in Byzantine history. Even though the Seljuk Turks did not adequately follow up their great triumph, the disaster emasculated the Empire by breaking the age-long Byzantine hold on Asia Minor. In the same fatal year of 1071, the Normans of southern Italy conquered the vital Byzantine Adriatic port of Bari, marking the virtual end of Byzantium's presence in the West. By now, Western Christendom was acquiring the wealth and power of a great civilization, and prostrate Byzantium was forced to beg aid from the papacy and the Franks. The century of Manzikert ended with the First Crusade and the fall of Jerusalem (1099), not to Byzantine warriors but to French and Norman crusaders. Byzantium tottered on until the mid-fifteenth century, but it was never again the same. Its years of expansion were over, and its energies were thenceforth consumed in its struggle to endure.

Yet Byzantine culture survived the blow of Manzikert. Art and learning continued, and even at the very close of its long history, in 1453, Byzantium was in the midst of an impressive classical-humanist revival that made a significant impact on the Italian Renaissance.

To the end, Byzantium revered its classical heritage. As a custodian of Greco-Roman culture, the Eastern Empire provided an invaluable service to the emerging civilization of Western Europe. Roman law and Greek philosophy and letters were studied in Constantinople at a time when they were all but unknown in the West. The influence of Byzantine art on medieval Western Christendom was, in the words of a modern historian, "far-flung and everywhere beneficial: and whatever else the west disliked and despised about the east, its mosaics and enamels, its textiles and ivories, its pearl and onyx, its painting and its gold work were eagerly coveted and jealously guarded in western treasuries."*

Yet Byzantium's government was never able to transcend the stifling autocracy of the late Roman Empire or the fundamentally defensive mood that it implied. Byzantium's creative impulses were all too often stunted by its remorseless conservatism, and creative originality was less valued than the preservation of a priceless heritage.

Byzantium's lasting contribution to European history lies above all in its conversion of Russia and the Balkans. Eastern Orthodox Christi-

---

* Romily Jenkins, *Byzantium, The Imperial Centuries*, Vintage Books, New York, 1969, p. 385.

anity is similar in basic doctrine to the traditional religions of Western Europe, yet it differs in numerous important ways. The culture of Orthodox Eastern Europe, deriving as it does from Byzantium, is more open to Westernizing influences than, say, the culture of the Islamic or Hindu or Buddhist peoples. Eastern Europe today is Westernized, yet not fully Western. Its culture is similar, yet different, industrialized but not fully at ease with parliamentary democracy on the Western pattern. Its historic traditions are varied and complex, but the tradition of Byzantium is not the least among them.

4

the barbarian west

The ignorance and savagery of the early medieval West stand in sharp contrast to the urbanity of Byzantium. Yet Western Europe had the inestimable advantage of a fresh start. It was inspired and enriched by the classical heritage, but not shackled by it.

In the aftermath of the Germanic invasions Western Europe found itself cut adrift from the government of the Roman Empire. The Church survived to carry on much of the old classical legacy. But Germanic kings and nobles were generally incapable of preserving the political and economic institutions of the Roman past. Towns had been declining in Western Europe ever since the third century; by A.D. 600 they were shrunken phantoms of what they once had been. North of the Alps the municipal governments of antiquity had disappeared without a trace. But many of the towns themselves managed to endure, after a fashion, as centers of ecclesiastical administration. They remained the headquarters of episcopal government and the sites of the bishops' cathedral churches. Many towns became important pilgrimage centers, for the more important cathedral churches possessed relics—portions of the bodies or clothing of departed saints—which were regarded as agents of spiritual and physical healing. The cathedral at Tours, for example, possessed the bones of the noted miracle-worker, St. Martin, which were said to heal any who touched them.

These episcopal centers played only a minor role in the culture and economy of the barbarian successor states. Far more important were the monastery, the peasant village, and the great farm or villa owned by some wealthy Roman or Germanic aristocrat and divided into small plots worked by semi-free tenant farmers. A small-scale luxury trade persisted, but by and large the economy of the sixth and seventh centuries was local and self-contained. Small agrarian communities produced most of their own needs, for their life was meager and their needs were few.

Except in Britain and northeastern Gaul the barbarians tended to become absorbed into the older indigenous population. Free Germanic farmers often descended into the ranks of the semi-servile peasantry that had survived from Roman times. But at the aristocratic level the pattern of life was set by the barbarian warrior nobility, and consequently the civility of the Roman villa gradually disappeared. The Roman and barbarian nobility were fused through intermarriage into one class—hard-bitten and warlike—far more Germanic than Roman.

Government; Intellectual Life

With the exception of Theodoric, the barbarian kings proved incapable of perpetuating the Roman administrative traditions which they inherited. They allowed the Roman tax system to break down; they permitted the privilege of minting coins to fall into private hands. The power and wealth of the state declined, not because the kings were generous but because they were ignorant. They lacked the slightest conception of responsible government and regarded their kingdoms as private estates to be exploited or alienated according to their whims. They made reckless gifts of land and public authority to nobles and churchmen and regarded what remained as their personal property, to be exploited for the sole purpose of their own enrichment. In brief, they succeeded in combining the worst features of anarchy and tyranny.

During the late Roman Empire Western Europe had been ruthlessly overgoverned; now it was radically undergoverned. The Germanic monarchs did precisely nothing to enliven the economy or ameliorate the general impoverishment. The Church strove to fill the vacuum by dispensing charity and glamorizing the virtue of resignation, but it was ill-equipped to cope with the chaos of the barbarian West. Its organization was confined largely to the defunct towns and walled monasteries. Only gradually were rural parishes organized to meet the needs of the countryside. Not until after the eighth century did the country parish become a characteristic feature of the Western Church. In the meantime a peasant was fortunate if he saw a priest once a year. The monarchy and the Church, the two greatest land-holders in the barbarian states, were better known among the peasantry as acquisitive landlords than as fountains of justice and divine grace. Rural life was harsh, brutish, and short, and the countryside was politically and spiritually adrift.

The intellectual life of the barbarian West was almost as backward as its political and economic life. The culture of old Rome was rotting, and the new civilization of Western Europe had scarcely begun to develop. The intellectual level of the sixth and seventh centuries can best be appreciated by looking at a few leading scholars of the period. Bishop Gregory of Tours (d. 594), whose *History of the Franks* is our best source for the reigns of Clovis and his successors, must be counted one of the leading historians of his age. Yet Gregory's *History* is written in ungrammatical Latin and is filled with outrageous and silly miracles. The world portrayed by Gregory of Tours was dominated by savage cruelty and naked force and beclouded by magic and superstitious fantasy. Both the story that he presents and the way in which he presents it attest to the decline of civilization in sixth-century Gaul.

Pope Gregory the Great (d. 604) was awarded a place alongside Ambrose, Jerome, and Augustine as one of the four Doctors of the Latin Church. But his writings, although marked by the profound practical wisdom and psychological insight of a potentially brilliant man, suffered from the cultural decadence of his age and are incomparably below the level of the fourth-century doctors in philosophical and scholarly sophistication. Pope Gregory watered down Augustinian theology for the benefit of his own naive contemporaries. The lofty theological issues with which Augustine grappled are overshadowed in Pope Gregory's thought by a concentration on such secondary matters as angels, demons, and relics.

Bishop Isidore of Seville (d. 636) was known as the foremost intellectual of his generation. His most impressive work, the *Etymologies*, was intended to be an encyclopedia of all knowledge. It was a valuable work for its time and was studied by many generations thereafter. But its value was diminished by Isidore's lack of critical powers. He included every scrap of information that he could find, whether likely or unlikely, profound or absurd. It can perhaps be said that he was victimized by the credulity of the ancient writers on whom he depended, and was left adrift by the weakness of the Roman scientific tradition. Nevertheless, as the greatest mind of his age he was naive. On the subject of monsters he writes as follows:

The Cynocephali are so called because they have dogs' heads and their very barking betrays them as beasts rather than men. These are born in India. The Cyclopses, too, hail from India, and they are so named because they have a single eye in the midst of the forehead. . . . The Blemmyes, born in Lybia, are believed to be headless trunks, having mouth and eyes in the breast; others are born without necks, with eyes in the shoulders . . . . They say the Panotii in Sythia have ears of so large a size that they cover the whole body with them . . . . The race of the Sciopodes is said to live in Ethiopia. They have one leg apiece, and are of a marvelous swiftness, and . . . in summertime they lie on the ground on their backs and are shaded by the greatness of their feet.

Finally, with a touch of skepticism, Isidore concludes,

Other fabulous monstrosities of the human race are said to exist, but they do not; they are imaginary.

In fairness to Isidore it should be said that his treatment of monsters fails to show him to best advantage, and that it was drawn from earlier materials dating from the ancient world. But he combined and synthesized these materials with an intellectual abandon typical of his age.

The Barbarian Kingdoms

The century between A.D. 500 and 600 witnessed important changes in the political structure of Western Christendom. In A.D. 500 Theodoric's Ostrogothic regime dominated Italy, the Vandals ruled North Africa, the Visigoths governed Spain, Clovis and his Franks were conquering Gaul, and the Anglo-Saxons were beginning their settlements in Britain. A century later, two of these states had been destroyed by Justinian's armies: North Africa was now Byzantine rather than Vandal, and the Ostrogothic kingdom of Italy had collapsed.

By 600 the Anglo-Saxon tribes had occupied much of Britain, enslaving many of the indigenous Celtic inhabitants and driving others into the western mountains of Wales, or across the Channel to Brittany. Anglo-Saxon Britain was now a confused medley of small, independent heathen kingdoms in which the process of Christian conversions was just beginning.

Gaul in 600 was thoroughly dominated by the Franks under the cruel and incompetent successors of Clovis, founder of the *Merovingian* dynasty.* This dynasty followed the Germanic custom of dividing the kingdom among the sons of a deceased ruler. Often the sons would engage in bitter civil war until, as it sometimes happened, one of them emerged as sole monarch of the Franks. At his death, the kingdom would be divided among his own sons, and the bitter comedy would be repeated. Merovingian government became more and more predatory and unenlightened, and the Frankish Church became increasingly disorganized and corrupt.

Corruption was also paralyzing Church and state in Visigothic Spain. The monarchy, which shed its Arianism and embraced Catholicism in 589, was able at length to reconquer its Mediterranean shore from feeble Byzantium (*c.* 624). But the inept Visigothic kings allowed their power to slip little by little into the hands of a greedy and oppressive landed aristocracy. The worm-eaten regime was an easy prey for the conquering Muslims in the early 700s.

The century since Theodoric's reign had been a disastrous one for Italy. The horrors of Justinian's Gothic wars were followed by the invasion of the Lombards. By 600 the decimated peninsula was divided between the Byzantines in Ravenna and the south, and the Lombards in the north. The papacy, under nominal Byzantine jurisdiction, dominated the lands around Rome and sought to preserve its fragile independence by playing Lombard against Byzantine. At critical moments, however, it looked to the Byzantines as its defenders.

Creative Forces

Such was the condition of Western Europe in 600. At first glance one can see little to hope for in the all-prevailing gloom. Yet this was the society out of which Western civilization was born. This was the formative epoch—the age of genesis—in which apparently minor

---

* Named after Clovis' half-mythical ancestor, Merovech.

trends would one day broaden into the powerful traditions that would govern the course of European history. Even in 600 there were glimmerings of light in the darkness. Classical culture still survived, if only in a sadly vulgarized form. Isidore of Seville was no Augustine, but he was far more than a mere barbarian. The Church, although tainted by the ignorance and corruption of its environment, still retained something of its power to inspire, enlighten, and civilize.

Far to the north, Ireland had been won for Christianity by St. Patrick in the fifth century; by 600 it had developed an astonishingly creative Celtic-Christian culture. Irish scholars were familiar with both Greek and Latin literature at a time when Greek was unknown elsewhere in the West. By the later seventh century Irish artists were producing magnificent illuminated manuscripts in a flowing, curvilinear Celtic style. Irish Christianity, isolated from the continental Church by the heathen Anglo-Saxon kingdoms, developed distinctive customs. It was organized around the monastery rather than the diocese, and its leader were abbots rather than bishops. Irish monks were famous for their learning, the austere holiness of their lives, and the vast scope of their missionary activities. They converted large portions of Scotland to their own form of Christianity and by the early 600s were conducting missionary activities on the Continent itself.

Monasticism was the most dynamic and significant institution in the Early Middle Ages. The impulse toward monastic life is not peculiar to Christianity but is found in many religions—Buddhism and Judaism, to name but two. The Essenes, for example, whose cult may have produced the famous Dead Sea scrolls, constituted a kind of Jewish monastic order. There have always been religious souls who long to withdraw from the world and devote their lives to uninterrupted communion with God, but among Christians this impulse was particularly strong. Monasticism came to be regarded as the most perfect form of the Christian life—the consummate embodiment of Christ's own words: "And every man that has forsaken home, or brothers, or sisters, or father, or mother, or wife, or children, or lands for my name's sake, shall receive his reward a hundredfold, and obtain everlasting life" (Matt., XIX, xxix).

The impulse toward withdrawal and denunciation first affected Christianity in the later third century when the Egyptian St. Anthony retired to the desert to live the ascetic life of a godly hermit. In time the fame of his sanctity spread, and a colony of ascetics gathered around him to draw inspiration from his holiness. Saint Anthony thereupon organized a community of hermits who lived together but had no communication with one another, like apartment dwellers in a large American city. Similar hermit communities soon arose throughout Egypt and spread into other regions of the Empire. Hermit saints abounded in the fourth and fifth centuries. One of them, St. Simeon Stylites, achieved the necessary isolation by living atop a sixty-foot pillar for thirty years, evoking widespread admiration and imitation.

In the meantime a more down-to-earth type of monasticism was developing. Beginning in early fourth-century Egypt and then expanding quickly throughout the Roman Empire, monastic communities, based on a cooperative rather than a hermit life, were attracting numerous fervent Christians who found insufficient challenge in the increasingly complacent post-Constantine Church. The holy individualism of the desert and pillar saints thus gave way to a more ordered monastic life. Still, the early communities remained loosely organized and continued to emphasize ascetic practices of severe fasting, hair shirts, and purifying lashings, which had been pioneered by the ancient hermits and which fascinate the modern psychologists.

St. Benedict and His Rule

Saint Benedict of Nursia (c. 480–544) changed the course of Western monasticism, tempering its flamboyant holiness with common sense and realistic principles of organization. As a youth, St. Benedict fled corrupt Rome and took up the hermit life in a cave near the ruins of Nero's country palace. In time word of his saintliness circulated and disciples gathered around him. As it turned out, Benedict was more than a mere ascetic; he was a man of keen psychological insight—a superb organizer who slowly learned from the varied experience of his youth how the monastic life might best be lived. Born of a Roman aristocratic family, he brought to his task a practical genius and a sense of order and discipline that were typically Roman. He founded a number of monasteries which drew not only prospective saints but ordinary people as well—even the sons of wealthy Roman families. At length he established his great monastery of Monte Cassino atop a mountain midway between Rome and Naples. For centuries thereafter Monte Cassino was one of the chief centers of religious life in Western Europe. It became a model monastery, governed by a comprehensive, compassionate rule. In the midst of Justinian's Gothic Wars St. Benedict died, but his rule survived to inspire and transform Western Europe.

Pope Gregory the Great described the Rule of St. Benedict as "conspicuous for its discretion." Modern scholars have discovered that it was derived from an earlier, anonymous monastic rule, but St. Benedict gave it a novel quality of humane practicality. It provided for a busy, closely regulated life, simple but not ruthlessly ascetic. Benedictine monks were decently clothed, adequately fed, and seldom left to their own devices. Theirs was a life dedicated to God and the attainment of personal sanctity, yet it was also a life that could be led by any dedicated Christian. It was rendered all the more attractive by the increasing brutality of the outside world. The monastic day was filled with carefully arranged activities: communal prayer, devotional reading, and work—field work, household work, manuscript copying—according to the needs of the monastery and the ability of the monk. The fundamental obligations were chastity, poverty, and obedience: the monk must be celibate; he must discard all personal possessions; he must obey his abbot. The abbot, elected by the monks for life, was unquestioned master of the monastery, but he was to consult the monks in all his decisions. He was strictly responsible to God and was instructed to govern justly in accordance with the Rule. He was cautioned not to sadden or "overdrive" his monks or give them cause for "just murmuring." Here especially is the quality of discretion to which Pope Gregory alludes and which doubtless has been a major factor in the Rule's success.

Contributions of the Benedictines

Within two centuries of Benedict's death the Rule had spread throughout Western Christendom. The result was not a vast hierarchical monastic organization but rather a host of individual, autonomous monasteries sharing a single Rule and way of life but administratively unrelated. Benedict had visualized his monasteries as spiritual sanctuaries into which pious men might withdraw from the world. But the chaotic and illiterate society of the barbarian West, desperately in need of the discipline and learning of the Benedictines, could not permit them to abdicate from secular affairs.

In reality, therefore, the Benedictines had an enormous impact on the world they renounced. Their schools produced the vast majority of literate Europeans during the Early Middle Ages. They served as a cultural bridge, transcribing and preserving the writings of Latin antiquity. They spearheaded the penetration of Christianity into the forests of Germany and later into Scandinavia, Poland, and Hungary. They served as scribes and advisers to kings, and were drafted into high ecclesiastical offices. As recipients of gifts of land from pious donors over many generations they held and managed large estates which became models of intelligent agricultural organization and technological innovation. With the coming of feudalism, Benedictine abbots became great vassals, responsible for political and legal administration and military recruitment over the large areas under their control. Above all, as islands of security and learning in an ocean of barbarism the Benedictine monasteries were the spiritual and intellectual centers of the developing classical-Christian-Germanic synthesis that underlay European civilization. In short, Benedictine monasticism became the supreme influence in the barbarian West.

Pope Gregory the Great

The Benedictines carried out their civilizing mission with the enthusiastic and invaluable support of the papacy. The alliance between these two institutions was consummated by the first Benedictine pope, Gregory the Great, who recognized how effective the Benedictines might be in spreading the Catholic faith and extending papal leadership far and wide across Christendom.

We have already encountered Pope Gregory as a scholar—a popularizer of Augustinian thought. His theology, although highly influential in subsequent centuries, failed to rise much above the intellectual level of his age. His real genius lay in his keen understanding of human nature and his ability as an administrator and organizer. His *Pastoral Care*, a treatise on the duties and obligations of a bishop, is a masterpiece of practical wisdom and common sense. It answered a great need of the times and became one of the most widely read books in the Middle Ages.

Gregory loved the monastic life and ascended the papal throne with genuine regret. On hearing of his election he went into hiding and had to be dragged into the Roman basilica of St. Peter's to be consecrated. But once resigned to his new responsibilities, Gregory bent every energy to the extension of papal authority. He believed fervently that the pope, as successor of St. Peter, was the rightful ruler of the Church. He reorganized the financial structure of the papal estates and used the increased revenues for charitable works to ameliorate the wretched poverty of his age. His integrity, wisdom, and administrative ability won for him an almost regal position in Rome and central Italy, towering over the contemporary Lombards and Byzantines who were then struggling for control of the peninsula. The reform of the Frankish Church was beyond his immediate powers. But he set in motion a process that would one day bring both France and Germany into the papal fold when he dispatched a group of Benedictine monks to convert heathen England.

The Conversion of England

The mission to England was led by the Benedictine St. Augustine (not to be confused with the great theologian of an earlier day, St. Augustine of Hippo). In 597, Augustine and his followers arrived in the English kingdom of Kent and began their momentous work. England was then divided into a number of independent barbarian kingdoms of which Kent was momentarily the most powerful, and Augustine was assured a friendly reception by the fact that King Ethelbert of Kent had a Christian wife. The conversion progressed speedily, and on Whitsunday, 597, King Ethelbert and thousands of his subjects were baptized. The chief town of the realm, "Kent City" or Canterbury, became the headquarters of the new Church, and Augustine himself became Canterbury's first archbishop. Under his influence Ethelbert issued the first written laws in the Anglo-Saxon language.

During the decades that followed, the fortunes of English Benedictine Christianity rose and fell with the varying fortunes of the barbarian kingdoms. Kent declined after King Ethelbert's death, and by the mid-600s political power had shifted to the northernmost of the Anglo-Saxon states, Northumbria. This remote outpost became the scene of a deeply significant encounter between the two great creative forces of the age: Irish-Celtic Christianity moving southward from its monasteries in Scotland, and Roman-Benedictine Christianity moving northward from Kent.

Although the two movements shared a common faith, they had different cultural backgrounds, different notions of monastic life and ecclesiastical organization, and even different systems for calculating the date of Easter. At stake was England's future relationship with the Continent and the papacy; a Celtic victory might well have resulted in the isolation of England from the main course of Western Christian development. But at the Synod of Whitby in 664, King Oswy of Northumbria decided in favor of Roman-Benedictine Christianity and papal influence in England was assured. Five years later, in 669, the papacy sent the scholarly Theodore of Tarsus to assume the archbishopric of Canterbury and reorganize the English Church into a coherent hierarchical system. As a consequence of Northumbria's conversion and Archbishop Theodore's tireless efforts, England, only a century out of heathenism, became Europe's most vigorous and creative Christian society.

The Irish-Benedictine encounter in seventh-century Northumbria produced a significant cultural surge known as the Northumbian Renaissance. The two traditions influenced and inspired one another to such an extent that the evolving civilization of the barbarian West reached its pinnacle in this remote land. Boldly executed illuminated manuscripts in the Celtic curvilinear style, a new script, a vigorous vernacular epic poetry, an impressive architecture—all contributed to the luster of Northumbrian civilization in the late 600s and the early 700s. The Northumbrian Renaissance centered in the great monasteries founded by Irish and Benedictine missionaries, particularly in the Benedictine monastery of Jarrow. Here the supreme scholar of the age, St. Bede the Venerable, spent his life.

Bede entered Jarrow as a child and remained there until his death in 735. The greatest of his many works, the *Ecclesiastical History of England*, displays a keen critical sense far superior to that of Bede's medieval predecessors and contemporaries. The *Ecclesiastical History*, our chief source for early English history, is the first major historical work to employ the modern chronological framework based on the Christian era (A.D.—Anno Domini—the year of the Lord). And Bede's chronological innovation reflects his deep sense of historical unity and purpose: the transformation of the world—and particularly of England—through the spread of the Christian gospel and the monastic life. The *Ecclesiastical History* reflects a remarkable cultural breadth and a penetrating mind, and it establishes Bede as the foremost Christian intellect since Augustine of Hippo.

By Bede's death in 735 the Northumbrian kings had lost their political hegemony, and Northumbrian culture was beginning to fade. But the tradition of learning was carried from England back to the Continent during the eighth century by a group of Anglo-Saxon Benedictine missionaries. In the 740s the English monk St. Boniface reformed the Church of Frankland, infusing it with Benedictine idealism and binding it more closely to the papacy. Pope Gregory had now been in his grave for 140 years, but his spirit was still at work. St. Boniface and other English missionaries founded new Benedictine monasteries among the Germans east of the Rhine and began the long, difficult task of Christianizing and civilizing Germany, just as Augustine and his monks had once Christianized Kent. By the later 700s the cultural center of Christendom had shifted southward again from England to the rising empire of the Frankish leader Charlemagne.* Significantly, the leading scholar in Charlemagne's kingdom was Alcuin, a Benedictine monk from Northumbria, a student of one of Bede's own disciples.

* See below, p. 84 ff.

Cross Page from the Lindisfarne Gospels (c. A.D. 700), *illustrating the artistic illuminations typical of the Northumbrian Renaissance.*

The Church and Western Civilization

The barbarian West differed from the Byzantine East in innumerable ways, the most obvious being its far lower level of civilization. But just as important is the fact that the Western Church was able to reject Byzantine caesaropapism and to develop more or less independently of the state. Church and state often worked hand in hand, but religion and secular politics were never merged as they were in Constantinople and, indeed, in most ancient civilizations. The early Christian West was marked by a profound dichotomy—a separation between cultural leadership which was ecclesiastical and monastic, and political power which was in the hands of the barbarian kings. This dualism underlay the fluidity and dynamism of Western culture. It produced a creative tension which tended toward change rather than crystallization, toward an uninterrupted series of cultural climaxes, and toward ever-new intellectual and spiritual configurations. Like St. Augustine's two cities, the warrior culture of the Germanic states and the classical-Christian culture of church and monastery remained always in the process of fusion yet never completely fused. The interplay between these two worlds governed the development of medieval civilization.

5

the explosion of islam

Background and Origins

Islam, Byzantium, and Western Christendom were Rome's three heirs, and of the three, Western Christendom remained for many centuries the most primitive and underdeveloped. Medieval Europe had much to learn from Islam and Byzantium, and its developing synthesis of classical, Christian, and Germanic traditions was shaped in many ways by its two neighboring civilizations. The influence of these neighbors was impeded, however, by Europe's hostility toward the "infidel" Muslims and the "effete, treacherous" Byzantines. In the eighth and ninth centuries Western Europe's contacts with Islam were limited largely to the battlefield. Only after the turn of the millennium did the West begin to draw upon the rich legacy of Muslim thought and culture.

Islam today is a distinctive culture and a living religion extending across an immense stretch of South Asia, the Middle East, and north Africa—from Indonesia to Pakistan to the Arab world of southwest Asia and Mediterranean Africa. This vast Islamic belt was created by a militant, compelling religion that burst into the world in seventh-century Arabia and spread outward with remarkable speed. In the first hundred years of its existence, Islam shattered the Christian domination of the Mediterranean basin, destroyed the Persian Empire, seized Byzantium's richest provinces, absorbed Spain, pressed into the heartlands of France, and expanded far into Southern Asia.

Muhammad

For countless centuries prior to the time of the prophet Muhammad (c. 571-632), fierce nomadic tribes from the Arabian Peninsula (the modern Saudi Arabia) had repeatedly invaded the rich civilized districts of Palestine, Syria, and Mesopotamia to the north. Many Semitic invaders and empire builders of the ancient Near East had come originally from the Arabian Desert—the Amorites, the Chaldeans, the Canaanites, even the Hebrews. These peoples had quickly assimilated the ancient civilization of the Fertile Crescent and developed it in new, creative ways. But their kinsmen who stayed in Arabia remained primitive and disorganized.

In Muhammad's time most Arabians still clung to their nomadic ways and to their crude, polytheistic religion, but by then new civilizing influences were beginning to make themselves felt. A great caravan route running northward from southern Arabia served as an important link in a far-flung commercial network between the Far East and the Byzantine and Persian Empires. Along this route cities developed to serve the caravans, and with city life came a modicum of civilization. Indeed, the greatest of these trading cities, Mecca, became a bustling commercial center which sent its own caravans northward and southward and grew wealthy on its middleman profits. As the tribal life of Mecca and other caravan cities began to give way to commercial life, new, foreign ideas challenged old ways and old viewpoints. It was in Mecca, around the year 571, that the prophet Muhammad was born.

At Muhammad's birth the Emperor Justinian had been dead for six years. Muhammad's contemporaries include such men as Pope Gregory the Great and Bishop Isidore of Seville. When the Benedictine mission from Rome landed in Kent in 597 to begin the conversion of England, Muhammad was in his twenties, as yet unknown outside his own immediate circle.

The future architect of one of the world's great religions was born of a poor branch of Mecca's leading clan. With little formal education behind him, he became a caravan trader, and his travels brought him into close contact with Judaism, Christianity, and Persian Zoroastrianism. A high-strung, sensitive man with a powerful, winning personality, he underwent a mystical experience while in his late thirties and began to set forth his new faith by preaching and writing. He won little support in Mecca apart from his wife and relatives and a few converts from the underprivileged classes. The ruling businessmen of Mecca were immune to the teaching of this "low-born upstart." They seem to have feared that his new religion would discredit the chief Meccan temple, the *Kaaba,* which housed a sacred meteoritic stone and was a profitable center of pilgrimages. Their belief that Muhammad's faith would ruin Mecca's pilgrim business was an ironic miscalculation, but their hostility to the new teaching forced Muhammad to flee Mecca in 622 and settle in the town of Medina, 280 miles northward on the caravan route.

The flight to Medina, known among the Muslims as the Hegira (He-jī′-ra) was a momentous turning point in the development of Islam and marks the beginning date of the Muslim calendar. Muhammad quickly won the inhabitants of Medina to his faith, and became the city's political chief as well as its religious leader. Indeed, under Muhammad's direction religious and civil authority were fused so that the sacred community was at once a state and a church. In this respect Muhammad's community at Medina foreshadowed the great Islamic state of later years.

The Medinans made war upon Mecca, raiding its caravans and blockading its trade. In 630 Medina conquered Mecca and incorporated it into the sacred community. During the two remaining years of his life Muhammad, now an almost legendary figure in Arabia, received the voluntary submission of many tribes in the peninsula. By the time of his death in 632 he had united the Arabians as never before into a coherent political-religious group, well-organized, well-armed, and inspired by a powerful new monotheistic religion. The violent energies of these desert people were now channeled toward a single goal: the conquest and conversion of the world.

The Islamic Religion

Faith was the cement with which Muhammad unified Arabia. The new faith was called *Islam,* the Arabic word for "surrender." Muhammad taught that his followers must surrender to the will of Allah, the single, almighty God of the universe. Allah's attributes of love and mercy were overshadowed by those of power and majesty, and the greatest good was to submit to Allah's commands. Muhammad did not regard himself as divine but rather as the last and greatest of a long line of prophets of whom he was the "seal." Among his predecessors were Moses, the Old Testament prophets, and Jesus.

Islam respected the Old and New Testaments and was relatively tolerant toward Jews and Christians—the "people of the book." But the Muslims had a book of their own, the *Koran,* which superseded its predecessors and was believed to contain the pure essence of divine revelation. The *Koran* is the comprehensive body of Muhammad's writings, the bedrock of the Islamic faith: "All men and jinn in collaboration," so it was said, "could not produce its like." Muslims regard it as the word of Allah, *dictated* to Muhammad by the angel Gabriel from an original "uncreated" book located in heaven. Accordingly, its divine inspiration and authority extend not only to its precepts but also to its every letter (of which there are 323,621), making any translation a species of heresy. Every good Muslim must read the *Koran* in Arabic, and as Islam spread the Arabic language necessarily spread with it.

The *Koran* is perhaps the most widely read book ever written. More than a manual of worship, it was the text from which the non-Arabian Muslim learned his Arabic. And since it was the supreme authority not only in religion but also in law, science, and the humanities, it became the standard text in Muslim schools for every imaginable subject. Muhammad's genius is vividly illustrated by his success in adapting a primitive language such as seventh-century Arabic to the sophisticated religious, legal, and ethical concepts that one encounters in his sacred book.

Muhammad offered his followers the assurance of eternal salvation if they led upright, sober lives and followed the precepts of Islam. Above all, they were bound to a simple confession of faith: "There is no god but Allah, and Muhammad is his prophet." The good Muslim was also obliged to engage in ritual prayers and fasting, to journey as a pilgrim to Mecca at least once in his lifetime, and to work devoutly toward the welfare and expansion of the sacred community. Holy war was the supremely meritorious activity, for service to the faith was identical with service to the state. Public law in Islamic lands had a religious sanction, and the fusion of religion and politics which Muhammad created at Medina remained a fundamental characteristic of Islamic society. There was no Muslim priesthood, no Muslim "Church" apart from the state: Muhammad's political successors, the caliphs, were defenders of the faith and guardians of the faithful. The tension between Church and state which proved such a stimulus to medieval Europe was thus unknown in the Muslim world.

The Early Conquests: 632–655

In the year immediately after Muhammad's death the explosive energy of the Arabs, harnessed at last by the teachings of the Prophet, broke upon the world. The spectacular conquests resulted in part from the youthful vigor of Islam, in part from the weakness and exhaustion of its enemies. The Emperor Heraclius had just defeated the Persians, and both Byzantium and Persia were spent and enfeebled by their long, desperate conflict. And the Monophysites of Syria and Egypt remained deeply hostile to their orthodox Byzantine masters.

The Arabs entered these tired, embittered lands afire with religious zeal, lured by the wealth and luxuries of the civilized world. They had no master plan of conquest—most of their campaigns began as plundering expeditions—but their momentum grew with each unexpected victory. Moving into Byzantine Syria they annihilated a huge Byzantine army in 636, captured Damascus and Jerusalem, and by 640 had occupied the entire land, detaching it more or less permanently from Byzantine control. In 637 they inflicted an overwhelming defeat on the Persian army and entered the Persian capital of Ctesiphon, gazing in bewilderment at its opulence and wealth. Within another decade they had subdued all Persia and arrived at the borders of India. In later years they penetrated deeply into the Indian subcontinent and laid the foundations of the modern Muslim states of Pakistan and Bangladesh. The Persians gradually adopted the Islamic faith and learned the Arab language, exchanging Zoroaster for Muhammad and thus preparing themselves for the great role that they would later play in Islamic politics and culture.

Meanwhile Muslims were pushing westward into Egypt. They captured Alexandria in the 640s, absorbing into their cultural sphere the great metropolis that had served Greek civilization ever since Hellenistic times. With Egypt and Syria in their hands they took to the sea, challenging the long-established Byzantine domination of the eastern Mediterranean. They took the island of Cyprus, raided ancient

Rhodes, and in 655 won a major victory over the Byzantine fleet in the Battle of the Masts.

The Civil War: 655–661

In 655 Islamic expansion ceased momentarily as the new empire became locked in a savage dynastic struggle. The succession to the caliphate was contested between the Umayyads, a leading family in the old Meccan commercial oligarchy, late to join the Islamic bandwagon but no less ambitious for all that, and Ali, the son-in-law of Muhammad himself. Ali headed a faction that was to become exceedingly powerful in later centuries. His followers insisted that the caliph must be a direct descendant of the Prophet. As it happened, Muhammad had left no surviving sons and only one daughter, Fatima, who married the Prophet's cousin, Ali.

In 661 the Umayyad forces defeated Ali in battle and initiated an Umayyad dynasty of caliphs that moved the Islamic capital to Damascus in Syria and ruled there for nearly a century. But the legitimist faction that had once supported Ali persisted as a troublesome, dedicated minority, throwing its support behind various of the numerous descendants of Ali and Fatima. In time the political movement evolved into a heresy known as *Shi'ism* which held that the *true* caliphs—the descendants of Muhammad through Fatima and Ali—were sinless, infallible, and possessed of a body of secret knowledge not contained in the *Koran*. *Shi'ism* became an occult underground doctrine which occasionally rose to the surface in the form of civil insurrection. In the tenth century the Shi'ists gained control of Egypt and established a "Fatimid" dynasty of caliphs in Cairo. Shi'ism inspired a band of Moslem desperadoes known as the "Assassins" who used hashish as a means of divine illumination. The movement survives to this day in the Ismaili sect led by the Aga Khan.

The Umayyad Dynasty: 661–750

The intermission in the Moslem expansion ended with the Umayyad victory over Ali in 661. And even though the Islamic capital was now Damascus rather than Medina, the old Arabian aristocracy remained in firm control. Constantinople was now the chief military goal, but the great city repulsed a series of powerful Muslim attacks between 670 and 680. The Byzantine defense was aided by a secret weapon known as "Greek Fire"—a liquid that ignited on exposure to air and could not be extinguished by water, but only by vinegar or sand. In 717–718 a great Arab fleet and army assaulted Constantinople in vain, and having expended all their energies and resources without success the Muslims abandoned their effort to take the city. Byzantium survived for another seven centuries, effectively barring inroads into southeastern Europe until the late Middle Ages.

In the meantime, however, Muslim armies were enjoying spectacular success in the West. From Egypt they moved along the North African coast into the old Vandal kingdom, now ruled by distant Byzantium. In 698 the Muslims took Carthage. In 711 they crossed the Straits of Gibraltar into Spain and crushed the tottering Visigothic kingdom at a blow, bringing the Spanish Christians under their dominion and driving the Christian princes into the fastness of the Pyrenees Mountains. Next the Muslims moved into southern Gaul and threatened the kingdom of the Merovingian Franks. In 732, a century after the Prophet's death the Muslims were halted at last on a battlefield between Tours and Poitiers by a Christian army led by the able Frankish warrior, Charles Martel. The Christians at Tours were not the white-clad defenders of the Gospel that former generations imagined them. They were semi-barbarous Franks, long-haired and clad in wolfskins. But they managed to halt the momentum of militant Islam in Western Europe, just as the Byzantines had stopped it in the East.

The Muslim army at Tours was small and makeshift in comparison with the great force that had invested Constantinople in 717–718, but together, these two battles brought an end to the era of major Islamic encroachments against the territories of the two Christian civilizations. The remainder of the Middle Ages witnessed continued Christian-Islamic warfare and some territorial change—most of Spain, for example, reverted to Christian control in the twelfth and thirteenth centuries—but Islam, Byzantium, and Western Christendom had achieved a relative equilibrium by the mid-eighth century and remained in balance for centuries to come.

Throughout the rest of the middle ages, the three civilizations tended to expand not at one another's expense but away from each other—Byzantium into the Balkans and Russia, Islam into South Asia,

THE ISLAMIC EMPIRE

The Empire at Mohammed's death
Conquests under the first three Caliphs
Conquests under the Omayyads
The Byzantine Empire

Miles
0   200   400   600   800   1000

Indus

Aral Sea

Caspian Sea

ARMENIA

PERSIA

Bagdad
Mesopot.
Ctesiphon
Antioch
Tyre
SYRIA
Damascus
Jerusalem

Arabian Sea

Indian Ocean

ARABIA

Medina

Mecca

Black Sea

Constantinople

ASIA MINOR

CYPRUS

CRETE

Mediterranean Sea

Alexandria   Cairo

EGYPT

Nile R.

AFRICA

Danube

AVARS

KINGDOM OF THE FRANKS

Rhine

Tours
Poitiers

Toledo
Cordova

Gibraltar

MOROCCO

Rome
Naples

CORSICA

SARDINIA

Tunis

Carthage

66

Western Christendom into Germany, Scandinavia, Hungary, and Western Slavdom. The Crusades were, ultimately, only a minor exception to this generalization; the Christian reconquest of Spain and the victory of the Seljuk Turks in Asia Minor were much more important exceptions. But it was not until the fourteenth century, when the Islamic Ottoman Turks swept into the Balkans, that the balance of the three power blocs was seriously upset.

The Golden Age of the Abbasids

In 750, seventeen years after the battle of Tours, the Umayyads were overthrown by a new dynasty, the Abbasids, Arabian in family background but with a program of greater political participation for the highly civilized conquered peoples, now converting in large numbers to Islam. It was above all the Islamized Persian aristocracy whom the Abbasids represented, and shortly after the victory of the new dynasty the capital was moved from Damascus to Baghdad on the Tigris, deep within the old Persian Empire, not far from the ruins of ancient Babylon. This move was accompanied by an eastward shift in Islam's orientation which relieved some of the pressure against Constantinople and the West.

Baghdad, under the early Abbasids, became one of the world's great cities. It was the center of a vast commercial network spreading across the Islamic world and far beyond. Silks, spices, and fragrant woods flowed into its wharves from India, China, and the East Indies; furs, honey, and slaves were imported from Scandinavia, and gold, slaves, and ivory from tropical Africa. Baghdad was the nexus of a far-flung banking system with branches in other cities across the Islamic world. A check could be drawn in Baghdad and cashed in Morocco, 4000 miles to the west. The Abbasid imperial palace, occupying fully a third of the city, contained innumerable apartments and public rooms, annexes for eunuchs, harems, and government officials, and a remarkable reception room known as the "hall of the tree" which contained an artificial tree of gold and silver on whose branches mechanical birds chirped and sang.

The wealth and culture of Baghdad reached its climax under the Abbasid caliph, Harun-al-Rashid (786–809), whose opulence and power quickly became legendary. Harun was accustomed to receiving tribute from the Byzantine Empire itself. When on one occasion the tribute was discontinued he sent the following peremptory note to the emperor at Constantinople:

> *In the name of God, the merciful, the compassionate.*
> *From Harun, the commander of the faithful,*
>   *to Nicephorus, the dog of a Roman.*
> *Verily I have read thy letter, O son of an infidel mother.*
> *As for the answer, it shall be for thine eye to see,*
>   *not for thine ear to hear. Salaam.*

The letter was followed by a successful military campaign which forced the unlucky Byzantines to resume their tribute.

The era of Harun-al-Rashid was one of notable intellectual activity in which the learned traditions of Greece, Rome, Persia, and India were absorbed and synthesized. In Baghdad Harun's son and successor founded the House of Wisdom—a great intellectual institute that was at once a library, a university, and a translation center. Here and elsewhere Islamic scholars pushed their learning far beyond the point it had reached under the Umayyads. Drawing from various traditions—Greek, Persian, Hindu—Islamic culture had come of age with remarkable speed. At a time when Charlemagne was struggling desperately to civilize his semi-barbaric Franks, Harun reigned over glittering Baghdad.

The rise of the Abbasids marked the breakdown of the Arabian aristocracy's monopoly on political power. Now the government was run by a medley of races and peoples, often of humble origin. As one disgruntled aristocrat observed, "Sons of concubines have become so numerous amongst us; Lead me to a land, O God, where I shall see no bastards."

The Abbasid government drew heavily from the administrative techniques of Byzantium and Persia. A sophisticated, complex bureaucracy ran the affairs of state from the capital at Baghdad and kept in touch with the provinces through a multitude of tax-gatherers, judges, couriers, and spies. The government was enlightened up to a point, although no more sensitive to the demands of social justice than other governments of its day. The Abbasid regime undertook extensive irrigation works, drained swamps, and thereby increased the amount of land under cultivation. But the status of the peasant and unskilled laborer was kept low by the competition of vast numbers of slaves. The brilliance of Abbasid culture had little effect on the under-privileged masses who, aside from their fervent Islamic faith, retained much of the same primitive way of life that they had known for the last two millennia.

The Decline of Abbasid Power

The Abbasids were unable to maintain their power throughout the vast reaches of the Islamic empire. Communications were limited by the speed of sailing vessels and camels, and governors of remote provinces required sufficient independence and military strength to defend themselves from infidel attacks. Such local independence and power could easily ripen into full autonomy. The Abbasid revolution of 750 was followed by a long process of political disintegration as one province after another broke free of the control of the caliphs at Baghdad. Even in the palmy days of Harun-al-Rashid, the extreme western provinces—Spain, Morocco, and Tunisia—were ruled by independent local dynasties. Spain, indeed, had never passed under Abbasid control but remained under the domination of Umayyad rulers. And by the later ninth century the trend toward distintegration was gaining strong momentum as Egypt, Syria, and eastern Persia (Iran) broke free.

By then the Abbasid caliphs were slowly losing their grip on their own government in Baghdad. Ambitious army commanders gradually usurped power, establishing control over the tax machinery and the other organs of government. In the later tenth and eleventh centuries the Fatimid caliphate of Cairo rose to great power, extending its authority to Syria and briefly occupying Baghdad itself. Since about the mid-tenth century the Abbasid caliphs of Baghdad had been controlled by members of a local Persian aristocratic dynasty who took the title of "sultan" and ruled what was left of the Abbasid state. A century later, in 1055, the chief of the Seljuk Turks conquered Baghdad, assumed the title of "Grand Sultan," and then turned his forces against Byzantium with the devastating effects that we have already seen. Seljuk power declined in the twelfth century, to be followed by a period of further Islamic political disintegration concurrent with the Crusades. By the later twelfth century Islam recovered itself in Syria and Egypt, and in the course of the thirteenth century the crusaders were driven out. In that same century the emasculated Abbasid caliphate was destroyed. The Mongols took Baghdad in 1258, massacred a good part of its population (allegedly, 800,000 people), and brought to an end the dynasty and the office that had ruled Baghdad, in fact or in name, for half a millennium.

Economic and Religious Change

The political troubles that the Abbasids endured from about 950–1258 were accompanied by a serious economic decline. Trade dried up, money became scarce, and Islamic rulers, whether in Baghdad, Cairo, or Damascus, were forced to reward their political underlings with land or revenue rights rather than wages. Thus, imperialism gave way to localism, and wealth tended increasingly to be identified with land rather than with commerce.

The general unrest of the period encouraged waves of popular protest, both socioeconomic and religious. The Ismaili sect, an outgrowth of the earlier legitimist faction, embarked on widespread terrorism and revolution. At the same time a quasi-heretical mystical movement known as Sufism became immensely popular throughout the Islamic world. For centuries the Sufi movement, although never tightly coordinated, had provided the chief impetus to missionary work among the infidel. These Sufi mystics, often illiterate but always fervent, had achieved the conversion of millions of people in Africa, India, Indonesia, Central Asia, and China. And it was they, rather than the orthodox religious scholars and lawyers, who could bring hope to the Muslim masses in times of trouble. Drawing from the Neoplatonic notion that reality rests in God alone, the Sufis sought mystical union with the divine and stressed God's love over the orthodox emphasis on God's authority. The orthodox Islamic scholars contended vigorously against this mystical trend, but by the tenth century Sufism was the most powerful religious force among the people of Islam. It affects Islamic personal devotion to this day.

Islamic Culture:
Conversion and Diffusion

Throughout the epoch of political disintegration the Muslim world remained united by a common tongue, a common culture, and a common faith. It continued to struggle vigorously with Byzantium for control of the Mediterranean and managed, at various times between the ninth and eleventh centuries, to occupy the key islands of Crete, Sicily, Sardinia, and Corsica. As early as the reign of Harun-al-Rashid, most of the inhabitants of Syria, Egypt, and North Africa had converted to Islam, even though these lands had once supported enthusiastic and well-organized Christian churches. The Muslim did not ordinarily persecute the Christians; they merely taxed them. And it may well be that the prolonged tax burden was a more effective instrument of conversion than ruthless persecution would have been.

The brilliant intellectual awakening of Harun-al-Rashid's day continued unabated for another four centuries. The untutored Arab from the desert became the cultural heir of Greece, Rome, Persia, and India, and within less than two centuries of the Prophet's death, Islamic culture had reached the level of a mature, sophisticated civilization. Its mercurial rise was a consequence of the Arabs' success in absorbing the great civilized traditions of their conquered peoples and employing these traditions in a cultural synthesis both new and unique. Islam borrowed, but never without digesting. What it drew from other civilizations it transmuted and made its own.

The political disintegration of the ninth and tenth centuries was accompanied by a diffusion of cultural activity throughout the Muslim world. During the tenth century, for example, Cordova, the capital of Umayyad Spain, acquired prodigious wealth and became the center of a brilliant cultural flowering. With a population of half a million or more, Cordova was another Baghdad. No other city in Western Europe could even remotely approach it in population, wealth, or municipal organization. It was the wonder of the age—with its magnificent mansions, mosques, aqueducts, and baths, its bustling markets and shops, its efficient police force and sanitation service, its street lights, and its splendid, sprawling palace, flashing with brightly colored tiles and surrounded by graceful minarets and sparkling fountains.

All across the Islamic world, from Cordova to Baghdad and far to the east, Muslim scholars and artists were developing the legacies of past civilizations. Architects were molding Greco-Roman forms into a brilliant and distinctive new style. Philosophers were studying and elaborating the writings of Plato and Aristotle, despite the hostility of narrowly orthodox Islamic theologians. Physicians were expanding the ancient medical doctrines of Galen and his Greek predecessors, describing new symptoms and identifying new curative drugs. As-

Capilla de Villaviciosa in the Cordova Mosque (961–965).

tronomers and astrologers were tightening the geocentric system of Ptolemy, preparing accurate tables of planetary motions, and giving the stars Arabic names that are used to this day—names such as Altair, Deneb, Aldebaran, and (regretfully) Zubenelgenubi. The renowned astronomer-poet of eleventh-century Persia, Omar Khayyam, devised a calendar of singular accuracy. Muslim mathematicians borrowed creatively from both Greece and India. From the Greeks they learned geometry and trigonometry, and from the Hindus they appropriated the so-called Arabic numerals, the zero, and algebra, which were ultimately passed on to the West to revolutionize European mathematics.

Islamic literature produced no long, systematic masterpieces but excelled in short works of poetry and prose. The individual anecdote took precedence over the extended narrative. Muslim poets endeavored to perfect individual verses rather than to create long, coherent poems. The quatrains of Omar Khayyam's *Rubaiyat* seem to have been arranged in alphabetical order rather than conforming to any overall plan. The chapters of the Koran itself, which had been left completely unorganized by Muhammad, were assembled shortly after his death in order of decreasing length, with no attempt at structural unity. The enduring value of these works lies in the power and beauty of their individual chapters and verses.

The Arab conquests during the century after Muhammad changed the historical course of North Africa and Southwest Asia decisively and permanently. The Arabs conquered their vast territories thrice over: with their armies, their faith, and their language. In the end, the term "Arab" applied to every Muslim from Morocco to Iraq, regardless of his ethnic background. Within its all-encompassing religious and linguistic framework, Arab culture provided a new stimulus and a new orientation to the long-civilized peoples of former empires. With its manifold ingredients, the rich Islamic heritage would one day provide invaluable nourishment to the voracious mind of the twelfth- and thirteenth-century West. Later, Islamic armies would bring Byzantium to an end and make Constantinople a Muslim city. Later still, in the sixteenth and seventeenth centuries, they would be at the gates of Vienna. Only in the nineteenth century did Islam become clearly subordinate to the West militarily and politically. And today there are signs that this subordination is ending.

MUSLIM CHRONOLOGY

c.571– 632:	Muhammad
622:	The Hegira
632– 655:	The First Conquests
655– 661:	Civil War: Umayyads versus Ali
661– 750:	Umayyad Dynasty: New Conquests
717– 718:	Arabs besiege Constantinople
732:	Arabs defeated at Tours
750–1258:	Abbasid dynasty at Baghdad
786– 809:	Harun-al-Rashid; Zenith of Abbasid power

6

carolingian europe

The Significance of the Carolingian Age

In the course of the eighth century Western Christendom began to emerge as a coherent civilization. It did so under the aegis of the Carolingian Empire—a vast constellation of territories welded together by the Frankish king Charlemagne and his talented predecessors. Here for the first time the various cultural ingredients—classical, Christian, and Germanic—that went into the making of European civilization achieved a degree of synthesis. Charlemagne was a Germanic king who surrounded himself with Germanic warrior-aristocrats. But he also drew churchmen and classical scholars around him and took very seriously his role as protector and sustainer of the Western Church. Although his empire was fundamentally Germanic, its intellectual life, limited though it was, drew heavily from the classical-Christian tradition. The fusion of these cultural ingredients was evident in the life of the Carolingian court, in the rising vigor of the Carolingian Church, and in the person of Charlemagne himself.

Charlemagne's Frankland stood in sharp contrast to contemporary Byzantium and the Abbasid Empire of Islam. Baghdad and Constantinople were the centers of brilliant, opulent, mercantile civilizations. Charlemagne's Franks were a half-barbarized agrarian people struggling toward political and intellectual coherence. But eighth-century western Europeans were steadily moving toward a life of larger meaning for themselves and for those who came after them. For the first time it began to dawn on a few of them that they were a people apart, that they were *Europeans*—agents of a new, distinctive civilization with its roots in Athens and Jerusalem, Germany, and Rome, bound together—much as the Byzantines and Muslims were—

74

by a common faith, a common scholarly language, and a common heritage.

The new Europe was spiritually and intellectually enlivened by the wide-ranging Benedictines, who disseminated a cultural tradition based on the Bible, the writings of the Latin Doctors and their contemporaries, and the surviving masterpieces of Latin literature. This evolving culture was bound together politically by a new dynasty of Frankish monarchs, the Carolingians.*

Carolingian Europe differed profoundly from the western Roman Empire of old. It was a land without large cities, thoroughly agrarian in its economic organization, with its culture centered on the monastery, the cathedral, and the perambulatory royal court rather than the forum. And although Charlemagne extended his authority into Italy, the center of his activities and his interests remained northern Frankland. In a word, the new Europe no longer faced the Mediterranean; its axis had shifted northward.

Agricultural Technology

The relative brightness of the Age of Charlemagne was the product of creative processes that had been at work during the preceding dark centuries. From the economic standpoint the most interesting of these processes was the gradual evolution of a new agrarian technology which increased the productivity of northern European farmlands.

By the opening of the eighth century the ineffective scratch plow of the ancient Mediterranean world had been superseded throughout the northern districts of the West by a heavy compound plow with wheels, colter, plowshare, and moldboard, which cut deeply into the soil, pulverized it, and turned it aside into ridges and furrows. The development of this heavy plow was complex and gradual; the basic idea may perhaps have been brought into western Europe by the Slavs in the sixth or seventh century. Its introduction into the West opened up vast areas of rich, heavy soil in which the older scratch plow was ineffective, and accentuated the tendency toward dividing fields into long strips cultivated by the eight-ox teams which the heavy plow required. Peasants pooled their oxen and their labor in

* They were so named by later historians after their most illustrious representative. Charles the Great or Charlemagne (Latin: *Carolus Magnus*).

order to exploit the new plow; in so doing they laid the foundation for the cooperative agricultural communities of medieval Europe with strong village councils to regulate the division of labor and resources. In these village communities the medieval peasantry learned the attitude of responsible, voluntary cooperation—an attitude that may well have influenced the rise of capitalist enterprise many centuries later.

The gain in productivity brought about by the introduction of the heavy compound plow made possible a change in the method of rotating crops. By the Carolingian age parts of northern Europe were beginning to adopt the three-field system in place of the two-field system typical of Roman times. Formerly a typical farm had been divided into two fields, one of which was planted each year and allowed to lie fallow the second year. But it was found that the rich northern soils, opened by the heavy plow, did not require a full year's rest between crops. Instead, they were sometimes divided into three fields, each of which underwent a three-year cycle of autumn planting, spring planting, and fallow. The shift from two fields to three had an important impact on the European economy, for it increased food production and brought a degree of prosperity to northern Europe. It is possible that the heavy plow and the three-field system, which could not be employed efficiently in the light, dry soils of the Mediterranean South, contributed to the northward shift in the economic and cultural orientation of Carolingian Europe.

The Age of Charlemagne also profited from a trend toward mechanization. The water mill, which was used occasionally in antiquity for grinding grain, had now come into more widespread use and was often to be seen on Carolingian farms. During the centuries following Charlemagne's death the water mill was put to new uses—to power the rising textile industry of the eleventh century, and to drive triphammers in forges. Thus, the technological progress of Merovingian and Carolingian times continued into the centuries that followed. By 1000 the development of the horseshoe and a new, efficient horse collar, both apparently imported from Siberia or central Asia, made possible the very gradual replacement of the ox by the more energetic horse as the chief draught animal on the farms of northwestern Europe. And in the twelfth century the windmill made its debut in the European countryside. These new advances resulted in still greater productivity and underlay the prosperous civilization of northern Europe in the High Middle Ages (c. 1050–1300). Slowly the custom of human slavery declined as human power gave way more and more to animal and machine power.

Carolingian Europe gained from the earlier phase of this drawn-out revolution in agrarian technology, but even so the peasants of the Carolingian age remained near the level of subsistence, owing in part to the rise of population along with productivity. During a great famine of 791, for example, peasants were driven to cannibalism and were even reported to have eaten members of their own family. Conditions may have been improving, but only very gradually, and a single bad year could be disastrous.

The Rise of the Carolingians

The dynasty of Clovis, the Merovingians, had declined over the centuries from cruel autocrats to crowned fools. By the later 600s all real power had passed to the aristocracy. Meanwhile, as a consequence of the Merovingian policy of dividing royal authority and crown lands among the sons of a deceased king, Frankland had split into several distinct districts, the most important of which were Neustria (Paris and northwestern France), Austrasia (the heavily Germanized northeast including the Rhinelands), and Burgundy in the southeast (see map, p. 89.

During the seventh century a great landholding family, known to historians as the Carolingians, rose to power in Austrasia. The Carolingians became "mayors" of the itinerant royal household; that is, they held the chief administrative post in the Austrasian government (such as it was) and made their office hereditary. As the Merovingians grew increasingly inept the Carolingians became the real masters of Austrasia. The Carolingian mayor built up his power by gathering around him a considerable number of trained warriors somewhat in the tradition of the old Germanic comitatus (see p. 89). These men became his vassals, placing themselves under his protection and maintenance and swearing fealty to him. Other nobles also had their private vassalic armies. But the Carolingians, with far the greatest number of followers, dominated the scene. In 687 a Carolingian mayor named Pepin of Heristal led his Austrasian army to a decisive victory over the Neustrians at Tertry, and the Carolingians thenceforth were the leading family in Frankland. With Neustria under their control they were able to dominate Burgundy, and when

Illuminations from the Flemish Hours of the Virgin (c. 1515): on the left, the month of July; on the right, the month of September. Note two examples of medieval technological achievement: the windmill and the compound plow with moldboard.

the Muslims moved into Gaul in the early 730s the Franks were able to unite against them under the able leadership of Pepin of Heristal's son, the vigorous Carolingian mayor Charles Martel.

Charles Martel ("The Hammer"): 714–741

This able, ruthless warrior not only turned back the Muslims at the battle of Tours (732); he also won victory after victory over Muslims and Christians alike, consolidating his power over the Franks and extending the boundaries of the Frankish state. Like the Adams family in American history, the Carolingians of the seventh and eighth centuries had the good fortune to produce exceedingly able

men over several generations. Martel's father, Pepin of Heristal, had
conquered Neustria. Martel himself defeated the Muslims and, indeed, almost everybody he faced. His son, Pepin the Short, gained
the Frankish crown, and his grandson, Charlemagne, won an empire.

The Carolingians followed the same policy of divided succession among male heirs that had so weakened the Merovingians. But
here, too, Carolingian luck played a crucial role in history. For as it
happened, the Carolingian mayors and later kings, over several generations, had only one long-surviving heir. Frankish unity was maintained not by policy but in spite of it. When Charles Martel died in
741 his lands and authority were divided among his two sons, Carloman and Pepin the Short. But Carloman ruled only six years, retiring
to a Benedictine monastery in 747—leaving the field to his brother
Pepin. Carloman represented a new kind of barbarian ruler, deeply
affected by the spiritual currents of his age, whose piety foreshadowed
that of numerous saint-kings of later centuries. Christian culture and
Germanic political leadership were beginning to draw together.

Missions from Northumbria

The fusion of these two worlds was carried still further by Pepin the
Short (741–768) who supported a Benedictine Christian revival in
Frankland and consummated an alliance of far-reaching consequences
between the Frankish monarchy and the papacy. By the time of
Charles Martel's death in 741 English Benedictine monks had long
been engaged in evangelical work among the heathen Germanic
peoples east of the Rhine. The earliest of these missions were directed
at the Frisians, a maritime people who were settled along the coast of
the Netherlands. The first of the Benedictine evangelists were monks
from Northumbria who brought to the Continent not only the strict
organizational discipline and devotion to the papacy that had been
characteristic of the Northumbrian Benedictines but also the peripa-
tetic missionary fervor which the Celtic monks had contributed to
the Northumbrian revival. So it was that Benedictine monks such as
Wilfrid of Ripon and Willibrord left their Northumbrian homeland
during the later 600s to evangelize the Frisians. The course of Western Civilization was deeply affected by the transference to Frankland
and Germany of the vital force of Northumbrian Christianity, with
its vibrant culture, its Roman-Benedictine discipline, and its spiritual

commitment. Wilfrid of Ripon, Willibrord, and their devoted followers represent the first wave of a movement that was ultimately to infuse the Frankish empire of Charlemagne with the spiritual life that had developed in Anglo-Saxon England during the century following St. Augustine's mission. The dynamic thrust of Roman-Benedictine Christianity, having leapt from Rome to Kent and thence to remote Northumbria, was returning to the Continent at last.

Saint Boniface in Germany

The key figure in this cultural movement was St. Boniface, an English Benedictine from Wessex. Reared in monasteries of southern England, Boniface left Wessex in 716 to do missionary work among the Frisians. From then until his death in 754 he devoted himself above all other tasks to Christianizing the heathen Germanic peoples. Boniface was a man of boundless energy and considerable learning, a wise and magnetic leader of men. He worked in close cooperation with both the papacy and the Anglo-Saxon church; a great number of his letters survive, many of which request support from his compatriots in Wessex and advice from Rome. On three occasions he visited Rome to confer with the pope, and from the beginning his work among the heathens was performed under papal commission. In 732 the papacy appointed him archbishop in Germany. Some years later he was given the episcopal see at Mainz as his headquarters. Throughout his career he was a devoted representative of the Anglo-Saxon church, the Benedictine Rule, and the papacy. As he put it, he strove "to hold fast the Catholic faith and unity, and to yield submission to the Church of Rome as long as life shall last for us."

Boniface also worked with the backing of the Frankish mayors—Charles Martel, Carloman, and Pepin the Short. Armed with the Christian faith and the Benedictine rule, and supported by England, Frankland, and Rome, Boniface labored among the Germanic tribes in Frisia, Thuringia, Hesse, and Bavaria. There he won converts, founded new Benedictine monasteries in the German wilderness, and erected the organizational framework of a disciplined German church. He suffered moments of discouragement, as when he wrote to an English abbot, "Have pity upon an old man tried and tossed on all sides by the waves of a German sea." Yet Boniface accomplished much, and the monasteries which he established—particularly the great house of Fulda in Hesse—were to become centers of learning and evangelism which played a great role in converting and civilizing the peoples of Germany.

Reform of the Frankish Church

During the decade following Charles Martel's death in 741 Boniface devoted much of his energy to Frankland itself, for the Frankish church of the early eighth century stood in desperate need of reform. On the whole it was corrupt, disorganized, and ignorant—the product of several centuries of Merovingian misrule. Many areas of Frankland had no priests at all; numerous Frankish peasants were scarcely removed from heathenism. Priests themselves are reported to have sacrificed animals to the gods and shared their beds with concubines. Charles Martel, although willing enough to support Boniface's missionary endeavors among the Germanic heathens, had no taste for ecclesiastical reforms within his own Frankish church. Indeed, he weakened the church by confiscating a considerable amount of ecclesiastical property and granting it to his military vassals. Carloman and Pepin, however, encouraged Boniface to work toward the reform of the Frankish church, and beginning in 742 he held a series of synods for that purpose. Working in close collaboration with the papacy, Boniface remodeled the Frankish ecclesiastical organization on the disciplined pattern of Anglo-Saxon England and papal Rome. He reformed Frankish monasteries along the lines of the Benedictine Rule, saw to the establishment of monastic schools, encouraged the appointment of dedicated prelates, and worked toward the development of an adequate parish system to bring the Gospel to the country folk. Thus Boniface laid the groundwork for both the new church in Germany and the reformed church in Frankland. In doing so, he served as one of the chief architects of the Carolingian cultural revival.

The Franco-Papal Alliance

Boniface's introduction of Roman discipline and organization into the Frankish church was followed almost immediately by the consummation of a political alliance between Rome and Frankland. It may well have been at Boniface's prompting that the Carolingian mayor Pepin the Short sought papal support for his seizure of the Frankish crown. Although the Merovingian monarchs retained the enormous prestige always enjoyed by a Germanic royal dynasty, they had long been shadowy, do-nothing kings. Even so, if the Carolingians hoped to replace the Merovingians on the Frankish throne, they would have to call upon the most potent spiritual sanction available to their age: papal consecration. In supporting Boniface and his fellow Benedictines the Carolingian mayors had fostered papal influence in the Frankish church. Now, seeking papal support for a dynastic revolution, Pepin the Short could reasonably expect a favorable response in Rome.

For their part, the popes had been seeking a strong, loyal ally against the untrustworthy Byzantines and the aggressive Lombards who had long been contending for political supremacy in Italy. The Carolingians, with their policy of aid to the Benedictine missionaries and their support of Boniface's reform measures, must have seemed strong candidates for the role of papal champion. And by mid-eighth century a champion was desperately needed. Traditionally the papacy had followed the policy of turning to Byzantium for protection against the Lombards who, although they had by now adopted Trinitarian Christianity, remained an ominous threat to papal independence. By 750 the popes could no longer depend on Byzantine protection for two reasons: (1) the Byzantine emperors had recently embraced a doctrine known as *iconoclasm* which the papacy regarded as heretical, and (2) Lombard aggression was rapidly becoming so effective that the Byzantine army could no longer be counted on to defend the papacy.

The iconoclastic controversy was the chief religious dispute of the Christian world in the eighth century. It was a conflict over the use in Christian worship of statues and pictures of Christ and the saints. These icons had gradually come to assume an important role in Christian worship. Strictly speaking, Christians might venerate them as symbols of the holy persons whom they represented, but in fact there was a strong tendency among the uneducated to worship the objects themselves. A line of reform emperors in Constantinople, beginning with Leo the Isaurian (717–741), sought to end the superstitious practice of worshiping images—vigorously fostered by the numerous monks of the Eastern empire—by banning icons altogether. This sweeping decree served the interests of the Byzantine emperors by weakening the power of the Eastern monasteries, which controlled far too much land and wealth for the empire's good, but it offended a great many Byzantines, image worshipers and intelligent traditionalists alike. In the West little or no support was to be found for the policy of iconoclasm; the papacy in particular opposed it as heretical and contrary to the Christian tradition. Although it ultimately failed in the Byzantine Church,* iconoclasm in the 750s was a vital issue and a storm center of controversy which aroused intense enmity between Rome and Constantinople. The papacy was deeply apprehensive of depending on the troops of a heretical emperor for its defense.

Even without the iconoclastic controversy it was becoming increasingly doubtful that the papacy could count on the military power of Byzantium in Italy. For by 750 the Lombards were on the rampage once again, threatening not only Byzantine holdings but also the territories of the pope himself. In 751 the Lombards captured Ravenna, which had long served as the Byzantines' Italian capital, and the papal position in Italy became more precarious than ever. If Pepin the Short needed the support of the papacy, the papacy needed Pepin's support even more.

Accordingly the alliance was struck. Pepin sent messengers to Rome with the far from theoretical question, "Is it right that a powerless ruler should continue to bear the title of king?" The pope answered that by the authority of the Apostle Peter, Pepin was henceforth to be king of the Franks, and ordered that he should be anointed into his royal office by a papal representative. The anointing ceremony was duly performed at Soissons in 751. It had the purpose of buttressing the new Carolingian dynasty with the strongest of spiritual sanctions. Not by mere force, but by the supernatural potency of the royal anointing was the new dynasty established on the Frankish throne. Appropriately, this ceremony—the symbolic junction of the power of Rome and Frankland—was performed by the aged Boniface.

With Pepin's coronation the last of the Merovingians were shorn of their long hair and packed off to a monastery. Three years there-

* That is, it failed in its extreme form. Eventually a compromise was reached that permitted flat representations of holy persons but not their representation in the round.

after Boniface, now nearing 80, returned to his missionary work in Frisia and met a martyr's death. In the same year, 754, the pope himself traveled northward to Frankland where he personally anointed Pepin and his two sons at the royal monastery of Saint-Denis, thereby conferring every spiritual sanction at his disposal upon the upstart Carolingian monarchy. At the same time he sought Pepin's military support against the Lombards.

Pepin obliged, leading his armies into Italy, defeating the Lombards, and granting a large portion of central Italy to the papacy. This "Donation of Pepin" was of lasting historical significance. It had the immediate effect of relieving the popes of the ominous Lombard pressure. In the long run, it became the nucleus of the Papal States, which were to remain a characteristic feature of Italian politics until the later nineteenth century. For the moment, the papacy had been rescued from its peril. It remained to be seen whether the popes could prevent their new champion from becoming their master.

Pepin the Short, like all successful monarchs of the Early Middle Ages, was an able general. As the first Carolingian king he followed in the warlike traditions of his father. Besides defeating the Lombards in Italy he drove the Muslims from Aquitaine and maintained domestic peace. He died in 768, leaving Frankland larger, more powerful, and better organized than he had found it.

Charlemagne (768–814)

Pepin was a talented monarch, but he was overshadowed by his even greater son. Charlemagne was a phenomenally successful military commander, a statesman of rare ability, a friend of learning, and a monarch possessed of a deep sense of responsibility for the welfare of the society over which he ruled. In this last respect he represents a tremendous advance over his Merovingian predecessors whose relationship to their state was that of a leech to his host.

Charlemagne towered over his contemporaries both figuratively and literally. He was 6'3½" tall, thick-necked and pot-bellied, yet imposing in appearance for all that. Thanks to his able biographer, Einhard, whose *Life of Charlemagne* was written a few years after the emperor's death, Charlemagne has come down to posterity as a three-dimensional figure. Einhard, who was dwarfish in stature, wrote enthusiastically of his oversized hero. The Roman historian Suetonius

Contemporary bronze figure of Charlemagne.

was Einhard's model, and he lifted whole passages from Suetonius's *Lives of the Twelve Caesars*, adapting many other phrases from the work to his own purposes. Yet there is much in Einhard's *Life* that represents his own appraisal of Charlemagne's deeds and character. Reared at the monastery of Fulda, Einhard served for many years in Charlemagne's court and so gained an intimate knowledge of the emperor. Einhard's warm admiration for Charlemagne emerges clearly from the biography, yet the author was able to see Charlemagne's faults as well as his virtues: Charles was temperate in eating and particularly so in drinking, for he hated drunkenness in anybody, particularly in himself and those of his household. But he found it difficult to abstain from food, and often complained that fasts injured his health. . . . His meals usually consisted of four courses not counting the roast, which his huntsmen used to bring in on the spit. He was fonder of this than of any other dish. While at the table he listened to reading or music. The readings were stories and deeds of olden times; he was also fond of St. Augustine's books, and especially of the one entitled *The City of God*. So moderate was he in the use of wine and all sorts of drink that he rarely allowed himself more than three cups in the course of a meal.*

Einhard provides a full account of Charlemagne's military and political career; but the most fascinating passages in the biography deal with the emperor's way of life and personal idiosyncrasies which reveal him as a human being rather than a shadowy hero of legend:

While he was dressing and putting on his shoes, he not only gave audience to his friends, but if the Count of the Household told him of any suit in which his judgment was necessary, he had the parties brought before him forthwith, considered the case, and gave his decision, just as if he were sitting on the judgment seat.

Einhard was also at pains to show Charlemagne's thirst for learning. He portrays the emperor as a fluent master of Latin, a student of Greek, a speaker of such skill that he might have passed for a teacher of rhetoric, a devotee of the liberal arts, and in particular a student of astronomy who learned to calculate the motions of the heavenly bodies. Einhard concludes this impressive discussion of Charlemagne's

---

* The size of the cup is not provided.

scholarship with a final tribute which unwittingly discloses the emperor's severe scholastic limitations:

He also tried to write, and used to keep tablets and blank pages in bed under his pillow so that in his leisure hours he might accustom his hand to form the letters; but as he did not begin his efforts at an early age but late in life, they met with poor success.

Charlemagne could be warm and talkative, but he could also be hard, cruel, and violent, and his subjects came to regard him with both admiration and fear. He was possessed of a strong, if superficial, piety that prompted him to build churches, collect relics, and struggle heroically for a Christian cultural revival in Frankland. But it did not prevent him from filling his court with concubines and other disreputable characters. In short Charlemagne, despite his military and political genius, was a man of his age, in tune with its most progressive forces yet by no means removed from its past.

The Expansion of the Empire

Above all else Charlemagne was a warrior-king. He led his armies on yearly campaigns as a matter of course. When his magnates and their retainers assembled around him annually on the May Field the question was not whether to go to war but whom to fight. Traditionally the Franks had fought on foot; but the epoch of Charles Martel and Pepin the Short had witnessed the rise of cavalry as the elite force in the Frankish army. This momentous shift, which amounted in effect to the birth of the medieval mounted knight, was perhaps associated with the coming of the stirrup to Frankland in the earlier 700s. For the stirrup gave stability to the mounted warrior and made possible the charge of cavalrymen with lances braced against their arms which was such an effective feature of later feudal warfare. In any case, the conquering armies of Charlemagne were built around a nucleus of highly trained horsemen. Such warriors were still something of a novelty in the age of Charlemagne, and under his masterful leadership they struck fear in their foes and acquired a reputation for invincibility.

It was only gradually, however, that Charlemagne developed a coherent scheme of conquest built on a notion of Christian mission and addressed to the goal of unifying and systematically expanding the Christian West. At the behest of the papacy Charlemagne followed his father's footsteps into Italy. There he conquered the Lombards completely in 774, incorporated them into his growing state, and assumed for himself the Lombard crown. Thenceforth he employed the title, "King of the Franks and the Lombards."

Between 778 and 801 Charlemagne conducted a series of campaigns against the Spanish Muslims which met with only limited success. He did manage to establish a frontier district, the "Spanish March," on the Spanish side of the Pyrenees. In later generations the southern portion of Charlemagne's Spanish March evolved into the county of Barcelona which remained more receptive to the influence of French institutions and customs than any other district in Spain. A relatively minor military episode in Charlemagne's Spanish campaign of 778—an attack by a band of Christian Basques against the rearguard of Charlemagne's army as it was withdrawing across the Pyrenees into Frankland—became the inspiration for one of the great epic poems of the eleventh century: the *Song of Roland*. The unknown author or authors of the poem transformed the Basques into Muslims and made the battle a heroic struggle between the rival faiths. Charlemagne was portrayed as a godlike conqueror, phenomenally aged, and Roland, the warden of the Breton March and commander of the rearguard, acquired a fame in literature far out of proportion to his actual historical importance.

Charlemagne devoted much of his strength to the expansion of his eastern frontier. In 787 he conquered and absorbed Bavaria, organizing its easternmost district into a forward defensive barrier against the Slavs. This East March or *Ostmark* became the nucleus of a new state later to be called Austria. In the 790s Charlemagne pushed still farther to the southeast, destroying the rich and predatory Avar state which had long tormented eastern Europe. For many generations the Avars had been enriching themselves on the plunder of their victims and on heavy tribute payments from Byzantium and elsewhere. Charlemagne had the good fortune to seize a substantial portion of the Avar treasure; it is reported that 15 four-ox wagons were required to transport the hoard of gold, silver, and precious garments back to Frankland. The loot of the Avars contributed significantly to the resources of Charlemagne's treasury and broadened the scope of his subsequent building program and patronage to scholars and churches.

THE CAROLINGIAN EMPIRE

PICTS

SCOTS

North Sea

SWEDES

DANISH KINGDOM

ANGLO-SAXON KINGDOMS

FRISIA

SAXONY

SLAVS

Rhine R.

Cologne

Aachen

Fulda

Elbe R.

Rouen

Rheims

AUSTRASIA

BRITTANY

NEUSTRIA

Paris

Orleans

Danube R.

Angers

Loire R.

Tours

BAVARIA

Poitiers

St. Gall

AVARS

AQUITAINE

Rhône R.

BURGUNDY

LOMBARDY

Pavia

Po R.

Venice

SLAVS

Ravenna

PYRENEES MTS

SPANISH MARCH

Ebro R.

CORSICA

Rome

Monte Cassino

BALEARIC IS.

SARDINIA

MILES
0   100   200   300   400

Byzantine Empire

Indeed, it placed him on a financial footing comparable to that of the Byzantine emperors themselves.

Charlemagne's most prolonged military effort was directed against the heathen Saxons of northern Germany. With the twin goals of protecting the Frankish Rhinelands and bringing new souls into the Church, he campaigned for some 32 years (772–804), conquering the Saxons repeatedly and baptizing them by force, only to have them rebel when his armies withdrew. In a fit of savage exasperation he ordered the execution of 4500 unfaithful Saxons in a single bloody day in 782. At length however, Saxony submitted to the remorseless pressure of Charlemagne's soldiers and the Benedictine monks who followed in their wake. By about 800 Frankish control of Saxony was well established, and in subsequent decades Christianity seeped gradually into the Saxon soul. A century and a half later Christian Saxons were governing the most powerful state in Europe and were fostering a significant artistic and intellectual revival that was to enrich the culture of tenth-century Christendom.

The Imperial Coronation of A.D. 800

Charlemagne's armies, by incorporating central Germany into the new civilization, had succeeded where the legions of Augustus and his successors had failed. No longer a mere Frankish king, Charlemagne, by 800, was the master of the West. A few small Christian states such as the principalities of southern Italy and the kingdoms of Anglo-Saxon England remained outside his jurisdiction, but with these exceptions Charlemagne's political sway extended throughout Western Christendom. He was, in truth, an emperor, and on Christmas Day, 800, his immense accomplishment was given formal recognition when Pope Leo III placed the imperial crown upon his head and acclaimed him "Emperor of the Romans." From the standpoint of legal theory this dramatic act reconstituted the Roman Empire in the West after an interregnum of 324 years. In another sense it was the ultimate consummation of the Franco-Papal Alliance of 751.

The imperial coronation of Charlemagne is difficult to interpret and has evoked heated controversy among historians. According to Einhard, Pope Leo III took Charlemagne by surprise and bestowed upon him an unwanted dignity. Charlemagne had such an aversion to the titles of Emperor and Augustus, so Einhard reports, "that he declared he would not have set foot in the Church the day that they were conferred, although it was a great feast day, if he could have forseen the design of the pope."

Many modern historians have tended to be skeptical of this assertion. It has been argued that Charlemagne was too powerful—too firmly in control of events—to permit a coronation that he did not wish. It has been pointed out that scholars in Charlemagne's court, beguiled by the dream of empire, may well have urged their emperor on. Some historians have stressed the fact that Byzantium lacked an emperor in 800 and that Charlemagne disclosed his interest in the Roman imperial crown by engaging unsuccessfully in marriage negotiations with the Byzantine empress Irene. Conversely, it has recently been suggested that the coronation was largely a product of internal Roman politics during the years 799–800.* In any event, the acclamation that Charlemagne received from the people of Rome immediately after his coronation had obviously been well rehearsed, and it is hard to believe that Charlemagne did not know what was afoot.

Most likely Charlemagne's imperial coronation of 800, like the royal coronation of Pepin the Short in 751, represents a coalescence of papal and Carolingian interests. For some years Charlemagne had been attempting to attain a status comparable to that of the Byzantine emperors. In 794 he had abandoned the practice, traditional among Germanic kings, of traveling constantly with his court from estate to estate, and had established his permanent capital at Aachen in Austrasia. Here he sought, though vainly, to create a Constantinople of his own. Aachen was called "New Rome," and an impressive palace church was built in the Byzantine style—almost literally a poor man's Sancta Sophia. Even though Charlemagne's "Mary Church" at Aachen was a far cry from Justinian's masterpieces at Constantinople and Ravenna, it was a marvel for its time and place and made a deep impression on contemporaries. Einhard describes it as a beautiful basilica adorned with gold and silver lamps, with rails and doors of solid brass, and with columns and marbles from Rome and Ra-

* See Geoffrey Barraclough, *The Medieval Papacy* (New York: Harcourt Brace Jovanovich, 1968), pp. 52–54.

venna. It was evidently the product of a major effort on Charlemagne's part—an effort not only to create a beautiful church but also to ape the Byzantines. The coronation of 800 may well have been an expression of this same imitative policy.

The papacy, on the other hand, may well have regarded the coronation as an opportunity to regain some of the initiative it had lost to the all-powerful Charlemagne. To be sure, the Carolingians had been promoted from kings to emperors; but their empire thenceforth bore the stamp, "Made in Rome." In later years the popes would insist that what they gave they could also take away. If the papacy could make emperors it could also depose them. Indeed, it was only shortly before that the papal chancery had produced a famous forged document called the "Donation of Constantine"* in which the first Christian emperor allegedly gave to the pope the imperial diadem and governance over Rome, Italy, and all the West. The pope is alleged to have returned the diadem but kept the power of governance. Later popes, drawing on the "Donation of Constantine," regarded the Holy Roman emperors as stewards exercising political authority by delegation from the papacy, wielding their power in the interests of the Roman Church. So convincing was this theory of papal supremacy in the eyes of the papacy that it justified the use of any documentation to support its case. The "Donation of Constantine," therefore, was not an effort to rewrite history but an attempt to buttress the papal position by manufacturing evidence for an event that had actually occurred, so the papacy imagined, but was unfortunately not documented.

Though Charlemagne always respected the papacy he was unwilling to cast himself in the subordinate role which papal theory demanded of him. He was careful to retain the title, "King of the Franks and the Lombards" alongside his new title of "Emperor". When the time came to crown his son emperor, Charlemagne excluded the pope from the ceremony and did the honors himself. In these maneuvers we are witnessing the prologue to a long, bitter struggle over the correct relationship between empire and papacy—a struggle that reached its crescendo in the eleventh, twelfth, and thirteenth centuries. At stake was the mastery of Western Christendom.

---

* Probably sometime in the 740s.

Interior of the "Mary Church" in Aachen (796–804). The Byzantine arches and the structural formation are very similar to Justinian's basilica of San Vitale in Ravenna.

But during the reign of Charlemagne the struggle remained latent. Charlemagne's power was unrivaled, and the popes were much too weak to oppose him seriously. Indeed, the warm Carolingian-papal relations of Pepin's day continued, and the papacy was nearly smothered in Charlemagne's affectionate embrace.

Carolingian Theocracy

At no time since has Europe been so nearly united as under Charlemagne. And never again would Western Christendom flirt so seriously with theocracy. The papal anointing of Pepin and Charlemagne gave the Carolingian monarchy a sacred, almost priestly quality. Charlemagne used his immense authority to govern not only the body politic but the imperial Church as well. The laws and regulations of his reign, known as *capitularies,* dealt with both ecclesiastical and secular matters. Although he did not claim to legislate on Church doctrine he felt a sense of responsibility for purifying and systematizing ecclesiastical discipline. He was a far greater force in the Carolingian Church than was the pope. He summoned a number of ecclesiastical synods and even presided over one of them. Indeed, the significant intellectual revival known as the "Carolingian Renaissance" was mostly a product of Charlemagne's concern for the welfare of the Church and the perpetuation of ecclesiastical culture.

The Carolingian Renaissance

The term "Carolingian Renaissance" can be misleading. Charlemagne's age produced no lofty abstract thought, no original philosophical or theological system, no Thomas Aquinas or Leonardo da Vinci. If we look for a "renaissance" in the ordinary sense of the word, we are bound to be disappointed. The intellectual task of the Carolingian age was far less exalted, far more rudimentary: to rescue continental culture from the pit of ignorance into which it was sinking.

As with so many other aspects of the era the Carolingian Renaissance bears the stamp of Charlemagne's will and initiative. It was he who saw the desperate need for schools in his kingdom and sought to provide them. There could be no question of establishing institutions of higher learning. None existed north of the Alps, and none would emerge until the High Middle Ages. It was for the Carolingians to build a system of primary and secondary education, and this was an immensely difficult task. Frankland had no professional class of teachers either lay or clerical. The only hope for pedagogical reform lay with the Church, which had an almost exclusive monopoly on literacy. So Charlemagne tried to force the cathedrals and monasteries of his realm to operate schools which would preserve and disseminate the rudiments of classical-Christian culture. A capitulary of 789 commands that

In every episcopal See and in every monastery, instruction shall be given in the psalms, musical notation, chant, the computation of years and seasons, and grammar, and all books used shall be carefully corrected.

A curriculum of the sort described in this capitulary can hardly be described as intellectually sophisticated or demanding, yet many Carolingian monasteries and cathedrals fell considerably short of the modest standards that it sought to establish. Still, Charlemagne succeeded in improving vastly the quantity and quality of schooling in his empire. There was even an attempt to make village priests provide free instruction in reading and writing. Only a minute fraction of Charlemagne's subjects acquired literacy. But those few provided an all-important learned nucleus which kept knowledge alive and transmitted it to future generations. It was above all in the monastic schools that learning flourished—in houses such as Fulda, Tours, and Reichenau. During the turbulent generations following Charlemagne's death many of these monastic schools survived to become seedbeds of the far greater intellectual awakening of the eleventh and twelfth centuries. In sum, Charlemagne's pedagogical reforms insured that learning in Europe would never again descend to the pre-Carolingian level.

As an integral part of his effort to raise the intellectual standards of his realm and sustain Christian culture, Charlemagne assembled scholars at his court from all over Europe. One such scholar was the emperor's biographer, Einhard, from eastern Frankland. Another was the poet-historian Paul the Deacon, of the great Italian Benedictine house of Monte Cassino. Paul the Deacon's *History of the Lombards* provides an invaluable account of that Germanic tribe and its settlement in Italy. From Spain came Theodulf, later bishop of Orleans and abbot of Fleury, a tireless supporter of Charlemagne's pedagogical reforms as well as a poet of considerable talent. The most important of these Carolingian scholars was the Northumbrian Alcuin of York, the last significant mind to be produced by the Northumbrian Renaissance. Alcuin, along with his countrymen of an earlier generation Wilfrid of Ripon, Willibrord, and Boniface—represents the vital connecting link between the Christian cultural life of seventh- and eighth-century England and the intellectual upsurge of Carolingian Frankland.

Alcuin performed the essential task of preparing an accurate new edition of the Bible purged of the scribal errors which had crept into it over the centuries, thereby saving Christian culture from the confusion arising from the corruption of its most fundamental text. For many years the chief scholar in Charlemagne's court school, Alcuin spent his final years as abbot of St. Martin of Tours. He was extraordinarily well educated for his period, and his approach to learning typified the whole philosophy of the Carolingian Renaissance: to produce accurate copies of important traditional texts, to encourage the establishment of schools, and in every way possible to cherish and transmit the classical-Christian cultural tradition (without, however, adding to it in any significant way). Alcuin and his fellow scholars were neither intellectual innovators nor men of conspicuous holiness. Drawn by Charlemagne's wealth and power and enriched by his patronage, they struggled to improve the scholarly level of the Carolingian Church; but they showed little concern for deepening its spiritual life or exploring uncharted regions of speculative thought. They had the talents and inclinations—and the limitations—of the schoolmaster. At best they were scholars and humanists; in no sense could they be described as philosophers or mystics.

Accordingly, Alcuin, Theodulf, Einhard, Paul the Deacon, and others like them purified and regularized the liturgy of the Church and encouraged the preaching of sermons. They carried on some of the monastic reforms begun by Boniface and saw to it that every important monastery had a school. It was a question not of producing new Platos and Augustines but of preserving literacy itself. A new, standardized script was developed—the Carolingian minuscule—which derived in part from the Irish and Northumbrian scripts of the previous century. Thenceforth the Carolingian minuscule superseded the often illegible scripts earlier employed on the Continent. Throughout the realm monks set about copying manuscripts on an unprecedented scale. If classical-Christian culture was advanced very little by these activities it was at least preserved. Above all, its base was broadened. In the task they set themselves, these Carolingian scholars were eminently successful.

The Renaissance after Charlemagne

It is characteristic of the powerful theocratic tendencies of the age that this significant cultural-pedagogical achievement was accomplished through royal rather than papal initiative. Germanic monarchy and classical-Christian culture had joined hands at last. With the breakdown of European unity after Charlemagne's death the momentary fusion of political and cultural energies dissolved; yet the intellectural revival continued. A deeply spiritual movement of monastic reform and moral regeneration began in Aquitaine under the leadership of the ardent and saintly Benedict of Aniane. Soon the influence of this movement took hold at the court of Charlemagne's son and successor, Louis the Pious. Louis gave St. Benedict of Aniane the privilege of visiting any monastery in the empire and tightening its discipline in whatever way he chose. And in 817 a significantly elaborated version of the old Benedictine Rule, based on the strict monastic regulations of Benedict of Aniane, was promulgated for all the monasteries of the empire and given the weight of imperial law. Benedict of Aniane's reform represents a marked shift from the spiritually superficial monastic regulations of Charlemagne's day to a deep concern for the Christ-centered life. The elaborated Benedictine Rule of 817 lost its status as imperial law on Louis the Pious's death in 840, but it remained an inspiration to subsequent monastic reform movements in the centuries that followed. Thenceforth the Benedictine life par excellence was based on Benedict of Aniane's modification of the original Rule.

While Carolingian spiritual life was deepening in the years after Charlemagne's death, Carolingian scholarship continued to flourish in the cathedral and monastic schools. A vigorous controversy over the question of free will and predestination testifies to the vitality of Carolingian thought in the early and middle decades of the ninth century. And in keeping with the Carolingian intellectual program of preserving the classical-Christian tradition, learned churchmen of the Carolingian Renaissance's "second generation" devoted themselves to the preparation of encyclopedic compilations of received knowledge, unoriginal but important none the less in the process of cultural transmission. For example, Raban Maur (d. 856), abbot of the great monastery of Fulda, provided an elaborate encyclopedia on the pattern of Isidore of Seville's *Etymologies*, entitled *De Universo*. He also carried forward the Carolingian pedagogical tradition by writing a handbook on the instruction of the clergy—*De Clericorum Institutione* —which had a significant influence on the operation of monastic schools.

John Scotus

The most interesting scholar in this "second generation" was the Irishman, John Scotus Erigena, who stands as the one original thinker of the whole Carolingian age. John Scotus, or John the Scot (the "Scots" in his day were inhabitants of Ireland rather than Scotland), served for years in the court of Charlemagne's grandson, Charles the Bald. Not only a brilliant speculative thinker, he was also a precocious wit, at least if we can give credence to the later legend of a dinner-table conversation between John the Scot and King Charles the Bald. The King, intending to needle his court scholar, asked the rhetorical question, "What is there that separates a Scot from a sot," to which John is alleged to have replied, "Only the dinner table."

John Scotus was a profound student of Neoplatonism and the only western European scholar of his age to master the Greek tongue. He translated into Latin an important Greek philosophical treatise, *On the Celestial Hierarchy*, written by an anonymous late-fifth-century Christian Neoplatonist known as the Pseudo-Dionysius. This author was incorrectly identified in the Middle Ages as Dionysius the Areopagite, the first-century Athenian philosopher who is described in the *Acts of the Apostles* as being converted to Christianity by St. Paul. He was further misidentified as St. Denis, evangelist of the Gauls and first bishop of Paris, who was decapitated by the pagans and in whose honor the great royal monastery of St. Denis was built. Accordingly, the writings of the Pseudo-Dionysius, even though tinged with pantheism, passed into the Middle Ages with the powerful credentials of an early Christian author, a Pauline convert, and a martyred missionary who brought Christianity to Gaul. In reality, the importance of the Pseudo-Dionysius lay in his providing a Christian dimension to the philosophical scheme of Plotinus and other pagan Neoplatonists. The unknowable and indescribable Neoplatonic god—the center and source of the concentric circles of reality—was identified with the God of the Christians. Such a god could not be approached intellectually but only by means of a mystical experience;

hence, the Pseudo-Dionysius became an important source of inspiration to later Christian mystics.

Stimulated by the work of the Pseudo-Dionysius, which he translated, John Scotus went on to write a highly original Neoplatonic treatise of his own, *On the Divisions of Nature*. In its blurred distinction between God and the created world, the treatise reflected the Neoplatonic tendency toward pantheism. It was condemned as heretical in the thirteenth century but made little impact on contemporaries who lacked both the interest and the background to understand it. John Scotus is a lonely figure in intellectual history, without any immediate predecessors or successors. He founded no schools of thought and carried on no real philosophical dialogue with his contemporaries who were scholars, poets, and pedants rather than abstract thinkers. He figures as the supreme intellect in the West between St. Augustine and the philosophers of the High Middle Ages, yet being neither the direct product of earlier intellectual currents nor the cause of subsequent ones, he played a minor role in the evolution of thought. He remains, nevertheless, the one interesting philosopher of the Carolingian epoch.

The intellectual revival instigated by Charlemagne reverberated down through subsequent generations. John Scotus' Neoplatonism may have been generally ignored and quickly forgotten. Yet in the monasteries and cathedrals of the ninth and tenth centuries, particularly in the German districts of Charlemagne's old empire, documents continued to be copied, schools continued to operate, and commentaries and epitomes of ancient texts continued to appear. By the eleventh century Europe was ready to build on her sturdy Carolingian foundations.

The Carolingian State

Charlemagne's empire was an ephemeral thing, arising from a chaotic past and disintegrating in the turbulent age that followed. It is far easier to understand why the empire broke up than to explain how such a vast, primitive, amorphous state was able to coalesce even briefly. The answer is to be found above all in the person of Charlemagne himself. It was Charlemagne who held his empire together, and he did so by the quality of his leadership and the strength of his personality. In an era of primitive roads and wretched communications he was obliged to depend heavily on the competence and loyalty of the counts, dukes, and margraves who administered his provinces. He kept some control over these magnates by sending pairs of inspectors known as *missi dominici* (envoys of the lord) from his court into the provinces to insure the implementation of his will. The *missi dominici*, consisting normally of one churchman and one layman, typified the theocratic trend of Charlemagne's age. They were moderately effective in binding the empire together, but only because they were received respectfully in the provinces as representatives of a fear-inspiring monarch. The allegiance of Charlemagne's counts and dukes was mostly a product of their respect for Charlemagne himself. They obeyed his commands and submitted to his capitularies not out of patriotism to his state but because of their devotion to his person. In sum, the administrative institutions of the Carolingian Empire were grossly inadequate to the needs of a great state. Beneath the military and cultural veneer Carolingian Europe was still semi-barbaric. Alcuin was yielding to illusion when he told Charlemagne, "If your intentions are carried out, it may be that a new Athens will arise in Frankland, and an Athens fairer than of old, for our Athens, ennobled by the teachings of Christ, will surpass the wisdom of the Academy." Alcuin's vision was a mirage; the Carolingian state remained a land of untutored warriors and peasants just emerging from barbarism.

Charlemagne's "Roman Empire" was a faint shadow of the Augustan state, yet one must admire this Carolingian who could do so much with so little; who could make such an effort to transcend his own barbaric past; who as an adult struggled vainly to learn how to write and to master the subtleties of Augustine's *City of God*. The historian Christopher Dawson caught the spirit of Charlemagne's achievement perfectly when he wrote, "The unwieldy empire of Charles the Great did not long survive the death of its founder, and it never really attained the economic and social organization of a civilized state. But, for all that, it marks the first emergence of the European culture from the twilight of prenatal existence into the consciousness of active life."*

* Christopher Dawson, *The Making of Europe* (New York: World Publishing Co., Meridian Books, 1957), p. 187.

7

the new invasions

Tentative though it was, the economic and cultural revival under Charlemagne might conceivably have evolved in the direction of a vital though authoritarian civilization had it not been for the new invasions that followed Charlemagne's death in 814. Until then the Carolingian realm had enjoyed relative internal peace. Intellectual life, although still rudimentary, was in the process of reawakening, and with the stimulus of the silver coinage which Charlemagne issued, commerce quickened. One historian has even suggested that under the bracing influence of Charlemagne's economic policy towns were beginning to grow and flourish once again. But these hopeful signs proved to be a false dawn. During the ninth and tenth centuries Europe was obliged to fight against the triple thrust of alien invaders—the semi-nomadic Hungarians from the east, the piratical Saracens (Muslims) from the south, and the wide-ranging Vikings from the north. The maturing of a higher civilization was delayed in Europe for another two centuries.

Louis the Pious (814–840)

It would be wrong to ascribe the political fragmentation of the Carolingian Empire entirely to these outside pressures. Charlemagne himself, in keeping with Frankish tradition, planned to divide his state among his several sons. As it happened, however, Charlemagne outlived all but one of them. The luck of the Carolingians was still running, and when the great conqueror died in 814 his realm passed intact to his remaining heir, Louis the Pious.

Although Louis was by no means incompetent, his military and political talents were distinctly inferior to those of his father Charlemagne, his grandfather Pepin the Short, and his great-grandfather Charles Martel. Carolingian unity continued but Carolingian leadership showed signs of faltering. Louis the Pious was well named. He ran Charlemagne's minstrels and concubines out of the imperial court and replaced them with priests and monks. Far more than his hardheaded father, Louis committed himself to the dream of a unified Christian Empire—a City of God brought down to earth. Yet he was far less suited than Charlemagne to the Herculean task of maintaining unity and cohesion in the immense, heterogeneous empire that the Carolingians had won. He was the first of his line to conceive the notion of bequeathing supreme political authority to his eldest son and thereby making the unity of the kingdom a matter of policy rather than chance. Ironically, he turned out to be the last Carolingian to rule an undivided Frankish realm. His bold plan for a single succession was foiled by the ambitions of his younger sons who rebelled openly against him and plunged the empire into civil war.

The Treaty of Verdun

When Louis the Pious's unhappy reign ended in 840 his three surviving sons struggled bitterly for the spoils. The eldest of the three, Lothar, claimed the indivisible imperial title and hegemony over the entire realm. The other two sons, Louis the German and Charles the Bald, fought to win independent royal authority in East and West Frankland respectively. In the end Lothar had to yield to the combined might of his younger brothers. The controversy was settled by the Treaty of Verdun in 843, which permanently divided the empire and foreshadowed the political structure of modern Europe. Lothar was permitted to keep the imperial title but was denied any superior jurisdiction over the realms of Louis the German and Charles the Bald. Louis ruled East Frankland, which became the nucleus of the modern German state. In a very real sense, he was Germany's first king. Charles the Bald became king of West Frankland, which evolved into modern France. Lothar retained a long, narrow strip of territory that stretched for some thousand miles northward from Italy through Burgundy, Alsace, Lorraine, and the Netherlands, embracing considerable portions of western Germany and eastern France. This

PARTITION OF THE EMPIRE
TREATY OF VERDUN, 843

Kingdom of Charles the Bald
Kingdom of Lothar
Kingdom of Louis

SLAVIC PEOPLES

AVARS

Baltic Sea

North Sea

Atlantic Ocean

ANGLO-SAXON KINGDOMS

FRISIA

SAXONY

Elbe R.

Fulda

AUSTRASIA

Rhine R.

Danube R.

Danube R.

BAVARIA

St. Gall

Cologne
Aachen

Verdun

Rouen
Rheims
Paris
NEUSTRIA
Angers
Tours
Orléans
Poitiers

AQUITAINE

Ebro R.

SPANISH MARCH

LOMBARDY

Rhône R.

Pavia
Po R.
Ravenna

Venice

Rome

Monte Cassino

Adriatic Sea

CORSICA

Mediterranean Sea

Scale of Miles
0 50 100 200 300 400

CAROLINGIAN CHRONOLOGY

687: Pepin of Heristal, Carolingian mayor of Austrasia, defeats Neustria; Carolingian hegemony established.

714–741: Rule of Charles Martel.

732: Arabs defeated at Tours.

741–768: Rule of Pepin the Short.

751: Pepin crowned king of the Franks. Merovingian Dynasty ends.

754: Death of St. Boniface.

768–814: Reign of Charlemagne.

772–804: Charlemagne's Saxon Wars.

800: Charlemagne crowned Roman Emperor.

814–840: Reign of Louis the Pious.

843: Treaty of Verdun.

Middle Kingdom included the two "imperial capitals"—Rome and Aachen—but its exposed frontiers were difficult to defend, and it lacked unity. At Lothar's death in 855 it was subdivided among his three sons, one of whom inherited Carolingian Italy and the increasingly insignificant imperial title. From the ninth century to the twentieth, fragments of Lothar's middle kingdom have been the source of endless bitter territorial disputes between Germany and France.

The struggles among Charlemagne's grandsons occurred against a background of Viking, Hungarian, and Saracen invasions, which accelerated the tendency toward political fragmentation brought about by internal weaknesses. But even without the invasions, and without the Frankish tradition of divided succession, Charlemagne's huge, unwieldy empire could not have long remained intact once his iron hand had been removed from control. As it turned out, even the more modest political units arising from the Treaty of Verdun were too large—too far removed from the desperate realities of the countryside—to cope successfully with the lightning raids of Viking shipmen or Hungarian horsemen. During the ninth and tenth centuries Carolingian leadership was visibly failing. The incapacity of the later Carolingians was nowhere better illustrated than in their names: Charles the Fat, Charles the Simple, Louis the Child, Louis the Blind.

The Impact of the Invasions

The Saracens, Hungarians, and Vikings, who plundered the declining Carolingian state, were in part drawn by the growing political vacuum, and in part impelled by forces operating in their own homelands. Europe suffered much from their marauding, yet it was strong enough in the end to survive and absorb the invaders. And these invasions were the last that Western Christendom was destined to endure. From about A.D. 1000 to the present the West has had the unique opportunity of developing on its own, sheltered from alien attacks that have so disrupted other civilizations over the past millennium. As the historian Marc Bloch said, "It is surely not unreasonable to think that this extraordinary immunity, of which we have shared the privilege with scarcely any people but the Japanese, was one of the fundamental factors of European civilization. . . ."*

Yet in the ninth and tenth centuries Europe's hard-pressed peoples had no way of knowing that the invasions would one day end. A Frankish historian of the mid-ninth century wrote, perhaps with a touch of melodramatic exaggeration, "The number of ships grows larger and larger; the great host of Northmen continually increases; on every hand Christians are the victims of massacres, looting, and incendiarism—clear proof of which will remain as long as the world itself endures. The Northmen capture every city they pass through, and none can withstand them." In southern Gaul people prayed for divine protection against the Saracens: "Eternal Trinity . . . deliver thy Christian people from the oppression of the pagans." To the north they prayed, "From the savage nation of the Northmen, which lays waste our realms, deliver us, O God." And in northern Italy: "Against the arrows of the Hungarians be thou our protector."

Saracens and Magyars

The Saracens of the ninth and tenth centuries, unlike their Muslim predecessors in the seventh and early eighth, came as brigands rather than conquerors and settlers. From their pirate nests in Africa, Spain, and the Mediterranean islands they preyed on shipping, plundered coastal cities, and sailed up rivers to carry their devastation far inland.

* March Bloch, *Feudal Society*, trans. L. A. Manyon (Chicago: The University of Chicago Press, 1961), p. 56.

Saracen bandit lairs were established on the southern coast of Gaul, from which the marauders conducted raids far and wide through the countryside and kidnapped pilgrims crossing the Alpine passes. Charlemagne had never possessed much of a navy, and his successors found themselves helpless to defend their coasts. In 846 Saracen brigands raided Rome itself, profaning its churches and stealing its treasures. As late as 982 a German king was severely defeated by Saracens in southern Italy; but by then the raids were tapering off. Southern Europe, now bristling with fortifications, had learned to defend itself and was even beginning to challenge Saracen domination of the western Mediterranean.

The Hungarians, or Magyars, fierce nomadic horsemen from the Asiatic steppes, settled in the land now known as Hungary. From the late 800s to 955 they terrorized Germany, northern Italy, and eastern Gaul. Hungarian raiding parties ranged across the land, seeking defenseless settlements to plunder, avoiding fortified towns, outriding and outmaneuvering the armies sent against them. In time, however, they became more sedentary, gave more attention to their farms, and lost much of their nomadic savagery. In 955 King Otto the Great of Germany crushed a large Hungarian army at the battle of Lechfeld and brought the raids to an end at last. Within another half-century, the Hungarians had adopted Christianity and were becoming integrated into the community of Christian Europe.

Vikings

The Vikings, or Norsemen, were the most fearsome invaders of all. These redoubtable warrior-seafarers came from Scandinavia, the very land that had, centuries before, disgorged many of the Germanic barbarians into Europe. Thus the ninth century Vikings and the Germanic invaders of Roman times had similar ethnic backgrounds. But to the ninth-century European—the product of countless Germanic-Celtic-Roman intermarriages, tamed by the Church and by centuries of settled life—the heathen Vikings seemed a hostile and alien people.

Then, as now, the Scandinavians were divided roughly into three groups: Danes, Swedes, and Norwegians. During the great age of Viking expansion in the ninth and tenth centuries the Danes, who were brought cheek to jowl with the Carolingian Empire by Charlemagne's conquest of Saxony, focused their attention on Frankland and England. The Norwegians raided and settled in Scotland, Ireland, and the North Atlantic. The Swedes concentrated on the East—the Baltic shores, Russia, and the Byzantine Empire. Yet the three Norse peoples had much in common, and the distinctions between them were by no means sharp. It is therefore proper to regard their raids, their astonishing explorations, and their far-flung commercial enterprises as a single great international movement.

Though the breakdown of Carolingian leadership doubtless acted as a magnet to Viking marauders, their raids on the West began as early as Charlemagne's age. The basic causes for their outward thrust must be sought in Scandinavia itself. Since pre-tenth-century Scandinavia is almost a closed book to historians, our explanations for the Viking outburst are little more than educated guesses. It is likely, however, that the Scandinavian population, once sharply reduced by the outward migrations of Roman times, had increased by the later 700s to a level which the primitive Norse agriculture was scarcely able to support. The pressure of over-population was probably aggravated by growing centralized royal power which cramped the more restless spirits and drove them to seek adventures and opportunities abroad. A third factor was the development of improved Viking ships, eminently seaworthy, propelled by both sail and oars, and capable of carrying crews of 40 to 100 warriors at speeds up to ten knots. In these longships the tall, muscular, reddish-haired Viking warriors struck the ports of Northern Europe. They sailed up rivers far into the interior, plundering the towns and monasteries of Frankland and England, sometimes stealing horses and riding across the countryside to spread their devastation still further.

The people of Europe were accustomed enough to warfare among their own nominally Christian warrior-nobility. But Christian barons tended to respect the sanctity of the monastaries, which, with their wealth, enticed the acquisitive Vikings and, with their near monopoly on literacy, produced almost all our information about the Viking raids. The monastic chroniclers of the time, accustomed to peace within their walls, doubtless exaggerated the violence of the Viking age and the size and ferocity of the Viking armies. Yet the Viking impact on northern France, England, and Russia was real, and it was lasting.

Attacks against England

England was the first to suffer from Viking attacks. About 789 three longships touched the Channel coast in Dorset and Vikings poured out of them to loot and sack a nearby town. Thenceforth the Anglo-Saxon kingdoms were tormented by incessant Viking raids. In 794 Norse brigands annihilated the Northumbrian monastery of Jarrow, where Bede had lived and died. Other great monastic centers of Northumbria suffered a similar devastation.

In 842 the Danes plundered London, and a few years thereafter they began to establish permanent winter bases in England which freed them from the necessity of returning to Scandinavia after the raiding season. By the later 800s they had turned from piracy to large-scale occupation and permanent settlement. One after another the Anglo-Saxon kingdoms were overrun until at length, in the 780s, only the southern kingdom of Wessex remained free of Danish control—and even Wessex came within a hair's breadth of falling to the Danes.

Attacks against the Continent

To mariners such as the Vikings, the English Channel was a boulevard rather than a barrier, and their raiding parties attacked the English and Frankish shores indiscriminately. They established permanent bases at the mouths of great rivers and sailed up them to plunder defenseless monasteries and sack towns. Antwerp was ravaged in 837, Rouen in 841, Hamburg and Paris in 845, Charlemagne's old capital at Aachen in 881.

But if some Europeans were driven to helpless resignation others fought doggedly to protect their lands. King Alfred the Great of Wessex saved his kingdom from Danish conquest in the late 870s and began the task of rolling back the Danish armies in England. King Arnulf of East Frankland won a decisive victory over the Norsemen in 891 at the battle of the Dyle and thereby decreased the Viking pressure on Germany—although it was at this very time that the Hungarian raids began. West Frankland continued to suffer for awhile, but in about 911 King Charles the Simple created a friendly Viking buffer state in northern France by concluding a treaty with a Norse chieftain named Rolf. The Vikings in Rolf's band had been

THE VIKING, HUNGARIAN
AND MUSLIM INVASIONS

ICELAND

Atlantic Ocean

VIKINGS

NORWAY

SWEDEN

Atlantic

SCOT-LAND

IRELAND

ENGLAND

DENMARK

Dnieper R.

Kiev R.

Aachen

Rouen

Rhine R.

Paris

Seine

Loire R.

Tours

Danube R.

HUNGARIANS

Danube R.

Black Sea

LOMBARDY

PROVENCE

Marseilles

Constantinople

CORSICA

Rome

Monte Cassino

Naples

SARDINIA

BALEARIC IS.

SICILY

MUSLIMS

Mediterranean Sea

	Vikings
	Muslims
	Hungarians

MILES

0   200   400   600   800

conducting raids from their settlement at the mouth of the Seine River. Charles, less simple than his name would imply, reasoned that if he could make Rolf his ally the Seine settlement might prove an effective barrier against further raids. Rolf became a Christian, married Charles the Simple's daughter, and recognized at least in some sense the superiority of the West Frankish monarchy. Thus his state acquired legitimacy in the eyes of Western Christendom. Expanding gradually under Rolf and his successors, it became known as the land of the Northmen, or "Normandy." Over the next century and a half the Normans became as good Christians as the Franks. They adopted French culture and the French language, yet retained much of their old energy. In the eleventh century Normandy was producing some of Europe's most vigorous warriors, Crusaders, administrators, and monks.

Ireland, Greenland, North America

France, England, and Germany formed only a part of the vast Viking world of the ninth and tenth centuries. By the mid-800s Norwegians and Danes had conquered the greater part of Ireland, and between 875 and 930 they settled remote Iceland. There a distinctive Norse culture arose which for several centuries remained only slightly affected by the main currents of Western civilization. In Iceland the magnificent oral tradition of the Norse saga flourished and was eventually committed to writing. The Icelandic Norsemen were perhaps the greatest sailors of all. They settled on the coast of Greenland in the late 900s, and in the eleventh century they established temporary settlements on the northern coasts of North America itself, anticipating Columbus by half a millennium.

Russia

To the east Swedish Vikings overran Finland and penetrated far southward across European Russia to trade with Constantinople and Baghdad. The Byzantine emperors took pride in the tall Norse mercenaries who served in their imperial guard. In Russia a Swedish dynasty established itself at Novgorod in the later ninth century, ruling over the indigenous Slavic population. In the tenth century a

Norse prince of Novgorod captured the south-Russian city of Kiev, which became the capital of the powerful, well-organized state of Kievan Russia. Deeply influenced by the culture of its subjects, the dynasty at Kiev became more Slavic than Scandinavian. Around the turn of the millennium, as we have already seen, Prince Vladimir of Kiev adopted Byzantine Christianity and submitted himself and his people to the Patriarch of Constantinople, thereby opening Russia to the influence of Byzantine culture (see pp. 32–41).

Twilight of the Viking Age

The development of centralized monarchies in Denmark, Norway, and Sweden, which may well have been a factor in driving enterprising Norse seamen to seek their fortunes elsewhere, ultimately resulted in taming the Viking spirit. As Scandinavia became increasingly civilized its kings discouraged the activities of roaming independent warrior bands, and its social environment gave rise to a somewhat more humdrum, sedentary life. Far into the eleventh century England continued to face the attacks of Norsemen, but these invaders were no longer pirate bands; rather, they were royal armies led by Scandinavian kings. The nature of the Scandinavian threat had changed, and by the late eleventh century the threat had ceased altogether. Around the year 1000 Christianity was winning converts all across the Scandinavian world. In Iceland, in Russia—even in the kingdoms of Scandinavia itself—the Norsemen were adopting the religion of the monks who had once so feared them. Scandinavia was becoming a part of western European culture.

Even at the height of the invasions the Norsemen were by no means pure barbarians. They excelled at commerce as well as piracy. They were the greatest seafarers of the age. They introduced Europe to the art of ocean navigation and enlarged the horizons of Western Christendom, injecting a spirit of enterprise and cosmopolitanism into the conservative, parochial outlook of Carolingian civilization.

8

europe survives the siege

Response to the Invasions: England

The invasions of the ninth and tenth centuries wrought significant changes in the political and social organization of western Europe. Generally speaking, political authority tended to crumble into small local units as unwieldly royal armies failed to cope with the lightning raids. This was true in France, but it was less so in Germany, where the monarchy, after a period of relative weakness, underwent a spectacular recovery in the tenth century. In England, paradoxically, the hammerblows of the Danes had the ultimate result of unifying the several Anglo-Saxon states into a single kingdom.

In the later eighth century, on the eve of the Viking invasions, England was politically fragmented, as it had been ever since the Anglo-Saxon conquests. But over the centuries the several smaller kingdoms had gradually passed under the control of three larger ones: Northumbria in the north, Mercia in the Midlands, and Wessex in the south. The Danish attacks of the ninth century, by destroying the power of Wessex's rivals, cleared the field for the Wessex monarchy and thereby hastened the trend toward consolidation that was already underway. But if the Danes were doing the Wessex monarchy a favor, neither side was aware of it during the troubled years of the later ninth century. For a time it appeared that the Danes might conquer Wessex itself.

King Alfred

At the moment of crisis a remarkable leader rose to the Wessex throne: Alfred the Great (871–99). Alfred did everything in his power to save his kingdom from the Vikings. He fought ferocious battles against them. He even resorted to bribing them. In the winter of 878 the Danes, in a surprise attack, invaded Wessex and forced Alfred to take refuge, with a handful of companions, on the isle of Athelney in a remote swamp. Athelney was England's Valley Forge. In the following spring Alfred rallied his forces and smashed a Danish army at the battle of Edington. This victory turned the tide of the war; the Danish leader agreed to take up Christianity, to withdraw from the land, and to accept a "permanent" peace. Wessex was never again seriously threatened.

But other Danes under other leaders refused to honor the peace, and Alfred, in his later campaigns, conquered Kent and most of Mercia and captured London—even then England's chief city. In the 880s a new peace treaty gave Wessex most of southern and south-western England. The remainder of England—the "Danelaw"—remained hostile, but all non-Danish England was now united under King Alfred.

Like all successful leaders of the age, Alfred was an able warrior. But more than that, he was a brilliant, imaginative organizer who systematized military recruitment and founded the English navy, seeing clearly that Christian Europe could not hope to drive back the Vikings without challenging them on the seas. He filled his land with fortresses which served both as defensive strongholds and as places of sanctuary for the agrarian population in time of war. And gradually, as the Danish tide was rolled back, additional fortresses were built to secure the territories newly reconquered. Alfred clarified and rationalized the laws of his people, enforced them strictly, and ruled with an authority such as no Anglo-Saxon king had exercised before his time.

King Alfred was also a scholar and a patron of learning. His intellectual environment was even less promising than Charlemagne's. The great days of Bede, Boniface, and Alcuin were far in the past, and by Alfred's time, Latin—the key to classical Christian culture—was almost unknown in England. Like Charlemagne, Alfred gathered scholars from far and wide—England, Wales, the continent—and set

ENGLAND ABOUT 885

Scale of Miles
0 20 40 60 80 100

SCOTS

Picts

Tay

North

Firth of Forth

ENGLISH NORTHUMBRIA

•LINDISFARNE

Sea

Picts

Tees

Whitby

York

IRELAND

Irish Sea

DANELAW

WALES

Trent

ENGLISH MERCIA

Severn R.

Ouse

EAST ANGLIA

Thames R.

London

SURREY

KENT

Canterbury

WESSEX

SUSSEX

DEVON

CORNWALL

English Channel

them to work teaching Latin and translating Latin classics into the Anglo-Saxon language. Alfred himself participated in the work of translation, helping to render such works as Boethius's *Consolation of Philosophy*, Pope Gregory's *Pastoral Care*, and Bede's *Ecclesiastical History* into the native tongue. In his translation of Boethius, Alfred added a regretful comment of his own: "In those days one never heard of ships armed for war." And in his preface to the *Pastoral Care* he alluded with nostalgia to the days "before everything was ravaged and burned, when England's churches overflowed with treasures and books." Alfred's intellectual revival, even more than Charlemagne's, was a salvage operation rather than an outburst of originality. He was both modest and accurate when he described himself as one who wandered through a great forest collecting timber with which others could build.

Alfred's task of reconquest was carried on by his able successors in the first half of the tenth century. By mid-century all England was in their hands, and the kings of Wessex had become the kings of England. Great numbers of Danish settlers still remained in northern and eastern England—the amalgamation of Danish and English customs required many generations—but the creative response of the Wessex kings to the Danish threat had transformed and politically united the Anglo-Saxon world. Out of the agony of the invasions the English monarchy was born.

The Renewal of the Danish Attacks

For a generation after the conquest of the Danelaw, from about 955 to 980, England enjoyed relative peace and prosperity. English flotillas patrolled the shores, the old fortresses began to evolve into commercial centers, and churchmen addressed themselves to the task of monastic reform. But the Danish inhabitants of northern and eastern England remained only half committed to the new English monarchy, and with the accession of an incompetent child-king, Ethelred the Unready (978–1016), Danish invasions resumed.

The new invasions evolved into a campaign of conquest directed by the Danish monarchy. The English defense was characterized by incompetence, treason, and panic. In 991 Ethelred began paying a tribute to the Danes, known thereafter as "danegeld." In later years the danegeld evolved into a land tax which was exceedingly profitable to the English monarchy, but at the time it was a symbol of humiliation. In 1016 Ethelred fled the country altogether, and in the following year King Canute of Denmark became the monarch of England.

Canute (1017–1035)

Canute has been described as nearly a dwarf and nearly a genius. He conquered Norway as well as England, and joining these two lands to his kingdom of Denmark, he became the master of a huge empire centering on the North Sea. A product of the new civilizing forces at work in eleventh-century Scandinavia, Canute was no bloodthirsty Viking. He issued law codes, practiced Christianity, and kept the peace. Devoting much of his time to England, he cast himself as an English king in the old Wessex tradition. He respected and upheld the ancient customs of the land and gave generously to the monasteries. Despite his Danish background, he was a far better English monarch than Ethelred. His reign was a continuation of the past, and he added luster to the crown that Alfred's dynasty had forged. English religion and culture prospered as before: "Merry sang the monks of Ely as Canute the king rowed by."

Canute's Danish-Norwegian-English empire was hopelessly disunited and failed to survive his death in 1035. When the last of his sons died in 1042 the English realm fell peacefully to Edward the Confessor, a member of the Old Wessex dynasty who had grown up in exile in Normandy.

The Aftermath

Though a poor general and a mediocre administrator, Edward the Confessor was a man of piety who won the support of his people despite his political ineptitude. His childless marriage ensured a disputed succession upon his death in 1066 and set the stage for the Norman conquest. When William the Conqueror, duke of Normandy, invaded England and won its crown in 1066, he inherited a prosperous kingdom with strong, well-established political and legal traditions—a kingdom still divided by differences in custom but with a deep-seated respect for royal authority. Ethelred the Unready notwithstanding, the Wessex dynasty had done its work well. With the timber that Alfred collected, his successors had built an ample and sturdy edifice.

Response to the Invasions: French Feudalism

In England the invasions stimulated the trend toward royal unification; in France they encouraged a shattering of political authority into small local units. This paradox can be explained in part by the fact that France, unlike England, was far too large for the Vikings to conquer. Although many of them settled in Normandy, the chief Norse threat to France came in the form of plundering expeditions rather than large conquering armies. Distances were too great, communications too primitive, and the national territorial army too unwieldy for the king to take the lead in defending his realm. Military responsibility descended to local lords who alone could hope to protect the countryside from the swift Viking assaults. The French Carolingians became increasingly powerless until at length in 987 the crown passed to a new dynasty—the Capetians. During the twelfth and thirteenth centuries the Capetian family produced some of France's most illustrious kings, but for the time being the new dynasty was as powerless as the old one. After 987, as before, the nobles overshadowed the king. About all one can say of the French monarchy in these dark years is that it survived.

The Viking Age witnessed the birth of feudalism in France. In a very real sense feudalism was a product of France's response to the invasions. Yet in another sense the Franks had long been drifting in a feudal direction. The roots of feudalism ran deep: one root was the honorable bond of fidelity and service of a warrior to his lord—which characterized the lord-vassal relationship of late-Merovingian and early-Carolingian times, and the still earlier comitatus of the Germanic barbarians. Another root was the late-Roman and early-medieval concept of land-holding in return for certain services to the person who granted the land. An estate granted to a tenant in return for service was known as a *benefice*.

Charles Martel took an important step toward feudalism by joining the institutions of benefice and vassalage. He undertook heavy confiscations of Church property and granted the appropriated estates to his military vassals. One reason for this step was the shortage of money in the Early Middle ages; it was almost impossible for a ruler to support his soldiers with wages. Often the vassals of an important Frankish lord were fed and sheltered in his household. Indeed, the "household knight" persisted throughout the feudal age. But as their military importance grew these warrior-vassals exhibited an ever-increasing hunger for land. Their lords were therefore under considerable pressure to grant them estates—benefices—in return for their loyalty and service.

This tendency was associated with a shift in Frankish military tactics. The Franks had originally been infantrymen, but gradually cavalry became increasingly important. The Frankish warrior *par excellence* became the armored, mounted knight, more effective than the infantrymen, but also far more expensive to support. The knight needed a fine mount, heavy armor and weapons, several attendants, and years of training. Hence the tendency for a lord to support his knightly vassals by granting them estates in return for their service. The knight did not, of course, labor on his own fields; rather he administered them and collected dues, chiefly in kind, from his peasants.

The Carolingian military vassal was typically a knight. As knightly tactics came more and more to dominate warfare, the custom of vassalage spread widely. Frankish magnates of Charlemagne's time had pledged their allegiance to their emperor and had thereby recognized that they were his vassals and he their lord. Moreover, these royal vassals had vassals of their own who owed primary allegiance to their immediate lords rather than to the emperor. Charlemagne himself approved of this practice of private lordship and encouraged the free men of his realm to become vassals of his magnates. In time of war these vassals of vassals (or subvassals) were expected to join their lords' contingents in the royal army. The disintegrative tendencies implicit in such an arrangement are obvious. Yet Charlemagne, lacking a coherent civil service or adequate funds to hire a professional army of his own, was obliged to depend on this potentially unstable hierarchy of authority and allegiance.

With the removal of Charlemagne's commanding personality, and under the pressure of the invasions, the rickety hierarchy began to collapse into its component parts. Charlemagne's old territorial officials, the dukes, counts, and margraves, backed by their own vassals, tended increasingly to usurp royal rights. They administered justice and collected taxes without regard for the royal will. In time they built castles and assumed all responsibility for the defense of their districts. Nominally these feudal magnates remained vassals of the kings of France, but they soon became too powerful to be coerced by the crown. Their authority was limited chiefly by the independence of their own vassals, who began to create subvassals or sub-subvassals of their own. At the height of the feudal age the lord-vassal relationship might run down through some ten or twenty levels; there was scarcely a vassal to be found who was not the lord of some still lower vassal.

The ultimate consequences of these developments have been described as "feudal anarchy." In a sense the term is well chosen, but it should not mislead us into thinking of feudalism simply as a "bad thing." Given the instability of the Carolingian Empire and the vulnerability of France in the Viking era, feudalism emerges as a successful accommodation to the realities of the age. Roman Europe succumbed to barbarian invasions; feudal Europe survived its invaders and ultimately absorbed them.

French feudalism reached its height in the tenth and eleventh centuries. Its key institution was the military benefice, the estate granted by a lord to his vassal in return for allegiance and service—primarily knightly military service. This military benefice was commonly known as a *fief* (rhyming with beef). It was a practical response to the requirements of local defense, the breakdown of central authority, and the scarcity of money which necessitated the paying for service in land rather than wages. A great lord would grant an estate—a fief—to his vassal. The vassal might then grant a part of the estate—another fief—to a vassal of his own. And so on and on, down and down, the process of enfeoffment went. The result was a hierarchically organized landed knightly aristocracy. Each knight gave homage and fealty—that is, pledged his personal allegiance—to his immediate lord; each lived off the labor and dues of a dependent peasantry which tilled the fields that his fief embraced; each administered a court and dispensed justice to those below him.

Such were the essential ingredients of feudalism. The term is extremely difficult to define and has often been abused and misunderstood. The great French scholar Marc Bloch described feudalism in these words:

A subject peasantry; widespread use of the service tenement (that is, the fief) instead of a salary, which was out of the question; the supremacy of a class of specialized warriors; ties of obedience and protection which bind man to man and, within the warrior class, assume the distinctive form called vassalage; fragmentation of authority—leading inevitably to disorder; and in the midst of all this, the survival of other forms of association, family and state . . . —such then seem to be the fundamental features of European feudalism.*

With this description in mind it may be helpful to emphasize some of the things that feudalism was not. It was not, for one thing, a universal and symmetrical system. Born in northern France in the Viking age, it took on many different forms as it spread across Europe. In northern France itself it varied widely from one region to another. It by no means encompassed all the land, for even at its height many landowners owed no feudal obligations and had no feudal ties. The feudal hierarchy, or feudal "pyramid," was riddled with ambiguities: a single vassal might hold several fiefs from several lords; a lord might receive a fief from his own vassal. The degree of confusion possible in feudalism is well illustrated by this twelfth-century act of enfeoffment:

I, John of Toul, affirm that I am the vassal of the Lady Beatrice, countess of Troyes, and of her son Theobald, count of Champagne, against every creature living or dead, excepting my allegiance to Lord Enjourand of Coucy, Lord John of Arcis, and the count of Grandpré. If it should happen that the count of Grandpre should be at war with the countess and count of Champagne in his own quarrel, I will aid the count of Grandpre in my own person, and will aid the count and countess of Champagne by sending them the knights whose services I owe them from the fief which I hold of them.

Feudalism was not, in its heyday, associated with the romantic knight errant, the many-turreted castle, or the lady fair. The knight of the ninth, tenth, and eleventh centuries was a rough-hewn warrior. His armor was simple, his horse was tough, his castle was a crude wooden tower atop an earthen mound, and his lady fair was any available wench. Chivalry developed after a time, but not until the foundations of the old feudal order were being eroded by the revival of commerce, royal government, and infantry tactics. Only

---

* Bloch, op. cit., p. 446.

then did the knight compensate for his declining usefulness by turning to elaborate armor, courtly phrases, and fairy-tale castles.

Feudalism was not exclusively a military institution. The vassal owed his lord not only military service but a variety of additional obligations as well. Among these were the duty to join his lord's retinue on tours of the countryside; to serve in his lord's court of justice; to feed, house, and entertain his lord and his lord's retinue on their all-too-frequent visits; to give money to his lord on a variety of specified occasions; to contribute to his lord's ransom should he be captured in battle. Early in its history the fief became hereditary. The lord, however, retained the right to confiscate it should his vassal die without heirs, to supervise and exploit it during a minority, and to exercise a power of veto over the marriage of a female fief-holder. In return for such rights as these the lord was obliged to protect and uphold the interests of his vassals. The very essence of feudalism was the notion of reciprocal rights and obligations, and the feudal outlook played a key role in steering medieval Europe away from autocracy.

Feudalism was both a military and a political system. With military responsibility went political power. As the central government of West Frankland demonstrated an ever-increasing incapacity to cope with the invasions or keep peace in the countryside, sovereignty tended to sink to the level of the greater feudal lords. Although nominally loyal vassals, these magnates were powers unto themselves, ruling their own territories without royal interference and maintaining their own courts and administrative systems as well as their own armies. In the days of the Viking raids many of these magnates had extreme difficulty in controlling their own turbulent vassals; feudal tenants several steps down in the pyramid were often able to behave as though they had no real superiors. Subvassals with their own courts and armies were frequently in a position to defy their lords. Accordingly, it is hard to identify the real locus of political power in early feudal France. Sovereignty was spread up and down the aristocratic hierarchy, and a lord's real power depended on his military prowess, his ambition, and the firmness of his leadership.

Specialists in medieval history are inclined to limit "feudalism" to the network of rights and obligations existing among members of the knightly aristocracy—the holders of fiefs. Although resting on the labor of peasants, the feudal structure itself encompassed only the warrior class of lords and vassals. There was, in other words, a world of difference between a vassal and a serf. Beneath the level of the feudal warrior class, 80 or 90 percent of the population continued to labor on the land, producing the food that sustained society. Yet the peasants were scorned by the nobility as boors and louts, and were largely ignored by the chroniclers of the age.

The feudal chaos of the ninth and tenth centuries, with its fragmentation of sovereign power and its incessant private wars, gradually gave way to a somewhat more orderly regime. Great territorial magnates such as the counts of Anjou and Flanders and the duke of Normandy extended their frontiers at the expense of weaker neighbors and tightened their control over their own vassals and subvassals. But not until the twelfth and thirteenth centuries did the French monarchs began to rise above the level of their greater magnates and assert real authority over the realm. The high noon of feudalism was a period of virtual eclipse for the French crown.

Response to Invasions: Germany

In England the invasions brought royal unification; in France, feudal particularism. The response of Germany differed from those of both England and France, owing to the special character of the invasions that Germany faced and the unique conditions prevailing in Germany itself. Although East Frankland (Germany) was subject to Viking attacks, the real threat came from the Hungarian horsemen of the East. When the late Carolingian kings of Germany proved incapable of coping with the Hungarian raids, authority descended, as in France, to the great magnates of the realm. But these magnates were not the dukes and counts of Carolingian officialdom. Most of Germany had remained outside Frankish control until the Carolingian conquests of the eighth century, and the Frankish system of local administration was relatively ephemeral there. The ancient tribal consciousness of Saxons, Bavarians, and Swabians was still strong. In the critical decades of the late ninth and early tenth centuries ambitious noblemen exploited this tribal patriotism by grasping leadership over the old tribal districts. These men of the hour assumed the title of duke, and the regions that they ruled came to be known as tribal duchies. The "tribal" dukes sought to dominate the local ecclesiastical organizations, to seize the royal Carolingian estates in their duchies, and to usurp royal powers. It was they who stood up to the Hungarian thrust.

In the early tenth century Germany was dominated by five tribal duchies: Saxony, Swabia, Bavaria, Franconia, and Lorraine. The first three had been incorporated only superficially into the Carolingian state, whereas the western duchies of Franconia and Lorraine were much more strongly Frankish in outlook and organization. The five "tribal" dukes might well have become the masters of Germany. Their ambitions were frustrated by two closely related factors: (1) their failure to curb the Hungarians, and (2) the reinvigoration of the German monarchy under an able new dynasty. The Carolingian line came to an end in Germany in 911 with the death of King Louis the Child. He was succeeded first by the duke of Franconia and then, in 919, by the duke of Saxony—the first of an illustrious line of kings whose power was based on their domination of the powerful Saxon duchy.

Otto I

The Saxon kings struggled vigorously to assert their authority over the tribal duchies. With the duchy of Saxony under the authority of the monarchy, the Saxon kings quickly won direct control over Franconia as well. But the semi-independent dukes of the two southern duchies, Swabia and Bavaria, presented problems. The real victory of the Saxon monarchy occurred in the reign of the second and greatest of the Saxon kings, Otto I (963–973).

Otto I, or "Otto the Great," directed his considerable talents toward three goals: (1) the defense of Germany against the Hungarian invasions; (2) the establishment of royal power over the remaining tribal duchies; and (3) the extension of German royal control to the crumbling, unstable Middle Kingdom that the Treaty of Verdun had assigned to Emperor Lothar back in 843. We have already seen how this Middle Kingdom began to fall to pieces after Lothar's death. By the mid-tenth century it had become a political shambles. Parts of it had been taken over by Germany and France but its southern districts—Burgundy and Italy—retained a chaotic independence. The dukes of Swabia and Bavaria both had notions of seizing these territories. Otto the Great, in order to forestall the development of an unmanageable rival power to his south, led his armies into Italy in 951 and assumed the title "King of Italy."

From 951 onwards events developed rapidly. Otto the Great had to leave Italy in haste to put down a major uprising in Germany. His victory over the rebels enabled him to establish his power there more strongly than ever. In 955 he won the crucial battle of the age when he crushed a large Hungarian army at Lechfeld, bringing the Hungarian raids to an end at last. Lechfeld served as a vivid demonstration of royal power—a vindication of the monarch's claim that he, not the "tribal" dukes, was the true defender of Germany. With the Hungarians defeated, Germany's eastern frontier now lay open to the gradual penetration of German-Christian culture. The day of the tribal duchies was over; the monarchy was supreme. Otto the Great now towered over his contemporaries as the greatest monarch of the West and the most powerful ruler since Charlemagne. The invasions of Germany, which had begun by uplifting the tribal duchies, ended with the revival of royal authority.

Not long after his victory at Lechfeld, Otto I turned his attention to still another crisis. Since his departure from Italy, a Lombard magnate had seized the Italian throne and was harassing the pope. In response to a papal appeal—which dovetailed with his own interests—Otto returned to Italy in force and recovered the Italian throne. In 962 the pope hailed Otto as Roman Emperor and placed the imperial crown on his head. It is this momentous event, rather than the coronation of Charlemagne in 800, that marks the true genesis of the medieval Holy Roman Empire.

Although the events of 962 are reminiscent of 800, Otto's empire was vastly different from Charlemagne's. Above all, Otto and his imperial successors exercised no universal jurisdiction over France or the remainder of Western Christendom. The medieval Holy Roman Empire had its roots deep in the soil of Germany, and most of the emperors subordinated imperial interests to those of the German monarchy. From its advent in 962 to its long-delayed demise in the early nineteenth century the Holy Roman Empire remained fundamentally a German phenomenon.

The German orientation of Otto's empire is illustrated by the fact that neither he nor the majority of his successors over the next two centuries made any real effort to establish tight control in Italy. Only when they marched south of the Alps could they count on the obedience of the Italians; when they returned to Germany they left be-

The Holy Roman Emperor with orb and sceptre: manuscript illumination from the Gospel Book of Otto III, A.D. *1000*

hind them no real administrative structure but depended almost solely on the fickle allegiance of certain Italian magnates and bishops. The German emperors were never successful in straddling the Alps.

In Germany conditions were quite different. There the coming of feudalism was delayed for more than a century after Otto's imperial coronation. The great magnates became vassals of the king but normally had no vassals of their own. The chief tool that Otto and his successors used in governing their state was the Church. In an era of a weak papacy the German kings dominated the churchmen within their realm and kept close control over important ecclesiastical ap-

THE HOLY ROMAN EMPIRE IN 962

North Sea

Baltic Sea

K. OF DEN.

SLAVS

FRISIA

SAXONY

Elbe R.

River

LORRAINE

FRANCONIA

BOHEMIA

FRANCE

SWABIA

Lechfeld

BAVARIA

CARINTHIA

HUNGARIANS

Danube R.

Rhone R.

KINGDOM OF BURGUNDY

KDM. OF ITALY

Venice

KDM. OF CROATIA

SERVIA

CORSICA

Rome

BENEVENTO

APULIA

SARDINIA

0   100   200   300 MILES

The Holy Roman Empire

The Five Stem Duchies

CALABRIA

SICILY

pointments. Otto had successfully wrested control of the Church in the various tribal duchies from the defunct dukes, and in a very real sense the great bishops and abbots of Germany were the king's men. They made ideal royal lieutenants. They could not pass on their estates to heirs, and when a bishop or abbot died his successor was handpicked by the king. Thus the loyalty and political capacity of the king's administrator-churchmen was assured. After 962 the German monarchy was, on occasion, even successful in appointing popes. There would come a time when churchmen would rebel at such treatment; but in Otto's reign the time was still far off.

Otto's claims to proprietorship of the imperial Church were supported by both tradition and theory. Otto was regarded as more than a mere secular monarch. He was *rex et sacerdos*, king and priest, sanctified by the holy anointing ceremony which accompanied his coronation. He was the vicar of God—the living symbol of Christ the king—the "natural" leader of the Church in his empire. And in the closing years of his reign his actual political powers over church and state came close to matching his exalted pretensions.

The Ottonian Renaissance

Otto's reign provided the impulse for an impressive intellectual revival which reached its culmination under his two successors, Otto II (973–83) and Otto III (983–1002). This "Ottonian Renaissance" produced a series of able administrators and scholars, the greatest of whom was the brilliant churchman Gerbert of Aurillac—later Pope Sylvester II (d. 1003). Gerbert visited Spain and returned with a comprehensive knowledge of Islamic science. With this event the infiltration of Arab thought into Western Christendom began.

Gerbert had an encyclopedic, though unoriginal, mind. A master of classical literature, logic, mathematics, and science, he astonished his contemporaries by teaching the Greco-Arab doctrine that the earth was spherical. It was widely rumored that he was a wizard in league with the Devil—but the rumors were dampened by his elevation to the papacy. Gerbert was no wizard but an advance agent of the intellectual awakening that Europe was about to undergo—a harbinger of the High Middle Ages.

Although successors of Otto the Great were no longer troubled by the tribal duchies or the Hungarians, they were obliged to cope with

CHRONOLOGY OF THE AGE OF SIEGE AND ITS AFTERMATH

England	France	Germany
c.787: First Danish raid	814–840: Louis the Pious	814–840: Louis the Pious
	840–877: Charles the Bald	840–876: Louis the German
871–899: Reign of Alfred	843: Treaty of Verdun	843: Treaty of Verdun
878: Battle of Edington	911: Normandy recognized	891: Vikings defeated by Arnulf
c.954: Reconquest of Danelaw completed		936–973: Reign of Otto the Great
		955: Otto defeats Hungarians at Lechfeld
978–1016: Reign of Ethelred	987: Capetians replace Carolingians	962: Otto crowned Roman Emperor
1017–1035: Reign of Canute		973–983: Reign of Otto II
1042–1066: Reign of Edward the Confessor		983–1002: Reign of Otto III
1066: Norman Conquest of England		1003: Gerbert of Aurillac dies
		1039–1056: Reign of Henry III

new problems and devise new solutions. In 1024 the Saxon dynasty died out and was replaced by a Franconian line known as the Salian dynasty (1024–1125). The "tribal" dukes gave way to a new, particularistic aristocracy whose impulse toward independence taxed the ingenuity of the emperors. Still, the early Salian kings were generally successful in maintaining their power. Working hand in glove with the German church, the Salians improved and expanded the royal administration and ultimately came to exercise even greater authority than Otto I. In the mid-eleventh century the strongest of the Salian emperors, Henry III (1039–56), ruled unrivaled over Germany and appointed popes as freely as he selected his own bishops. In 1050, at a time when France was still a mixup of feudal principalities and England, under Edward the Confessor, was relatively small and more-or-less isolated, the German Emperor Henry III dominated central Europe and held the papacy in his palm.

The Organization of Agriculture

Beneath the social layer of emperor, kings, and nobles, the great majority of Europeans labored on the soil. To discuss the typical medieval manor is as difficult as to discuss the typical American business. Medieval agrarian institutions were almost infinitely diverse; medieval agriculture exhibited countless variations. Nevertheless some features of agrarian life recur throughout much of the more fertile and heavily populated portions of northern Europe. Certain generalizations can be made about medieval agrarian institutions if we bear in mind that numerous exceptions to any of them can always be found.

Any discussion of medieval husbandry must begin by distinguishing between two fundamental institutions: the village and the manor. The village, the basic unit of the agrarian economy, consisted of a population nucleus ranging from about a dozen to several hundred peasant families living in a cluster. In some of the poorer or more isolated districts, peasant families lived in separate farms or hamlets; but village life was the norm.

The manor, on the other hand, was an artificial unit—a unit of jurisdiction and economic exploitation controlled by a single lord. The lord might be a king, or a great baron, with numerous manors under his control. Or he might be a simple knight, at the bottom of the feudal pyramid, with only one or two manors at his disposal. The manor—the unit of jurisdiction—was often geographically identical with the village; but some manors embraced two or more villages, and, on occasion, a village might be divided into two or more manors. In any case the agrarian routine of plowing, planting, and harvesting was based on the village organization, whereas the peasants' dues, obligations, and legal and political subordination were based on the manor.

The Village

The ordinary village consisted of a grouping of peasants' huts surrounded by open fields. There would normally be either two or three such fields. Two was the traditional number but, as we have seen, the agrarian economy had been shifting in many districts of northern Europe from a two-field to a three-field system of rotation. The peasants of a three-field village would plant one field in the spring for fall harvesting, plant one field in the fall for early summer harvesting, and let the third field lie fallow throughout the year. The next year the fields would be rotated and the process repeated.

The arable lands surrounding the village were known as *open fields*, because they were unfenced. They were divided into strips about 220 yards long, separated from one another by furrows. Each peasant possessed several strips scattered throughout the fields, but the peasant community labored collectively, pooling their plows, their draught animals, and their toil. Collective husbandry was necessary because plows were scarce and had to be shared and because no one peasant owned sufficient oxen or horses to make up the team of eight beasts necessary to draw the heavy plow. The details of this collective process were usually worked out in the village council and were guided by immemorial custom.

The shape, contour, and method of cultivation of the open fields was determined by the topography of the region and the fertility of the soil and varied enormously from place to place. The strips themselves were products of the heavy plow and the necessity of reversing the eight-ox team as seldom as possible. The length of the strips was determined by the distance a team could draw the plow without rest. A group of four strips, which constituted the normal day's work of a plow team, became the basis of our modern acre.

The open fields were fundamental to the village economy and, indeed, to the entire agrarian economic system of the Middle Ages. But there was more to the village community than the cluster of peasants' huts and encircling fields. Besides his scattered strips in the fields, a peasant ordinarily had a small garden adjacent to his hut where vegetables and fruits could be raised and fowl kept to provide variety to his diet. The village also included a pasture where the plow animals might graze, and a meadow from which hay was cut to sustain the precious beasts over the winter. Some village communities kept sheep on their pasture as a source of cheese, milk, and wool. Certain districts, particularly in Flanders and northern England, took up sheep raising on a scale so large as almost to exclude the growing of grains.

Attached to most village communities was a wooded area from which fuel and building materials could be gathered. It also served as a forage for pigs, which provided most of the meat in the peasants' diet. There was commonly a stream or pond nearby which supplied the community with fish, a water mill for grinding grain, and a large oven which the community used for baking bread. By the eleventh century most village communities were organized as parishes. Each parish possessed a village church supervised by a priest who was drawn from the peasant class and had land of his own scattered among the strips of the open fields.

The village community has often been described as a closed system, economically self-sufficient, capable of sustaining the material and spiritual needs of the villagers without much contact with the outside world. From the foregoing discussion it should be clear enough why this was so. The economy of the Early Middle Ages, lacking a vigorous commercial life and a significant urban population, failed to provide villages with much incentive to produce beyond their immediate needs. There was only the most limited market for surplus grain. Accordingly, village life tended to be uneventful, tradition-bound, and circumscribed by the narrowest of horizons. On the other hand, gradual but profound changes were occurring in medieval civilization which eventually made a deep impact upon the village. The medieval innovations in agrarian technology significantly increased agricultural efficiency and productivity. Moreover the commercial and urban revival of the High Middle Ages provided an ever-expanding market for surplus grain. These developments in turn eroded village parochialism, freed the village economy from its self-sufficiency by incorporating it into a regional economic system, and provided enterprising peasants with a means of acquiring considerable money. They also encouraged the expansion of villages and fields through the clearing of forests and wilderness and the drainage of marshes. Timeless though it might have seemed, the village economy was changing.

The Manor

Superimposed on the economic structure of the village was the political-juridical structure of the manor. The average peasant was bound to a manorial lord. A few agrarian laborers were outright slaves, but slavery was in decline throughout the Early Middle Ages and had practically disappeared by the end of the eleventh century. Some peasants were of free status, owing rents to their lord but little or nothing more. A few were landless laborers working for a wage. But the great middle stratum of the medieval peasantry consisted of serfs—men of unfree status, bound to the land like the peasantry of late Roman times, and possessed of strips of their own in the open fields. They owed various dues to their manorial lord, chiefly in kind, and were normally expected to labor for a certain number of days per week—often three—on the lord's fields.

The lord drew his sustenance from the dues of his peasants and from the produce of his own fields. The lord's fields were strips scattered among the strips of the peasants, and were known collectively as his demesne. Theoretically, then, the fields of the manor were divided into two categories: the lord's demesne (perhaps one-fourth to one-third of the total area) and the peasants' holdings. But in fact the demesne strips and the peasants' strips were intermixed. The demesne was worked by the peasants who also paid their lord a percentage of the produce of their own fields and rendered him fees for the use of the pasture, the woods, and the lord's mill and oven. Such were some of the more common peasant obligations on many manors. But such obligations were exceedingly diverse.

The lord also enjoyed significant political authority over his peasants—authority that flourished and grew in rhythm with the disintegration of sovereign power which occurred in late Carolingian times. The administrative center of the manor was the manorial court, usually held in the lord's castle or manor house. Here a rough, custom-based justice was meted out, disputes settled, misdeeds punished, and obligations enforced. Since most lords possessed more than one manor, authority over individual manors was commonly exercised by an agent of the lord known as a bailiff or steward. It was he who supervised the manorial court, oversaw the farming of the demesne, and collected the peasants' dues. In addition to the peasants' agrarian obligations, the lord was also entitled to certain payments deriving from his political and personal authority over his tenants. He might levy a *tallage*—an arbitrary manorial tax which was theoretically unlimited in frequency and amount but was in fact circumscribed by custom. He was normally entitled to payments when a peasant's son inherited the holdings of his father, and when a peasant's daughter married outside the manor.

In general the serfs had no standing before the law. The lord was prevented from exploiting them arbitrarily only by the force of custom. But custom was strong in the Middle Ages and protected the serf in many different ways. He was by no means a chattel slave. He could not be sold, nor could his own hereditary fields be taken from him. After paying his manorial dues he was entitled to keep the produce of his own fields. Although hardly enviable, his situation could have been worse.

In the eleventh century the manorial regime was only incompletely established in England and was scarcely evident at all in Scandinavia and in parts of northern Germany and southern France. Although the two-field system was common in Southern Europe and the three-field system in the north, many northern villages had only two fields. Others had four or five or even more, all subject to complex rotation arrangements. Vital and endlessly diverse, medieval agriculture proved capable of expanding sufficiently to support the soaring new economy and the rich civilization of the High Middle Ages.

The Post-Carolingian Church

The existence of parish churches in the villages of the eleventh century illustrates the deeply significant fact that the long process of Christianizing Europe was by now far advanced. Whatever were the intellectual and moral shortcomings of the village priests, they were at least representatives of the international Church operating at the most immediate local levels throughout the European counryside. At a rather more elevated level was the work and influence of the Benedictines. They offered prayers to God, copied manuscripts, taught in their schools, supplied knights to secular armies, and served as prelates and counsellors under counts, dukes, and kings. While continuing their traditional spiritual activities they played, even more than in early Carolingian times, a major role in lay political life.

The greatest Benedictine house of the later tenth and earlier eleventh centuries was Cluny in Burgundy. Founded in 910 by the duke of Aquitaine, Cluny was free of local episcopal jurisdiction, subject to the pope alone, and blessed with a series of remarkably able

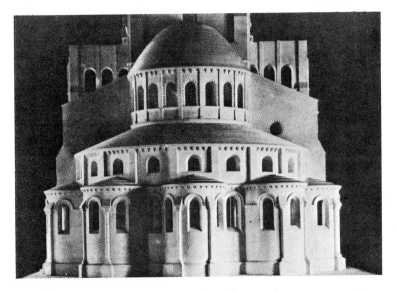

Model of the Abbey Church at Cluny showing Romanesque apse.

and long-lived abbots. Cluny followed Benedict of Aniane's modifications of the original Benedictine Rule. Its monks, shunning field work, devoted themselves to an elaborate sequence of daily prayers and liturgical services, and a strict, godly life. This strictness was relative, falling short of the austere regimes of several of the more ascetic orders of the High Middle Ages. Yet the Cluniacs were successful in avoiding the abuses and corruption that flourished in many monasteries of their day.

Richly endowed, holy, and seemingly incorruptible, Cluny became famous and widely admired. In time it began to acquire daughter houses. Gradually it became the nucleus of a great congregation of reform monasteries extending throughout Europe—all of them obedient to the abbot of Cluny. In the mid-eleventh century the Congregation of Cluny was both powerful and wealthy, and its new abbey church completed in the early twelfth century was the most splendid building of its time in all Europe. Cluny's high ideals were tempered by a sense of dignity—and perhaps also by a comfortable feeling of spiritual success and social acceptance. Enriched and supported by the lay aristocracy, it was by no means in radical opposition to secular society; rather it tended on the whole to uphold the social system of its day and to worship the Lord God without disparaging the lords of men.

Cluny's attitude typified that of the entire Church in the earlier eleventh century. As the lay world became more and more exposed to Christianity, as pious kings such as Edward the Confessor in England and Henry III in Germany demonstrated their concern for the welfare of their churches, the Church itself tended increasingly to come to terms with lay society. Through the ceremony of anointing, kings became virtual priest-kings. Indeed, contemporary political theory taught that the Church and the world were one—a single, God-oriented organism in which churchmen and lay lords each had appropriate roles to play.

Apart from Cluny, the monasteries and bishoprics of eleventh-century Europe were largely under lay control. They were dependent on lay patronage and were often entangled in the feudal system. Their prelates were appointed by lay lords in much the same way that village priests were chosen and controlled by manorial lords. Although not free, the Church was wealthy, respected, and comfortable, and few churchmen were inclined to challenge the situation. Those few, however, were to undertake in the later eleventh century a political-spiritual revolution which severely undermined the long established church-state entente.

Europe on the Eve of the High Middle Ages

During the centuries between the fall of the Roman Empire in the West and the great economic and cultural revival of the later eleventh century, the foundations were built on which Western Civilization rose. Kingdoms were forming, distinctive customs and institutions were developing, and a classical-Christian intellectual tradition was gradually being absorbed, adapted, and broadened. At the bottom of the social scale, the peasant had become firmly attached to the soil and his productivity was rising.

By 1050 both England and Germany were comparatively stable, well-organized kingdoms. The Church was poised for a great movement of reform and centralization. The French monarchy was still weak, but within another century it would be on its way toward dominating France. Meanwhile feudal principalities such as Normandy, Champagne, Flanders, and Anjou were well on the road to political coherence. Warfare was still endemic, but it was beginning to lessen as Europe moved toward political stability. Above all, the invasions were over—the siege had ended. Hungary and the Scandinavian world were being absorbed into Western Christendom, and Islam was by now on the defensive. The return of prosperity, the increase in food production, the rise in population, the quickening of commerce, the intensification of intellectual activity, all betokened the coming of a new era. Western civilization was on the threshold of an immense creative surge.

Suggested Readings

The asterisk indicates a paperback edition.

GENERAL HISTORIES

*Christopher Dawson, *The Making of Europe*. New York: Meridian Books, 1946. A thoughtful, sympathetic analysis of early medieval culture, stressing the central role of the Catholic faith.

Margaret Deanesly, *A History of Early Medieval Europe: 476–911*. 2nd ed. New York: Barnes & Noble, 1960. Accurate and highly detailed.

*M. L. W. Laistner, *Thought and Letters in Western Europe: A.D. 500–900*. Ithaca, N.Y.: Cornell Univ. Press, 1957, from the revised edition of 1936. Still the best intellectual history of the period.

*Robert Latouche, *The Birth of Western Economy*. New York: Harper & Row, 1966. A provocative account of early medieval economic trends, emphasizing the importance of the small farm.

*Archibald R. Lewis, *Emerging Medieval Europe: A.D. 400–1000*. New York: Alfred A. Knopf, 1967. A short, provocative survey covering both Eastern and Western Europe.

*Robert S. Lopez, *The Birth of Europe*. New York: M. Evans, 1967. A treatment of the entire medieval period, rich in insight, stressing social and economic history and devoting much more attention than usual to southern Europe.

*J. M. Wallace-Hadrill, *The Barbarian West: 400–1000*. New York: Harper & Row, 1962. A skillful condensation and popularization by England's foremost authority on early-medieval Frankland.

CHRISTIANITY

*Peter Brown, *Augustine of Hippo: A Biography*. Berkeley: Univ. of California Press, 1969. A splendid recent study.

*C. N. Cochrane, *Christianity and Classical Culture*. New York: Oxford Univ. Press, 1944. A penetrating study, sympathetic to the mystical viewpoint.

*Jean Daniélou and Henri Marrou, *The Christian Centuries*, Vol. I, *The First Six Hundred Years*. London: Darton, Longman, and Todd, 1964. Clear, comprehensive, and in total control of recent scholarship.

*Jeffrey B. Russell, *A History of Medieval Christianity*. New York: Thomas Y. Crowell, 1968. A short, lucid work of interpretation examining the Church's response to the opposing forces of property and order.

THE LATER EMPIRE AND THE GERMANIC INVASIONS

*Peter Brown, *The World of Late Antiquity: A.D.150–750*. New York: Harcourt Brace Jovanovich, 1971. A well-written, well-illustrated work treating with sympathy this era of profound social and cultural change in Eastern and Western Europe and the Near East.

*J. B. Bury, *History of the Later Roman Empire*. 2 vols. New York: Dover Publications, 1957. A reprint of a classic older study, full and scholarly.

*Edward Gibbon, *The Triumph of Christianity in the Roman Empire*. New York: Harper & Row, 1958. Chapters 15–20 of Gibbon's late-eighteenth-century masterpiece, *The Decline and Fall of the Roman Empire*. The entire work is available in a three-volume Modern Library edition.

*Ferdinand Lot, *The End of the Ancient World and the Beginnings of the Middle Ages*. New York: Harper & Row, 1961. A reprint of a masterful scholarly study stressing economic factors in Rome's decline. A valuable introduction by Glanville Downey summarizes the state of scholarship on the problem of the "decline and fall."

BYZANTIUM

*J. M. Hussey, *The Byzantine World*. New York: Harper & Row, 1961. A brief, skillful summary of Byzantine civilization.

*Romily Jenkins, *Byzantium: The Imperial Centuries*. New York: Random House, 1969. A fine, up-to-date account of the period from Heraclius to the battle of Manzikert, particularly valuable on the age of the Macedonian emperors.

George Ostrogorsky, *History of the Byzantine State*. Rev. ed. New Brunswick, N.J.: Rutgers Univ. Press, 1969. The most comprehensive single-volume history of Byzantium.

*Speros Vryonis, *Byzantium and Europe*. New York: Harcourt Brace Jovanovich, 1967. A short, well-illustrated interpretive survey picturing Byzantium as "a society and culture midway between those of Islam and the Latin west."

THE WEST BEFORE THE CAROLINGIANS

*Eleanor Duckett, *The Wandering Saints of the Early Middle Ages*.

New York: W. W. Norton, 1964. Perceptive biographical portraits of Patrick, Boniface and other early-medieval missionaries.

*Bryce Lyon, *The Origins of the Middle Ages: Pirenne's Challenge to Gibbon*. New York: W. W. Norton, 1972. A recent study on conflicting historical interpretations of the early-medieval West.

*Henri Pirenne, *Mohammed and Charlemagne*. New York: Meridian Books, 1955. The firmest statement by the great Belgian scholar of his controversial thesis that Roman civilization endured in the West until the eighth century. This book should be read in connection with Lyon (above).

*J. M. Wallace-Hadrill, *Early Germanic Kingship in England and on the Continent*. Oxford: Clarendon Press, 1971. Lucid, authoritative studies of kingship from the early Germanic tribes through Charlemagne and Alfred.

J. M. Wallace-Hadrill, *The Long-Haired Kings and Other Studies in Frankish History*. New York: Barnes & Noble, 1962. A collection of illuminating studies on the Merovingian era.

ISLAM

*G. E. von Grunebaum, *Medieval Islam*. 2nd ed. Chicago: Univ. of Chicago Press, 1963. A learned and original work; the best on the subject.

*P. K. Hitti, *History of the Arabs*. 6th ed. New York: St. Martin's Press, 1958. Broad, yet full; a monumental work. For a short survey by the same author, see *The Arabs: A Short History*. Chicago: Henry Regnery, 1956.

*Archibald Lewis, *The Islamic World and the West: A.D. 642–1492*. New York: John Wiley, 1970. A thoughtful collection of essays by modern historians and original sources in English translation.

*W. M. Watt and Pierre Cachia, *A History of Islamic Spain*. Garden City, N.Y.: Doubleday Anchor, 1967. A good, short survey from the fall of the Visigoths to the fall of Granada, particularly full on the tenth-century golden age of Cordova.

CAROLINGIAN AND POST-CAROLINGIAN EUROPE

*Frank Barlow, *Edward the Confessor*. Berkeley: Univ. of California Press, 1970. Barlow, the world's chief living authority on Edward the Confessor, shows that Edward's sanctity was largely a matter of posthumous reputation.

*Geoffrey Barraclough, *The Origins of Modern Germany*. New York: Capricorn Books, 1963. A general account of German constitutional history that places particular emphasis on the medieval period.

*Marc Bloch, *Feudal Society*, translated by L. A. Manyon. 2 vols. Chicago: Univ. of Chicago Press, 1961; originally published in 1940. A masterly work, challengingly written and boldly original in its conclusions. Bloch treats feudalism in a broad sociological sense.

*Marc Bloch, *French Rural History*, translated by Janet Sondheimer. Berkeley: Univ. of California Press, 1966. A seminal study of agrarian life and institutions in medieval and early-modern France. Originally published in French in 1931, this book has changed our ways of looking at history.

*Jacques Boussard, *The Civilization of Charlemagne*. New York: McGraw-Hill, 1968. This important French work, which was immediately translated into English by Frances Partridge, is now the best single book in English on the age of Charlemagne.

*Johannes Brøndsted, *The Vikings*. Baltimore: Penguin Books, 1965. A comprehensive social history.

*Eleanor Duckett, *Alfred the Great: The King and His England*. Chicago: Univ. of Chicago Press, 1956. "This is a very simple book," the author states. It is also short, sound, and exceptionally well-written.

*Eleanor Duckett, *Carolingian Portraits*. Ann Arbor: Univ. of Michigan Press, 1969. Sensitive biographical sketches of ninth-century figures.

*F. L. Ganshof, *Feudalism*, translated by P. Grierson. 2nd ed. New York: Harper & Row, 1961. A short, somewhat technical, and authoritative survey of medieval feudal institutions by a great Belgian scholar.

F. L. Ganshof, *Frankish Institutions under Charlemagne*, translated by Bryce and Mary Lyon. Providence: Brown Univ. Press, 1968. A masterful work of institutional history.

*Sidney Painter, *French Chivalry*. Ithaca, N.Y.: Cornell Univ. Press, 1957. Short, witty, and perceptive.

Sir Frank Stenton, *Anglo-Saxon England*. 3rd ed. New York: Oxford Univ. Press, 1971. A massive masterpiece.

*Carl Stephenson, *Medieval Feudalism*. Ithaca, N.Y.: Cornell Univ. Press, 1956. Brief, semipopular, and lucid; a well-organized account, broader than Ganshof's and less detailed.

*Lynn White, Jr., *Medieval Technology and Social Change*. New York: Oxford Univ. Press, 1962. This important pioneering work covers the whole of the Middle Ages. Beautifully written and opulently annotated, it stresses technological progress in the development of medieval civilization.

SOURCES

*St. Augustine's *Confessions* has been published in several paperback editions. For *The City of God*, see the good paperback abridgement by Vernon I. Bourke (New York: Doubleday-Image).

*Bede, *A History of the English Church and People*, translated by Leo Shirley-Price. Baltimore: Penguin Books, 1955.

*Einhard, *Life of Charlemagne*, translated by S. E. Turner. Ann Arbor: Univ. of Michigan Press, 1960.

*Eusebius, *The History of the Church*, translated by G. A. Williamson. Baltimore: Penguin Books, 1965.

*Gregory of Tours, *History of the Franks*, translated by Ernest Brehaut. New York: W. W. Norton, 1969.

*Gregory the Great, *Dialogues, Book II: St. Benedict*, translated by Myra L. Uhfelder. Indianapolis: Bobbs-Merrill, 1967. Pope Gregory I's biography of St. Benedict of Nursia.

*Boyd Hill, ed., *The Rise of the First Reich: Germany in the Tenth Century*. New York: John Wiley, 1969. Original sources and modern historians' interpretations in English translation.

There are a number of general collections of medieval sources in translation. Among the best are:

*Robert Brentano, ed., *The Early Middle Ages; 500–1000*. New York: Free Press, 1964.

*Carolly Erickson, ed., *The Records of Medieval Europe*. Garden City, N.Y.: Doubleday Anchor, 1971.

*David Herlihy, ed., *Medieval Culture and Society*. New York: Harper & Row, 1968.

part II The High Middle Ages: the first flowering of european culture

9

economic revolution and new frontiers

The High Middle Ages: 1050–1300

History, it has often been said, is a seamless web. But the human mind can only cope with the flow of historical reality by chopping it into chronological slices, forcing it into compartments of the historian's own making. In this sense every historical "period" is a kind of falsehood—an affront to the continuity of human development. Yet unless we concoct historical epochs, unless we invent ages, unless we tame the past with some relatively tidy chronological framework, we cannot make history intelligible to the human mind. Thus the historian speaks of "Classical Antiquity," "The Early Middle Ages," "The Renaissance," etc. These are artifices, but necessary ones. Without them the past would have little meaning, but we should never forget that they are inventions of our own.

The term *High Middle Ages* has been applied to the economic and cultural surge of the later eleventh, twelfth, and thirteenth centuries. Yet no spectacular event occurred in 1050 to signal the advent of the new era; no cataclysm occurred in 1300 to mark its end. The transition from Early Middle Ages to High Middle Ages was gradual and uneven. It might be argued that the High Middle Ages came to Germany as early as the tenth century under the Ottos. Ever since the waning of the Viking, Hungarian, and Saracen invasions, many decades prior to 1050, Europe had been pulsing with new creative energy. Broadly speaking, though, the scope and intensity of the revival did not become evident until the later eleventh century. By

145

the century's end, Europe's lively commerce and bustling towns, its intellectual vigor and political inventiveness, its military expansion, and its heightened religious enthusiasm left no doubt that vital new forces were at work—that Western Christendom had at last become a great creative civilization. As the historian might say, a new age had dawned.

The causes of cultural awakening such as occurred in the High Middle Ages are far too complex to be identified precisely or listed in order of importance. One essential element was the ending of the invasions and the increasing political stability that followed. We know that in the eleventh century Europe's population was beginning to increase significantly and that its food production was rising. Whether increased productivity led to increased population or vice-versa is difficult to say. But productivity could not have risen as it did without the revolutionary developments in agricultural technology: the three-field system which spread across much of northern Europe, the windmill, the water mill (by 1086 there were over 5000 water mills in England alone), the heavy, wheeled plow, the horseshoe and improved horse collar which transformed horses into efficient draught animals, and the tandem harness which made it possible to employ horses and oxen in large teams to draw plows or to pull heavy wagons. These and numerous related inventions came to the West gradually over the centuries, but they had a powerful cumulative influence on the economic boom of the High Middle Ages.

Towns and Commerce

The rise in productivity and population was accompanied by a commercial revival and a general reawakening of urban life. In turn, the new towns became the foci of a brilliant, reinvigorated culture. The intimate human contacts arising from town life stimulated European thought and art. The cathedral and the university, perhaps the two greatest monuments of high medieval culture, were both urban phenomena. The Franciscan order, possibly the most dynamic monastic institution of the new age, devoted itself chiefly to evangelical work among the new urban population, and its founder was the son of an urban merchant. The towns were also, and above all, centers of commercial and industrial enterprise. The European economy in the High Middle Ages remained fundamentally agrarian, but the towns were the economic and cultural catalysts. In them God and mammon stood face to face and often worked hand in hand.

There had been towns in Europe ever since antiquity. The administrative-military town of the Roman Empire gave way in time to the far humbler cathedral town of the Early Middle Ages. But both had one crucial thing in common: both were economic parasites living off the blood, labor and taxes of the countryside; both—like modern government-cities such as Washington, D.C., and Sacramento, California —consumed more than they produced. The towns of the High Middle Ages, on the other hand, represented something radically new to western Europe. With few exceptions, they were true commercial entities that earned their own way, living off the fruits of their merchant and industrial activities. Small, foul, disease-ridden, and often torn by internal conflict, they were nevertheless western Europe's first cities in the modern sense.

The new towns brought with them a new way of life and a new, urban class in which were merged such attitudes as acquisitiveness, piety, and civic pride. These last two qualities are memorialized to this day in the great urban cathedrals of the High Middle Ages. And civic pride could drive townsmen to the point of rhapsodic exaggeration. Medieval London, the metropolis of England, with a population of 35,000 or so, was no less crowded, foul, or riotous than other "large" cities of its time, yet the twelfth-century writer William Fitz Stephen could describe it in these enthusiastic words:

Among the noble and celebrated cities of the world, London, the capital of the kingdom of the English, is one which extends its glory farther than all the others and sends its wealth and merchandise more widely into distant lands. Higher than all the rest does it lift its head. It is happy in the healthiness of its air; in its observance of Christian practice; in the strength of its fortifications; in its natural situation; in the honor of its citizens; and in the modesty of its matrons. It is cheerful in its sports, and the fruitful mother of noble men.*

The commercial towns arose in rhythm with the upsurge of international commerce and the development of vigorous markets for local

---

* William Fitz Stephen, "Description of the City of London (1170–1183)," in *English Historical Documents*, ed. David C. Douglas and George W. Greenaway, 12 vols. (London: Eyre & Spottiswoode, 1953), 2:956.

agrarian products. Often they began as suburbs of older cathedral towns or as humble settlements outside the walls of some of the many fortresses that had risen in ninth- and tenth-century Europe. These fortresses were generally known by some form of the Germanic word *burgh*, and in time the term came to apply to the town itself rather than the fortress that spawned it. By the twelfth century a burgh, or *borough*, was an urban commercial center, inhabited by *burghers* or *burgesses*, who constituted a new class known later as the *bourgeoisie*.

In the later eleventh century towns were developing rapidly all over Europe. They were thickest in Flanders and northern Italy where the immense opportunities of international commerce were first exploited. The greatest Italian city of the age was Venice, long a Byzantine colony but now an independent republic, whose merchants carried on a lucrative trade with Constantinople and the East. Other Italian coastal towns—Genoa, Pisa, and Amalfi—soon followed Venice into the profitable markets of the eastern Mediterranean, and the ramifications of their farflung trade brought vigorous new life to the towns of interior Italy, such as Milan and Florence. During the High Middle Ages the Muslims were virtually driven from the seas and Italian merchants dominated the Mediterranean.

Meanwhile the towns of Flanders were growing wealthy from the commerce of the North—from trade with northern France and the British Isles, the Rhineland and the shores of the Baltic Sea. Flanders itself was a great sheep-growing district; its towns became centers of woolen textile production. In time, the towns were processing more wool than Flemish sheep could supply so that from the twelfth century onward Flemish merchants began to import wool on a large scale from England. By then Flanders was the great industrial center of northern Europe, and its textile industry the supreme manufacturing enterprise of the age.

The new urban class emerged from a society that had heretofore been almost exclusively agrarian. The burgher class was drawn from vagabonds, runaway serfs, avaricious minor noblemen and, in general, the surplus of a mushrooming population. At an early date ambitious traders began to form themselves into merchant guilds in order to protect themselves against confiscatory tolls and other exactions levied by a hostile landed aristocracy. A town was almost always situated on the territories of some lord—sometimes a duke or even a king—and the merchants found that only by collective action could they win the privileges essential to their calling: personal freedom from serflike status, freedom of movement, freedom from inordinate tolls at every bridge or feudal boundary, the rights to own property in the town, to be judged by a town court, to execute commercial contracts, and to buy and sell freely. By the twelfth century, a number of lords, recognizing the economic advantages of having flourishing commercial centers on their lands, were issuing town charters which guaranteed many of these rights. Indeed, some farsighted lords began founding and chartering new towns on their own initiative.

At first the urban charters differed greatly from one another, but in time it became customary to pattern them after certain well-known models. The charter granted by King Henry I of England to Newcastle-on-Tyne, and that of the French king Louis VI to the community of Lorris, were copied repeatedly throughout England and France. In effect these charters created semi-autonomous political and legal entities, each with its own local government, its own court, its own tax-collecting agencies, and its own customs. These urban communes paid well for their charters and continued to render regular taxes to their lord. But—and this is all-important—they did so as political units. Individual merchants were not normally subject to the harassments of their lords' agents. These townsmen enforced their own law in their own courts, collected their own taxes, and paid their dues to their lord in a lump sum. In short, they had won the invaluable privilege of handling their own affairs.

One should not conclude, however, that the medieval towns were even remotely democratic. It was the prosperous merchants and master craftsmen who profited chiefly from the charters, and it was they who came to control the town governments, ruling as narrow oligarchies over the towns' less exalted inhabitants. Some towns witnessed the beginnings of a significant split between large-scale producers and wage-earning workers. Indeed, the medieval town was the birthplace of European capitalism. For as time progressed towns tended to become centers of industry as well as commerce. Manufacturing followed in the footsteps of trade. And although most industrial production took place in small shops rather than large factories, some enterprising businessmen employed considerable numbers of workers to produce goods, usually textiles—on a large scale. Normally, these workers did not labor in a factory but rather in their own shops or homes. Since the entrepreneur sent his raw materials out to his workers, rather than bringing the workers to the materials, this mode of production has been called the "putting-out system." As a direct antecedent of the factory system, it was a crucial phase in the early history of capitalism.

The more typical medieval manufacturer worked for himself in his own shop, producing his own goods and selling them directly to the public. As early as the eleventh century, these craftsmen were organizing themselves into craft guilds, as distinct from merchant guilds. In an effort to limit competition and protect their market, the craft guilds established strict admission requirements and stringent rules on prices, wages, standards of quality, and operating procedures. A young craftsman would learn his trade as an apprentice in the shop of a master craftsman. After a specified period, sometimes as long as seven years, he ended his apprenticeship. With good luck and rich parents he might then become a master himself. But normally he had to work for some years as a day laborer—a journeyman—improving his skills and saving his money, until he was able to demonstrate sufficient craftsmanship to win guild membership and accumulate enough money to establish a shop of his own. Toward the end of the High Middle Ages, as prosperity waned and urban society crystallized, it became increasingly common for journeymen to spend their whole lives as wage earners, never becoming masters at all. Accordingly, the town became the scene of bitter class feeling which erupted from time to time into open conflict.

There were many who made their fortunes in commerce and manufacturing. Europe was astir with new life; for a clever, enterprising man the possibilities were vast. In the twelfth and thirteenth centuries, merchants were moving continuously along the roads and rivers of Europe. Italians crossed the Alps bringing spices and luxury goods from the Near East and the Orient to the aristocracy of France and Germany. French, Flemish, and German merchants carried goods far and wide across the continent, "buying cheap and selling dear." To William Fitz Stephen's London "merchants from every nation under heaven delight to bring their trade by sea. The Arabian sends gold; the Sabean sends spice and incense; the Sythian brings arms; and from the rich, fat lands of Babylon comes palm oil. The Nile Valley sends precious stones; the men of Norway and Russia send furs and sables. Nor is China absent with purple silk. The French come with their wine."*

* Douglas and Greenaway, op. cit., 2:959.

A series of annual fairs along the overland trade routes provided the long-distance merchants with excellent opportunities to sell their goods. As large-scale commerce grew, credit and banking grew with it, and by the thirteenth century several banking families had amassed immense fortunes. It may seem paradoxical that the period which is often regarded as the supreme age of faith witnessed the rise of large-scale commerce and a money economy. Yet it was money that built the Gothic cathedrals and supported the Crusades, that financed the pious charities of St. Louis and gave substance to the magnificent religious culture of the thirteenth century—money and, of course, an ardent faith. In time, faith itself would fall victim to the acquisitive spirit which was evolving in the towns, but during the High Middle Ages the townsmen, by and large, exhibited a piety that was far more vibrant and intense than that of the peasantry and the aristocracy. Indeed, the powerful surge of lay piety among the European townsmen became a crucial factor in the evolution of medieval Christianity.

Changes in Feudalism

Feudalism, based as it was on hereditary land tenure in return for service, was a characteristic product of a money-poor society which could not afford to pay wages to its warriors. With the rise of a money economy in Europe, the basic feudal relationship began to dissolve. The deep impact of feudal custom on the European mind is demonstrated by the various ingenious ways in which the aristocracy sought to adapt feudalism to the new economic realities. Indeed, during the eleventh and twelfth centuries the feudal system spread from France into England, Germany, and the Crusader States of the Holy Land. At the same time, however, kings and dukes were resorting increasingly to the hiring of mercenaries for warfare, and professional judges and civil servants for the administration of their realms. As the twelfth century progressed the feudal vassal was, oftener than not, asked to pay a tax in lieu of his personal service in the feudal army. With the income from this tax, which was sometimes called *scutage*, a monarch could hire professional warriors who were better trained, better disciplined, and more obedient than the landed knights. The feudal aristocracy retained its lands and power for centuries to come, and continued to produce warriors. But the knights of the new age expected to be paid. They no longer served at their own expense in return for their fiefs. Once the paying of taxes had replaced personal service as the vassal's primary obligation—and this was the case almost everywhere by the thirteenth century—feudalism had lost its original purpose.

The Evolution of Agrarian Life

The new social and economic conditions of the High Middle Ages wrought a transformation in the European countryside. The most spectacular change was the immense expansion of arable land. The great primeval forest of northern Europe was reduced to isolated patches, swamps and marshes were drained, and extensive new territories were opened to cultivation. This prodigious clearing operation was stimulated by the soaring population and the rising money economy. Agricultural surpluses could now be sold to townsmen and thereby converted into cash. Consequently, the peasant was motivated to produce as far in excess of the consumption level as he possibly could. Every new field put into operation was likely to bring a profit.

A second change, no less significant than the first, was the elevation of the peasant's status. Slavery, which was rare in Carolingian times, had virtually disappeared from Europe by the eleventh century. The tillers of the land were chiefly freemen and serfs. Often the freeman owned his own small farm, but the serf was generally to be found on a manor. Normally, it will be remembered, the manor included the peasants' fields and the lord's fields (demesne), the produce of which went directly to the lord. Among the obligations which the serf normally owed his lord was labor service for a stipulated number of days on the lord's demesne. In Carolingian times, manorial lords had augmented the part-time serf labor by using slaves. As slavery gradually died out, the lord was faced with a severe labor shortage on his demesne.

As a result of this problem, and in keeping with the trend toward transforming service obligations into money payments, the lords tended to abandon demesne farming altogether. They leased out their demesne fields to peasants and, in return for a fixed money payment, released their serfs from the traditional obligation of working part-time on the demesne. At about the same time they translated the serf's rent-in-kind from his own fields into a money rent. By freeing the serf of his labor obligation they transformed him, in effect, into a tenant farmer, thereby improving his status immensely. The obligations of the serf, like those of the feudal vassal, were gradually being placed on a fiscal basis.

The abandonment of demesne farming was a slow, uneven trend which progressed much more rapidly in some areas than in others. In thirteenth-century England, a countertrend developed whereby many lords successfully reclaimed and enlarged their demesnes. But on the continent the demesne gradually disappeared and in quite a literal sense, the peasant inherited the earth.

When the lords transformed the dues and services of their serfs into fixed money rents, they failed to reckon with inflation. The booming economy of the High Middle Ages was accompanied by an upward spiral of prices and a concomitant decline in the purchasing power of money. Hence, the real value of the peasants' rents steadily diminished. Many lords of the later Middle Ages came to regret the bargains their ancestors had made, and endeavored to revise peasant rents upward.

Inflation ruined more than one lord, but it had a beneficent effect on the medieval peasantry. The lords could do little to recoup their losses; indeed, they were often obliged to improve the condition of their peasants still more in order to keep them from fleeing to the towns or the newly cleared lands. The peasant was in demand, and the enterprising land developers who were turning woods and marshes into fields competed for his services. As a consequence, the High Middle Ages witnessed the elevation of innumerable peasants from servile status to freedom. Rural communes emerged—peasant villages whose lords had granted them charters closely paralleling those of townsmen. One should not idealize the lot of the thirteenth-century peasant—it was still impoverished and brutish by present standards— yet it was far better than peasant life in the Early Middle Ages. The terrifying peasants' rebellions of Early Modern Europe were products of a later and different era when the expansion and prosperity of the High Middle Ages had given way to an epoch of recession and closed frontiers.

The New Frontiers

European frontiers were open and expanding in the High Middle Ages. The clearing of forests and draining of swamps represents the conquest of a great internal frontier. It is paralleled by an external expansion all along the periphery of Western Christendom which brought areas of the Arab, Byzantine, and Slavic worlds within the ballooning boundaries of European civilization and added wealth to the flourishing economy.

Western Europe had been expanding ever since Charles Martel repelled the Arabs in 732. Charlemagne had introducd Frankish government and Christianity into much of Germany and had established a Spanish bridgehead around Barcelona. The stabilization and conversion of Hungary and Scandinavia around the turn of the millennium pushed the limits of Western civilization far northward and eastward from the original Carolingian core. Now, in the eleventh, twelfth, and thirteenth centuries, the population boom produced multitudes of landless aristocratic younger sons who sought land and military glory on Christendom's frontiers. And the ever-proliferating European peasantry provided a potential labor force for the newly conquered lands. While the Christian warrior of the frontier was carving out new estates for himself, he was also storing up treasures in heaven, for as a result of his aggressive militancy Christendom was everywhere expanding—into Muslim Spain, Sicily, and Syria, and into great tracts of Slavic Eastern Europe. Land, gold, and eternal salvation—these were the alluring rewards of the medieval frontier.

Spain

So it was that knightly adventurers from all over Christendom—and particularly from feudal France—flocked southwestward into Spain during the eleventh century to aid in the reconquest of the Iberian Peninsula from Islam. The powerful Moorish Caliphate of Cordova had broken up after 1002 into small, warring fragments, thereby providing the Christians with a superb opportunity. The Christians, however, were themselves divided into several kingdoms which consumed more energy fighting one another than fighting the Moors. Taking the lead in the reconquest, the Christian kingdom of Castile captured the great Muslim city of Toledo in 1085. In later years Toledo became a crucial contact point between Islamic and Christian culture. Here Arab scientific and philosophical works were translated into Latin and then disseminated throughout Europe to challenge and invigorate the mind of the West.

THE RECONQUEST OF SPAIN

Early in the twelfth century the Spanish Christian kingdom of Aragon contested the supremacy of Castile and undertook an offensive of its own against the Moors. In 1140 Aragon was strengthened by its unification with the county of Barcelona—the Spanish March of Charlemagne's time. During the greater part of the twelfth century Aragon, Castile, and the smaller Christian kingdoms exhausted themselves fighting one another and the reconquest stalled. But in 1212 Pope Innocent III proclaimed a crusade against the Spanish Muslims, and the king of Castile advanced from Toledo with a pan-Iberian army, winning a decisive victory over the Moors at the battle of Las Navas de Tolosa. Thereafter Moorish power was permanently crippled. Cordova itself fell to Castile in 1236, and by the later thirteenth century the Moors were confined to the small southern kingdom of Granada where they remained until 1492. Castile now dominated central Spain, and the work of re-Christianization proceeded

apace as Christian peasants were imported en masse into the reconquered lands. Aragon, in the meantime, was conquering the Muslim
islands of the western Mediterranean and establishing a powerful
maritime empire.

Thus, the High Middle Ages witnessed the Christianization of
nearly all the Iberian peninsula and its organization into two powerful Christian kingdoms and several weaker ones. The long crusade
against the Muslims was the chief factor in the molding of Spanish
life in the Middle Ages, and its ultimate result was to produce the
intense blend of piety and patriotism which inspired the saints,
soldiers, and *conquistadores* of Spain's sixteenth-century Golden Age.

Southern Italy and Sicily

The most vigorous and militant force in Europe's eleventh-century
awakening was the warrior-aristocracy of Normandy—largely Viking
in ancestry but now thoroughly adapted to French culture. These
Norman knights, French in tongue, Christian in faith, feudal in
social organization, plied their arms across the length and breadth of
Europe: in the reconquest of Spain, on the Crusades to the Holy
Land, on the battlefields of England and France, and in southern
Italy and Sicily. Normandy itself was growing in prosperity and
political centralization, and an ever-increasing population pressure
drove the greedy and adventurous Norman warriors far and wide on
distant enterprises. The impression which they made on contemporaries is suggested by a passage from an Italian chronicler:

The Normans are a cunning and revengeful people; eloquence and deceit
seem to be their hereditary qualities. They can stoop to flatter, but unless
curbed by the restraint of law they indulge in the licentiousness of nature
and passion and, in their eager search for wealth and power, despise whatever they possess and seek whatever they desire. They delight in arms and
horses, the luxury of dress, and the exercise of hawking and hunting, but
on pressing occasions they can endure with incredible patience the in-
clemency of every climate and the toil and privation of a military life.

Early in the eleventh century the Normans began to try their luck
in the chaotic politics of southern Italy. Here, Byzantine coastal cities
—a legacy of Justinian's conquests—struggled with old Lombard principalities and rising seaport republics such as Naples and Amalfi. The

great offshore island of Sicily was controlled by the Muslims—or rather it was divided among several mutually hostile Muslim princes who had been compounding the confusion of southern Italy by mounting raids against it. The whole area was a bewildering mixture of four peoples: Greek, Lombard, Latin-Italian, and Arab—and three major religions: Roman Catholic, Eastern Orthodox, and Islamic—in addition to which there existed an important and vigorous Jewish minority. It was, in short, a chaotic melting pot, politically unstable and, from the standpoint of the Normans, enormously promising.

First hiring themselves out as mercenaries to one side or another, the Norman adventurers quickly began to found states of their own. During the 1030s and 1040s a group of eight brothers, sons of an insignificant Norman lord named Tancred d'Hauteville, began wandering into southern Italy and gradually assumed leadership in the movement of conquest. These eight d'Hauteville brothers illustrate vividly the dynamism engendered in Europe by the adventurous enterprises of landless younger sons of the north European nobility. For although they were nobodies in Normandy the d'Hautevilles rose to supreme power in southern Italy. In the early 1040s the district of Apulia was thrown into chaos by a Lombard insurrection against Byzantine control; when the dust had cleared, it was found that most of Apulia was dominated by neither Byzantines nor Lombards but by three of Tancred d'Hauteville's sons, bearing the formidable names: William Iron-Hand, Humphrey, and Drogo.

The papacy, fearing the ominous rise of Norman power to the south of the Papal States and spurred on by stories of Norman atrocities, mounted an army against the Normans and engaged them in battle at Civitate in 1053. The Normans defeated the army, captured the pope himself, and, after paying him due reverence, obliged him to confirm their conquests and become their lord—in short, to legitimize them. No longer freebooters, the Normans now enjoyed the status of respectable landholders and vassals of St. Peter.

In the meantime the greatest of the d'Hauteville brothers, Robert Guiscard (the Cunning), had arrived in the area and had carved out a patrimony for himself in the southern province of Calabria. Robert was proud, ambitious, ruthless, calculating, and dishonest—possessed, in other words, of all the qualities of the successful empire builder. As master of Calabria he lived like a brigand, inviting distinguished guests to dinner and having them robbed. In 1054 he won control of Apulia and thereby rose to a position of dominance in Norman

Italy. A treaty which he executed with the papacy in 1059 gave him the title, "By the grace of God and St. Peter, duke of Apulia, Calabria, and hereafter Sicily." This last phrase was in effect a papal license for Robert and his fellow Normans to direct their energies to the conquest of the Sicilian Muslims.

The Capella Palatina in Palermo (1132–1140); note the mosaics on the inside of the arches and on the floor.

Robert Guiscard's newly-born duchy was wealthy and powerful by the standards of the age. It included an important center of medical studies at Salerno and several thriving commercial cities such as Amalfi which carried on an extensive trade with Africa, Arabia, and Constantinople. But the Normans, who "despise whatever they possess and seek whatever they desire," were not satisfied with dominion over Apulia and Calabria. In 1060 Guiscard, taking up the papal challenge, landed with a Norman army in Sicily. Shortly afterward he turned the enterprise over to his brother Roger, the youngest of the d'Hautevilles. In later years Guiscard, although hard pressed to suppress the incessant revolts of his Norman-Apulian nobles, found time to launch a major attack against Byzantine lands and to come to the papacy's rescue by driving a hostile Holy Roman emperor from Rome.* His death in 1085 terminated a career that reflected in full measure the limitless confidence, enterprise, and ambition of his age.

While Robert Guiscard was occupied in his farflung projects, his

* See p. 205.

Mosaic of Christ from the Cathedral in Monreale.

brother Roger was proceeding with the subjugation of Sicily. The Norman conquest of the island was difficult and prolonged, but in 1072 Roger captured the rich Sicilian city of Palermo, with one of the finest harbors in the Mediterranean. By 1092 the conquest was completed and Roger d'Hauteville stood as undisputed master of Sicily.

By now the entire area of Sicily and southern Italy was in Norman hands, yet it remained for a time politically divided. Robert Guiscard's heterogeneous, rebellious state passed first to his son, then to his grandson who died without direct heirs in 1127. Under these two successors, southern Italy became ever more turbulent. Sicily, on the contrary, was much less prone to rebellion. Roger d'Hauteville wisely instituted a policy of toleration which placated the Sicilian Muslims and won their support for the new Norman dynasty. When Roger died in 1101 he passed on to his heirs a well-organized state and a sophisticated administration that combined Muslim, Byzantine, and feudal elements and was backed by an obedient Saracen army.

In 1105 Sicily passed to Roger d'Hauteville's son, Roger II, "the Great" (d. 1154), a brilliant administrator and empire builder of a rather different type than Guiscard. Roger the Great was able, ambitious, tolerant, and cruel—less the adventurous feudal warrior than his predecessors had been, and far more sophisticated than they. In 1127 Roger undertook a campaign for the mastery of southern Italy, and by 1129 he assumed control of all the Norman domains, Apulia and Calabria as well as Sicily. In the following year he was elevated to royal status by papal coronation and the lands won by the Normans were fused into a kingdom.

Although Roger the Great's new realm embraced both Sicily and southern Italy it was called simply the Kingdom of Sicily; it would later be called the Kingdom of the Two Sicilies. Roger ruled strongly but tolerantly over the assorted peoples of his realm with their variety of faiths, customs, and languages. The Sicilian capital of Palermo, with its superb harbor and magnificent palace, its impressive public buildings and luxurious villas, was at once a great commercial center and a crucial point of cultural exchange. Known as the city of the threefold tongue, Palermo drew its administrators and scholars from the Latin, Byzantine, and Arabic cultural traditions.

The legal structure of the kingdom included elements from Justinian's *Corpus Juris* and subsequent Byzantine law, from Lombard law, and from Norman feudalism. The royal court, or *curia*, was the core of an efficient, centralized bureaucracy with special departments of justice and finance. The administration profited from the inclusion of an important non-noble professional class, devoted to the king and to the efficient execution of its duties. Drawing on the long experience of Byzantium and Islam, Roger's government was far in advance of most other states in Latin Christendom.

The kingdom's splendid and varied architecture was similarly multicultural in inspiration. The Capella Palatina (palace church) at Palermo, built on a marble foundation and opulently decorated with mosaics, was a source of wonder and admiration and remains so to this day. Not far from the capital, the magnificent cathedral at Monreale, begun several decades after Roger's death, synthesizes Italian, Norman-French, Moslem, and Byzantine artistic traditions with wonderful artistry. The nave of the cathedral is built on the pattern of the Italian basilica, but the building is enlivened with rich Islamic and Byzantine decorations. It contains a remarkable set of brass doors executed in the Byzantine style, and its interior sparkles with some 70,000 square feet of Byzantine mosaics. This remarkable structure, the cathedral church of the archbishop of Sicily, remains today in an excellent state of preservation. It epitomizes in stone the multiform civilization of twelfth-century Norman Sicily.

Under Roger and his successors the kingdom enjoyed a vital and diverse intellectual life. Its history was well chronicled by talented contemporary historians—in particular, Hugo Falcandus who produced an illuminating biography of Roger the Great. The Muslim scholar Idrisi, the greatest geographer of his age, contributed a comprehensive geographical work which drew from classical and Islamic sources. Characteristically, Idrisi dedicated his masterpiece to Roger the Great, and the work bears the title, "The Book of Roger." Sicily, like Spain, became a significant source of translations from Arabic and Greek into Latin. The Sicilian translators provided western European scholars with a steady stream of texts drawn from both classical Greek and Islamic sources, and these texts, together with others passing into Europe from Spain, served as the essential foundations for the impressive intellectual achievements of thirteenth-century Christendom.

In many ways Norman Sicily was western Europe's most interesting and fruitful frontier state. Having been carved out partially at

Muslim expense, it was representative of twelfth-century Europe's advancing territorial frontier, and as a vibrant center of cultural interplay it demonstrated that the frontier was not only advancing but also open. Europe besieged had given way to a new Europe—buoyant, expanding, and exposed to the invigorating influences of surrounding civilizations, and nowhere was this stimulating cultural contact more intense than in Norman Sicily. East and West met in Roger the Great's glittering, sundrenched realm, and worked creatively side by side to make his kingdom the most sophisticated European state of its day.

The Crusades

The Crusades to the Holy Land were the most spectacular and self-conscious acts of Western Christian expansionism in the High Middle Ages, although by no means the most lasting. They arose in response to a major political crisis in the Near East. During the eleventh century a new warlike tribe from Central Asia, the Seljuk Turks, had swept into Persia, taken up the Islamic faith, and turned the Abbasid caliphs of Baghdad into their pawns. In 1071 the Seljuk Turks had inflicted a nearly fatal blow on the Byzantine Empire, smashing a Byzantine army at the battle of Manzikert and seizing Asia Minor, the essential reservoir of Byzantine manpower.* Stories began filtering into the West of Turkish atrocities, against Christian pilgrims to Jerusalem, and when the desperate Byzantine emperor, Alexius Comnenus, swallowed his pride and appealed to the West for help, Europe, under the leadership of a reinvigorated papacy, was only too glad to respond.

The Crusades represented a fusion of three characteristic impulses of medieval man: piety, pugnacity, and greed. All three were essential. Without Christian idealism the Crusades would be inconceivable, yet the dream of liberating Jerusalem and the Holy Land from the infidel and reopening them to Christian pilgrims was reinforced mightily by the lure of new lands and unimaginable wealth. The Crusades provided a superb opportunity to perform their knightly skills in God's service—and to make their fortunes in the bargain.

* For a discussion of the Seljuk Turks and the battle of Manzikert see p. 42.

It was to Pope Urban II that Emperor Alexius Comnenus sent his envoys asking for military aid against the Turks, and Urban II, a masterful reform pope, was quick to grasp the opportunity. The Crusade presented many advantages to the Church. It enabled the papacy to put itself at the forefront of an immense popular movement and grasp the moral leadership of Europe. Moreover, the Church may well have seen in the Crusade a partial solution to the problem of endemic private warfare in Europe. The Church had long been trying to pacify the warrior nobility; through such principles as the "Truce of God" it had sought to outlaw warfare on holy days and during holy seasons. The Crusade promised to be a far more effective means of domestic pacification, drawing off warlike and restive members of the European nobility and turning their ferocity outward against the Muslims rather than inward against each other. When Urban proclaimed the Crusade he also proclaimed a peace throughout Christendom. Then, too, as a rescue mission to Byzantium, the Crusade opened the possibility of reuniting the Eastern and Western churches which had been in schism for more than a generation. Finally, Urban shared with many other Europeans of his day the beguiling dream of winning Jerusalem for Christendom.

Accordingly in 1095 Pope Urban summoned the European nobility to take up the Cross and reconquer the Holy Land. He delivered a powerful address to the Frankish aristocracy at Clermont-Ferrand, calling upon them to emulate the brave deeds of their ancestors, to avenge the Turkish atrocities (which he described in gory detail), to win the Biblical "land of milk and honey" for Christendom and drive the infidel from the holy city of Jerusalem. Finally, he promised those who undertook the enterprise the highest of spiritual rewards: "Undertake this journey for the remission of your sins, with the assurance of the imperishable glory of the kingdom of Heaven."

The response was overwhelming. With shouts of "God wills it!" Frankish warriors poured into the crusading army. By 1096 the First Crusade was under way. A great international military force—with a large nucleus of feudal knights from central and southern France, Normandy, and Sicily—made their way across the Balkans and assembled at Constantinpole. Altogether the warriors of the First Crusade numbered around twenty-five or thirty thousand, a relatively modest figure by modern standards but immense in the eyes of contemporaries. Emperor Alexius was gravely disturbed by the magnitude

of the western European response. Having asked for a certain amount
of military support, he had, as he put it, a new barbarian invasion on
his hands. Cautious and apprehensive, he demanded and obtained
from the Crusaders a promise of homage for all the lands they might
conquer.

From the beginning there was friction between the Crusaders and
the Byzantines. They differed in temperament and also in aim, for
the Byzantines wished only to recapture the lost provinces of Asia
Minor whereas the Crusaders were determined on nothing less than
the conquest of the Holy Land. Alexius promised military aid, but it
was never forthcoming, and not long after the Crusaders left Constantinople they broke with the Byzantines altogether. Hurling themselves southeastward across Asia Minor into Syria, they encountered
and defeated Muslim forces, captured ancient Antioch after a long
and complex siege, and in the summer of 1099 took Jerusalem itself.
Urban, who had remained behind, died just before the news of
Jerusalem's fall reached Rome.

The Crusaders celebrated their capture of Jerusalem by plundering
the city and pitilessly slaughtering its inhabitants. As a contemporary
Christian eyewitness describes it,

If you had been there you would have seen our feet colored to our ankles
with the blood of the slain. But what more shall I relate? None of them
were left alive; neither women nor children were spared. . . . Afterward,
all, clergy and laymen, went to the Sepulcher of the Lord and His glorious temple, singing the ninth chant. With fitting humility they repeated
prayers and made their offering at the holy places that they had long
desired to visit.

With the capture of Jerusalem, after only three years of vigorous
campaigning, the goal of the First Crusade had been achieved. No
future crusade was to enjoy such success as the first, and during the
two centuries that followed, the original conquests were gradually
lost. For the moment, however, Europe rejoiced at the triumph of its
Crusaders. Some of them returned to their homes and received
heroes' welcomes. Others remained in Latin Syria to enjoy the fruits
of their conquests. A long strip of territory along the eastern Mediterranean shore had been wrested from Islam and was now divided,
according to feudal principles, among the Crusader knights. These

warriors consolidated their conquests by erecting large, elaborate castles whose ruins still excite the admiration of travelers.

The conquered lands were organized into four Crusader States: the Country of Edessa, the Principality of Antioch (under a dynasty of south-Italian Normans), the Country of Tripolis, and the Kingdom of Jerusalem. This last was the most important of the four states, and the king of Jerusalem was theoretically the feudal overlord of all the crusader territories. In fact, however, he had difficulty enforcing his authority outside his own kingdom, and sometimes even within it. Indeed, the feudal knights who settled in the Holy Land were far too proud and warlike for their own good, and the Crusader States

THE CRUSADER STATES

were characterized from the beginning by dangerous rivalries and dissensions.

Gradually over the years the Muslims began to reconquer their lost lands. In 1144 the County of Edessa fell before Islamic pressure, and the disaster gave rise to a renewal of crusading fervor in Europe. The renowned twelfth-century abbot, St. Bernard of Clairvaux, preached the crusade across Europe, and described the enthusiastic response to his preaching as nothing less than miraculous. The Second Crusade (1147–48) was led by King Louis VII of France and Emperor Conrad III of Germany. Louis transported his army by sea while Conrad's forces took the land route. They met in Jerusalem and at once encountered friction with the established Christian residents who had learned to live alongside the Muslims, who imitated their dress and customs, and who lacked the zeal of the newly-arrived warriors. This contrast in mood between established residents and new crusaders was to be a recurring problem in the Holy Land.

Rather than moving on Edessa, the Crusaders decided to besiege the great inland caravan center of Damascus. It was a wise plan, in theory, for possession of Damascus would have added much to the strategic and commercial stability of the Crusader States, but Damascus proved impregnable and the siege failed. The Crusaders returned to Europe emptyhanded, prompting St. Bernard to describe the campaign as "an abyss so deep that I must call him blessed who is not scandalized thereby."

The 1170s and 1180s witnessed the rise of a new, unified Islamic state centered in Egypt and galvanized by the skilled leadership of a Kurdish warrior-prince named Saladin. Chivalrous as well as able, Saladin at first engaged in a truce with the Crusader States, but the rise of his new principality was nevertheless an ominous threat to Latin Syria. The truce was broken by a Christian robber baron, a typical product of the feudal environment, who persisted in attacking Muslim caravans. Saladin now moved on Jerusalem, and in 1187 he captured it. Jerusalem was not to be retaken by a Christian army for the remainder of the Middle Ages.

This new catastrophe resulted in still another major crusading effort. The Third Crusade (1189–92) was led by three of medieval Europe's most illustrious monarchs: Emperor Frederick Barbarossa of Germany, King Philip Augustus of France, and King Richard the

Lion-Hearted of England.* Frederick Barbarossa had a long and successful career behind him as Holy Roman Emperor; Philip Augustus was later to become the architect of the great thirteenth-century Capetian monarchy in France; and Richard the Lion-Hearted was already a warrior of immense renown on the battlefields of Europe. Yet for all that, and notwithstanding the abundant growth of legend and romance that has sprung up around the Third Crusade, the enterprise can hardly be described as successful. Frederick Barbarossa never reached the Holy Land at all. He drowned while crossing a river in Asia Minor and the greater part of his army returned to Germany. Philip and Richard, who had been enemies at home, were hostile toward one another from the beginning. They joined forces in besieging and capturing the important coastal city of Acre, but shortly thereafter King Philip returned to France to plot against Richard. There followed a series of encounters between the forces of Saladin and Richard the Lion-Hearted during which the two chivalrous antagonists developed a degree of mutual admiration. Richard won several battles but failed to retake Jerusalem, and in the end he settled for a pact with Saladin, granting Christian pilgrims free access to the holy city. It was, all in all, a miserably disappointing conclusion to such an immense undertaking. As an ironic postscript, King Richard fell into hostile hands on his return journey and became the prisoner of Frederick Barbarossa's son, Emperor Henry VI, who released his royal captive only after England had paid the immense sum of 100,000 pounds—quite literally, a king's ransom.

Within another decade Europe was ready for still another attempt on Jerusalem. Although lacking the distinguished royal leaders of the previous campaign, the Fourth Crusade (1201–4) had as its instigator the most powerful of the medieval popes: Innocent III. Like the First Crusade, it was led not by kings but by great feudal lords such as Baldwin IX, count of Flanders. It was, withal, the oddest of the Crusades. It never reached the Holy Land at all, yet in its own way it was spectacularly successful.

The Crusaders resolved to avoid the perils of overland travel by crossing to the Holy Land in Venetian ships. The doge of Venice, a Christian but also a man of business, demanded as payment for the

---

* All three will be encountered in subsequent chapters.

service of his ships a sum of money greater than the Crusaders could afford. He agreed, however, to take what money the Crusaders had and to transport them to the Holy Land if in return they would do him an errand on the way. They were to capture for Venice the port of Zara which had recently come into the hands of the king of Hungary. Pope Innocent III was infuriated by this bargain which diverted the crusading army against a king who was not only a Christian but a papal vassal. The Crusaders were automatically excommunicated when they attacked Zara, and Innocent repudiated the entire enterprise.

Nevertheless, the warriors went doggedly ahead. Capturing Zara in 1202, they were then diverted still again, this time by a political dispute in Constantinople involving the succession to the Byzantine throne. One of the two claimants, having recently fled to the West, contacted the Crusaders and begged their support, promising them immense wealth, aid against the Muslims and reunion of the Eastern and Western churches under Rome. Rising to the challenge, the Crusaders moved on Constantinople. The emperor-in-residence panicked and fled the city, and a delegation of citizens, realizing that further resistance was useless, opened Constantinople's gates to the Crusaders. Their imperial claimant was installed in power but was murdered shortly afterwards by one of his anti-Latin countrymen. Meanwhile the Crusaders had withdrawn from the city as a result of growing hostility and violence between Greeks and Latins. But now, having expended considerable effort in what was apparently a fruitless cause, they resolved to take the city for themselves, to elect a new Byzantine emperor from their own ranks, and to divide the Eastern Empire among them.

Accordingly, the Crusaders besieged Constantinople and took it by storm in 1204. The impregnable Byzantine capital had fallen at last to enemy conquerors; the Crusaders had succeeded where hordes of Muslims, Persians, and barbarians had failed. Count Baldwin IX of Flanders became emperor, and he and his heirs ruled in Constantinople for more than half a century. A nucleus of the old Byzantine state held out in Asia Minor, gathering its strength, until in 1261 the Latin empire was overthrown and Greek emperors reigned once again in Constantinople. But the Fourth Crusade had delivered a blow from which Byzantium never entirely recovered.

The wealth of Constantinople permanently diverted the warriors of the Fourth crusade from the Holy Land. The Eastern and Western churches were temporarily reunited, however. A Latin patriarch now sat in Constantinople, and a Latin hierarchy presided over a captive Greek church. Innocent III, who had absolved the Crusaders from excommunication after the fall of Zara and had excommunicated them anew for attacking Constantinople, readmitted them once again to communion when he realized the "great blessings" that had befallen Christendom by the capture of the schismatic city. The Crusaders, for their part, returned to Europe with immense booty from Constantinople—precious gems, money, and gold such as few of them had imagined. But the greatest prize of all was the immense store of relics which the Westerners liberated from the Byzantine capital and brought to their homeland. Bones, heads, and arms of saints, the crown of thorns, St. Thomas the Apostle's doubting finger, and many similar treasures passed into western Europe at this time. Perhaps more important, the West was given additional access to the intellectual legacy of Greek and Byzantine civilization. But the old hostility between Greeks and Latins was aggravated by the events of the Fourth Crusade into a virtually insurmountable wall of hatred.

During the thirteenth century, crusading fervor gradually waned. Crusades against the Muslim Near East were generally unsuccessful, and the papacy weakened the crusading ideal by calling for repeated crusades not only against the Muslims in the Holy Land but also against the Muslims in Spain, the Albigensian heretics of southern France, and even the Holy Roman emperor. In 1212 a visionary and ill-organized enterprise known as the "Children's Crusade" ended in disaster. Thousands of boys and girls flocked into the ports of southern Europe, gripped by religious fervor and convinced that the Mediterranean would dry up before them and provide them a miraculous pathway into the Holy Land. Many of them were obliged to abandon the enterprise and return home disillusioned; the remainder were sold into Muslim slavery.

The next major effort against the Muslims of the Near East, the Fifth Crusade (1217–1221), was directed not at the Holy Land but against the real center of Muslim power: Egypt. The Crusaders captured the important Egyptian port of Damietta in 1219 and refused a Muslim offer to trade Jerusalem for it. But dissension tore the crusader ranks, and when they moved against Cairo they were caught between a Muslim army and the flooding Nile. The results were military disaster, the abandonment of Damietta, and the failure of the Crusade.

Three additional crusades of importance were undertaken in the thirteenth century. The first of these, led by the brilliant emperor Frederick II, was at once the most fruitful and least violent of the three. Frederick negotiated with the sultan of Egypt rather than fighting him, and in 1229 obtained possession of Jerusalem by treaty. The triumph was ephemeral, however, for Jerusalem fell into Muslim hands once again in 1244. And because of the lack of fighting, Frederick II's crusade was never dignified by being given a number.

The Sixth and Seventh crusades were led by the saint-king of France, Louis IX. One was undertaken against Egypt in 1248, the other against Tunisia in 1270. Both failed, and the second cost St. Louis his life. Crusades continued to be organized and mounted in subsequent generations, but as the thirteenth century closed it was obvious that crusading enthusiasm was waning and the movement dying out. In 1291, the fall of Acre—the last Christian bridgehead on the Syrian coast—brought an end to the Crusader States in the Holy Land.

Yet the Crusades were more than simply a romantic failure. During the greater part of the High Middle Ages Christian lords ruled portions of the Holy Land. Their activities caught the imagination of Europe and held it for two centuries, uniting Western Christendom in a single vast effort. At the same time European merchants established permanent bases in Syria and enormously enlarged their role in international commerce. Knights and barons who participated in the crusades broadened their perspective through contacts with other civilizations. The effect of such contacts in dissolving the provincial narrowmindedness of the European nobility is incalculable.

The Crusades gave rise to several semimonastic orders of Christian warriors bound by monastic rules and dedicated to fighting the Muslims and advancing the crusading cause in every possible way. One such order was the Knights Hospitalers, which drew chiefly on the French for its membership. Another was the Knights Templars, an international brotherhood that acquired great wealth through pious gifts and intelligent estate management, and gradually became involved in far-flung banking activities. A third order, the Teutonic Knights, was composed chiefly of Germans. In the thirteenth century the Teutonic Knights transferred their activities from the Holy Land to northern Germany where they devoted themselves to the eastward thrust of German-Christian civilization against the Slavs. Orders of a similar sort arose on other frontiers of Western Christendom. The Knights of Santiago de Compostella, for example, were dedicated to fighting the Muslims in Spain and aiding in the Christian reconquest of the Iberian peninsula. These crusading orders, bridging as they did the two great medieval institutions of monasticism and knighthood, represented the ultimate synthesis of the military and the Christian life. They brought the Church into worldly affairs as never before.

The German Eastward Expansion

Eastern Germany was still another of medieval Europe's expanding frontiers. The German eastward drive was not a product of active royal policy but rather a movement led by enterprising local aristocrats and, in particular, the dukes of Saxony. It was a slow movement with a great deal of momentum behind it. Over a long period between 1125 and 1350, it succeeded in pushing the eastern boundary of Germany from the Elbe River past the Oder to the Vistula at Slavic expense. The gains were consolidated by the building of innumerable agrarian villages and a massive eastward migration of German peasants. Consequently, the new areas were not only conquered; they were in large part Christianized and permanently Germanized. As an indirect consequence of the movement, the Slavic kingdom of Poland was converted to Catholic Christianity and incorporated into the fabric of Western Christendom.

The later phases of the German push were spearheaded by the Teutonic Knights who penetrated temporarily far northward into Lithuania, Latvia, and Estonia, and even made an unsuccessful bid to conquer Russia. During the fourteenth and fifteenth centuries the Teutonic Knights lost some of their conquests, but much of the German expansion proved to be permanent. The epoch between 1125 and 1350 witnessed the conquest and Germanization of what ultimately became the eastern two-fifths of pre-World-War-II Germany.

In the later thirteenth and early fourteenth centuries European expansion was coming to an end. The internal frontiers of forest and swamp had by then been won, and the external frontiers were everywhere hardening, sometimes even receding, as in the holy land. The closing of the frontiers was accompanied by diminishing prosperity

THE GERMAN EASTWARD PENETRATION

German before 800
800–1400
Large minorities 1400
Small minorities 1400

FINNS

SWEDES

Baltic Sea

ESTONIANS

Dvina R.

LETTS

DANES

RUSSIANS

Königsberg

Lübeck

Niemen R.

Elbe R.

Berlin

GERMANS

Magdeburg

Weser R.

Leipzig

Oder R.

Vistula R.

POLES

Dresden

Breslau

Rhine R.

Prague

BOHEMIANS

Cracow

Dniester

MORAVIANS

Danube R.

Vienna

Buda

Theiss R.

HUNGARIANS

ITALIANS

Drave R.

Venice

CROATS

Po R.

Adriatic Sea

Danube R.

Scale of Miles

0   100   200   300   400

and cultural change. For the culture of the High Middle Ages was the product of a buoyant, expanding frontier society, fired by a powerful religious confidence, driven by immense ambitions, and captivated by a world in which, so it seemed, anything was possible.

CHRONOLOGY OF THE EUROPEAN FRONTIER MOVEMENT

Spain	*Sicily*	*Holy Land*
1002: Breakup of Caliphate of Cordova	c. 1016: Norman infiltration begins	
	1060–91: Sicily conquered	
1085: Capture of Toledo	1085: Death of Robert Guiscard	1095: Calling of First Crusade
1140: Aragon unites with Catalonia	1130: Coronation of Roger the Great	1099: Crusaders take Jerusalem
	1154: Death of Roger the Great	1187: Crusaders lose Jerusalem
1212: Christian victory at Las Navas de Tolosa		1204: Crusaders take Constantinople
1236: Castile takes Cordova		1291: Crusaders driven from Holy Land

10

new dimensions in medieval christianity

The Church in the High Middle Ages

The expansion of civilization during the High Middle Ages has been viewed thus far as a series of advancing economic and territorial frontiers. In a broader sense, however, frontiers of all sorts were being explored and extended. Scholars were pioneering in new intellectual frontiers, artists and writers were adding ever-new dimensions to Western culture. Administrators were pushing forward the art of government. And underlying all these phenomena—which will be ex-explored in the next chapters—was a deepening of the religious impulse which manifested itself in many different ways: in the rise of a vigorous papacy dedicated to reform and the creation of a Christian world order,* in the development of new forms of monasticism, in the rapid expansion of ecclesiastical administration and Church activities, in the intensification of lay piety, and in the growth of heresy.

Medieval religion followed many different paths. It could be devoutly orthodox, it could be anticlerical, and it could be openly heretical. Yet its basic institutional expression was the Catholic Church, and the most obvious thing that the preponderant majority of Western Christians had in common was their Catholicism. Nationalism was scarcely yet alive, and the allegiance of Europeans tended to be at once local and international. In the twelfth and thirteenth centuries the majority of Europeans were still intensely paro-

* See p. 198 ff.

chial in their outlook, only vaguely aware of what was going on beyond their immediate surroundings. But alongside their localism was an element of cosmopolitanism—a consciousness of belonging to the international commonwealth of Western Christendom, fragmented politically, but united culturally and spiritually by the Church.

The Church in the High Middle Ages was a powerful unifying influence. It had made notable progress since the half-heathen pre-Carolingian era. A flourishing parish system was by now spreading across the European countryside to bring the sacraments and a modicum of Christian instruction to the peasantry. New bishoprics and archbishoprics were formed, and old ones were becoming steadily more active. The papacy never completely succeeded in breaking the control of kings and secular lords over their local bishops, but by the twelfth century it was coming to exercise a very real authority over the European episcopacy, and the growing efficiency of the papal bureaucracy evoked the envy and imitation of the rising royal governments.

The Sacraments

The buoyancy of high medieval Europe is nowhere more evident than in the accelerating impact of Christian piety on European society. The sacraments of the Church introduced a significant religious dimension into the life of the typical European layman: his birth was sanctified by the sacrament of *baptism* in which he was cleansed of the taint of original sin and initiated into the Christian fellowship. At puberty he received the sacrament of *confirmation,* which reasserted his membership in the Church and gave him the additional grace to cope with the problems of adulthood. His wedding was dignified by the sacrament of *matrimony.* If he chose the calling of the ministry, he was spiritually transformed into a priest and "married" to the Church by the sacrament of *holy orders.* At his death he received the sacrament of *extreme unction,* which prepared his soul for its journey into the next world. And throughout his life he could receive forgiveness from the damning consequences of mortal sin by repenting his past transgressions and humbly receiving the comforting sacrament of *penance.* Finally, he might partake regularly of the central sacrament of the Church—the *eucharist*—receiving the body of Christ into his own body by consuming the eucharistic bread. Thus, the church, through its seven sacraments, brought God's grace to all Christians, great and humble, at every critical juncture of their lives. The sacramental system, which only assumed final form in the High Middle Ages, was a source of comfort and reassurance: it brought hope of salvation not simply to the saintly elite but to the sinful majority; it made communion with God not merely the elusive goal of a few mystics but the periodic experience of all believers. And, of course, it established the Church as the essential intermediary between God and man.

The Evolution of Piety

The ever-increasing scope of the Church, together with the rising vigor of the new age, resulted in a deepening of popular piety throughout Europe. The High Middle Ages witnessed a profound shift in religious attitude from the awe and mystery characteristic of earlier Christianity to a new emotionalism and dynamism. This shift is evident in ecclesiastical architecture, as the stolid, earthbound Romanesque style gave way in the later twelfth century to the tense, upward-reaching Gothic.* A parallel change is evident in devotional practices as the divine Christ sitting in judgment gave way to the tragic figure of the human Christ suffering on the Cross for man's sins. And it was in the High Middle Ages that the Virgin Mary came into her own as the compassionate intercessor for hopelessly lost souls. No matter how sinful a person might be, he could be redeemed if only he won the sympathy of Mary, the "Mother of God," for what son could refuse the petition of his mother? Indeed, a legend of the age told of the devil complaining to God that the tender-hearted Queen of Heaven was cheating Hell of its most promising candidates. Christianity became, as never before, a doctrine of love, hope, and compassion. The God of Justice became the merciful, suffering God who died in agony to atone for the sins of men and to bring them everlasting life.

Like all other human institutions, the medieval Church fell far short of its ideals. Corrupt churchmen were in evidence throughout the age, and certain historians have delighted in cataloguing instances of larcenous bishops, gluttonous priests, and licentious nuns. But cases

* See p. 276 ff.

such as these were clearly exceptional. The great shortcoming of the high-medieval Church was not gross corruption but rather a creeping complacency which resulted sometimes in a shallow, even mechanical attitude toward the Christian religious life. The medieval Church had more than its share of saints, but among much of the clergy the profundity of the Faith was often lost in the day-to-day affairs of the pastoral office, the management of far-flung estates, disputes over land and privileges, and ecclesiastical status seeking.

The Crisis in Benedictinism

The drift toward complacency has been a recurring problem in Christian monasticism—as in most human organizations. Again and again, the lofty idealism of a monastic reform movement has been eroded and transformed by time and success until, at length, new reform movements arose in protest against the growing worldliness of the old ones. This cycle has been repeated countless times. Indeed, the sixth-century Benedictine movement was itself a protest against the excesses and inadequacies of earlier monasticism. St. Benedict had regarded his new order as a means of withdrawing from the world and devoting full time to communion with God. But Benedictinism, despite Benedict's ideal, quickly became involved in teaching, evangelism, and ecclesiastical reform, and by the tenth and eleventh centuries the whole Benedictine movement had become deeply immersed in worldly affairs. Benedictine monasteries controlled vast estates, supplied significant contingents of knights in their service to feudal armies, and worked closely with secular princes in affairs of state. Early in the tenth century the Cluniac movement, which was itself Benedictine in spirit and rule, arose as a protest against the worldliness and complacency of contemporary Benedictine monasticism.* But by the later eleventh century the Congregation of Cluny had come to terms with the secular establishment and was beginning to display traces of the very complacency against which it had originally rebelled. Prosperous, respected, and secure, Cluny was too content with its majestic abbeys and priories, its elaborate liturgical program, and its bounteous fields to give its wholehearted support to the radical transformation of

* See pp. 133–135.

Christian society for which many Christian reformers were now struggling.

St. Benedict had sought to create monastic sanctuaries in which Christians might retire from the evils and temptations of society, but the High Middle Ages witnessed an endeavor to sanctify society itself. The new goal, pioneered by the reform papacy of the eleventh century, was not *withdrawal* but *conversion*. Rather than making Christians safe from the world, the world would be made safe for Christianity. During the eleventh and twelfth centuries, these two contrary tendencies—withdrawal and conversion—both had a profound impact upon monastic reform.

In the early generations of the High Middle Ages the Benedictine movement was showing signs of exhaustion. During the long, troubled centuries of the Early Middle Ages, Benedictine teachers and missionaries, scribes and political advisors, had provided indispensable services to society. Benedictine monasteries had served as the spiritual and cultural foci of Christendom. But in the twelfth century the Benedictines saw their pedagogical monopoly broken by the rising cathedral schools and universities of the new towns. These urban schools produced increasing numbers of well-trained scholars who gradually superseded the Benedictine monks as scribes and advisers to princes. In other words, the urbanizing impulse of the High Middle Ages drastically diminished the traditional Benedictine contribution to society.

Still, the Benedictines retained their great landed wealth. The Benedictine monastery was scarcely the sanctuary from worldly concerns that St. Benedict had planned. Nor was it any longer the vital force it once had been in Christianizing the world. Twelfth-century Benedictinism followed neither the path of withdrawal nor the path of conversion, and even in the arena of secular affairs it was losing its grip. The Benedictine life was beginning to appear tarnished and unappealing to sensitive religious spirits caught up in the soaring piety of the new age.

Carthusians and Cistercians

The monastic revolt against Benedictinism followed the two divergent roads of uncompromising withdrawal from society and ardent participation in the Christianization of society. The impulse toward withdrawal pervaded the Carthusian order which arose in eastern France in the later eleventh century and spread across Christendom in the twelfth. Isolated from the outside world, the Carthusians lived in small groups, worshiping together in communal chapels but otherwise living as hermits in individual cells. This austere order has survived to the present day and, unlike most monastic movements, its severe spirituality has seldom waned. Yet even in the spiritually-charged atmosphere of the twelfth century it was a small movement, offering a way of life for only a minority of heroically holy men. Too ascetic for the average Christian, the Carthusian order was much admired but seldom joined.

The greatest monastic order of the twelfth century, the Cistercian, managed for a time to be both austere and popular. The mother house of the order, Citeaux, was established by a little group of religious radicals in 1098 on a wild, remote site in eastern France. The Cistercian order grew slowly at first, then gradually acquired momentum. In 1115 it had four daughter houses; by the end of the century it had 500.

The success of the Cistercians demonstrates the immense appeal of withdrawal to the Christians of the twelfth century. Like Citeaux, the daughter houses were deliberately built in remote wilderness areas. The abbeys themselves were stark and primitive in contrast to the elaborate Cluniac architecture. Cistercian life was stark and primitive too—less severe than that of the Carthusians but far more so than that of the Cluniacs. The Cistercians sought to resurrect the strict, simple life of primitive Benedictinism, but in fact they were more austere than Benedict himself. The numerous Cistercian houses were bound together, not by the authority of a central abbot as at Cluny, but by an annual council of all Cistercian abbots meeting at Citeaux. Without such centralized control it is unlikely that the individual houses could have clung for long to the harsh, ascetic ideals on which the order was founded.

The key figure in twelfth-century Cistercianism was St. Bernard, who joined the community of Citeaux in 1112 and three years later became the founder and abbot of Clairvaux, one of Citeaux's earliest daughter houses. St. Bernard of Clairvaux was the leading Christian of his age—a profound mystic, an eloquent religious orator, and a crucial figure in the meteoric rise of the Cistercian order. His moral influence was so immense that he became Europe's leading arbiter of political and ecclesiastical disputes. He persuaded the king of France and the Holy Roman emperor to participate in the Second Crusade. And he persuaded Christendom to accept his candidate in the years following a hotly disputed papal election in 1130. On one occasion he even succeeded in reconciling the two great warring families of Germany, the Welfs and Hohenstaufens. He rebuked the pope himself: "Remember, first of all, that the Holy Roman Church, over which you hold sway, is the mother of churches, not their sovereign mistress —that you yourself are not the lord of bishops but one among them. . . ." And he took an uncompromising stand against one of the rising movements of his day: the attempt to reconcile the Catholic faith with human reason, led by the brilliant twelfth-century philosopher, Peter Abelard. In the long run Bernard failed to halt the growth of Christian rationalism, but he succeeded in making life miserable for Abelard and in securing the official condemnation of certain of Abelard's teachings.*

Above and beyond his obvious talents as a persuader of men, St. Bernard won the devotion and admiration of twelfth-century Europe through his reputation for sanctity. He was widely regarded as a saint in his own lifetime, and stories of his miracles circulated far and wide. Pilgrims flocked to Clairvaux to be healed by his touch. This aspect of Bernard's reputation made his skillful preaching and diplomacy even more effective that it would otherwise have been. For here was a holy man, a miracle worker, who engaged in severe fasts, overworked himself to an extraordinary degree, wore coarse clothing, and devoted himself totally to the service of God.

On one occasion St. Bernard commanded Duke William of Aquitaine to reinstate certain bishops whom the Duke had driven from their sees. When, after much persuasion, the Duke proved obdurate, St. Bernard celebrated a High Mass for him. Holding the consecrated host in his hands, Bernard advanced from the altar toward the Duke and said, "We have besought you, and you have spurned us. The united multitude of the servants of God, meeting you elsewhere, have entreated you and you have scorned them. Behold! Here comes to you the Virgin's Son, the Head and Lord of the Church which you persecute! Your Judge is here, at whose name every knee shall bow. . . . Your Judge is here, into whose hands your soul is to pass! Will you

* See pp. 302–303.

spurn him also? Will you scorn him as you have scorned his servants?" The Duke threw himself on the ground and submitted to Bernard's demands.

Bernard's career demonstrates the essential paradox of Cistercianism. For although the Cistercians strove to dissociate themselves from the world, Bernard was drawn inexorably into the vortex of secular affairs. Indeed, as the twelfth century progressed, the entire Cistercian movement became increasingly worldly. Like the later Puritans, the Cistercians discovered that their twin virtues of austere living and hard work resulted in an embarrassing accumulation of wealth and a corrosion of their spiritual simplicity. Their efforts to clear fields around their remote abbeys placed them in the vanguard of the internal frontier movement. They became pioneers in scientific farming and introduced notable improvements in the breeding of horses, cattle, and sheep. The English Cistercians became the great wool producers of the realm. Altogether the Cistercians exerted a powerful, progressive influence on European husbandry and came to play a prominent role in the European economy. Economic success brought ever-increasing wealth to the order. Cistercian abbey churches became more elaborate, and the primitive austerity of Cistercian life was progressively relaxed. In later years there appeared new offshoots, such as the Trappists, which returned to the strict observance of original Cistercianism.

Monasticism in the World

The Cistercians had endeavored to withdraw from the world, but despite their goal they became a powerful force in twelfth-century Europe. At roughly the same time, other orders were being established with the deliberate aim of participating actively in society and working toward its regeneration. The Augustinian Canons, for example, submitted to the rigor of a rule, yet carried on normal ecclesiastical duties in the world, serving in parish churches and cathedrals. The fusion of monastic discipline and worldly activity culminated in the twelfth-century Crusading orders—the Knights Templars, the Knights Hospitalers, the Teutonic Knights, and similar groups—whose ideal was a synthesis of the monastic and the military life for the purpose of expanding the political frontiers of Western Christendom. These and other efforts to direct the spiritual vigor of monastic life toward the Christianization of society typify the bold visions and lofty hopes of the new emotionally-charged religiosity that animated twelfth-century Europe.

Heresies and the Inquisition

The surge of popular piety also raised serious problems for the Church and society, for it resulted in a flood of criticism against churchmen. It was not that churchmen had grown worse, but rather that laymen had begun to judge them by more rigorous standards. Popular dissatisfaction toward the workaday Church manifested itself in part in the rush toward the austere twelfth-century monastic orders. Yet the majority of Christians could not become monks, and for them, certain new heretical doctrines began to exert a powerful appeal.

The heresies of the High Middle Ages flourished particularly in the rising towns of southern Europe. The eleventh-century urban revolution had caught the Church unprepared. The new towns were becoming the real centers of the burgeoning lay piety, yet the Church, with its roots in the older agrarian feudal order, seemed unable to minister effectively to the vigorous and widely literate new burger class. Too often the urban bishops appeared as political oppressors and enemies of burghal independence rather than spiritual directors. Too often the Church failed to understand the townsmen's problems and aspirations or to anticipate their growing suspicion of ecclesiastical wealth and power. Although the vast majority of medieval townsmen remained loyal to the Church, a minority, particularly in the south, turned to new, anticlerical sects. In their denunciation of ecclesiastical wealth, these sects were doing nothing more than St. Bernard and the Cistercians had done. But many of the anticlerical sects crossed the line between orthodox reformism and heresy by preaching without episcopal or papal approval; far more important, they denied the exclusive right of the priesthood to perform sacraments.

One such sect, the Waldensians, was founded by a merchant of Lyons named Peter Waldo who, around 1173, gave all his possessions to the poor and took up a life of apostolic poverty. He and his followers worked at first within the bounds of orthodoxy, but gradually their anticlericalism and their denial of special priestly powers earned them the condemnation of the Church. Similar groups, some orthodox, some heretical, arose in the communes of Lombardy and were known as the *Humiliati*. These groups proved exceedingly troublesome and embarrassing to the local ecclesiastical hierarchies, but generally they escaped downright condemnation unless they themselves took the step of denying the authority of the Church. Many of them did take that step, however, and by the opening of the thirteenth century heretical, anticlerical sects were spreading across northern Italy and southern France, and even into Spain and Germany.

The most popular heresy in southern France was sponsored by a group known as the *Cathari* (the pure) or the Albigensians—after the town of Albi where they were particularly strong. The Albigensians represented a fusion of two traditions: (1) the anticlerical protest against ecclesiastical wealth and power, and (2) an exotic theology derived originally from Persia. The Albigensians recognized two gods: the god of good who reigned over the universe of the spirit, and the god of evil who ruled the world of matter. The Old Testament God, as creator of the material universe, was their god of evil; Christ, who was believed to have been a purely spiritual being with a phantom body, was the god of good. Albigensian morality stressed a rigorous rejection of all material things—of physical appetites, wealth, worldly vanities, and sexual intercourse—in the hope of one day escaping from the prison of the body and ascending to the realm of pure spirit. In reality this severe ethic was practiced only by a small elite known as the *perfecti*; the rank and file normally begat children, and participated only vicariously in the rejection of the material world —by criticizing the affluence of the Church. Indeed, their opponents accused them of gross licentiousness, and it does seem to be true that certain Provençal noblemen were attracted to the new teaching by the opportunity of appropriating Church property in good conscience.

However this may be, Albigensianism was spreading rapidly as the thirteenth century dawned and was becoming a dangerous threat to the unity of Christendom and the authority of the Church. Pope Innocent III, recognizing the gravity of the situation, tried with every means in his power to eradicate Albigensianism. At length, in 1208, he responded to the murder of a papal legate in southern France by summoning a crusade against the Albigensians. The Albigensian Crusade was a ruthless, savage affair which succeeded in its purpose but only at the cost of ravaging the vibrant civilization of Southern France. The French monarchy intervened in the Crusade's final stages, brought it to a bloody conclusion, and thereby extended the sway of the Capetian kings to the Mediterranean. The Albigensian Crusade was an important event in the development of French royal power, and it succeeded in reversing the trend toward heresy in southern Europe. It also disclosed the brutality of which the Church was capable when sufficiently threatened.

In the years immediately following the Albigensian Crusade, there emerged an institution that will always stand as a grim symbol of the medieval Church at its worst: the Inquisition. The Christian persecution of heretics dates from the later fourth century, but it was not until the High Middle Ages that heterodox views presented a serious problem to European society. Traditionally, the problem of converting or punishing heretics was handled at the local level, but in 1233 the papacy established a permanent central tribunal for the purpose of standardizing procedures and increasing efficiency in the suppression of heresies. The methods of the Inquisition included the use of torture, secret testimony, conviction on the testimony of only two witnesses, the denial of legal counsel to the accused, and other procedures offensive to the Anglo-American legal tradition but not especially remarkable by standards of the times. Indeed, many of these procedures—including torture—were drawn from the customs of Roman law. In defense of the Inquisition it might be said that convicted heretics might escape death by renouncing their "errors," and that far from establishing a reign of terror, the Inquisition seems to have enjoyed popular support.

Some historians have adduced other arguments in an attempt to defend an indefensible institution. Let us say here merely that the Christian faith was far more important to the people of medieval Europe than national allegiance—that the medieval Church, with its elaborate charitable activities, its hospitals and universities, and its other social services, performed many of the functions of the modern state, and that therefore medieval heresy was analogous to modern treason. To the medieval Catholic, heresy was a hateful, repugnant thing, an insult to Christ, and a source of contamination to others. An Albigensian preaching in the streets of thirteenth-century Paris would have been approximately as popular as a Ku Klux Klansman preaching white supremacy on a modern campus. Today, when political and economic doctrines are more important to most people than religious creeds, the closest parallels to medieval Waldensianism or Albigensianism are to be found in the Communist and Nazi parties in modern America, Zionism in Soviet Russia, and revisionist Marxism in Peking. In examining opposition to movements such as these, we can gain an inkling of the state of mind that produced the medieval Inquisition.

Mendicantism

The thirteenth-century church found an answer to the heretical drift which was far more compassionate and effective than the Inquisition. In the opening decades of the century two radically new orders emerged—the Dominican and the Franciscan—which were devoted to a life of poverty, preaching, and charitable deeds. Rejecting the life of the cloister, they dedicated themselves to religious work in the world—particularly in the towns. Benedictines and Cistercians had traditionally taken vows of personal poverty, but the monastic orders themselves could and did acquire great corporate wealth. The Dominicans and Franciscans, on the contrary, were pledged to both personal and corporate poverty and were therefore known as mendicants (beggars). Capturing the imagination of thirteenth-century Christendom, they drained urban heterodoxy of much of its former support by demonstrating to the townsmen of Europe that Christian orthodoxy could be both relevant and compelling.

The Dominicans

St. Dominic (1170–1221), a well-educated Spaniard, spent his early manhood as an Augustinian canon at a cathedral in Castile. In his mid-thirties he traveled to Rome, met Pope Innocent III, and followed the pope's bidding to preach in southern France against the Albigensians. For the next decade, between 1205 and 1215, he worked among the heretics, leading an austere, humble life, and winning considerable renown for his eloquence and simplicity. For the most part the Albigensians seem to have been unaffected by Dominic's preaching; they respected him but did not follow him.

The Dominican Order evolved out of a small group of volunteers who joined Dominic in his work among the Albigensians. Gradually Dominic came to see the possibility of a far greater mission for his followers: to preach and win converts to the faith throughout the world. In 1215 Dominic's friend the bishop of Toulouse gave the group a church and a house in the city, and shortly thereafter the papacy recognized the Dominicans as a separate religious order and approved the Dominican rule.

The congregation founded by Dominic was to be known as the Order of Friars Preachers. It assumed its permanent shape during the years between its formal establishment in 1216 and Dominic's death in 1221 by which time it had grown to include some 500 friars and 60 priories organized into eight provinces embracing the whole of western Europe. The Dominicans stood in the vanguard of thirteenth-century piety. Their order attracted men of imagination and unusual religious dedication, men who could not be satisfied with the enclosed and tradition-bound life of earlier monasticism but who were challenged by the austerity of the Dominican rule, the disciplined vitality of the order, and the stimulating goal of working toward the moral regeneration of society rather than withdrawing from the world.

The Dominican rule drew freely from the earlier rule of the Augustinian Canons which Dominic had known in his youth, but added new elements and provided a novel direction for the religious life. The order was to be headed by a minister-general, elected for life, and a legislative body that met annually and consisted sometimes of delegates from the Dominican provinces, sometimes of priors from all the Dominican houses. The friars themselves belonged not to a particular house or province but to the order, and their place of residence and activity was determined by the minister-general. Their life, strictly regulated and austere, included such rigors as midnight services, total abstinence from meat, frequent fasts, and prolonged periods of mandatory silence. And the entire order was strictly bound by the rule of poverty which Dominic had learned from his contemporary, St. Francis. Not only should poverty be the condition of individual Dominicans as it was of individual Benedictines; it was to be the condition of the order itself. The Dominican order was to have no possessions except churches and priories. It was to have no fixed incomes, no manors, but was to subsist through charitable gift. It was, in short, a mendicant order.

The Dominican order expanded at a phenomenal rate during the course of the thirteenth century. Dominican friars carried their evangelical activities across Europe and beyond, into the Holy Land,

Central Asia, Tartary, Tibet, and China. Joining the faculties of the rising universities they became the leading proponents of Aristotelian philosophy and included in their numbers such notable scholars as St. Albertus Magnus and St. Thomas Aquinas. Dominic himself had insisted that his followers acquire broad educations before undertaking their mission of preaching and that each Dominican priory include a school of theology. Within a few decades after his death his order included some of the foremost intellects of the age.

The Dominicans were, above all, preachers, and their particular mission was to preach among heretics and non-Christians. Their contact with heretics brought them into close involvements with the Inquisition, and in later years their reputation was darkened by the fact that they themselves became the leading inquisitors. The grand inquisitor of Spain, for example, was customarily a Dominican. They acquired the nickname *"Domini canes"*—hounds of God—by their willingness to supplement St. Dominic's policy of persuasion with the easier and crueler policy of force.

The Dominican order still flourishes. The rule of corporate poverty was softened increasingly and finally, in the fifteenth century, dropped altogether, in deference to the great truth that full-time scholars and teachers cannot beg or do odd jobs or be in doubt as to the source of their next meal. But long after their original mendicant ideals were modified, the Dominicans remained faithful to their essential mission of championing Catholic orthodoxy by word and pen.

Saint Francis

Dominic's remarkable achievement was overshadowed by that of his contemporary, St. Francis (*c.* 1182–1226)—a warm, appealing man who is widely regarded as Christianity's ideal saint. Francis was a product of the medieval urban revolution. He was the son of a wealthy cloth merchant of Assisi, a northern Italian town with an influential Albigensian minority. As a youth he was generous, high-spirited, and popular, and in time he became the leader of a boisterous but harmless teen-age gang. He was by no means dissolute but rather, as one writer has aptly expressed it, he "seems altogether to have been rather a festive figure."

In his early twenties St. Francis underwent a profound religious conversion that occurred in several steps. It began on the occasion of a banquet which he was giving for some of his friends. After the banquet Francis and his companions went into the town with torches, singing in the streets. Francis was crowned with garlands as king of the revellers, but after a time he disappeared and was found in a religious trance. Thereafter he devoted himself to solitude, prayer, and service to the poor. He went as a pilgrim to Rome where he is reported to have exchanged clothes with a beggar and spent the day begging with other beggars. Returning to Assisi, he encountered an impoverished leper and, notwithstanding his fear of leprosy, he gave the poor man all the money he was carrying and kissed his hand. Thenceforth he devoted himself to the service of lepers and hospitals.

To the confusion and consternation of his bourgeois father, Francis now went about Assisi dressed in rags, giving to the poor. His former companions pelted him with mud, and his father, fearing that Francis's almsgiving would consume the family fortune, disinherited him. Francis left the family house singing a French song and spent the next three years of his life in the environs of Assisi, living in abject poverty. He ministered to lepers and social outcasts and continued to embarrass his family by his unconventional behavior. It was at this time that he began to frequent a crumbling little chapel known as the Portiuncula. One day in the year 1209, while attending Mass there, he was struck by the words of the Gospel that the priest was reading: "Everywhere on your road preach and say, 'The kingdom of God is at hand.' Cure the sick, raise the dead, cleanse the lepers, drive out devils. Freely have you received; freely give. Carry neither gold nor silver nor money in your belts, nor bag, nor two coats, nor sandals, nor staff, for the workman is worthy of his hire."* Francis at once accepted this injunction as the basis of his vocation and immediately thereafter—even though a layman—began to preach to the poor.

Disciples now joined him, and when he had about a dozen followers he is said to have remarked, "Let us go to our Mother, the Holy Roman Church, and tell the pope what the Lord has begun to do through us and carry it out with his sanction." This may have seemed a naive approach to the masterful, aristocratic Pope Innocent III, yet when Francis came to Rome in 1210, Innocent sanctioned his work. Doubtless the pope saw in the Franciscan Mission a potential orthodox counterpoise to the Waldensians, Albigensians, and other

* Matt. 10:7–10.

This much-restored painting of St. Francis, ascribed to the half-legendary thirteenth-century Italian painter Cimabue (c. 1240–1302), is taken from a series of frescoes in the Upper Church of St. Francis in Assisi.

heretical groups who had been winning masses of converts from the Church by the example of their poverty and simplicity. For here was a man whose loyalty to Catholicism was beyond question and whose own artless simplicity might bring erring souls back into the Church. Already Innocent III had given his blessing to movements similar to that of Francis. An orthodox group of Humiliati had received his sanction in 1201, and in 1208 he permitted a converted Waldensian to found an order known as the "Poor Catholics," which was dedicated to lay preaching. In Francis's movement the pope must have seen still another opportunity to encourage a much-needed wave of radical reform within the orthodox framework. And it may well be that Francis's glowing spirituality appealed to the sanctity of Innocent himself, for the pope, even though a great man of affairs, was genuinely pious. However this may be, thirteenth-century Europe deserves some credit for embracing a movement that in many other ages would have been persecuted or ridiculed. Rome crucified Christ; high medieval Europe took Francis to its heart and made him a saint. But the hard edges of Franciscan religious austerity were blunted in the process.

Immediately after the papal interview Francis and his followers returned to the neighborhood of Assisi. They were given the Portiuncula as their own chapel, and over the years it continued to serve as the headquarters of the Franciscan movement. Around it the friars built huts of branches and twigs. The Portiuncula was a headquarters but not a home, for the friars were always on the move, wandering in pairs over the country, dressed in peasants' clothing, preaching, serving, and living in conscious imitation of the life of Christ. During the next decade the order expanded at a spectacular rate. Franciscans were soon to be found throughout northern Italy; by 1220 Franciscan missions were active in Germany, France, Spain, Hungary, and the Holy Land, and the friars numbered in the thousands. The captivating personality of Francis himself was doubtless a crucial factor in his order's popularity, but it also owed much to the fact that its ideals were singularly relevant to the highest religious aspirations of the age. Urban heresy lost some of its allure as the cheerful, devoted Franciscans began to pour into Europe's cities, preaching in the crowded streets and setting a living example of Christian sanctity.

The Franciscan ideal was based above all on the imitation of Christ. Fundamental to this ideal was the notion of poverty, both individual and corporate. The Franciscans subsisted by working and serving in return for their sustenance. Humility was also a part of the ideal; Francis named his followers the Friars Minor (little brothers). Preaching was an important part of their mission, and it answered an urgent need in the rising cities where the Church had hitherto responded inadequately to the deepening religious hunger of townsmen. Perhaps most attractive of all was the quality of joyousness, akin to the joyousness that Francis had shown prior to his conversion, but directed now toward spiritual ends. Contemporaries referred to Francis affectionately as "God's own troubadour."

Pious men of other times have fled the world; the Albigensians renounced it as the epitome of evil. But Francis embraced it joyfully as the handiwork of God. In his "Song of Brother Sun" he expressed poetically his holy commitment to the physical universe:

> *Praise be to Thee, my Lord, for all thy creatures,*
> *Above all Brother Sun*
> *Who brings us the day, and lends us his light;*
> *Beautiful is he, radiant with great splendor,*
> *And speaks to us of Thee, O most high.*
> *Praise to Thee, my Lord, for Sister Moon and for the stars;*
> *In heaven Thou hast set them, clear and precious and fair.*
> *Praise to Thee, my Lord, for Brother Wind.*
> *For air and clouds, for calm and all weather*
> *By which Thou supportest life in all Thy creatures.*
> *Praise to Thee, my Lord, for Sister Water*
> *Which is so helpful and humble, precious and pure.*
> *Praise to Thee, my Lord, for Brother Fire,*
> *By whom Thou lightest up the night.*
> *And fair is he, and gay and mighty, and strong.*
> *Praise to Thee, my Lord, for our sister, Mother Earth,*
> *Who sustains and directs us,*
> *And brings forth varied fruits, and plants*
> *and flowers bright.*
> *Praise and bless my Lord, and give Him thanks,*
> *And serve Him with great humility.*

. . . .

Early Franciscanism was too good to last. The order was becoming too large to retain its original disorganized simplicity. Francis was a saint rather than an administrator, and well before his death the movement was passing beyond his control. In 1219–20 he traveled to Egypt in an effort to convert its Muslim inhabitants—a hopeless task, but Francis was never dismayed by the impossible—and while he was away it became apparent that his order required a more coherent organization than he had seen fit to provide it. Many perplexing questions now arose: With thousands of friars invading the begging market, what would become of the common tramp? Would Europe's generosity be overstrained? Above all, how could these crowds of friars be expected to cleave to the ideal without an explicit rule and without Francis's personal presence to inspire and guide them? In short, could the Franciscan ideal be practical on a large scale? For the movement was proliferating at a remarkable rate. Besides the Friars Minor themselves, a Second Order was established—a female order directed by Francis's friend, St. Clare—known as the Poor Clares. And there was a peripheral group of part-time Franciscans, known as Tertiaries, who dedicated themselves to the Franciscan way while continuing their former careers in the world. The little band of Franciscan brothers had evolved into a multitude.

On his return from the Near East Francis prevailed on a powerful friend, Cardinal Hugolino—later Pope Gregory IX—to become the order's protector. On Hugolino's initiative a formal rule was drawn up in 1220 which provided a certain degree of administrative structure to the order. A novitiate was established, lifetime vows were required, and the rule of absolute poverty was softened. In 1223 a shorter, somewhat laxer rule was instituted, and over the years and decades that followed, the movement continued to evolve from the ideal to the practical.

St. Francis himself withdrew more and more from involvement in the order's administration. At the meeting of the general chapter in 1220 he resigned his formal leadership of the movement with the words, "Lord, I give thee back this family that Thou didst entrust to me. Thou knowest, most sweet Jesus, that I have no more the power and the qualities to continue to take care of it." In 1224, St. Francis underwent a mystical experience atop Mt. Alverno in the Apennines, and legend has it that he received the *stigmata** on

---

* The stigmata, which have been attributed to several saints, consist in wounds or scars, supposedly of supernatural origin, that correspond to those sustained by Christ in his crucifixion.

that occasion. It is not entirely clear how St. Francis reacted to the evolution of his order, but in his closing years his mysticism deepened, his health declined, and he kept much to himself. At his death in 1226 he was universally mourned, and the order which he had founded remained the most powerful and attractive religious movement of its age.

As Franciscanism became increasingly modified by the demands of practicality it also became increasingly rent with dissension. Some friars, wishing to draw on Francis's prestige without being burdened with his spiritual dedication, advocated an exceedingly lax interpretation of the Franciscan way. Others insisted on the strict imitation of Francis's life and struggled against its modification. These last, known in later years as "Spiritual Franciscans," sought to preserve the apostolic poverty and artless idealism of Francis himself; by the fourteenth century they had become vigorously antipapal and anticlerical.

The majority of Franciscans, however, were willing to meet reality halfway. Although Francis had disparaged formal learning as irrelevant to salvation, Franciscan friars began devoting themselves to scholarship and took their places alongside the Dominicans in the thirteenth- and fourteenth-century universities. Indeed, Franciscan scholars such as Roger Bacon in thirteenth-century England played a crucial role in the revival of scientific investigation, and the minister-general of the Franciscan order in the later thirteenth century, St. Bonaventure, was one of the most illustrious theologians of the age. The very weight and complexity of the Franciscan organization forced it to compromise its original ideal of corporate poverty. Although it neither acquired nor sought the immense landed wealth of the Benedictines or Cistercians, it soon possessed sufficient means to sustain its members. It is interesting to see how the minister-general Bonaventure, a holy man and also a brilliant philosopher, instituted and justified some of the changes that the order underwent in the thirteenth century. Although an intense admirer of St. Francis, Bonaventure was not himself a beggar by nature, nor a wandering minstrel, nor a day laborer, but a scholar-administrator burdened with the task of adapting a way of life designed for a dozen friars living in huts of twigs to an international order of many thousands. Contrary to Francis, Bonaventure encouraged scholarship as an aid to preaching and evangelism. St. Francis had urged his followers that "manual labor should be done with faith and devotion." Bonaventure, after demonstrating the superiority of contemplation to manual labor, concluded that Franciscans were under no compulsion to engage in physical work, although if any wished to do so he should by all means do it, "with faith and devotion."

Necessary though they were, these compromises robbed the Franciscan movement of a good measure of the radical idealism that Francis had instilled in it. In the progress from huts of twigs to halls of ivy something very precious was left behind. The Franciscans continued to serve society, but by the end of the thirteenth century they had ceased to inspire it.

The Passing of the High Middle Ages

The pattern of religious reform in the High Middle Ages is one of rhythmic ebb and flow. A reform movement is launched with high enthusiasm and lofty purpose, it galvanizes society for a time, then succumbs gradually to complacency and gives way to a new and different wave of reform. But with the passing of the High Middle Ages one can detect a gradual waning of spiritual vigor in orthodox Catholicism. The frontiers were closing as the fourteenth century dawned. Western political power was at an end in Constantinople and the Holy Land, and the Spanish reconquest had stalled. The

CHRONOLOGY OF HIGH MEDIEVAL MONASTICISM AND HETERODOXY

910: Founding of Cluny
1084: Establishment of Carthusian Order
1098: Establishment of Citeaux
1112–53: Career of St. Bernard of Clairvaux as a Cistercian.
1128: Original rule of the Knights Templars.
c. 1173: Beginning of the Waldensian sect.
1208: Innocent III calls the Albigensian Crusade.
1210: Innocent III authorizes the Francisan Order.
1216: Dominican Rule sanctioned by the papacy.
1226: Death of St. Francis.
1233: Inquisition established.

economic boom was given way to an epoch of depression, declining population, peasants' rebellions, and debilitating wars. And until the time of the Protestant Reformation, no new religious order was to attain the immense social impact of the thirteenth-century Franciscans and Dominicans. Popular piety remained strong, particularly in northern Europe where succeeding centuries witnessed a significant surge of mysticism. But in the south a more secular attitude was beginning to emerge. Young men no longer flocked into monastic orders; soldiers no longer rushed to crusades; papal excommunications no longer wrought their former terror. The electrifying appeal of a St. Bernard, a St. Dominic, and a St. Francis was a phenomenon peculiar to their age. By the fourteenth century, their age was passing.

11

empire
and
papacy

Papacy and Church
in the Mid-Eleventh Century

The role of the papacy in the changing religious configurations of the High Middle Ages was scarcely touched upon in the previous chapter, for although it was fundamental to the spiritual development of the period it was also closely associated with the politics of empire and kingdom which is the central topic of this chapter. Therefore we must go back to the mid-eleventh century, the age when Cluny still stood in the vanguard of European monasticism, when Citeaux was yet an untouched wilderness and the mendicant movement lay in the distant future.

With the dawning of the High Middle Ages there emerged a newly invigorated papacy, dedicated to ecclesiastical reform and the spiritual regeneration of Christian society. Almost at once the reform papacy became involved in a struggle with the Holy Roman Empire—a tragic conflict that dominated European politics for more than two centuries. On the eve of the conflict, Germany was the mightiest monarchy in Western Christendom and the German king or Holy Roman Emperor dominated the papacy. By 1300 Germany was fragmented and the papacy, after 250 years of political prominence, was exhausted and on the brink of a prolonged decline.

Prior to the beginnings of papal reform in the mid-eleventh century, a chasm had existed between the papal theory of Christian society and the realities of the contemporary Church. The papal theory, with a venerable tradition running back to the fifth-century pope, Leo the Great,* envisaged a sanctified Christian commonwealth in which lords and kings accepted the spiritual direction of priests and bishops who, in turn, submitted to the leadership of the papacy. The popes claimed to be the successors—the vicars—of St. Peter. Just as St. Peter was the chief of Christ's apostles, they argued, the pope was the monarch of the apostolic Church. And as eternal salvation was more important than earthly prosperity—as the soul was more important than the body—so the priestly power was greater than the power of secular lords, kings, and emperors. The properly ordered society, the truly Christian society, was one dominated by the Church which, in turn, was dominated by the pope. In the intellectual climate of the High Middle Ages this view had great pertinence and caught the imagination of many thoughtful men. It provided the papal monarchy with a persuasive justification.

The reality of mid-eleventh-century society was far different. Almost everywhere the Church was under the control of aristocratic lay proprietors. Petty lords appointed their priests; dukes and kings selected their bishops and abbots. As we have seen, the Holy Roman Emperors used churchmen extensively in the administration of Germany. In France, the Church provided warriors from its estates for the feudal armies, clerks for the feudal chanceries, and shrewd political advisers for the feudal princes. The Church played a vital role in the operation of tenth- and early-eleventh-century society but it was usually subordinate to the lay ruling class. Its spiritual and sacramental role was compromised by its secular administrative responsibilities. As was bound to happen under such conditions, the Church tended to neglect its sacred mission. From the lay standpoint it was an effective administrative tool, but from the spiritual standpoint it was inadequate and sometimes corrupt. Monasteries all too frequently ignored the strict Benedictine rule. Some priests had concubines, and many had wives, despite the canonical requirement of priestly celibacy. Lay lords often sold important ecclesiastical offices to the highest bidder, and the new prelate customarily recouped the expense of buying his office by exploiting his tenants and subordinates. This commerce in ecclesiastical appointments was known as *simony*. It was regarded by some contemporary reformers as the arch sin of the age.

* See p. 25.

Ecclesiastical corruption was nowhere more evident than in Rome itself. The papacy of the earlier eleventh century had fallen into the soiled hands of the Roman nobility and had become a prize disputed among the several leading aristocratic families of the city. In 1032 the prize fell to a young aristocratic libertine who took the name of Benedict IX. His pontificate was scandalous even by contemporary Roman standards. Benedict sold the papacy, then changed his mind and reclaimed it. By 1046 his right to the papal throne was challenged by two other claimants; the papacy had fallen into a three-way schism.

Ecclesiastical Reform

Such were the conditions of the European Church as the mid-eleventh century approached. A Church dominated by lay proprietors had long existed in Europe and had long been accepted. But with the upsurge of lay piety that accompanied the opening of the High Middle Ages, the comfortable church-state relationship of the previous epoch seemed monstrously wrong to many sensitive spirits. This was the epoch in which Christians were beginning to join hermit groups such as the Carthusians; they would soon be flocking into the new, austere Cistercian order. Such men as these were responding to the spiritual awakening of their age by following the path of withdrawal from worldly society. Others chose the more novel and adventurous approach of *conversion* and took up the task of reforming the Church and the world. The dream of sanctifying society, which was later to find such vivid expression in the career of St. Francis, was shared by many Christians of the High Middle Ages. During the second half of the eleventh century it manifested itself in a powerful movement of ecclesiastical reform which was beginning to make itself felt across Western Christendom. At the heart of this movement was the reform papacy.

In general, the reformers fell into two groups: (1) a moderate group which sought to eliminate simony, enforce clerical celibacy, and improve the moral calibre of churchmen, but without challenging the Church's traditional subordination to the lay aristocracy—a subordination that had been sweetened by countless generous gifts of lands and powers to submissive prelates, and (2) a radical group which sought to demolish the tradition of lay control and to rebuild society on the pattern of the papal monarchy theory. The radical reformers struggled to establish an ideal Christian commonwealth in which laymen no longer appointed churchmen—in which kings deferred to bishops and a reformed papacy ruled the Church. The moderate reformers endeavored to heal society; the radicals were determined to overturn it.

The Congregation of Cluny, firm in its spiritual rectitude yet at peace with the existing social order, was one of the chief centers of moderate reform in the eleventh century. Its ideals were shared by several of the more enlightened rulers of the age, among them, Emperor Henry III, the powerful Salian monarch of Germany. Shocked by the antics of Pope Benedict IX and the three-way tug-of-war for the papal throne, Henry III intervened in Italy in 1046, arranged the deposition of Benedict and his two rivals, and drastically improved the quality of the papal leadership by appointing the first of a series of reform popes. The ablest of these imperial appointees, Pope Leo IX (1049–54), carried on a vigorous campaign against simony and clerical marriage, holding yearly synods at Rome, sending legates far and wide to enforce reform, and traveling constantly himself to preside over local councils and depose guilty churchmen. Leo's reform pontificate opened dramatically when, at the Roman Synod of 1049, the bishop of Sutri was condemned for simony and promptly fell dead in the presence of the whole assembly—a victim, it was assumed, of the divine wrath.

Leo IX labored mightily for reform, and his pontificate constitutes the opening phase in the evolution of the high-medieval papacy. His concern for a secure territorial position in central Italy prompted him to lead an army against the enterprising Norman adventurer to the south, Robert Guiscard, but being defeated and captured at Civitate he was forced to recognize the Normans and give them the status of papal vassals.* His vigorous assertion of papal authority aggravated the long and deepening hostility between the churches of Rome and Constantinople, and in 1054 two of his legates placed a papal bull on the high altar of Sancta Sophia excommunicating the Eastern patriarch. More than anything else, Leo struggled to enforce canon law and to purge the Church of simony and incontinence. In most of his enterprises, he could count on the support of Emperor Henry III. In these early years empire and papacy worked hand in glove to raise the moral level of the European Church.

But however successful this reform movement might have been,

* See p. 157.

there were those who felt that it was not going far enough. The real evil, in the view of the radical reformers, was lay supremacy over the Church. Henry III's domination of papal appointments, however well-intentioned, was the supreme example of a profound social sin. A number of ardent reformers were to be found among the cardinals whom Pope Leo appointed and gathered around him. These new men, who dominated the reform papacy for the next several decades, came for the most part from monastic backgrounds. Many of them were deeply influenced by the strong piety surging throughout the towns of eleventh-century northern Italy, a piety that was stimulating the widespread revival of hermit monasticism.

One such man was St. Peter Damiani, a leader of the northern-Italian hermit movement before he was brought to Rome by Leo IX and made a cardinal. Zealous and saintly, Damiani was deeply respected by his contemporaries. He was a mystic and, like St. Bernard after him, a vigorous opponent of the growing tendency among Christian intellectuals to elucidate the Faith by reason and logic. Damiani served the reform papacy tirelessly, traveling far and wide to enforce the prohibitions against simony and incontinence and to reform the clergy. Yet he drew back from what seemed to him the irresponsible efforts of his more radical brethren to challenge and destroy the social order. Aflame with the new piety and deeply dedicated to the papacy, Damiani was nevertheless one of the less extreme of Leo IX's new cardinals.

The real leaders of the radical group were Humbert and Hildebrand. Both were cardinals under Leo; both had, like Damiani, left monastic lives to join the Roman curia. Humbert was a German from Lorraine, probably of aristocratic background, who used his subtle, well-trained intellect to support papal reform in its most radical aspect. He was one of Pope Leo's legates to Constantinople during the dispute with the Eastern Church, where his uncompromising attitudes on papal supremacy clashed with the equally intransigent views of the Eastern patriarch. Indeed, it was Humbert himself who instigated the schism of 1054 by laying a bull excommunicating the patriarch on the high altar of Sancta Sophia. A few years later Humbert produced a bitter, closely reasoned attack against the lay-dominated social order in the West, *Three Books Against the Simoniacs*, in which he extended the meaning of simony to include not merely the buying or selling of ecclesiastical offices but any instance of lay interference in clerical appointments. In Humbert's view the Church ought to be utterly free of lay control and supreme in European society.

Hildebrand, an Italian, lacked the originality and intellectual depth of Humbert but had a remarkable ability to draw ideas from the minds of others and formulate them into a clearly articulated program. Intellectually, Hildebrand was a disciple of Humbert, but as a leader and man of action he was second to none. Contemporaries described him as a small, ugly, pot-bellied man, but they also recognized that a fire burned inside him—a holy or unholy fire depending on one's point of view, for Hildebrand was the most controversial figure of his age. Consumed by the ideal of a Christian society dominated by the Church and a Church dominated by the papacy, Hildebrand served with prodigious vigor and determination under Pope Leo IX and his successors. At length he became pope himself, taking the name Gregory VII (1073–85). His pontificate was to be one of the greatest and most tragic of the Middle Ages.

So long as Henry III lived, radicals such as Humbert and Hildebrand remained in the background. But in 1056 the emperor died in the prime of life, leaving behind him a six-year-old heir, Henry IV, and a weak regency government. Henry III's death was a catastrophe for the empire and a godsend to the radicals who longed to wrest the papacy from imperial control. At the death of Henry III's last papal appointee in 1057, the reform cardinals began electing popes on their own. In 1059, under the influence of Humbert and Hildebrand, they issued a daring declaration of independence known as the *Papal Election Decree*, which stated that thenceforth the pope would be chosen by cardinals. The Emperor and the Roman laity would merely give formal approval to the candidate whom the cardinals elected. In the years that followed, this revolutionary proclamation was challenged by both the empire and the Roman aristocracy, but in the end the cardinals won out. The papacy had broken free of lay control and was in the hands of the reformers. For now the cardinals elected the pope* and the pope appointed the cardinals. The Decree of 1059 created at the apex of the ecclesiastical hierarchy a reform oligarchy of the most exclusive sort.

---

* Strictly speaking, the Decree of 1059 provided that the pope should be elected not by all the cardinals but by the cardinal bishops alone. The other cardinals—cardinal priests and cardinal deacons—were empowered to participate in papal elections by a decree of the twelfth century.

The Investiture Controversy

The next step in the program of the radical reformers was infinitely more difficult. It involved nothing less than the annihilation of lay control over the entire Church. At a time when the Church possessed untold wealth, including perhaps a third of the land in Europe, the total realization of such a goal would cripple secular power and revolutionize European society. Yet only by its realization, so the radical reformers believed, could a justly-ordered Christian commonwealth be achieved.

One of the first arenas of conflict was the ancient city of Milan with its proud archbishopric, renowned since St. Ambrose's time. Milan was in the grip of the new commercial revival and, like many other Lombard towns of the eleventh century, was seething with activity. The Lombard towns of this era were, as a rule, dominated by their bishops—who were inclined to cooperate with the Holy Roman Empire—and by an élite of landed noblemen. As a group, the Lombard bishops tended to ignore the new wave of reform, and some were themselves guilty of simony. Throughout Lombardy, and in Milan in particular, the rule of the nobles and episcopacy was being challenged by the growing lower classes of artisans, day workers, and peasants. In Milan and elsewhere, this revolutionary lower-class group was called, by its enemies, the *patarenes* (ragpickers). Hostile to the domination of the traditional ruling group and fired by a new piety, the patarenes made common cause with the reform papacy against their unreformed and oppressive masters. The reformers in Rome had no sympathy for the Lombard bishops and were especially antagonistic toward the archbishop of Milan who was, in effect, an imperial agent and who, by condoning simony and incontinence among his clergy, symbolized the old proprietary Church at its worst.

In 1059 Cardinal Peter Damiani journeyed to Milan to enforce reform. Backed by the patarenes and the authority of Rome, he humbled the archbishop and the higher clergy, made them confess their sins publicly, and wrung promises of amendment from them. Thus, the Milanese church, despite its traditional cooperation with the Empire and independence of Roman authority, was made to submit to the power of the papacy. Over the next 15 years struggle between the patarenes and the noble-ecclesiastical ruling group continued, and the city was torn by murder and mob violence. When, in 1072, the young Emperor Henry IV ordered the consecration of an antireformer as archbishop of Milan, he was at once faced with the combined wrath of the papacy and patarenes. The patarenes rioted and the pope excommunicated Henry's counselors. The most significant aspect of this entire affair is the way in which it typifies the close alliance between radical urban piety and papal reform. During the second half of the eleventh century the papacy managed to place itself at the forefront of the new piety and to draw upon the vital energy of the revolutionary social-spiritual movement that was sweeping across Europe. At odds with much of the traditional ecclesiastical establishment, the radical reformers in Rome were nevertheless in tune with the most vigorous spiritual forces of the age.

The struggle over lay control of ecclesiastical appointments broke out in earnest in 1075 when Hildebrand, now Pope Gregory VII, issued a proclamation banning lay investiture. Traditionally, a newly chosen bishop or abbot was invested by a lay lord with a ring and a pastoral staff, symbolic of his marriage to the Church and his duty toward his Christian flock. Gregory attacked this custom of lay investiture as the crucial symbol of lay authority over churchmen. Its prohibition was a challenge to the established social order. It threatened to compromise the authority of every ruler in Christendom, and none more than the Holy Roman Emperor himself, whose administrative system was particularly dependent on his control of the German church. By Gregory VII's time Henry IV had grown to vigorous manhood and was showing promise of becoming as strong a ruler as his father, Henry III. Refusing to accept the decree against lay investiture, Henry sent a flaming letter of defiance to Rome, asserting his right as a divinely appointed sovereign to lead the German church without papal interference and challenging Gregory's very right to the papal throne. The letter was addressed to Gregory under his previous name, "Hildebrand, not pope but false monk." It concluded with the dramatic words, "I, Henry, king by grace of God, with all my bishops, say to you: 'Come down, come down, and be damned throughout the ages.'"

Henry's letter was in effect a defense of the traditional social order of divinely ordained priest-kings ruling over a docile church. Gregory's view of society was vastly different: he denied the priestly qualities of kings and emperors, suggested that most of them were gangsters destined for Hell, and repudiated their right to question his status or his decrees. Emperors had no power to appoint churchmen, much less depose popes, but the pope, as the ultimate authority in Christendom, had the power to depose kings and emperors. Accordingly, Gregory responded to Henry's letter with a startling and unprecedented exercise of spiritual authority which was, nevertheless, perfectly in accord with his conception of Christian society: he excommunicated and deposed Henry. It was for the pope to judge whether or not the king was fit to rule, and Gregory had judged. His judgment was nothing less than revolutionary, for in banning lay investiture and deposing the king of Germany he was putting into practice the papal theory in its most radical form and striking at the very bedrock of the traditional order.

Radical though it was, the deposition was effective. Under the relatively calm surface of Salian monarchical authority in Germany, a powerful aristocratic opposition had long been gathering force. Subdued during the reign of Henry III, local and regional particularism asserted itself during the long regency following his death, and Henry IV, on reaching maturity, had much ground to recover. In 1075 he succeeded in stifling a long, bitter rebellion in Saxony and seemed to be on his way toward reasserting his father's power when the investiture controversy exploded. Gregory VII's excommunication and deposition—awesome spiritual sanctions to the minds of eleventh-century Christians—unleashed in Germany all the latent hostility that the centralizing policies of the Salian dynasty had evoked. Many Germans, churchmen and laymen alike, refused to serve an excommunicated sovereign. The German nobles took the revolutionary step of threatening to elect a new king in Henry's place, thereby challenging the ingrained German tradition of hereditary kingship with the counterdoctrine of elective monarchy. The elective principle, which crippled the later-medieval and early-modern German monarchy, had its real inception at this moment.

Desperate to keep his throne, Henry crossed the Alps into Italy to seek the pope's forgiveness. In January 1077, at the castle of Canossa in Tuscany, the two men met in what was perhaps medieval history's most dramatic encounter—Henry IV humble and barefoot in the snow, clothed in rough, penitential garments; Gregory VII torn between his conviction that Henry's change of heart was a mere political expedient and his priestly duty to forgive a repentant sinner. Finally, Gregory lifted Henry's excommunication and the monarch, promising to amend his ways, returned to Germany to rebuild his authority.

Down through the centuries Canossa has symbolized the ultimate royal degradation before the power of the Church. Perhaps it was. But in the immediate political context it was a victory, and a badly needed one, for Henry IV. It did not prevent a group of German nobles from electing a rival king, nor did it restore the powerful centralized monarchy of Henry III; but it did save Henry IV's throne. Restored to communion, he was able to rally support, to check for a time the forces of princely particularism, and to defeat the rival king.

As his power waxed, Henry ignored his promises at Canossa and resumed his support of lay investiture. In 1080 Gregory excommunicated and deposed him a second time, only to find that these potent spiritual weapons were losing their strength through overuse. In the early 1080s Henry returned to Italy, this time with an army. Gregory summoned his vassal and ally, the Norman Robert Guiscard, to rescue him from his situation, but Robert's boisterous Normans, although they frightened Henry away, became involved in a destructive riot with the Roman townspeople. The commoners of Rome had always supported Gregory, but now they turned furiously against him and he was obliged, for his own protection, to accompany the Normans when they withdrew to the south. In 1085 Gregory died at Salerno, consumed by bitterness and a conviction of failure. His last words were these: "I have loved justice and hated iniquity; therefore I die in exile."*

Although Gregory VII failed to transform Europe into what he conceived to be a proper Christian society, his theory of papal monarchy retained its potency. The reform papacy soon fell into the able hands of Urban II (1088–99), a former prior of Cluny, who seized the moral leadership of Europe by calling the First Crusade. Urban steered a more moderate course than Gregory had done, yet he and his successors continued to harass the unlucky Henry, stirring up rebellions in Germany and eroding the power of the imperial government. In 1106 Henry died as unhappily as Gregory had. In the end Henry's own son and heir, Henry V, led an army of hostile nobles against his father. As Henry IV died, his empire seemed to be collapsing around him.

---

* An ironic twist to Psalm 45, verse 7: "You have loved justice and hated iniquity; therefore God, your God, has anointed you with the oil of gladness, above all your rivals."

Henry V (1106–25) enjoyed a happier reign than his father's, but only because he foresook his father's struggle to recover the fullness of imperial power as it had existed in the mid-eleventh century. The independence-minded aristocracy consolidated the gains it had made during the preceding era of chaos, and Henry V could do little about it.

Toward the end of his reign, Henry V worked out a compromise settlement with the Church which brought the Investiture Contest to an end at last. Already the controversy had been settled by compromise in England and France where the church-state struggle had been considerably less bitter than in Germany. As time progressed both papacy and empire tended to draw back from the extreme positions they had taken during Gregory VII's pontificate, and in 1122 they reconciled their differences in the Corcordat of Worms. Henry agreed that the investiture ceremony would no longer be performed by laymen, but the pope conceded to the emperor the important privilege of bestowing on the new prelate the symbols of his *territorial* and *administrative* jurisdiction. Bishops and abbots were thenceforth to be elected according to the principles of canon law, by the monks of a monastery or the canons of a cathedral, but the emperor had the right to be present at such elections and to make the final decision in the event of a dispute. These reservations enabled the emperor to retain a considerable degree of de facto control over the appointment of important German churchmen. The exercise of royal control over a "canonical election" is illustrated in a twelfth-century charter of King Henry II of England to the monks at Winchester: "I order you to hold a free election, but nevertheless I forbid you to elect anyone except Richard, my clerk, the archdeacon of Poitiers."

There was no real victory in the Investiture Controversy. The Church had won its point—lay investiture was banned—but monarchs still exercised very real control over their churches. The theory of papal monarchy over a reconstituted Christian society remained unrealized, and the old tradition of peaceful cooperation between kings and prelates was badly shaken. The papacy, however noble its intentions, had become politicized as never before, and by asserting its authority in deeds and treatises it evoked hostile countertrends of royalist political propaganda and growing anticlericalism.

Still, the papal-imperial balance of power had changed radically since the mid-eleventh century. The papacy was now a mighty force in Europe, and the power of the emperor had declined sharply. During the chaotic half-century between the onset of the Investiture Controversy in 1075 and Henry V's death in 1125, feudalism came to Germany. In these decades of civil strife a powerful new aristocracy emerged. Ambitious landowners rose to great power, built castles, extended their estates, and usurped royal rights. They forced minor neighboring noblemen to become their vassals and, in some instances, forced free peasants to become their serfs. The monarchy was helpless to curb this ominous process of fragmentation.

The Investiture Controversy resulted in the crippling of imperial authority in northern Italy. The fierce patarene struggle of Milan was repeated throughout Lombardy, and in the anarchy wrought by the papal-imperial conflict the pro-imperial Lombard bishops lost the wide jurisdictional rights that they had formerly exercised over their cities and the surrounding countryside. Everywhere the pious and vigorously independent Lombard townsmen took up the cause of papal reform, rebelled against the control of nobles, bishops, and emperor alike, and established quasi-independent city states. By 1125, Milan and her sister cities were free urban communes, and imperial authority in Lombardy had become virtually nominal.

In Germany and Italy alike, imperial power was receding before the whirlwind of local particularism, invigorated by the Investiture Controversy and the soaring popular piety of the age. Well before the Concordat of Worms, the decline of the medieval empire had begun.

The Age of Frederick Barbarossa

The Salian dynasty died out with the passing of Henry V in 1125. During the next quarter century Germany reaped the harvest of princely particularism. The nobles disparaged the principle of hereditary royal succession and reverted to the elective principle that they had asserted at the time of Canossa. Their choice always fell to a man of royal blood but never to the most direct heir. In the turbulent decades between 1125 and 1152 a rivalry developed between two great families that had risen to power in the anarchic era of the Investiture Controversy: the Welfs of Saxony and the Hohenstaufens of Swabia. In 1152 the princes elected as king a powerful and talented Hohenstaufen, Frederick I, "Barbarossa" (the Red-Bearded), duke of Swabia, who took as his mission the revival and reconstruction of the German monarchy.

Emperor Frederick Barbarossa recognized that the mighty imperial structure of Henry III was beyond recovery. His goal was to harness the new feudal forces of his age to the royal advantage. He actually encouraged the great princes of the realm to expand their power and privileges at the expense of the lesser lords, but at the same time he forced them to recognize his own feudal lordship over all the kingdom. In other words, he succeeded in establishing an effective lordship over the leading feudal magnates, making them his obedient vassals—his tenants-in-chief. He was the supreme overlord at the apex of the feudal pyramid.

But as the sorry state of the early French monarchy well illustrates, feudal overlordship was an ephemeral thing if the royal overlord lacked the power and resources to support his position. Therefore, Frederick Barbarossa set about to increase his revenues and extend the territories under his direct authority. A strong feudal monarchy required a substantial territorial core under exclusive royal control— an extensive royal demesne to act as a counterweight to the great fiefs of the chief vassals of the realm. Frederick enlarged his demesne territories, most of which were concentrated in Swabia, by bringing many of the new monasteries and rising towns under imperial jurisdiction. The crux of his imaginative policy was the reassertion of imperial authority over the wealthy Lombard cities. With Lombardy under his control and its revenues pouring into the imperial treasury, no German lord could challenge him.

Barbarossa's Lombard policy earned him the hostility of the papacy which had always feared the consolidation of imperial power in Italy, and of the intensely independent Lombard cities, which were determined to give up as little of their wealth and autonomy as they possibly could. And should he become too deeply involved in Italy, Barbarossa exposed himself to rebellion on the part of the German aristocrats and high nobility—in particular, the Welf family which was vigorously represented at the time by Duke Henry the Lion of Saxony.

The papacy of the mid-twelfth century was having problems of its own. Pope Hadrian IV (1154–59), who was to become one of Frederick Barbarossa's most ardent foes, was faced at the beginning of his pontificate with the problem of maintaining the papacy's hold on

Rome itself. A gifted man of humble origins, Hadrian IV was the one Englishman ever to occupy the papal throne. Rome was turbulent during his years, for the patarene movement had reached the Holy City and had turned violently antipapal. The revolutionary social forces that had earlier allied with the papacy in breaking the power of an archbishop in Milan were now challenging the pope's authority over Rome. In the 1140s the city was torn by a lower-class rebellion whose leaders struggled to drive out the pope and dreamed of reestablishing the ancient Roman Republic. Very quickly this anti-papal communal movement spread to other cities in the Papal States, and for a time the papacy itself was forced into exile.

Before long, the Roman rebellion fell under the leadership of Arnold Brescia, a gifted scholar and spiritual revolutionary, whose goal it was to strip the Church of its wealth and secular authority. Suppressed by the Norman troops of Roger the Great in the 1140s, Arnold's revolution reasserted itself under Hadrian, and the pope was driven to the desperate expedient of placing Rome itself under interdict, ordering the suspension of church services throughout the city. The interdict proved an effective weapon. Among other things, it severely curtailed the influx of pilgrims and thereby had an adverse effect on Rome's economy. The revolution collapsed and Arnold was driven from the city. Hadrian and Barbarossa joined forces to hunt him down, and, once he fell into their hands, he was hanged, burned, and thrown into the Tiber (1155). Thus, Arnold of Brescia was emphatically eliminated and his relics were put out of the reach of any future admirers. But his movement persisted as an anti-clerical heresy —an early example of the opposition to ecclesiastical wealth and power that was soon to find expression among the Waldensians and Albigensians and, by implication, among the Franciscans.

The growing split between the papacy and the Roman townsmen was an ominous indication that papal leadership over urban reform movements was at an end. The papacy was no longer able to make common cause with the explosive forces of popular piety, as it had done in the age of Gregory VII, but was now beginning to suppress them. Pope Hadrian actually had little choice but to defend himself in whatever way possible against Arnold of Brescia, yet, in laying Rome under interdict, he was following a path that would lead within a century to the Albigensian Crusade and the Inquisition. This schism between papal leadership and popular piety was a factor of no small importance in the ultimate downfall of the later medieval papacy.

Hadrian IV and Frederick Barbarossa first met on the occasion of the imperial coronation in Rome in 1155. The two men had collaborated against Arnold of Brescia, but thereafter they became enemies. At their initial encounter, Hadrian insisted that Frederick follow ancient tradition and lead the papal mule.* At first Frederick refused to humble himself in such a manner, but when it appeared that there would be no coronation at all he grudgingly submitted. This small conflict was symbolic of far greater ones, for Hadrian and his successors proved to be implacable opponents of Frederick's drive to win control of the Lombard cities.

The Lombard struggle reached its height in the pontificate of Alexander III (1159–81), Hadrian's successor. Wise, shrewd, and learned, Alexander was the greatest pope of the twelfth century and Frederick Barbarossa's most formidable opponent. Whereas most of the early reform popes had been monks, Alexander and many of his successors were canon lawyers. Hildebrand himself had urged the study of canon law and the formulation of canonical collections in order to provide intellectual ammunition to support papal claims. During the later eleventh and twelfth centuries the study of canon law was pursued vigorously in northern Italian schools, particularly the great law school at Bologna, and a good number of twelfth and thirteenth century popes were products of these schools. Alexander III was one of the ablest of them.

Determined to prevent Frederick Barbarossa from establishing himself strongly in northern Italy, Alexander rallied the Lombard towns which had long been engaged in intercity warfare but now combined forces against the empire. They formed an association called the Lombard League and organized a powerful interurban army to oppose Frederick. The emperor had meanwhile thrown his support behind a rival claimant to the papal throne, and Alexander responded by excommunicating and deposing him. There followed a prolonged struggle involving Alexander, Barbarossa, and the Lombard League, which ended in the total victory of the Lombard army at the battle of Legnano in 1176.

---

* The tradition of the ceremonial mule-leading seems to have originated in the eighth-century forgery, the "Donation of Constantine."

THE HOLY ROMAN EMPIRE
IN 1190

North Sea

Baltic Sea

KINGDOM OF DENMARK

LITHUANIA

Lübeck

SAXONY

POMERANIA

PRUSSIANS

BRANDENBURG

KINGDOM OF POLAND

RUSSIA

Cologne

NASSAU

Elbe

KINGDOM OF FRANCE

LORRAINE

BOHEMIA

Worms

FRANCONIA

ALSACE

MORAVIA

Danube

SWABIA

Augsburg

Constance

KINGDOM OF BURGUNDY

BAVARIA

KINGDOM OF HUNGARY

Milan

LOMBARDY

Venice

Pisa

TUSCANY

Adriatic Sea

BULGARIANS

Danube

CORSICA

Subi

SERBIA

Rome

Anagni

SARDINIA

BYZANTINE EMPIRE

KINGDOM OF SICILY

Mediterranean Sea

Palermo

MILES
0 100 200 300 400

Barbarossa submitted as graciously as he could, granting de facto independence to the Lombard cities in return for their admission of a vague imperial overlordship. Pope and emperor tearfully embraced; Barbarossa led Alexander's mule and promised to be a dutiful son of the Roman See.

Barbarossa had lost the battle but not the war. Leaving Lombardy severely alone, he shifted his operations southward to Tuscany, establishing administrative control over this rich province immediately to the north of the Papal States. At the same time he arranged a fateful marriage between his son and the future heiress of the Norman Kingdom of southern Italy and Sicily—a marriage which ultimately brought that opulent kingdom within the imperial fold. The papacy had been outwitted and was in grave danger of being encircled and stifled. In 1180 Barbarossa consolidated his power in Germany by crushing the greatest and most hostile of his vassals, Henry the Lion, the Welf duke of Saxony. After Alexander III's death in 1181, the papacy ceased for a time to be a serious threat, and the far-sighted emperor was at the height of his power in 1190 when he died while leading his army toward the Holy Land on the Third Crusade.

Henry VI: 1190–97

Barbarossa had taken pains to circumvent the princely policy of elective monarchy by forcing the princes, prior to his death, to elect his son, Henry VI. In 1190 Henry succeeded to the German throne without difficulty, and in 1194 he made good his claim to the Kingdom of Sicily. The Papal States were now an island completely surrounded by Holy Roman Empire, and the papacy was powerless to alter the situation. The bounteous revenues of southern Italy and Sicily fattened the imperial purse. The territories under imperial rule had never been so extensive.

But for an age in which the emperor had to remain ever vigilant against the centrifugal forces of local particularism and, above all, against the ambitions of the great German vassals, the imperial frontiers had become dangerously overextended. It remained uncertain whether a single man could rule Italy and Germany concurrently. Whether Henry VI might have accomplished this task we shall never know, for he died prematurely in 1197 leaving as his heir his infant son, Frederick II. The problems the empire faced in 1197 would have taxed the ablest of leaders, yet at this crucial moment imperial leadership failed. The papacy had its opportunity.

The High Noon of the Medieval Papacy: Innocent III

During the twelfth century, the papacy lost much of its former zealous reform spirit as it evolved into a huge, complex administrative institution. Revenues flowed into its treasury from all the states of Western Christendom; bishops traveled vast distances to make their spiritual submission to the Roman pontiff; the papal curia served as a court of last appeal for an immense network of ecclesiastical courts. Papal authority over the European Church had increased immeasurably since the mid-eleventh century. As the dream of a papal monarchy came ever nearer realization, the traditional theory of papal supremacy over Christian society was increasingly magnified and elaborated by the canon lawyers. These subtle ecclesiastical scholars were beginning to dominate the papal curia and, like Alexander III, to occupy the papal throne itself.

Innocent III (1198–1216), the greatest of all the lawyer popes, came to power in the year following Emperor Henry VI's death. It was he who seized the opportunity offered by the succession of an infant to the throne of the overextended empire. Innocent was history's most powerful pope—a brilliant, astute diplomat, an imperious, self-confident aristocrat who, although genuinely pious, was distinctly aloof from the surging religious emotionalism of the humbler folk of his age. He had the wisdom and sensitivity to support the Franciscans, and the ruthlessness to mount the Albigensian Crusade.*

Animated by the theory of papal monarchy in its most uncompromising form, Innocent forced his will on the leading monarchs of Europe, playing off one ruler against another with consummate skill. In the course of a long struggle with King John of England over the appointment of an archbishop of Canterbury, Innocent laid John's entire kingdom under interdict, threatened to depose John himself, and asked King Philip Augustus of France to send an army against

* See pp. 183–184.

him. The struggle ended with John's complete submission, the installation of Innocent's man in the archbishopric of Canterbury, and the establishment of papal lordship over England.

Innocent had earlier clashed with Philip Augustus over the king's refusal to repudiate an uncanonical second marriage and return to his first wife. After laying France under interdict and excommunicating Philip, Innocent obtained his submission.* It has already been shown how Innocent instigated the Fourth Crusade, which was aimed at Jerusalem but ended in Constantinople, and how he mounted crusades against the Albigensians and the Spanish Moors. These diverse activities illustrate the unprecedented political and moral sway which Innocent exercised over Christendom.

A mighty force in the secular politics of his age, Innocent also dominated the Church more completely than any of his predecessors had done. In 1215 he summoned a general Church council in Rome —the Fourth Lateran Council—which produced a remarkable quantity of significant ecclesiastical legislation: clerical habit was strictly regulated, a moratorium was declared on new religious orders, clerics were forbidden to participate in the ancient Germanic legal procedure of the ordeal,† fees for the administration of sacraments were forbidden, cathedral churches were ordered to maintain schools and to provide sermons at their chief services, and all Catholics were bound to receive the sacraments of penance and the eucharist at least once a year. The efficient organization of the Fourth Lateran Council, and the degree to which Pope Innocent dominated and directed it are illustrated by the fact that the churchmen in attendance—more than 1200 bishops, abbots, and priests—produced their important new legislation in meetings that lasted a total of only three weeks. By contrast, the fifteenth-century Council of Basel met off and on for 18 years and the Council of Trent for 19.

The range of Innocent III's activities was seemingly boundless, but throughout his pontificate one political issue took precedence over all others: the problem of the German imperial succession. It was a marvellously complex problem which taxed even Pope Innocent's

---

* Philip Augustus's submission was less complete, however, than might have been wished. His controversial second wife had died—conveniently but naturally—and his reconciliation with his first wife was a mere formality.

† See pp. 19–20.

diplomatic skill. Involved were the questions of whether or not the kingdom of Sicily would remain in imperial hands, whether the imperial throne would pass to the Welfs or the Hohenstaufens, and whether an accommodation could be achieved between the traditionally hostile forces of papacy and empire. The German succession problem also touched the interests of the French and English monarchies: the Welf claimant, Otto of Brunswick, was a nephew of King John of England and could usually count on his support, whereas the Hohenstaufens enjoyed the friendship of the French king, Philip Augustus.

The direct Hohenstaufen heir was the infant Frederick, son of the late Henry VI. But since a child could hardly be expected to wage a successful fight for the throne in these turbulent years, the Hohenstaufen claim was taken up by Frederick's uncle, Philip of Swabia, brother of the former emperor. The young Frederick remained in Sicily while Philip of Swabia and the Welf, Otto of Brunswick, contended for the imperial throne. Innocent recognized the German princes' right to elect their own monarch but, as it happened, Philip and Otto had both been elected, each by a different group of nobles. In the case of a disputed election such as this, Innocent claimed the right to intervene by virtue of the traditional papal privilege of crowning the emperor. He delayed his decision considerably, and in the meantime, civil war raged in Germany. At length he settled on Otto of Brunswick. Otto had promised to support the papal interests in Germany and to abandon almost entirely the policy of imperial control of the German church. Further, a Welf emperor would have no claim on the Hohenstaufen kingdom of Sicily, and Otto's coronation would therefore realize the papal goal of separating the two realms.

Despite Innocent's decision, the civil war continued in Germany until, in 1208, Philip of Swabia died. Otto was crowned emperor in 1209, but now, having no rival to oppose him, he repudiated his promises to Innocent, asserted his mastery over the German church, and even launched an invasion of southern Italy. Innocent responded to this breach of faith by deposing and anathematizing Otto and throwing his support behind the young Frederick. From the beginning, the kingdom of Sicily had been, at least nominally, a papal vassal state, and Innocent, as overlord, claimed the feudal privilege of guardianship over its minor king. Frederick, in other words, was Innocent's ward. Before undertaking to back Frederick, Innocent wrung a number of promises from him, making him swear to abdicate as king of Sicily and sever the Sicilian kingdom from the empire, to go on a crusade, to follow the spiritual direction of the papacy, and in general to confirm the promises that Otto of Brunswick had made and later broken.

Innocent's decision in favor of Frederick resulted in a revival of the Hohenstaufen cause in Germany and a renewal of the civil war. Innocent employed all his diplomatic skill and leverage to win over German nobles to Frederick's cause. He was supported in these maneuverings by King Philip Augustus of France, now on friendly terms with the papacy, traditionally sympathetic to the Hohenstaufens, and hostile to the English and their Welf allies.

The complex currents of international politics in Innocent's pontificate reached their climax and their resolution in 1214. King John invaded France from the west while Otto of Brunswick led a powerful army against Philip Augustus from the east—an army heavily subsidized by England and consisting of the combined forces of pro-Welf princes from Germany and the Low Countries. John's invasion bogged down and accomplished nothing; Otto's army met the forces of Philip Augustus in pitched battle at Bouvines and was decisively defeated. The battle of Bouvines of 1214 was an epoch-making engagement. Philip Augustus emerged as Europe's mightiest monarch, Otto's imperial dreams were demolished, and Frederick became emperor in fact as well as in theory. Bouvines was a triumph not only for Philip Augustus and Frederick but also for Innocent III. His ward was now emperor-elect and was pledged to sever the kingdom of Sicily from Germany and free the German Church of imperial control.

Germany itself was in a state of chaos. The solid achievements of Frederick Barbarossa, which might have served as the foundation for a powerful revival of imperial power, were compromised by the subsequent imperial involvement in the affairs of the Sicilian kingdom and were demolished by 19 years of civil strife during which the German princes usurped royal privileges and royal lands on a vast scale. By the time of Innocent's death the imperial authority that Barbarossa had achieved was almost beyond recovery.

The policies of Innocent III were everywhere triumphant. Yet Innocent, by the very range and breadth of his political activities, had involved the papacy in secular affairs to such a degree that its spiritual authority was becoming tarnished. Innocent had won his battles, but he had chosen a dangerous battleground. His successors, lacking his skill and his luck, could do little to arrest the gradual decline of papal political authority during the middle and later decades of the thirteenth century and over the centuries that followed. For papal power was based ultimately on spiritual prestige, and the thirteenth-century popes, despite their piety, despite their continuing concern for ecclesiastical reform, were lawyers, administrators, and diplomats rather than charismatic spiritual leaders. The papacy was a mighty force in the world of the thirteenth century, but it was failing more and more to satisfy the spiritual hunger of devoted Christians. Piety remained strong, but many of the pious were coming to doubt that the papal government, with its vast wealth and bureaucratic efficiency, was indeed the true spiritual center of the apostolic Church and the citadel of Christ's kingdom on earth. The popes were doing what they had to do, and in playing the game of international politics they continued to dream of a regenerated Christian society led and inspired by the Church. But as time went on they dreamed less and plotted more, permitting their political means to overshadow their spiritual ends.

The impressive diplomatic success of Innocent III's pontificate ended abruptly with his death in 1216. Once Innocent was gone, his former ward, Frederick II, now a grown man, made it clear that he would ignore his promises as completely as Otto of Brunswick had earlier done. Frederick ruled exactly as he pleased, and as his reign progressed he became the medieval papacy's most ferocious adversary. In choosing Frederick and supporting his candidacy to the imperial throne, Innocent III had made a fearful miscalculation.

Frederick II (1211–1250)

Frederick II, whose Sicilian childhood exposed him to several faiths, grew up to be a brilliant, anticlerical skeptic, more concerned with his harem and his exotic menagerie than with his soul. He dazzled his contemporaries and earned the name *Stupor Mundi*, the "Wonder of the World." His vision of unifying all Italy and making it the nucleus of the empire won him the hatred of the papacy. Some churchmen regarded Frederick quite literally as the incarnate antichrist.

Frederick II was a talented, many-sided man—perhaps the most flamboyant product of an intensely creative age. He was a writer of considerable skill and an amateur scientist, curious about the world around him, but in some matters deeply superstitious. After much delay he kept his promise to lead a crusade (1228), but instead of fighting the Muslims he negotiated with them, and did so with such success that Jerusalem itself came into his hands for a time. The amicable spirit of Frederick's crusade against the infidel struck many churchmen as unholy, and its success infuriated them.

Frederick II ruled his kingdom of Sicily in the autocratic but enlightened manner of a Renaissance despot, establishing a uniform legal code, tightening and broadening the centralized administrative system of his Norman-Sicilian predecessors, encouraging agriculture, industry, and commerce, abolishing interior tariffs and tolls, and founding a great university in Naples. He had promised Innocent III that he would cut Sicily off from his Empire, but he made no effort to keep his word. He had always preferred his urbane, sunny Sicilian homeland to the cold forests and gloomy castles of Germany. Although he tried to follow Frederick Barbarossa's policy of strengthening the royal demesne and enforcing the feudal obligations of his great German vassals, he did so half-heartedly. To him, Germany was important chiefly as a source of money and military strength with which to carry out his policy of bringing all Italy under his rule.

As it happened, this policy proved disastrous to the Holy Roman Empire. Frederick's aggressions in Italy evoked the opposition of a revived Lombard League and the implacable hostility of the papacy. He gave up lands and royal rights in Germany with an almost careless abandon in order to keep the peace with the German princes and win their support for his persistent but inconclusive Italian campaigns. In the end, he was even obliged to tax his beloved Sicily to the point of impoverishment in order to support his endless wars. Astute lawyer-popes such as Gregory IX and Innocent IV devoted all their diplomatic talents and spiritual sanctions to blocking Frederick's enterprises, building alliances to oppose him and hurling anathemas against him. In 1245 Innocent IV presided over a universal council of the Church at Lyons, which condemned and excommunicated the emperor. Frederick was deposed, a rival emperor was elected in his place, and a crusade was called to rid the empire of its ungodly tyrant. Revolts now broke out against Frederick throughout his empire. The royal estates in Germany slipped more and more from his grasp, and his Italian holdings were ridden with rebellion. Against this unhappy background Frederick II died in 1250.

The Decline of the Medieval Empire

In a very real sense, the hopes of the medieval empire died with him. His son succeeded him in Germany but died in 1254 after a brief and unsuccessful reign. For the next 19 years, Germany endured a crippling interregnum (1254–73) during which no recognized emperor held the throne. In 1273 a vastly weakened Holy Roman Empire reemerged with papal blessing under Rudolph of Habsburg, the first emperor of a family that was destined to play a crucial role in modern European history. Rudolph attempted to rebuild the shattered royal demesne and shore up the foundations of imperial rule, but it was much too late. The monarchy's one hope had been to strengthen and extend the crown lands, gradually transforming them into the nucleus of a modern state. This was the policy on which the medieval French monarchy had risen to a position of dominance in France; it was the policy that Frederick Barbarossa had pursued so promisingly in Germany. But it aroused the unremitting opposition of the great German princes who had no desire to see their own rights and territories eaten away by royal expansion and would much prefer to extend their own principalities at the expense of the crown.

The civil strife during Innocent's pontificate, the Italian involvements of Frederick II, and the Interregnum of 1254–73 gave the princes their opportunity, and by 1273 the crown lands were hopelessly shrunken and disorganized. Germany was now drifting irreversibly toward the loose confederation of principalities and the anemic elective monarchy which characterized its constitutional structure from the fourteenth to the later nineteenth century. The tragic failure of the medieval empire doomed Germany to 600 years of agonizing disunity—a heritage which may well have contributed to her catastrophic career in the twentieth century.

Italy, too, emerged from the struggles of the High Middle Ages hopelessly fragmented. The Papal States, straddling the peninsula, were torn with unrest and disaffection, and the papacy had trouble maintaining its authority over the turbulent inhabitants of Rome itself. North of the Papal States, Tuscany and Lombardy had become a chaos of totally independent warring city-states—Florence, Siena, Venice, Milan, and many others—whose rivalries would form the political backdrop of the Italian Renaissance.

The Kingdom of Sicily, established by the Normans and cherished by the Hohenstaufens, passed shortly after Frederick II's death to his illegitimate son, Manfred. The papacy, determined to rid Italy of Hohenstaufen rule, bent all its energies toward securing Manfred's downfall. At length it offered the Sicilian crown to Charles of Anjou, a younger brother of King Louis IX of France (St. Louis). The pope's intention was that the power of France be used to drive Manfred out of the Sicilian kingdom. Charles of Anjou—dour, cruel, and ambitious—defeated and killed Manfred in 1266 and established a new, French dynasty on the throne of the kingdom.

The inhabitants of the realm, particularly those on the island of Sicily, had become accustomed to Hohenstaufen rule and resented Charles of Anjou. They looked on his French soldiers as an army of occupation. When, on Easter Monday, 1282, a French soldier mishandled a young married woman on her way to evening vesper services in Palermo, he was struck down, and on all sides was raised the cry "Death to the French!" The incident resulted in a spontaneous uprising and a general massacre of the French which quickly spread throughout the island. When the French retaliated, the Sicilians offered the crown to Peter III of Aragon, Manfred's son-in-law, who claimed the Hohenstaufen inheritance and led an army to Sicily.

There ensued a long, bloody, indecisive struggle known by the romantic name, "The War of the Sicilian Vespers." For 20 years, Charles of Anjou and his successors, backed by the French monarchy and the papacy, fought against the Sicilians and Aragonese. In the end, southern Italy remained Angevin and its kings ruled from Naples, while Sicily passed under the control of the kings of Aragon. The dispute between France and Aragon over southern Italy and Sicily persisted for generations and was an important factor in the politics of early modern Europe.

The chaotic strife of the thirteenth century destroyed Sicilian prosperity. Once the wealthiest and most enlightened state in Italy, the kingdom of Sicily became backward, pauperized and divided—a victim of international politics and of the ruthless struggle between Church and state.

The Papacy After Innocent III

To judge by the disintegration of the Holy Roman Empire in the thirteenth century, one might conclude that the papacy had won an overwhelming victory. But the triumph was an empty one. For as popes like Innocent III, Gregory IX, and Innocent IV became increasingly involved in power politics, their spiritual role was more and more obscured. In the thirteenth century the papacy's international religious mission was being steadily subordinated to its local political interests. Slowly, almost imperceptibly, it was losing its hold on the hearts of European Christians. Papal excommunication, after several centuries of overuse—often for political purposes—was no longer the terrifying weapon it once had been. To call a crusade against Frederick II was doubtless an effective means of harassment, but the crusading ideal was debased in the process.

As the papacy became a great political power and a big business, it found itself in need of ever-increasing revenues. By the end of the thirteenth century the papal tax system was admirably efficient, with the result that the papacy acquired an unsavory reputation for greed. As one contemporary observer complained, the supreme pastor of Christendom was supposed to lead Christ's flock but not to fleece it. Ironically, the fiscal and political cast of the later medieval papacy came as a direct consequence of its earlier dream of becoming the spiritual dynamo of a reformed Christendom. Rising to prominence in the eleventh century upon the floodtide of the new popular piety, the papacy became in the twelfth and thirteenth centuries increasingly insensitive to the deeper spiritual aspirations of Christians as it became more and more absorbed in the problems of politics.

The papacy humbled the Empire only to be humbled itself by the rising power of the new centralized monarchies of northern Europe. By the end of the thirteenth century a new concept of royal sovereignty was in the air. The kings of England and France were finding it increasingly difficult to tolerate the existence of a semi-independent, highly privileged, internationally controlled Church within their realms. By endeavouring to bring these ecclesiastical "states within states" under royal control, the two monarchies encountered vigorous papal opposition. The issue of papal versus royal control of the Church was an old one, but the ancient controversy now took a new form. The growing monarchies of the late thirteenth century found themselves increasingly in need of money. This was particularly true after 1294 when England and France became locked in a series of costly wars. Both monarchies adopted the novel policy of systematically taxing the clergy of their realms, and Pope Boniface VIII (1294–1303) retaliated in 1296 with the papal bull *Clericis Laicos* that expressly forbade this practice. Once again, Church and state were at an impasse.

Boniface VIII was another lawyer-pope—a man of ability but not of genius—proud, aged, and intransigent, with a vision of absolute papal power that transcended even the notions of Innocent III, but with a fatal blindness to the momentous implications of the new centralized monarchies of late thirteenth-century Europe. His great weakness was his inability to bend his stupendous concepts of papal authority to the hard realities of contemporary European politics.

In King Philip the Fair* of France (1285–1314) Boniface had a powerful, ruthless antagonist. Philip ignored the papal bull prohibiting clerical taxation; he set his agents to work spreading scandalous rumors about the Pope's morals and exerted financial pressure on Rome by cutting off all papal taxes from his French realm. Boniface was obliged to submit for the moment, and Philip taxed his clergy unopposed. But a vast influx of pilgrims into Rome in the Jubilee year of 1300 restored the pope's confidence. He withdrew his concession to Philip the Fair on clerical taxation and in 1302 issued the famous bull *Unam Sanctam*, which asserted the doctrine of papal monarchy in uncompromising terms: ". . . We declare, announce, affirm, and define that for every human creature, to be subject to the Roman pontiff is absolutely necessary for salvation."

Philip the Fair now summoned an assembly of the realm and accused Boniface of every imaginable crime from murder to black magic. A small French military expedition crossed into Italy in 1303 and took Boniface prisoner at his palace at Anagni with the intention of bringing him to France for trial. Anagni, the antithesis of Canossa, symbolized the humiliation of the medieval papacy. The French plan failed—Boniface was freed by local townsmen a few days after his capture—but the proud old Pope died shortly thereafter, outraged and chagrined that armed Frenchmen should have dared to lay hands on his person.

The great age of the medieval papacy was now at an end. In 1305

*I.e., the handsome; see pp. 000–000.

CHRONOLOGY OF THE PAPAL-IMPERIAL CONFLICT

1039–1056: Reign of Henry III
1046: Henry III deposes 3 rival popes, inaugurates papal reform movement.
1049–1054: Pontificate of Leo IX
1056–1106: Reign of Henry IV
1059: Papal Election Decree
1073–1085: Pontificate of Gregory VII
1075: Gregory VII bans lay investiture.
1076: Gregory VII excommunicates and deposes Henry IV.
1077: Henry IV humbles himself at Canossa.
1080: Second excommunication and deposition of Henry IV.
1088–1099: Pontificate of Urban II
1106–1125: Reign of Henry V
1122: Concordat of Worms
1152–1190: Reign of Frederick I, "Barbarossa"
1154–1159: Pontificate of Hadrian IV
1155: Execution of Arnold of Brescia
1159–1181: Pontificate of Alexander III

1176: Lombards defeat Barbarossa at Legnano.
1180: Barbarossa defeats Duke Henry the Lion of Saxony.
1190–1197: Reign of Henry VI
1194: Henry VI becomes king of Sicily.
1198–1216: Pontificate of Innocent III
1211–1250: Reign of Frederick II
1214: Philip Augustus defeats Otto of Brunswick at Bouvines.
1215: Fourth Lateran Council
1227–1241: Pontificate of Gregory IX
1243–1254: Pontificate of Innocent IV
1245: Council of Lyons
1254–1273: Interregnum in Germany
1273–1291: Reign of Rudolph of Habsburg
1282–1302: War of the Sicilian Vespers
1294–1303: Pontificate of Boniface VIII
1302: Boniface VIII issues *Unam Sanctam*
1303: Boniface VIII humiliated at Anagni
1305–1314: Pontificate of Clement V. Papacy moves to Avignon.

the cardinals elected the Frenchman Clement V (1305–14), who pursued a policy of cautious subservience to the French throne. Clement submitted on the question of clerical taxation, repudiated *Unam Sanctam,* and abandoned faction-ridden Rome for a new papal capital at Avignon on the Rhone. Here the popes remained for the next several generations, their independence often limited by the power of the French monarchy and their spiritual prestige continuing to decline. The town of Avignon belonged to the papacy, not to the French Crown, yet France's enemies could never be confident of the Avignon papacy's political objectivity. The French kings were strong, and they were nearby.

It is easy to criticize the inflexibility of a Boniface VIII or the limpness of a Clement V, but the waning of papal authority in the later Middle Ages did not result primarily from personal shortcomings. Rather it stemmed from an ever-widening gulf between papal government and the spiritual hunger of ordinary Christians, combined with the hostility to Catholic internationalism on the part of increasingly powerful centralized states such as England and France. It would be grossly unfair to describe the high medieval papacy as "corrupt." Between 1050 and 1300 men of good intentions and high purposes sat on the papal throne. Not satisfied merely to chide the society of their day by innocuous moralizing from the sidelines, they plunged into the world and struggled to transform and sanctify it. Tragically, perhaps inevitably, they soiled their hands.

12

england and france

The Anglo-Norman Monarchy

While empire and papacy were engaged in their drawn-out struggle, England and France were evolving into centralized states. Strong monarchy came earlier to England than to France, yet in the long run it was the English who were the more successful in imposing constitutional limitations on the crown. French royal absolutism and English parliamentary monarchy are both rooted in the High Middle Ages.

More than that, the rise of effective royal law and administration was an early, crucial step in the evolution of the political orders that envelop us today. The secret of writing entertaining administrative history has yet to be discovered, but in the often tedious details of medieval governance in England and France we are witnessing the genesis of the modern state and all that it implies. These details can be overlooked only at the peril of missing one of the most fundamental medieval contributions to modern civilization.

The Anglo-Saxon period of English history came to an end when Duke William of Normandy won the English crown with his victory at Hastings in 1066. In the centuries that followed, England was more closely tied to the continent than before; her rulers dominated both England and significant portions of France. As kings of England they were masterless, but they held their French territories as vassals of the king of France. England's territorial involvement in France continued from 1066 until the mid-sixteenth century. It led to centuries of hostility and warfare between the two monarchies, but it was also a source of fiscal and cultural enrichment for England and its kings. Throughout much of the period between 1066 and 1204 England was merely one important component of a powerful trans-channel state which played a great role in twelfth-century politics. When the English monarchy lost its northern French dominions in 1204, it declined sharply in wealth and power and the kings of France became the supreme royal figures of Western Christendom in the thirteenth century.

The English kingdom that William the Conqueror won in 1066 was already centralized and well-governed by the standards of mid-eleventh-century Europe. Its kings had enjoyed the direct allegiance of all their subjects. Its army was subject only to the commands of the king or his representatives; private armies and private war were virtually unknown. A royal council of nobles and household officials known as the *witenagemot* advised the king on important matters and approved the succession of new kings. The chief officers in the royal household were gradually coming to assume important administrative responsibilities: issuing writs that carried royal commands to local officials in the countryside, administering the royal treasury, and performing other governmental functions. Although the pre-Conquest royal household was constantly on the move, traveling around England from one royal estate to another, the treasury had become fixed permanently at Winchester in Wessex.

England in 1066 had long been divided into regional units known as shires, each with its own shire court and administered by a royal officer called a "shire reeve", or sheriff. The sheriff presided over the shire court, the membership of which was drawn from important men of the district. The customs and procedures of the shire courts were rooted in the traditions of the locality rather than in royal mandates. In operation as in membership, the shire courts were local phenomena and are often described as folk courts. The sheriff, too, was usually a local figure whose sympathies were apt to be divided between his native shire and the king. The subtle interplay between local initiative and royal authority—a significant characteristic of Anglo-Saxon government—persisted over the post-conquest centuries to give medieval England a political balance lacking in many contemporary states.

The English shires were subdivided into smaller administrative units known as hundreds—deriving perhaps from the early days of the barbarian invasions when such a district might provide settlements for a hundred warriors. Each hundred had its own court which handled less important cases than those brought to the shire courts. Like the shire courts, the hundred courts were local in membership and legal custom yet were presided over by royal officials. By 1066 a number of hundreds had passed into the hands of private lords—lay or ecclesiastical—in which case the royal official was replaced by an official of the lord.

The sheriff was responsible for administering the unique Anglo-Saxon land tax, the danegeld, which varied somewhat in amount but in most instances provided the crown with about 10 pounds from each hundred. It was also the sheriff's task to assemble the shire's contingent when the king summoned the army—the *fyrd*, as it was then called. Our evidence suggests that by 1066 it had become customary for each hundred to provide about twenty armed men for the fyrd and to supply their sustenance during their period of duty.

Such were some of the more important institutions which William the Conqueror inherited when he won the English crown. He came to England not as an open aggressor but as a legitimate claimant to the throne, related (distantly) to the Anglo-Saxon royal family and designated—so he claimed—by King Edward the Confessor who died childless early in 1066. On the Confessor's death, the witenagemot had chosen an able warrior, Earl Harold Godwinson of Wessex, to succeed him, but William had always regarded Harold as a usurper, and when Harold was killed at Hastings and his army put to flight, William took the position that he was passing into his rightful inheritance. Although another five years were required to put down the last vestiges of English resistance, William was crowned king of England in London on Christmas Day, 1066, and turned at once to the problem of governing his new realm.

Taking up his role as Edward the Confessor's proper successor, William promised to preserve the laws and customs of Edward's day. Indeed, it was to his advantage to do so, since many of these customs were exceedingly beneficial to the monarchy. He maintained the danegeld, as well he might, continued to summon the fyrd whenever he needed it, perpetuated the folk courts of shire and hundred, and drew needed strength from the Anglo-Saxon custom of general allegiance to the Crown.

The Conqueror preserved much, but he also built energetically on the system that he inherited. The changes and additions that he introduced were products in part of the customs that he had known in Normandy, in part of his own creative imagination, and in part of his unique position as unquestioned master of a conquered land. If the government of Anglo-Saxon England was remarkably strong, the government of Norman England was far stronger, and its strength was, in some measure, a consequence of the political genius of William the Conqueror.

In the years immediately following the conquest, William divided much of England among the leading warriors of his victorious army, thereby introducing into the kingdom a new, knightly, French-speaking aristocracy. He established a feudal regime in England more-or-less on the Norman pattern, but more rationally organized and more directly subordinate to the royal will. Most English estates, both lay and ecclesiastical, were transformed into fiefs, held by crown vassals in return for a specified number of mounted knights and various other feudal services. He was careful to reserve about one sixth of the lands of England for his own royal demesne, so that he and his successors would never be mere nominal overlords like the early Capetians and the later Hohenstaufens.

The Crown vassals, or tenants-in-chief, in order to raise the numerous knights required by the monarchy, subdivided portions of their fiefs into smaller fiefs and granted them to knightly subvassals. In other words, the process of subinfeudation proceeded in much the way that it had centuries earlier on the continent, but more swiftly and systematically. As a natural byproduct of the establishment of feudalism in England, scores of castles were quickly erected across the land by the king and his barons.

Feudalism in England was by no means accompanied by political disintegration as it had been in Carolingian Frankland. With the resources of their vast royal domain on which to draw, the Norman kings of England were firmly established at the apex of the feudal pyramid and were generally successful in keeping their vassals under tight rein. Their authoritative position in the Anglo-Norman feudal structure owed much to the centralizing traditions of the Anglo-Saxon monarchy. The new barons esablished feudal courts, as had been their custom in Normandy, but alongside these baronial courts there persisted the far older courts of shire and hundred. The new feudal army could be an effective force, but when it proved inadequate or when barons rebelled against the monarchy, the Old English fyrd could be summoned or mercenaries could be hired.

Feudal particularism was attenuated by the Anglo-Saxon custom of general allegiance to the crown, which enabled the Norman kings to claim the direct and primary loyalty of every vassal and subvassal in the English feudal hierarchy. A knight's allegiance to his lord was now secondary to his allegiance to the crown. Private war between vassals was prohibited, and private castles could be built only by royal license. In brief, the new institution of feudalism was molded by the powerful Anglo-Saxon tradition of royal supremacy into something far more centralized—far less centrifugal—than the feudalism of the continent.

On the Conqueror's death, his kingdom passed in turn to his two sons, William II (1087–1100) and Henry I (1100–35). Both were strong, ruthless men, but Henry I was the abler of the two. A skillful general and brilliant legal and administrative innovator, Henry I rid England of rebellion and exploited the growing prosperity of his day by a policy of severe taxation. He was not a kindly man, but his was an age in which firmness and military skill were the chief requisites to successful rule and excessive geniality was a grave weakness. His great service to his English and Norman subjects was his pitiless enforcement of the peace.

The reigns of William the Conqueror and his sons witnessed a significant growth in royal administrative institutions. The unique survey of land holdings known as *Domesday Book*—the product of a comprehensive census of the realm undertaken by royal order in 1086—testifies to the administrative vigor of William the Conqueror. Between 1066 and 1135 the royal administration became steadily more elaborate and efficient. By the close of Henry I's reign, royal justices were traveling about England hearing cases in the shire courts, and thereby extending the king's jurisdiction far and wide across the land. The baronial courts and the ancient folk courts of the counties and hundreds continued to function. But the extension of royal jurisdiction under Henry I was the initial step in a long and significant process whereby folk justice and baronial justice were gradually overshadowed and finally superseded by the king's justice.

Administrative efficiency and royal centralization were the keynotes of Henry I's reign. Royal dues were collected systematically by local noblemen in the king's service—the sheriffs—who passed the money on to a remarkably effective new accounting agency known as the *exchequer*. A powerful royal bureaucracy was gradually coming into being. The growing efficiency of the exchequer and the expansion of royal justice were both motivated in part by the king's desire for larger revenues. For the more cases the royal justices handled, the more fines went into the royal coffers; the more closely the sheriffs were supervised, the less likely it was that royal taxes would stick to their fingers. The Norman kings discovered that strong government was good business.

The Anglo-Norman church was ornamented by two leaders of exceptional ability: Lanfranc (d. 1089) and St. Anselm (d. 1109). Both were theologians, both, in different ways, were deeply involved in the politics of their day, and both were Italians who migrated to the great Benedictine monastery of Bec in Normandy.

William the Conqueror drew Lanfranc from Normandy to become archbishop of Canterbury and primate of the English church. William and Lanfranc were contemporaries of Hildebrand and could not help but become involved in the raging controversy over ecclesiastical reform. The king and the archbishop were both sympathetic to reform, but neither was receptive to the Gregorian notions of an independent church and a new social order. William was more than willing to work toward the regeneration of the Anglo-Norman church, and Lanfranc supported him vigorously. But when Gregory VII demanded that William become his vassal, the Conqueror flatly refused: "I have not consented to pay fealty nor will I now, because I never promised it, nor do I find that my predecessors ever paid it to your predecessors."

Gregory VII, preoccupied with his struggle against the Holy Roman emperor, could not afford to alienate William, who was, after all, friendly toward reform. Accordingly, the specific issue of lay investiture did not emerge in England until after Gregory's death. It was raised by St. Anselm, who had followed Lanfranc to Bec and was chosen in 1093 to succeed him as archbishop of Canterbury. Lanfranc and William the Conqueror had worked in close cooperation with one another, but St. Anselm's relations with the Norman monarchy were turbulent. Already advanced in years when he reluctantly assumed the archbishopric, Anselm was the greatest theologian of his age and was, perhaps, the most profound philosopher that Western Christendom had produced since St. Augustine's time. He was also devoted to Gregorian notions of ecclesiastical independence, lay investiture, and papal monarchy.

These notions no Norman king could accept, and Anselm came into bitter conflict with both William II and Henry I. He spent much of his tenure as archbishop in exile, and it was not until 1107 that a compromise on the investiture issue was ratified between Henry, the papacy, and himself. As in the later Concordat of Worms, the agreement of 1107 prohibited lay investiture as such, but permitted the king to retain a certain control over important ecclesiastical appointments. Ecclesiastical tenants-in-chief were to continue their traditional practice of rendering homage to the king. More important than the settlement itself is the fact that Anselm died two years thereafter, and Henry, rid at last of his troublesome saint, dominated the English church through pressure and patronage. Anselm had won a point, but the Church remained generally subservient to the Norman monarchy.

Henry I's death in 1135 was followed by a period of unrest brought on by a disputed royal succession. Henry was survived by a daughter, Matilda, who was wed to Geoffrey Plantagenet, count of Anjou. Henry had arranged the marriage with the hope of healing the long rivalry between the two great powers of northern France: Normandy and Anjou. In the years just prior to Henry's death Matilda bore him two grandsons, the eldest of whom, Henry Plantagenet, would ultimately rule a vast territory including Anjou, Aquitaine, Normandy, and England. But when the old King died, Henry Plantagenet was still an infant, and the English crown was seized by Henry I's nephew, Stephen of Blois (1135–54). For two turbulent decades Stephen and Matilda struggled for control of England while the English barons, often shifting their allegiance from one side to the other, threw up unlicensed castles and usurped royal rights. English churchmen and commoners, tormented by the endemic warfare of the period, looked back longingly toward the peaceful days of Henry I.

Henry II 1154–1189

During Stephen's troubled reign Henry Plantagenet grew to vigorous manhood and established control over Anjou and Normandy. His territories were extended still further by his marriage to Eleanor, heiress of the large, southern French duchy of Aquitaine. And at King Stephen's death in 1154 Henry peacefully acquired the throne and became King Henry II of England (1154–89). He now held sway over an immense constellation of territories north and south of the English Channel, which has been called the Angevin Empire. On the map, the Angevin Empire dwarfs the modest territory controlled by the King of France. But Henry II, and his sons who succeeded him, had difficulty in keeping order throughout their vast, diverse territories. The Angevin Empire was a source of great wealth, power, and prestige to the English monarchy, but it was also a burden.

Henry was an energetic, brilliant, exuberant man—short, burly, and red-headed. Named after his grandfather, he was far more flamboyant than Henry I yet ruled in his imperious tradition and consciously imitated him. In many respects he was a creature of his age —a product of the great intellectual and cultural outburst of twelfth-century Europe. He was a literate monarch who consorted with scholars, encouraged the growth of towns, and presided over an age of economic boom. A chaos of feverish activity pervaded his court, which was constantly on the move and, in the opinion of one court scholar, was "a perfect portrait of Hell."

Henry pursued the interdependent goals of preserving the Angevin Empire, strengthening royal authority, and increasing his revenues. He began his reign by ordering the destruction of unlicensed baronial castles that had been thrown up during the previous anarchic period and was cautious thereafter in permitting new private castles to be built. At once he began to recover the royal privileges that had been eroding during Stephen's reign and, in some cases, to expand them considerably. During the 35 years of his rule the royal administration grew steadily in complexity and effectiveness. The maturity of Henry's exchequer is illustrated not only by a series of annual financial accounts—known as *Pipe Rolls*—but also by a comprehensive, detailed treatise on the exchequer's organization and methods—the *Dialogue of the Exchequer*—written by one of the king's financial officers. The royal secretarial office—the chancery— was similarly increasing in efficiency and scope. Indeed, the entire royal administration was growing more specialized, more professional, and more self-conscious. Separate administrative departments were evolving, and public records became fuller and more extensive. Many

THE ANGEVIN EMPIRE, 1154

WALES

ENGLAND

London

North Sea

Rhine R.

English Channel

FLANDERS

Bruges

HOLY ROMAN EMPIRE

Amiens

Rouen

Rheims

NORMANDY

St.Denis

Paris

CHAMPAGNE

St.Michel

BRITTANY

MAINE

Orleans

Seine R.

ANJOU

TOURAINE

Tours

BERRY

BURGUNDY

POITOU

Poitiers

Cluny

LA MARCHE

Bay of

Biscay

DUCHY OF AQUITAINE

Clermont

AUVERGNE

Lyons

Bordeaux

QUERCY

Rhone R.

GASCONY

TOULOUSE

Avignon

PROVENCE

Toulouse

Montpellier

NAVARRE

Ebro R.

ARAGON

Angevin Empire in 1154

Capetian Domain

Scale of Miles
50   100   150   200

233

Englishmen were delighted at the return of peace and order; others were uneasy over the steady rise of "Big Government."

Throughout the twelfth century, commerce was becoming ever more vigorous and the circulation of money was rapidly increasing. Under the pressure of royal ambition and the growing money economy, the older feudal relationship of service in return for land was giving way to wage service. By the time of Henry II it had become commonplace for feudal tenants-in-chief to pay scutage to the crown in lieu of their military-service obligation. Dues from the royal demesne estates were being collected in coin rather than in kind, and royal troops, servants, and administrators customarily served for wages. These trends can be traced back to the reign of Henry I and beyond, but under Henry II they were accelerating. The feudal hierarchy remained powerful, but feudal obligations were being translated into fiscal terms. Both the economy and the administration were steadily increasing in complexity and sophistication.

Of necessity, the authority of the king and the efficiency of his central administrative system depended upon an effective local government and the maintenance of strong bonds between court and countryside. The two were linked under Henry II, as under Henry I, by the activities of sheriffs and itinerant royal justices. Henry II broadened the scope of these itinerant justices and increased their organizational efficiency, thereby making royal justice more accessible to ordinary Englishmen than ever before. Itinerant royal justices now made periodic circuits of the countryside, bringing the king's law to considerable numbers of Englishmen who had previously been untouched by it.

The sheriffs were bound to enforce the king's orders which continued to issue from the chancery in the form of writs. It was also the sheriff's duty to collect royal dues and fines and to render a periodic accounting of them to the exchequer. Thus, the sheriffs were subordinated to the central administration and subjected to royal control. Nevertheless, most sheriffs were powerful local nobles with wide estates of their own and were by no means completely dependent on the royal favor. Many of them abused their power and displayed a degree of independence such as to challenge the king's authority. In 1170 Henry II ordered a searching investigation of his sheriffs' behavior—the Inquest of Sheriffs—and subsequently replaced most of them with new and more tractable men.

Henry II has been called the father of the English common law. Like his predecessors, he favored the extension of royal jurisdiction partly for its financial rewards to the crown, and in his quest for ever-greater judicial revenues he was able to advance the powers of the royal courts well beyond their former limits. His *Assize of Clarendon* of 1166 widened the scope of royal justice to include the indictment and prosecution of local criminals. It provided that regional inquest juries should meet periodically under royal auspices to identify and denounce notorious neighborhood criminals whose guilt or innocense was then to be determined by the ordeal of cold water.* The inquest jury was more akin to the modern grand jury than to the modern trial jury, for its duty was to investigate and indict rather than to judge guilt. Inquest juries had been used before: they were assembled under William the Conqueror to provide information for the Domesday survey; there is a reference to one such jury in the records of late Anglo-Saxon times, and bodies of a similar nature were employed in the administration of Carolingian Frankland. Never before, however, had they been used in such a systematic fashion.

Henry also extended royal jurisdiction over the vast, turbulent field of land disputes, employing local juries to determine the rightful possessors or heirs of disputed estates. The most important of Henry's "possessory assizes," the *Assize of Novel Disseisin*, was designed to curb local violence by providing a legal action against forcible dispossession of an estate. Regardless of whether the plaintiff had a just claim to the estate in question, if he was driven from his land by force he was entitled to purchase a royal writ commanding the sheriff to assemble a jury to determine the facts of the case. If the jury concluded that the plaintiff had indeed been violently dispossessed, the sheriff, acting with full royal authority, would see that the estate in dispute was restored to the plaintiff. Another of the new legal actions provide by Henry II—the *Grand Assize*—used a similar procedure of purchased writ and jury to determine not whether the plaintiff had been dispossessed but whether he had, in fact, the best title to the land in question.

These and similar assizes carried the king's justice into an area that had once been dominated by the feudal courts which usually settled questions of land possession by the crude procedure of trial

* See p. 20.

by combat. Previous kings had intervened in territorial quarrels, but never in such a consistent, systematic way. Now, Englishmen learned to turn to Henry's courts for quick, modern, rational justice. Feudal law, with its archaic and time-consuming procedures, lost out in the competition. Gradually the patchwork of local laws and customs which had so long divided England was giving way to a uniform royal law—a *common law* by which all Englishmen were governed. The *political* unification of the tenth century was consummated by a process of *legal* unification that advanced significantly under the Angevin kings.

Predictably, Henry II also sought to expand royal justice at the expense of the ecclesiastical courts. A separate system of ecclesiastical jurisdiction had long been in effect, distinct from the various secular courts—local, feudal, and royal. The ecclesiastical court system can be regarded as one manifestation of the complex government of the international Church, which—as it grew steadily more elaborate—came increasingly into conflict with the proliferating governmental structures of England and other secular states. The two governments, royal and ecclesiastical, were both expanding in the twelfth century, and conflicts between them were bound to occur. The first great conflict centered on Anselm, the second on Becket.

In 1162 Henry sought to bring the English church under strict royal control by appointing to the archbishopric of Canterbury his chancellor and good friend, Thomas Becket. But in raising Becket to the primacy, Henry had misjudged his man. As chancellor, Becket was a devoted royal servant, but as archbishop of Canterbury he became a fervent defender of ecclesiastical independence and an implacable enemy of the king. Henry and Becket became locked in a furious quarrel over the issue of royal control of the English church. In 1164 Henry issued a list of pro-royal provisions relating to church-state relations known as the *Constitutions of Clarendon,* which, among other things, prohibited appeals to Rome without royal license and established a degree of royal control over the Church courts. Henry maintained that the Constitutions of Clarendon represented ancient custom; Becket regarded them as novel encroachments on the freedom of the Church.

At the heart of the quarrel was the issue of whether churchmen accused of crimes should be subject to royal jurisdiction after being found guilty and punished by Church courts. The king complained that "criminous clerks" were often given absurdly light punishments by the ecclesistical tribunals. A murderer, for example, might simply be defrocked and released, and the Constitutions of Clarendon provided that such a person should then be remanded to a royal court for punishment. Becket replied that no man should be put in double jeopardy. In essence, Henry was challenging the competence of an agency of the international Church, and Becket, as primate of England, felt bound to defend the ecclesiastical system against royal encroachment. Two worlds were in collision.

Henry turned on his archbishop, accusing him of various crimes against the kingdom, and Becket, denying the king's right to try an archbishop, fled England to seek papal support. Pope Alexander III, who was in the midst of his struggle with Frederick Barbarossa, could ill afford to alienate Henry; yet neither could he turn against such an ardent ecclesiastical champion as Becket. The great lawyer-pope was forced to equivocate—to encourage Becket without breaking with Henry—until at length in 1170, the king and his archbishop agreed to a truce. Most of the outstanding issues between them remained unsettled, but Becket was permitted to return peacefully to England and resume the archbishopric. At once, however, the two antagonists had another falling out. Becket excommunicated a number of Henry's supporters; the king flew into a rage, and four overenthusiastic knights of the royal household went to Canterbury cathedral and murdered Becket at the high altar.

This dramatic crime made a deep impact on the age. Becket was regarded as a martyr; miracles were alleged to have occurred at his tomb, and he was quickly canonized. For the remainder of the Middle Ages, Canterbury was a major pilgrimage center and the cult of St. Thomas enjoyed immense popularity. Henry, who had not ordered the killing but whose anger had prompted it, suffered acute embarrassment. He was obliged to do penance by walking barefoot through the streets of Canterbury and submitting to a flogging by the Canterbury monks. But his campaign against the ecclesiastical courts was delayed only momentarily. Although forced to give in on specific matters such as royal jurisdiction over criminous clerks and unlicensed appeals to Rome, he obtained through indirection and maneuvering what he had failed to get through open conflict. He succeeded generally in arranging the appointment to high ecclesiastical offices of men friendly to the crown, and by the end of his reign royal justice had made significant inroads on the authority of the Church courts. The monarchy had succeeded in bringing the Enlish Church under tight rein. Here, as elsewhere, Henry was remarkably successful in steering England toward administrative and legal centralization.

Throughout his reign Henry divided his time between England and the other territories of the Angevin Empire. Strictly speaking, these territories did not constitute an "empire" in any real sense of the word. They were in fact a multitude of individual political units, each with its own customs and its own administrative structure, bound together by their allegiance to Henry Plantagenet. The French monarchy did what it could to break up this threatening configuration, encouraging rebellions on the part of Henry's dutiless sons and his estranged wife, Eleanor of Aquitaine. Henry put down the rebellions one by one, relegated Eleanor to comfortable imprisonment, and sought to placate his sons. It did little good. The rebellions persisted, and as Henry neared death in 1189 his two surviving sons, Richard and John, were both in arms against him. In the end the aged monarch was outmaneuvered and defeated by his offspring and their French allies; he died with the statement, "Shame, shame on a conquered king."

Richard and John

Although Henry's final days were saddened by defeat, the Angevin Empire remained intact, passing into the capable hands of his eldest surviving son, Richard I, "the Lion-Hearted" (1189–99). This illustrious warrior-king devoted himself chiefly to two great projects: defending the Angevin Empire against the French crown and crusading against the Muslims. He was a superb general who not only won renown on the Third Crusade but also foiled every attempt of the French monarchy to reduce his continental territories. He was far less impressive as an administrator and, indeed, spent less than six months of his ten-year reign in England. During his protracted absences, the administrative system of Henry II proved its worth; it governed England more or less satisfactorily for ten kingless years. Meanwhile Richard was engaging in his adventures in the Holy Land, and campaigning along the frontiers of the Angevin Empire against King Philip Augustus of France.

The fortunes of the Angevin Empire veered sharply with the accession of King John (1199–1216), Richard the Lion-Hearted's younger brother. John is an enigmatic figure—brilliant in certain respects, a master of administrative detail, but a suspicious and unscrupulous leader. He trusted nobody, and nobody trusted him. Consequently his subjects never supported him more than half-heartedly in moments of crisis.

In Philip Augustus of France (1180–1223) John had a shrewd, unremitting antagonist. Philip took full advantage of his position as feudal lord over John's continental possessions. In 1202 John was summoned to the French royal court to answer charges brought against him by one of his own Aquitainian vassals. When John refused to come, Philip Augustus declared his French lands forfeited and proceeded to invade Normandy. The duchy quickly fell into Philip's hands (1203–4) as John's demoralized vassals defected, one after another, and John himself fled to England. In the chaos that followed, Philip Augustus was able to wrest Anjou and most of the remaining continental possessions of the Angevin Empire from John's control. Only portions of distant Aquitaine retained their connection with the English monarchy. King John had sustained a monstrous political and military disaster.

For the next ten years John nursed his wounds and wove a dextrous web of alliances against King Philip in hopes of regaining his lost possessions. His careful plans were shattered by Philip's decisive victory over John's Flemish and German allies at the battle of Bouvines in 1214.[*] With Bouvines went John's last hope of reviving the Angevin Empire.

In the decade between the loss of Normandy and the catastrophe at Bouvines, John engaged in a bitter quarrel with Pope Innocent III. At stake was royal control over the appointment of an archbishop of Canterbury. According to canon law and established custom, a bishop or archbishop was to be elected by the canons of the cathedral chapter. The Investiture Controversy notwithstanding, such elections were commonly controlled by the king who would overawe the canons into electing the candidate of his choice. Canterbury differed from most other cathedrals in that a body of monks performed the functions that were ordinarily the responsibility of cathedral canons;

* See p. 216.

it was the monks who customarily elected the archbishop, but they, no less than canons, were usually susceptible to royal control. In 1205, however, the monks of Canterbury declined to wait for royal instructions and elected one of their own number as archbishop, sending a delegation to Rome to obtain Pope Innocent's confirmation. Going personally to Canterbury, John forced the monks to hold another election and to select his own nominee. In the course of events several delegations went from England to Rome, and Innocent, keenly interested in the enforcement of proper canonical procedures, quashed both elections. He ordered those Canterbury monks who were then in Rome—quite a number by this time—to hold still another election, and under papal influence they elected Stephen Langton, a learned Englishman who had spent some years as a scholar in Paris.

Furious that his own candidate should have been passed over, John refused to confirm Langton's appointment or to admit him into England. For the next six years, 1207–13, John held to his position while Innocent used every weapon at his disposal to make the king submit. England was laid under interdict; John retaliated by confiscating all ecclesiastical revenues. John was excommunicated, and Innocent even threatened to depose him. This threat, together with the danger of a projected French invasion of England with full papal backing, forced John to submit at last. In 1213 he accepted Stephen Langton as archbishop of Canterbury. Going still further, John conceded to Innocent the overlordship of England that Gregory VII had fruitlessly demanded of William the Conqueror long before. John agreed to hold his kingdom thenceforth as a papal fief and render a substantial annual tribute to Rome. Having lost the struggle over the archbishopric, John was anxious to transform his papal antagonist into a devoted friend, and his concession of the overlordship had precisely that effect.

John had won the papal friendship, but many of his own barons were regarding him with increasing hatred and contempt. The Bouvines disaster of 1214, coming at the end of a long series of expensive and humiliating diplomatic failures, destroyed what remained of John's royal prestige. It paved the way for the English baronial uprising that culminated on the field of Runnymede in 1215 with the signing of *Magna Carta*.

John's barons had good reason to oppose him. He had pushed the centralizing tendencies of his Norman and Angevin predecessors to new limits and was taxing his subjects as they had never been taxed before. The baronial reaction of 1215 was both a protest against John and an effort to reverse the trend toward royal authoritarianism of the past 150 years.

Magna Carta has been interpreted in contradictory ways: as the fountainhead of English constitutional monarchy, and as a reactionary, backward-looking document designed to favor the particularistic feudal aristocracy at the expense of the enlightened Angevin monarchy. In reality, Magna Carta was both feudal and constitutional, both backward-looking and forward-looking. Its more important clauses were designed to keep the king within the bounds of popular tradition and feudal custom. Royal taxes not sanctioned by custom, for example, were to be levied only by the common council of the kingdom. But implicit in the traditional feudal doctrine that the lord had to respect the rights of his vassals—and in the age-old Germanic notion that the monarch had to adhere to the customs of his people —was the constitutional principle of government under the law. In striving to make King John a good feudal lord, the barons in 1215 were moving uncertainly, perhaps unconsciously, toward constitutional monarchy. For this was the crucial moment when the English nobles were just beginning to represent a national viewpoint. In the past, baronial opposition to royal autocracy had taken the form of a selfish insistence on local aristocratic autonomy. But one finds in Magna Carta the notion that the king is bound by traditional legal limitations in his relations with all classes of free Englishmen. It would be misleading to lay too much stress on the underlying principles of this intensely practical document which was concerned primarily with correcting specific royal abuses of feudal custom. But it would be equally misleading to ignore the implication in Magna Carta derived from the feudal ideology, of an over-arching body of law which limited and circumscribed royal authority.

The chief constitutional problem in the years following Magna Carta was the question of how an unwilling king might be forced to stay within the bounds of law. A series of royal promises was obviously insufficient to control an ambitious monarch who held all the machinery of the central government in his grasp. Magna Carta itself relied on a committee of 25 barons who were empowered, should the king violate the charter, to call upon the English people "to distrain and distress him in every possible way." Thus, the monarch was to be restrained by the sanction of baronial and popular rebellion—a desperate and unwieldy weapon against an unscrupulous king.

John himself seems to have had no intention of carrying out his promises. He repudiated Magna Carta at the first opportunity, with the full backing of his papal overlord. The result was a full-scale revolt that ended only with John's death in 1216.

The crown now passed, without objection, to John's nine-year-old-son, Henry III (1216–72) who was supervised during his minority by a baronial council. In the decades that followed, Magna Carta was reissued many times, but the great task of the new age was to create political institutions capable of limiting royal autocracy by some means short of rebellion. The ultimate solution to this problem was found in Parliament.

Henry III

Henry III was a petulant, erratic monarch: pious without being holy, bookish without being wise. Surrounding himself with foreign favorites and intoxicated by grandiose, impractical foreign projects, he ignored the advice of his barons and gradually lost their confidence.

Ever since its beginning, the English monarchy had customarily arrived at important decisions of policy with the advice of a royal council of nobles, prelates, and officials. In Anglo-Saxon times, this council was called the witenagemot; after 1066 it was known as the *curia regis*. Its composition had always been vague, and it had never possessed anything resembling a veto power over royal decisions. But many Englishmen, particularly among the upper classes, put much importance in the fact that royal policies were framed in consultation with the lay and ecclesiastical magnates.

Traditionally, English royal councils were of two types. Ordinary royal business was conducted in a small council consisting of the king's household officials and whatever barons happened to be at court at the time. But in moments of crisis, or when some important decision was pending, the kings supplemented their normal coterie of advisers by summoning the important noblemen and churchmen of the realm to meet as a great council. It was this great baronial council that eventually evolved into Parliament.

A key factor in the evolution from great council to Parliament was the trend in the thirteenth century toward including representatives of the county gentry and the townsmen alongside the great barons and prelates. This development resulted from the royal policy, particularly evident after Magna Carta, of summoning the great council for the purpose of obtaining approval for some uncustomary tax. As wealth gradually seeped downward into the sub-baronial classes, the king found it expedient to obtain the consent of these lesser orders to new royal taxes by summoning their representatives to the great council.

The vigorous baronial opposition to Henry III arose from the fact that he summoned the great council not for the purpose of consulting his magnates on policy matters but chiefly for the purpose of obtaining their consent to new taxes. The barons resented being asked to finance chimerical foreign schemes in which they had not been consulted and of which they disapproved. They might well have chosen as their motto, "No taxation without consultation." They responded to Henry's fiscal demands with increasing reluctance, until at last in 1258 the monarch's soaring debts brought on a financial crisis of major proportions. In order to obtain desperately needed financial support from his barons, Henry submitted to a set of baronial limitations on royal power known as the *Provisions of Oxford.*

These Provisions went far beyond Magna Carta in providing machinery to force the king to govern according to good custom and in consultation with his magnates. The great council was to be summoned at least three times a year and was to include, along with its usual membership, 12 men "elected" by the "community"—in other words, chosen by the barons. These 12 were empowered to speak for the magnates in the great council, so that even if heavily outnumbered their authority would be great. The Provisions of Oxford also established a *Council of Fifteen,* chiefly baronial in composition, which shared with the king control over the royal administration. Specifically the council was given authority over the exchequer and was empowered to appoint the chancellor and other high officers of state.

The Provisions of Oxford proved premature, and the governmental system that they established turned out to be unworkable because of baronial factionalism. Their importance lies in the fact that they disclose clearly the attitude of many mid-thirteenth-century barons toward the royal administration. These magnates had no thought of abolishing the enlightened administrative and legal achievements of the past two centuries or of weakening the central government. Their interests were national rather than provincial, and they sought to exert a degree of control over the royal administration rather than dismantle it. Most of them acted as they did, not on the basis of theoretical abstractions, but because they thought it necessary to curb an incompetent, arbitrary, spendthrift king.

With the failure of the Provisions, Henry resumed exclusive control over his government and returned to the arbitrary policies that his barons found so distasteful. At length, baronial discontent exploded into open rebellion. The barons, led by Simon de Montfort, defeated the royal army at Lewes in 1264 and captured Henry himself. For the next 15 months Simon ruled England in the king's name, sharing authority with two baronial colleagues and a committee of magnates similar to that of the Provisions of Oxford. The rule of Simon de Montfort and his committee was augmented periodically by meetings of the great council—now commonly called "parliaments." Simon's government was a product of the same philosophy that underlay the Provisions of Oxford, and like the government of the Provisions, it was weakened and ultimately brought to ruin by baronial factionalism.

In 1265 the monarchy rallied under the leadership of Henry's talented son, Edward. A baronial army was defeated at Evesham, and Simon de Montfort's rebellion faltered and died.

The Evolution of Parliament

But the effect of the uprising proved to be lasting. England had undergone an interesting experience in baronial government and, far more important, a significant step had been taken in the development of Parliament. Earlier in 1265 Simon de Montfort had summoned a great council—a parliament—which included for the first time all three of the classes that were to characterize the parliaments of the later Middle Ages. Simon de Montfort's parliament included, in addition to the barons, two knights from every shire and two burghers from every town. Simon's chief motive in summoning this parliament was probably to broaden the base of his rebellion, but in later years parliaments were summoned for many purposes: to sit as a high court of law, to advise the king on important matters of policy, to declare their support in moments of crisis, and to give their consent to the ever-increasing royal taxes.

The English Parliament was built on a sturdy foundation of local government, and all three of the major parliamentary orders—barons, burghers, and shire knights—brought with them a wealth of local political experience. The burghers in Parliament were usually veterans of town government. The shire knights had long been involved in the administration of the counties and the county courts. Intermediate between the baronial nobility and the peasantry, these men constituted a separate class—a country gentry—rooted to their shires and their ancestral estates, experienced in local government, and well suited to represent their counties in Parliament.

In 1272 Henry III was succeeded by his son, Edward I (1272–1307), a far wiser man than his father. Edward I was a monarch of strong will and independence, but he had the sagacity to take the barons into his confidence and he was successful by and large in winning their support. Although he, like his father, regarded parliaments as means of winning approval for new taxes, he used them for many other purposes as well. He summoned parliaments often and experimented endlessly in their composition. In the later years of his reign shire knights and townsmen were frequently included. It was not until the fourteenth century, however, that the knights and burghers began meeting separately from the barons thereby giving birth to the great parliamentary division into Lords and Commons.

As the thirteenth century closed, the actual powers of parliaments remained vague and their composition was still fluid. At best, they might bargain discreetly with the king for concessions in return for financial aid. Still, a beginning had been made. The deep-rooted medieval concept of limited monarchy had given rise to an institution that would develop over the centuries into a keystone of representative government. There was nothing remotely democratic about the parliaments that Edward I summoned. He regarded them as instruments of royal policy and used them to aid and strengthen the monarchy rather than limit it. Yet ultimately, Parliament was to be the crucial institutional bridge between medieval feudalism and modern democracy.

Edward I

The reign of Edward I witnessed the culmination of many trends in English law and administration that had been developing throughout the High Middle Ages. Edward was a great systematizer, and in his hands the royal administrative structure and the common law acquired the shape and coherence that they were to retain in future centuries.

The four chief agencies of royal government under Edward I were the chancery, the exchequer, the council, and the household. Chancery and exchequer were by now both permanently established at Westminster. The chancery remained the royal secretarial office, and its chief officer, the chancellor, was the custodian of the great seal by which royal documents were authenticated. A staff of professional chancery clerks prepared the numerous letters and charters by which the king made his will known, and preserved copies of them for future reference. The exchequer, headed by a royal official known as the treasurer, continued to serve, as it had for nearly two centuries, as the king's accounting agency. By now it supervised the accounts not only of sheriffs but of many other local officials who were charged with collecting royal revenues.

Unlike the chancery and exchequer, the council and household accompanied the king on his endless travels. Since meetings of the great council were coming more and more to be referred to as "parliaments," the "council" in Edward's government is to be identified with the earlier "small council." It was a permanent group of varied and changing membership, consisting of judges, administrators, and magnates, who advised the king on routine matters. In the Provisions of Oxford the barons had endeavored to dominate the council, but in Edward's reign it was firmly under royal control. The household was a royal government in miniature, with its own writing clerks supervised by the keeper of the privy seal and its own financial office known as the "wardrobe." By means of his household administration the king could govern on the move, without the necessity of routing all his business through Westminster.

Royal government in the countryside continued to depend on sheriffs and itinerant justices, whose duties and responsibilities were defined and regularized as never before. But now other royal servants were working alongside them: coroners, who were charged with investigating felonies; keepers of the peace, whose duty it was to apprehend criminals; assessors, tax collectors, customs officials, and others—local men, for the most part, who were responsible for serving the king in their native districts.

The royal legal system was also taking permanent form. Cases of singular importance were brought before the king himself, sitting in Parliament or surrounded by his council. Less important cases were handled by the king's itinerant justices or by one of the three royal courts sitting at Westminster. These three were the courts of the *king's bench*, which heard cases of particular royal concern; *exchequer*, which, besides its fiscal responsibilities, heard cases touching on the royal revenues; and *common pleas*, which had jurisdiction over most remaining types of cases. These courts were all staffed with highly trained professionals—lawyers or, in the case of the exchequer, experienced accountants. By Edward I's day the royal judicial system had come of age.

Like his predecessors, Edward worked toward the expansion of royal justice over private justice. From the beginning of his reign he issued numerous writs of *quo warranto* (by what warrant?), which obliged noblemen who claimed the right of private legal jurisdiction to prove their claims. They might do so either by producing royal charters granting such jurisdictional privileges or by demonstrating that they and their predecessors had exercised such rights since before the reign of Richard I. In 1290 Edward issued the statute of *Quo Warranto*, which quashed all private jurisdictions unsupported by royal charter, no matter how ancient such jurisdiction might be. By means of these policies, Edward eliminated a good number of private jurisdictional franchises, and, perhaps more important still, made it clear that all remaining private franchises were exercised through royal license and royal suffrance. The absolute supremacy of royal jurisdiction was at last established beyond question.

Edward's reign was marked by the appearance of a great many royal statutes—issued by the king in Parliament—which elaborated and systematized royal administrative and legal procedures in many different ways. Law had formerly been regarded as a matter of custom; the king might interpret or clarify it, but he seldom made a new law. As ancient Germanic tradition had it, the king was bound by the customs of his people. It is not always possible to distinguish between the act of clarifying or elaborating old law and making new law, and many of Edward's predecessors had been lawmakers in fact if not in theory. But in the later thirteenth century the English government began to legislate on a larger scale than before. Even in Edward's day original legislation was such a solemn affair that the king issued his statutes only with the approval of the "community of the realm" as expressed in his parliaments. Edward dominated his parliaments, and his statutes were unquestionably products of the royal initiative, but it is nevertheless significant that the role of parliaments in the making of law was clearly conceded. In the course of the fourteenth century, Parliament employed its power of approving royal taxes to win control of the legislative process itself.

Thus, Edward I completed the work of his predecessors in creating an effective and complex royal administrative system, bringing feudal justice under royal control, and building a comprehensive body of common law. More than that, he solidified the concept of original legislation and nurtured the developing institution of Parliament, setting into motion forces that would have an immense impact on England's future.

Edward was also a skillful and ambitious warrior. He brought to a decisive end the centuries-long military struggle along the Welsh frontier by conquering Wales altogether in a whirlwind campaign of 1282–83. He granted his eldest son the title "Prince of Wales," which male heirs-apparent to the English throne have held ever since. By a ruthless exploitation of the traditional English overlordship over the Scottish realm he came very near to conquering Scotland and was foiled only by the dogged determination of the Scottish hero-king, Robert Bruce. His war with Philip IV of France was expensive and inconclusive, but it did succeed in preserving English lordship over Gascony which had been seriously threatened. These wars gradually exhausted the royal treasury, and during the latter portion of his reign, Edward was faced with growing baronial and popular opposition to his expensive policies. But the king was able to ride out this opposition by making timely concessions: reissuing Magna Carta and recognizing Parliament's right to approve all extraordinary taxation. At his death in 1307, Edward left behind him a realm exhausted by his prodigious foreign and domestic activities but firmly under his control. Edward's England was still, in spirit, a feudal kingdom rather than a modern nation, but feudalism was waning and the initial steps toward nationhood had been taken.

The most significant of all Edward's contributions was, in the long run, his policy of developing Parliament into an integral organ of government. It is ironic, therefore, that King Edward looked upon Parliament as a source of strength to the crown and a useful instrument for raising the necessary revenues to support his far-flung projects. He would have been appalled to learn that his royal descendants would one day be figurehead kings and that Parliament was destined to rule England.

The Early Capetians

When William of Normandy conquered England in 1066, the French monarchy exerted unsteady control over a modest territory around Paris and Orleans known as the Île de France and was virtually powerless in the lands beyond. To be sure, the French kings had as their vassals great feudal magnates such as the dukes of Normandy and Aquitaine and the counts of Anjou, Flanders, and Champagne, but vassalage was a slender bond when the king lacked the power to enforce his lordship. In theory the anointed king of the French was a mighty figure—with his priestly charisma, with the sovereign power traditionally associated with royalty, and with the supreme feudal overlordship. But in grim reality he was impotent to control his great vassals and unable to keep order in the Île de France itself.

Since 987 the French crown had been held by the Capetian dynasty. The achievement of the Capetians in the first century or so of their rule was modest enough. Their one triumph was their success in keeping the crown within their own family. The Capetians had gained the throne originally by virtue of being elected by the magnates of the realm, but from the first they sought to purge the monarchy of its elective character and to make it hereditary. This they accomplished by managing to produce male heirs at the right moment and by arranging for the new heir to be crowned before the old king died. They may have been aided by the fact that the crown was not a sufficiently alluring prize to attract powerful usurpers.

In the early twelfth century the Capetians remained no stronger than several of their own vassals. While vassal states such as Normandy and Anjou were becoming increasingly centralized, the Capetian Île de France was still ridden with fiercely insubordinate barons. If the Capetians were to realize the potential of their royal title they had three great tasks before them: (1) to master and pacify the Île de France; (2) to expand their political and economic base by bringing additional territories under direct royal authority; and (3) to make their lordship over the great vassals real rather than merely theoretical.

During the twelfth and thirteenth centuries a series of able Capetian kings pursued and achieved these goals. Their success was so complete that by the opening of the fourteenth century the Capetians controlled all France, either directly or indirectly, and had developed an efficient, sophisticated royal bureaucracy. They followed no hard and fast formula. Rather their success depended on a combination of luck and ingenuity—on their clever exploitation of the powers which, potentially, they had always possessed as kings and feudal overlords. They were surprisingly successful in avoiding the family squabbles that had at times paralyzed Germany and England. Unlike the German monarchs, they maintained comparatively good relations with the papacy. They had the enormous good fortune of an unbroken sequence of direct male heirs from 987 to 1328. Above all, they seldom overreached themselves: they avoided grandiose schemes and spectacular strokes of policy, preferring instead to pursue modest, realistic goals. They extended their power gradually and cautiously by favorable marriages, by confiscating the fiefs of vassals who died without heirs, and by dispossessing vassals who violated their feudal obligation toward the monarchy. Yet the majority of the Capetians had no desire to absorb the territories of all their vassals. Rather they sought to build a kingdom with a substantial core of royal domain lands surrounded by the fiefs of loyal, obedient magnates.

Philip I, Louis VI, and Louis VII

The first Capetian to work seriously toward the consolidation of royal control in the Île de France was King Philip I (1060–1108), a bloated, repugnant man who grasped the essential fact that the Capetian monarchy had to make its home base secure before turning to loftier goals. Philip's realistic policy was pursued far more vigorously by his son, Louis VI, "the Fat" (1108–37). Year after year, Louis the Fat battled the lords of the Île de France, besieged their castles one after another, and at last reduced them to obedience. At his death in

1137 the Île de France was relatively orderly and prosperous, and the French monarchy was stronger than it had been since Carolingian times.

Louis the Fat received invaluable assistance in the later part of his reign from Abbot Suger of the great royal monastery of Saint-Denis. This talented statesman served as chief royal adviser from 1130 to 1151 and labored hard and effectively to extend the king's sway, to systematize the royal administration, and, incidentally, to augment the wealth and prestige of Saint-Denis.

Suger provided an invaluable element of continuity between the reigns of Louis the Fat and his son, Louis VII (1137–80), who pursued his father's goals with less than his father's skill. Pious and gentle, Louis VII was, in the words of a contemporary observer, "a very Christian king, if somewhat simple-minded." When Abbot Suger died in 1151, Louis was left to face unaided a new and formidable threat to the French monarchy. The Angevin Empire was just then in the process of formation, and in 1154 the ominous configuration was completed when Henry Plantagenet, count of Anjou and duke of Normandy and Aquitaine, acceded to the English throne as King Henry II. Louis VII sought to embarrass his mighty vassal by encouraging Henry's sons to rebel, but his efforts were too halfhearted to be successful. Still, Louis's reign witnessed a significant extension of royal power. Indeed, as one historian has aptly said, it was under Louis VII that "the prestige of the French monarchy was decisively established."* The great vassals of the Crown, fearful of their powerful Angevin colleague and respectful of Louis's piety and impartiality, began for the first time to bring cases to the court of their royal overlord and to submit their disputes to his judgment. Churchmen and townsmen alike sought his support in struggles with the nobility. These developments resulted not so much from royal initiative as from the fundamental trends of the age toward peace, order, and growing commercial activity. Frenchmen in increasing numbers were turning to their genial, unassuming monarch for succor and justice. Little by little, Louis began to assume his rightful place as feudal suzerain and supreme sovereign of the realm.

---

* Robert Fawtier, *The Capetian Kings of France* (London: The Macmillan Co., 1960), p. 23.

Philip Augustus: 1180–1223

The French monarchy came of age under Louis VII's talented son, Philip II "Augustus." By remorseless insistence on his feudal rights and by a policy of dextrous opportunism, Philip Augustus enlarged the royal territories enormously and, beyond the districts of direct royal jurisdiction, transformed the chaotic anarchy of the vassal states into an orderly hierarchy subordinate to the king.

Philip Augustus's great achievement was the destruction of the Angevin empire and the establishment of royal jurisdiction over Normandy, Anjou, and their dependencies. For two decades he plotted with dissatisfied members of the Angevin family against King Henry II and King Richard the Lion-Hearted, but it was not until the reign of King John (1199–1216) that his efforts bore fruit. Against John's notorious faithlessness and greed, Philip was able to play the role of the just lord rightfully punishing a disobedient vassal. And when Philip Augustus moved against Normany in 1203–4, John's unpopularity played into his hands. The prize that Philip had sought so long was now won with surprising ease, and, once Normandy was conquered, John's remaining fiefs in northern France fell quickly. Ten years later, in 1214, Philip extinguished John's last hope of recovering the lost territories by winning his decisive victory over John's German allies at Bouvines.* Settling for good the question of Normandy and Anjou, Bouvines was also a turning point in the power balance between France and Germany in the High Middle Ages. Thereafter the Capetian monarchy overshadowed the faltering kingdom of Germany and the defunct Angevin Empire. France became the great power in thirteenth-century Christendom.

Under Philip Augustus and his predecessors significant developments were occurring in the royal administrative system. The curia regis had assumed its place as the high feudal court of France and was proving an effective instrument for the assertion of royal rights over the dukes and counts. Hereditary noblemen who had traditionally served as local administrators in the royal territories were gradually replaced by salaried officials known as *baillis*. These new officials, whose functions were at once financial, judicial, military, and administrative, owed their positions to royal favor and were

---

* See pp. 216, 239.

fervently devoted to the interests of the crown. Throughout the thirteenth century the baillis worked tirelessly and often unscrupulously to erode the privileges of the feudal aristocracy and extend the royal sway. This intensely loyal and highly mobile bureaucracy, without local roots and without respect for feudal or local traditions, became in time a powerful instrument of royal absolutism. The baillis stood in sharp contrast to the local officials in England—the sheriffs and the shire knights—who were customarily drawn from the local gentry and whose loyalties were divided between the monarch whom they served and the region and class from which they sprang.

Louis VIII: 1223–1226

The closing years of Philip Augustus's reign were concurrent with the Albigensian Crusade, called by Innocent III against the dualist heretics of southern France.* Philip Augustus declined to participate personally in the crusade, but his son, Prince Louis, took an active part in it. And when the Prince succeeded to his father's throne in 1223 as Louis VIII (1223–26), he threw all the resources of the monarchy behind the southern campaign. The crusade succeeded in eliminating the Albigensian heresy, but only by devastating large portions of Languedoc and exterminating the brilliant culture that had previously flourished there. Thenceforth southern France tended to be dominated by northern France, and the authority of the French monarchy was extended to the Mediterranean.

It may perhaps be surprising to discover that Louis VIII, who inherited a vastly expanded royal jurisdiction from his father and extended it still further himself, gave out about a third of the hard-won royal territories as fiefs to junior members of the Capetian family. These family fiefs, created out of the royal domain, are known as *apanages*. Their emergence should serve as a warning that the growth of the Capetian monarchy cannot be understood simply as a linear process of expanding the royal territories. The Capetians had no objection to vassals so long as they were obedient and subject to royal control. Indeed, given the limited transportation and communication facilities of twelfth and thirteenth-century France, the

---

* See pp. 183–184.

kingdom was far too large to be controlled directly by the monarchy. The new vassals, bound to the crown by strong family ties, played an essential role in the governance of the realm. For the time being, at least, they strengthened rather than weakened the effectiveness of Capetian rule.

St. Louis: 1226–1270

Louis VIII died prematurely in 1226, leaving the land in the capable hands of his stern and pious Spanish widow, Blanche of Castile, who acted as regent for the boy-king Louis IX (1226–70), later St. Louis. Even after St. Louis came of age in 1234 he remained devoted to his mother, and Queen Blanche continued for years to be a dominant influence in the royal government.

St. Louis possessed both his mother's sanctity and his mother's firmness. Unlike some saint-kings, he was a strong monarch, determined to rule justly and firmly and to promote moral rectitude throughout the kingdom of France. His sanctity, although thoroughly genuine, was perhaps too conventional. He punished heretics and crusaded against the Muslims. He once remarked that the only possible response for a Christian toward Jews who blasphemed was "to plunge his sword into their bellies as far as it would go." In asserting these attitudes he was mirroring the biases of his age. But in other respects his reign was far from conventional. Unlike most kings, he oriented his life not toward political ends but toward what he conceived to be religious ends. He believed in war against the infidel, but he believed just as fervently in peace among Christian rulers. Accordingly, he arranged treaties with Henry III of England and with the king of Aragon which settled all outstanding disputes. He played the role of peacemaker among Christian princes and was even called upon to arbitrate between Henry III and his barons. (He decided uncompromisingly in favor of royal authority, and the English barons were outraged.)

St. Louis was content, in general, to maintain the royal rights established by his predecessors. His baillis and other officials were actually far more aggressive than he in extending the royal power. As one modern historian puts it, "in this reign monarchical progress was the complex result of the sanctity of a revered ruler, and the patient and obstinately aggressive policy of the king's servants."

THE EXPANSION OF THE FRENCH ROYAL DOMAIN

1154

ENGLAND
FLANDERS
HOLY ROMAN EMPIRE
Rouen
Laon
Rheims
NORMANDY
CHAMPAGNE
CAPETIAN DOMAIN
Paris
MAINE
BLOIS
Orleans
BRITTANY
Tours
POITOU
BURGUNDY
Holdings of Henry II
Poitiers
Clermont
Bordeaux
AQUITAINE
AUVERGNE
GASCONY
LANGUEDOC
Montpellier
K. OF ARAGON

1223

Rouen
NORMANDY
Paris
MAINE
ANJOU
TOURAINE
Tours
POITOU
Poitiers
MARCHE
Clermont
UNDER PHILIP AUGUSTUS
Avignon

1270

Paris
UNDER LOUIS IX AND PHILIP III
LANGUEDOC
Toulou
Montpellier

1314

UNDER PHILIP IV
CHAMPAGNE

Indeed, St. Louis went to the length of establishing a system of itinerant royal inspectors—*enquêteurs*—who reported local grievances and helped keep the ambitious local officials in check.

In France under Louis IX medieval culture reached its climax. Town life flourished under St. Louis's rule, and in the towns magnificent Gothic cathedrals were being built. This was the great age of the medieval universities, and at the most distinguished university of the age, the University of Paris, some of the keenest intellects of medieval Europe—St. Bonaventure, St. Albertus Magnus, St. Thomas Aquinas—were assembled concurrently. The universities produced brilliant, subtle theologians, but they also produced learned and ambitious lawyers—men of a more secular cast who devoted their talents to the king and swelled the ranks of the royal bureaucracy. The Capetian government became steadily more complex, more efficient and, from the standpoint of the feudal nobility, more oppressive.

Philip the Fair: 1285–1314

St. Louis died in the midst of his last crusade. Under his successors the bureaucracy pursued its centralizing policies without restraint. The saint-king was succeeded by his inept son, Philip III (1270–85) and his frigid, inegmatic grandson, Philip IV, "the Fair" or "the Handsome" (1285–1314). Philip was a mysterious, silent figure, conventionally pious, but with a flair for choosing able, aggressive and thoroughly unprincipled ministers—chiefly middleclass lawyers from southern France—who devoted themselves singlemindedly to the exaltation of the French monarchy.

The reign of Philip the Fair was an age of unceasing royal aggression against the territories of neighboring states, against the papacy, and against the traditional privileges of the French nobility. Philip waged an indecisive war against King Edward I of England over Edward's remaining fiefs in southern France. He made a serious effort to absorb Flanders, imprisoning the Flemish count and ruling the district directly through a royal agent, but he was foiled by a bloody uprising of Flemish nobles and townsmen who won a stunning victory over him at the battle of Courtrai in 1302. He pursued a successful policy of nibbling aggression to the east against the Holy Roman Empire. He suppressed unscrupulously the rich crusading order of Knights Templars, ruined their reputation by an astonishingly modern campaign of vituperative propaganda, and confiscated their wealth. We have already seen how he struggled with Pope Boniface VIII, how his agents held Boniface captive for a brief time, and how he finally engineered the election of the pliable French

Pope Clement V, who took up residence at Avignon.* Against his nobles he pursued a rigorously anti-feudal policy. He short-circuited the feudal hierarchy and demanded direct allegiance and obedience from all Frenchmen. All these activities were manifestations of the prevailing political philosophy of his reign: that the French king was by rights the secular and spiritual master of France and the dominating figure in western Europe. We encounter this same philosophy in ambitious French statesmen of succeeding centuries: in Cardinal Richelieu; in Louis XIV; and, stripped of its monarchical trappings, in Napoleon and De Gaulle.

Throughout the thirteenth century the French royal bureaucracy had been developing steadily. The royal revenues came to be handled by a special accounting bureau, roughly parallel to the English exchequer, called the *chambre des comtes*. The king's judicial business became the responsibility of a high court known as the *Parlement of Paris*, which was to play a highly significant political role in later centuries. Under Philip the Fair the bureaucracy became a refined and supple tool of the royal interest, and its middleclass background and tenacious royalism gave the king a degree of independence from the nobility that was quite unknown in contemporary England.

Still, the king could not rule without a certain amount of support from his subjects. Philip's victory over the papacy on the issue of royal taxation of the clergy and his rape of the Knights Templars brought additional money into his treasury, but the soaring expenses of government and warfare forced him to seek ever-new sources of revenue and, as in England, to secure his subjects' approval of extraordinary taxation. But instead of summoning a great assembly —a parliament—for this purpose, he usually negotiated individually with various taxpaying groups.

Nevertheless it was under Philip the Fair that France's first great representative assemblies were summoned. Beginning in 1302, the *Estates General* was assembled from time to time, primarily for the purpose of giving formal support to the monarchy in moments of crisis—during the struggle with Pope Boniface VIII, for example, or in the midst of the Knights Templars controversy. The assembly included members of the three great social classes, or "estates": the

* See p. 224.

clergy, the nobility, and the townsmen. It continued to meet occasionally during the succeeding centuries, but it never became a real organ of government as did Parliament in England. Its failure resulted in part from a premature and unsuccessful bid for power during the fourteenth century in the midst of the Hundred Years' War. But even under Philip the Fair the Estates General lacked the potential of the contemporary parliaments of England. It had no real voice in royal taxation and was therefore not in a position to bargain with the king through increasing control of the purse strings. It was not, as in England, an evolutionary outgrowth of the royal council, but rather an entirely separate, exotic body. There was no real opportunity for the townsmen and the gentry to join ranks as in the English House of Commons; lacking the important responsibilities in local government which fell on the English shire knights, the

CHRONOLOGY OF THE ENGLISH AND FRENCH MONARCHIES IN THE HIGH MIDDLE AGES

England	*France*
1066: Norman Conquest of England	987–1328: Rule of the Capetian Dynasty
1066–1087: Reign of William the Conqueror	1060–1108: Reign of Philip I
1087–1100: Reign of William II	
1100–1135: Reign of Henry I	1108–1137: Reign of Louis VI, "the Fat"
1135–1154: Disputed succession; King Stephen	
1154–1189: Reign of Henry II	1137–1180: Reign of Louis VII
1189–1199: Reign of Richard I "the Lion-Hearted"	1180–1223: Reign of Philip II, "Augustus"
1199–1216: Reign of John	
1203–1204: Loss of Normandy	1214: Battle of Bouvines
1215: Magna Carta	1223–1226: Reign of Louis VIII
1216–1272: Reign of Henry III	1226–1270: Reign of St. Louis IX
1264–1265: Simon de Montfort's rebellion	1270–1285: Reign of Philip III
1272–1307: Reign of Edward I	1285–1314: Reign of Philip IV, "the Fair"

knights of France remained an inarticulate and subordinate part of the aristocratic class. Above all, the French nobility and bourgeoisie lagged far behind the English in developing a national consciousness or a feeling of cohesion. Late-thirteenth-century France was too large, too heterogeneous, and too recently consolidated under royal authority for its inhabitants to have acquired a meaningful sense of identification as a people. Their outlook remained provincial.

Yet despite the significant differences between the English Parliament and the French Estates General, the two institutions had much in common. Both were products of a European-wide evolution out of feudal monarchy and out of the vague but pervading medieval notion of government under the law or government by the consent of the realm. Similar representative institutions were emerging concurrently all over Western Christendom: in the Christian kingdoms of Spain, in Italy under Frederick II, in the rising principalities of Germany, and in innumerable counties, duchies, and communes across Europe. Of these many experiments only the English Parliament survives today. But Parliament was not merely the outgrowth of an isolated English experience; it was one particular expression of a broad and fundamental trend in medieval European civilization.

13

literature
and
art

The Dynamics of
High Medieval Culture

Thirteenth-century Paris has been described as the Athens of medieval Europe. And despite all the obvious and fundamental differences that separate the golden age of Pericles from the golden age of St. Louis, these two epochs did have something in common. Both developed within the framework of traditional beliefs and customs which had long existed but were being challenged and transformed by powerful new forces—a new rationalism, a new art, a burgeoning of commerce, an expansion of frontiers, and an influx of ideas from other cultures. The socio-religious world of the Early Middle Ages, like the socio-religious world of the early Greek polis, was parochial and tradition bound. As the two cultures passed into their golden ages, the values of the past were assailed by new intellectual currents, and the old economic patterns were expanded and transformed. Yet for a time, these dynamic new forces resulted in a heightened cultural expression of the old values. The Parthenon, dedicated to the venerable civic goddess Athena, and the Gothic cathedrals of Notre Dame (Our Lady) that were rising at Paris, Chartres, Reims, Amiens, and elsewhere, were all products of a new creativity harnessed to the service of an older ideology. In the long run, the new creative impulses would subvert the old ideologies, but for a time, both ancient Greece and medieval Europe achieved an elusive equilibrium between old and new. The results, in both cases, were spectacular.

Thus, twelfth and thirteenth-century Europe succeeded, by and large, in keeping its vibrant, audacious culture within the bounds of traditional Catholic Christianity. And the Christian world view gave form and orientation to the new creativity. Despite the intense dynamism of the period, it can still be called, with some semblance of accuracy, an Age of Faith.

Europe in the High Middle Ages underwent an artistic and intellectual awakening that affected every imaginable form of expression. Significant creative work was done in literature, architecture, sculpture, law, philosophy, political theory, even science. By the close of the period, the foundations of the Western cultural tradition were firmly established. The pages that follow will provide only a glimpse at the achievements of this fertile era.

Latin Literature

The literature of the High Middle Ages was abundant and richly varied. Poetry was written both in the traditional Latin—the universal scholarly language of medieval Europe—and in the vernacular languages of ordinary speech that had long been evolving in the various districts of Christendom. Traditional Christian piety found expression in a series of somber and majestic Latin hymns, whose mood is illustrated—through the clouded glass of translation—by these excerpts from "Jerusalem the Golden" (twelfth century):

> *The world is very evil, the times are waxing late,*
> *Be sober and keep vigil; the judge is at the gate.*
> . . . . .
> *Brief life is here our portion; brief sorrow, short-lived care.*
> *The life that knows no ending, the tearless life, is there.*
> . . . .
> *Jerusalem the Golden, with milk and honey blessed,*
> *Beneath thy contemplation sink heart and voice oppressed.*
> *Beneath thy contemplation sink heart and voice oppressed.*
> *I know not, O I know not, what social joys are there,*
> *What radiancy of glory, what light beyond compare.*

At the opposite end of the medieval Latin spectrum one encounters poetry of quite a different sort, composed by young, wandering scholars and older non-students. The deliberate sensuality and blasphemy of their poems is an expression of student rebelliousness against establishment ideals:

> *For on this my heart is set, when the hour is neigh me,*
> *Let me in the tavern die, with a tankard by me,*
> *While the angels, looking down, joyously sing o'er me. . . .*

One of these wandering-scholar poems is an elaborate and impudent expansion of the Apostles' Creed. The phrase from the Creed, "I believe in the Holy Ghost, the Holy [Catholic] Church . . ." is embroidered as follows:

> *I believe in wine that's fair to see,*
> *And in the tavern of my host*
> *More than in the Holy Ghost*
> *The tavern will my sweetheart be,*
> *And the Holy Church is not for me.*

These sentiments do not betoken a sweeping trend toward agnosticism. Rather, they are distinctively medieval expressions of the perennial student irreverence toward established institutions. A modern student activist shouting obscenities in a D.A.R. meeting would create much the same effect, though less cleverly.

Vernacular Literature; the Epic

For all its originality, the Latin poetry of the High Middle Ages was outstripped both in quantity and in variety of expression by vernacular poetry. The drift toward emotionalism, which we have already noted in medieval piety, was closely paralleled by the martial epics of the eleventh century to the delicate and sensitive romances of the thirteenth. Influenced by the sophisticated romanticism of the southern troubadour tradition, the bellicose spirit of northern France gradually softened.

In the eleventh and early twelfth centuries, heroic epics known as *chansons de geste* (songs of great deeds) were enormously popular among the feudal nobility of northern France. These chansons arose

out of the earlier heroic tradition of the Teutonic north that had produced such moody and violent masterpieces as *Beowulf*. The hero
Beowulf is a lonely figure who fights monsters, slays dragons, and
pits his strength and courage against a wild, windswept wilderness.
The chansons de geste reflect the somewhat more civilized and
christianized age of feudalism. Still warlike and heroic in mood, they
often consisted of exaggerated accounts of events in the reign of
Charlemagne. The most famous of all the chansons de geste, the
Song of Roland, tells of a heroic, bloody battle between a horde of
Muslims and the detached rearguard of Charlemagne's army as it was
withdrawing from Spain. Like old-fashioned Westerns, the chansons
de geste were packed with action, and their heroes tended to steer
clear of sentimental entanglements with women. Warlike prowess,
courage, and loyalty to one's lord and fellows-in-arms were the virtues
stressed in these heroic epics. The battle descriptions, often characterized by gory realism, tell of Christian knights fighting with almost
superhuman strength against fantastic odds. The heroes of the chansons are not only proud, loyal and skilled at arms, but also capable of
experiencing deep emotions—weeping at the death of their comrades
and appealing to God to receive the souls of the fallen. In short, the
chansons de geste mirror the bellicose spirit and sense of military
brotherhood that characterized the feudal knighthood of eleventh-
century Europe:

> *Turpin of Rheims, his horse beneath him slain,*
> *And with four lance wounds he himself in pain,*
> *Hastens to rise, brave lord, and stand erect.*
> *He looks on Roland, runs to him, and says*
> *Only one thing: "I am not beaten yet!*
> *True man fails not, while life in him is left."*
> *He draws Almace, his keen-edged steel-bright brand*
> *And strikes a thousand strokes amid the press.*
> . . . . .
> *Count Roland never loved a recreant,*
> *Nor a false heart, nor yet a braggart jack,*
> *Nor knight that was not faithful to his lord.*
> *He cried to Turpin—churchman militant—*
> *"Sir, you're on foot, I'm on my horse's back."*

> For love of you, here will I make my stand,
> And side by side we'll take both good and bad.
> I'll not leave you for any mortal man."
> . . . .
> Now Roland feels that he is nearing death;
> Out of his ears the brain is running forth.
> So for his peers he prays God call them all,
> And for himself St. Gabriel's aid implores.

Roland and his rear guard are slain to a man, but the Lord Charlemagne returns to avenge them, and a furious battle ensues:

> Both French and Moors are fighting with a will.
> How many spears are shattered! lances split!
> Both French and Moors are fighting with a will.
> Whoever saw those shields smashed all to bits,
> Heard the bright hauberks grind, the mail rings rip,
> Heard the harsh spear upon the helmet ring,
> Seen countless knights out of the saddle spilled,
> And all the earth with death and deathcries filled,
> Would long recall the face of suffering!

The French are victorious, Charlemagne himself defeats the Moorish emir in single combat, and Roland is avenged:

> The Muslims fly, God will not have them stay.
> All's done, all's won, the French have gained the day.

The Lyric

During the middle and later twelfth century the martial spirit of northern French literature was gradually transformed by the influx of the romantic troubadour tradition of southern France. In Provence, Toulouse, and Aquitaine a rich, colorful culture had been developing in the eleventh and twelfth centuries, and out of this vivacious society came a lyric poetry of remarkable sensitivity and enduring value. The lyric poets of the south were known as *troubadours*. Many of them were court minstrels, but some, including Duke William IX of Aquitaine, were members of the upper nobility. Their poems were far more intimate and personal than the chansons de geste, and placed much greater emphasis upon romantic love. The wit, delicacy, and romanticism of the troubadour lyrics disclose a more genteel and sophisticated nobility than that of the feudal north—a nobility that preferred songs of love to songs of war. Indeed, medieval southern France, under the influence of Islamic courtly poetry and ideas, was the source of the romantic-love tradition of Western civilization. It was from southern France that Europe derived such concepts as the idealization of women, the importance of male gallantry and courtesy, and the impulse to embroider relations between man and woman with potent emotional overtones of eternal oneness, undying devotion, agony, and ecstacy. One of the favorite themes of the lyric poets was the hopeless love—the unrequited love from afar:

> *I die of wounds from blissful blows,*
> *And love's cruel stings dry out my flesh,*
> *My health is lost, my vigor goes,*
> *And nothing can my soul refresh.*
> *I never knew so sad a plight,*
> *It should not be, it is not right.*
>
> . . . .
>
> *I'll never hold her near to me*
> *My ardent joy she'll ever spurn,*
> *In her good grace I cannot be*
> *Nor even hope, but only yearn.*
> *She tells me nothing, false or true,*
> *And neither will she ever do.*

The author of these lines, Jaufré Rudel (fl. 1148), unhappily and hopelessly in love, finds consolation in his talents as a poet, of which he has an exceedingly high opinion. The poem concludes on a much more optimistic note:

> *Make no mistake, my song is fair,*
> *With fitting words and apt design.*
> *My messenger would never dare*
> *To cut it short or change a line.*
>
> . . . .
>
> *My song is fair, my song is good,*
> *'Twill bring delight, as well it should.*

Many such poems were written in southern France during the twelfth century. The recurring theme is the poet's passionate love for a woman. Occasionally, however, the pattern is reversed, as in the following lyric poem by the poetress Beatritz de Dia (fl. 1160):

> *I live in grave anxiety*
> *For one fair knight who loved me so.*
> *It would have made him glad to know*
> *I loved him too—but silently.*
> *I was mistaken, now I'm sure,*
> *When I withheld myself from him.*
> *My grief is deep, my days are dim,*
> *And life itself has no allure.*
>
> *I wish my knight might sleep with me*
> *And hold me naked to his breast,*
> *And on my body take his rest,*
> *And grieve no more, but joyous be.*
> *My love for him surpasses all*
> *The loves that famous lovers knew.*
> *My soul is his, my body, too,*
> *My heart, my life, are at his call.*
>
> *My most beloved, dearest friend,*
> *When will you fall into my power?*
> *That I might lie with you an hour,*
> *And love you 'til my life should end!*
> *My heart is filled with passion's fire.*
> *My well-loved knight, I grant thee grace*
> *To hold me in my husband's place,*
> *And do the things I so desire.*

Not all the lyric poems of southern France took love or life quite so seriously. In some, one encounters a refreshing lightness and wit. The following verses, by Duke William IX of Aquitaine (1071–1127), typify the vivacious spirit of the South. They parody both the romantic seriousness of the love lyric and the heroic mood of the chansons de geste:

I'll make some verses just for fun,
Not of myself or anyone,
Nor of great deeds that knights have done
Nor lovers true.
I made them riding in the sun,
My horse helped, too.

Minstrels playing the harp, the flute, and the pipe and tabor.

When I was born, I'm not aware,
I'm neither gay nor in despair,
Nor stiff, nor loose, nor do I care,
Nor wonder why.
Since meeting an enchantress fair,
Bewitched am I.

Living for dreaming I mistake,
I must be told when I'm awake,
My mood is sad, my heart may break,
Such grief I bear!
But never mind, for heaven's sake,
I just don't care.

I'm sick to death, or so I fear,
I cannot see, but only hear.
I hope that there's a doctor near,
No matter who.
If he can heal me, I'll pay dear,
If not, he's through.

My lady fair is far away,
Just who, or where, I cannot say,
She tells me neither yea nor nay,
Yet I'm not blue,
So long as all those Normans stay
Far from Poitou.

My distant love I so adore,
Though me she has no longing for,
We've never met, and furthermore—
To my disgrace—
I've other loves, some three or four,
To fill her place.

This verse is done, as you can see,
And by your leave, dispatched 'twill be
To one who'll read it carefully
In far Anjou.
Its meaning he'd explain to me
If he but knew.

These verses, only a brief sampling of the fascinating lyrics of southern France—and distorted by translation—may provide some feeling for the rich civilization that flourished there in the twelfth century and disintegrated with the savage horrors of the Albigensian Crusade.

The Romance

Midway through the twelfth century, the southern tradition of courtly love was brought northward to the court of Champagne and began to spread rapidly across France, England, and Germany. As its influence grew, the northern knights discovered that more was expected of them than loyalty to their lords and a life of carefree slaughter. They were now expected to be gentlemen as well—to be courtly in manner and urbane in speech, to exhibit delicate, refined behavior in feminine company, and to idolize some noble woman. Such, briefly, were the ideals of courtly love. Their impact on the actual behavior of knights was distinctly limited, but their effect on the literature of northern Europe was revolutionary. Out of the convergence of vernacular epic and vernacular lyric there emerged a new poetic form known as the romance.

Like the chanson de geste, the romance was a long narrative, but like the southern lyric, it was sentimental and imaginative. It was commonly based on some theme from the remote past: the Trojan War, Alexander the Great, and, above all, King Arthur—the half-legendary sixth-century British king. Arthur was transformed into an idealized twelfth-century monarch surrounded by charming ladies and chivalrous knights. His court at Camelot, as described by the late-twelfth-century French poet, Chrétien de Troyes, was a center of romantic love and refined religious sensitivity where knights worshipped their ladies, went on daring quests, and played out their chivalrous roles in a world of magic and fantasy.

In the chanson de geste the great moral imperative was loyalty to one's lord; in the romance it was love for one's lady. Several romances portray the old and new values in conflict. An important theme in both the Arthurian romances and the twelfth-century romance of *Tristan and Iseult* is a love affair between a vassal and his lord's wife. Love and feudal loyalty stand face to face, and love wins out. Tristan loves Iseult, the wife of his lord, King Mark of Cornwall. King

Arthur's beloved knight Lancelot loves Arthur's wife, Guinevere. In both stories the lovers are ruined by their love, yet love they must— they have no choice—and although the conduct of Tristan and Lancelot would have been regarded by earlier standards as nothing less than treasonable, both men are presented sympathetically in the romances. Love destroys the lovers in the end, yet their destruction is romantic—even glorious. Tristan and Iseult die together, and in their very death their love achieves its deepest consummation.

Alongside the theme of love in the medieval romances, and standing in sharp contrast to it, is the theme of Christian purity and dedication. The rough-hewn knight of old, having been taught to be courteous and loving, was now taught to be holy. Lancelot was trapped in the meshes of a lawless love, but his son, Galahad, became the prototype of the Christian knight—pure, holy, and chaste. And Perceval, another knight of the Arthurian circle, quested not for a lost loved one but for the Holy Grail of the Last Supper.

The romance flourished in twelfth- and thirteenth-century France and among the French-speaking nobility of England. It spread also into Italy and Spain, and became a crucial factor in the evolution of vernacular literature in Germany. The German poets, known as Minnesingers, were influenced by the French lyric and romance, but developed these literary forms along highly original lines. The Minnesingers produced their own deeply sensitive and mystical versions of the Arthurian stories which, in their exalted symbolism and profundity of emotion, surpass even the works of Chrétien de Troyes and his French contemporaries.

Aucassin et Nicolette; the Romance of the Rose

As the thirteenth century drew toward its close, the romance was becoming conventionalized and drained of inspiration. The love story of *Aucassin et Nicolette*, which achieved a degree of popularity, was actually a satirical romance in which the hero was much less heroic than heroes usually are, and a battle is depicted in which the opponents cast pieces of cheese at each other. Based on earlier Byzantine material, *Aucassin et Nicolette* makes mortal love take priority over salvation itself. Indeed, Aucassin is scornful of Heaven:

For into Paradise go only such people as these: There go those aged priests and elderly cripples and maimed ones who day and night stoop before altars and in the crypts beneath the churches; those who go around in worn-out cloaks and shabby old habits; who are naked and shoeless and full of sores; who are dying of hunger and of thirst, of cold and of misery. Such folks as these enter Paradise, and I will have nothing to do with them. I will go to Hell. For to Hell go the fair clerics and comely knights who are killed in tournaments and great wars, and the sturdy archer and the loyal vassal. I will go with them. There also go the fair and courteous ladies who have loving friends, two or three, together with their wedded lords. And there go the gold and silver, the ermine and all rich furs, the harpers and the minstrels, and the happy folk of the world. I will go with these, so long as I have Nicolette, my very sweet friend, at my side.

Another important product of thirteenth-century vernacular literature, the *Romance of the Rose*, was in fact not a romance in the ordinary sense but an allegory of the whole courtly love tradition in which the thoughts and emotions of the lover and his lady are personified in actual characters such as Love, Reason, Jealousy, and Fair-Welcome. Begun by William of Lorris as an idealization of courtly love, the *Romance of the Rose* was completed after William's death by Jean de Meun, a man of limited talent and bourgeois origin. Jean's contribution was long-winded and encyclopedic, and the poem as a whole lacks high literary distinction, yet it appealed to contemporaries and enjoyed a great vogue.

Fabliaux and Fables

Neither epic, lyric, nor romance had much appeal below the level of the landed aristocracy. The inhabitants of the rising towns had a vernacular literature all their own. From the bourgeoisie came the high medieval *fabliaux*, short satirical poems, filled with vigor and crude humor, which devoted themselves chiefly to ridiculing conventional morality. Priests and monks were portrayed as lechers, merchants' wives were easily and frequently seduced, and clever young men perpetually made fools of sober and stuffy merchants.

Medieval urban culture also produced the fable, or animal story, an allegory in the tradition of Aesop in which various stock characters in medieval society were presented as animals—thinly disguised. Most of the more popular fables dealt with Renard the Fox and were known collectively as the *Romance of Renard*. These tales constituted a ruthless parody of chivalric ideals in which the clever, unscrupulous Renard persistently outwitted King Lion and his loyal but stupid vassals. Thus, paradoxically, the medieval town, which produced such powerful waves of piety, was responsible for literary forms characterized chiefly by secularism, lasciviousness, and the ridiculing of customs and conventions. To balance the impression conveyed by the fabliaux and fables one must consider the great Romanesque and Gothic cathedrals, the *Song of Brother Sun** composed by that illustrious son of a medieval merchant, St. Francis of Assisi, and the deeply religious poetry of the Florentine Dante.

Dante

Vernacular poetry matured late in Italy, but in the works of Dante (1265–1321) it achieved its loftiest expression. Dante wrote on a wide variety of subjects, sometimes in Latin, more often in the Tuscan vernacular. He composed a series of lyric poems celebrating his love for the lady Beatrice, which are assembled, with prose commentaries, in his *Vita Nuova* ("The New Life"). Dante's lyrics reflect a more mystical and idealized love than that of the troubadours:

> *A shining love comes from my lady's eyes,*
> *All that she looks on is made lovelier,*
> *And as she walks, men turn to gaze at her,*
> *Whoever meets her feels his heart arise.*
> . . . .
> *Humility, and hope that hopeth well,*
> *Come to the mind of one who hears her voice,*
> *And blessed is he who looks on her a while*
> *Her beauty, when she gives her slightest smile*
> *One cannot paint in words, yet must rejoice*
> *In such a new and gracious miracle.*

Firmly convinced of the literary potential of the Tuscan vernacular, Dante urged its use in his *De Vulgari Eloquentia*, which he wrote in Latin so as to appeal to scholars and writers who scorned the vulgar

---

* Above, p. 191.

tongue. And he filled his own vernacular works with such grace and beauty as to convince by example those whom he could not persuade by argument. In his hands the Tuscan vernacular became the literary language of Italy.

Dante was no mere disembodied writer, but a man immersed in the politics of his age. His experience brought him to the opinion that Italy's hope for peace lay in imperial domination and in divorcing the papacy from politics. Although futile and anachronistic in view of the Empire's impotence in Dante's time, these views were expressed forcefully in his great political essay, *On Monarchy*.

Dante's masterpiece was the *Divine Comedy*, written in the Tuscan vernacular. Abounding in allegory and symbolism, it encompasses in one majestic vision the entire universe of medieval man. Dante tells of his own journey through hell, purgatory, and paradise to the very presence of God. This device permits the poet to make devastating comments on past and contemporary history by placing all those of whom he disapproved—from local politicians to popes—in various levels of hell. Virgil, the archetype of ancient rationalism, is Dante's guide through hell and purgatory; the lady Beatrice, a symbol of purified love, guides him through the celestial spheres of paradise; and St. Bernard, the epitome of medieval sanctity, leads him to the threshold of God. The poem closes with Dante alone in the divine presence:

> *Eternal Light, thou in thyself alone*
> *Abidest, and alone thine essence knows,*
> *And loves, and smiles, self-knowing and self-known. . . .*
> . . . .
> *Here power failed to the high fantasy,*
> *But my desire and will were turned—as one—*
> *And as a wheel that turneth evenly,*
> *By Holy Love, that moves the stars and sun.*

The Romanesque Style

The High Middle Ages is one of the great epochs in the history of Western architecture. Stone churches, large and small, were built in prodigious numbers: in France alone, more stone was quarried during the High Middle Ages than by the pyramid and temple builders

Romanesque exterior: Sainte-Foy in Conques (c. 1050–c. 1120).

Romanesque interior: Saint-Etienne in Nevers (c. 1083–1097).

of ancient Egypt throughout its 3000-year history. But the real achievement of the medieval architects lay not in the immense scope of their activities but in the splendid originality of their aesthetic vision. Two great architectural styles dominated the age: the Romanesque style flourished in the eleventh century and early twelfth, and during the middle decades of the twelfth century gave way gradually to the Gothic style. From about 1150 to 1300 the greatest of the medieval Gothic cathedrals were built. Thereafter the Gothic builders, having exhausted the structural possibilities of their style, turned from basic innovation to decorative elaboration. But during the High Middle Ages Gothic architecture constituted one of humanity's most audacious and successful architectural experiments.

The evolution of high medieval architecture was shaped by two fundamental trends in medieval civilization. First, the great cathedrals were products of the urban revolution—of rising wealth, civic pride, and intense urban piety. Second, the evolution from Romanesque to Gothic parallels the shift in literature and piety toward emotional sensitivity and romanticism. Romanesque architecture, though characterized by an exceeding diversity of expression, tended toward the solemnity of earlier Christian piety and the rough-hewn power of the chansons de geste. The Gothic style, on the other hand, is dramatic, upward-reaching, aspiring. It embodies the heightened sensitivity that one finds in the romance; in certain respects it echoes contemporary attitudes on the idealization of women: a great many Gothic cathedrals were dedicated to Notre Dame.

The development from Romanesque to Gothic can be understood, too, as an evolution in the principles of structural engineering. The key architectural ingredient in the Romanesque churches was the

(a) *Barrel Vault.* (b) *Cross Vault.*

Romanesque tympanum: Sainte-Foy in Conques (c. 1130).

round arch, which appears in their portals, their windows, their arcades, and the massive stone vaulting of their roofs. Romanesque roof design was based on various elaborations of the round arch, such as the barrel vault and the cross vault (see illustration). The immense downward and outward thrusts of these heavy stone roofs required massive pillars and thick supporting walls.

The great engineering achievement of the Romanesque architects was to replace flat wooden ceilings with stone vaulting, thereby creating buildings less susceptible to fire and more organic. In achieving this goal, the Romanesque builders constructed stone vaults far larger than ever before. The glittering mosaics and wooden roofs, which characterized the churches of late-Roman, Byzantine, and Carolingian times, gave way to the domination of stone as the key material in both Romanesque architecture and Romanesque sculpture. Indeed, the inventive, fantastic religious sculpture of the age—ornamenting the capitals of Romanesque columns and the semicircular

"Adoration of the Magi," Cloister capital, Moissac (1100).

ROMANESQUE CAPITALS

Nave capital, Anzy-le-Duc (late eleventh century).

Detail of right portal, Vezelay (begun 1120).

Cloister capital, Moissac (1100).

279

areas between the lintels and round arches of the doors (the *tympana*)—were totally architectonic—completely fused into the structure of the church itself.

By the standards of the later Gothic style, the Romanesque interior is dark—characterized by heavy masses and relatively small windows. Graceful and richly decorated in southern Europe, the style tends to become increasingly severe as one moves northward. A church in the fully developed Romanesque style conveys a feeling of artistic unity and earthbound solidity. Its sturdy arches, vaults, and walls, and its somber, shadowy interior give the illusion of mystery and otherworldliness, yet suggest at the same time the steadfast might of the universal Church.

The Gothic Style

During the first half of the twelfth century new structural elements began to be employed in the building of Romanesque churches: first, ribs of stone that ran along the edges of the arched cross vaults and helped to support them; next, pointed arches that permitted greater flexibility and height in the vaulting. By the middle of the century these novel features—vault rib and pointed arch—were providing the basis for an entirely new style of architecture, no longer Romanesque but Gothic. They were employed with such effect by Abbot Sugar in his new abbey church of Saint-Denis near Paris around 1140 that Saint-Denis is regarded as the first true Gothic church.

French Gothic churches of the late twelfth century such as Notre Dame of Paris disclose the development of vault rib and pointed arch into a powerful, coherent style. During these exciting years, every decade brought new experiments and opened new possibilities in church building, yet Notre Dame of Paris and the churches of its period and region retain some of the heaviness and stolidity of the earlier Romanesque. Not until the thirteenth century were the full potentialities of Gothic architecture realized. The discovery of the vault rib and pointed arch, and of a third Gothic structural element—the flying buttress—made it possible to support weights and stresses in a new way. The traditional building, of roof supported by walls, was transformed into a radically new kind of building—a skeleton—in which the stone vault rested not on walls but on slender columns and

Nave looking east (showing vault ribs), Notre Dame in Paris (begun 1163).

High Gothic facade: Amiens Cathedral (showing the three west portals decorated with sculpture: thirteenth century).

High Gothic exterior: Reims Cathedral (showing the great clerestory windows around the rounded east end, and the decorated flying buttresses: thirteenth century).

graceful exterior supports. The walls became mere screens—structurally unnecessary. With the passage of time, they were replaced increasingly by huge windows of stained glass which flooded the church interiors with light and color. For concurrent with the Gothic architectural revolution was the development, in twelfth-century Europe, of the new art of stained-glass making. The glorious colored windows created in the twelfth and thirteenth centuries, with episodes from the Bible and religious legend depicted in shimmering blues and glowing reds, have never been equalled.

The Gothic innovations of vault rib, pointed arch, and flying buttress created the breathtaking illusion of stone vaulting resting on walls of glass. The new churches rose upward in seeming defiance of gravity, losing their earthbound quality and reaching toward the heavens. By about the mid-thirteenth century all the structural possibilities of the Gothic skeleton design were fully realized, and in the towns of central and northern France there now rose churches of

High Gothic interior: Amiens Cathedral looking east toward the rounded apse (east end: thirteenth century).

delicate, soaring stone with walls of lustrous glass. Never before in history had windows been so immense or buildings so lofty; and seldom since has European architecture been at once so assured and so daringly original.

Gothic sculpture, like Romanesque, was intimately related to architecture, yet the two styles differed markedly. Romanesque fantasy, exuberance, and distortion gave way to a serene, self-confident naturalism. Human figures were no longer crowded together on the capitals of pillars; often they stood as statues—great rows of them—in niches on the cathedral exteriors: saints, prophets, kings, and angels,

Christ and the Virgin, depicted as tall slender figures, calm yet warmly human, or as lovely young women, placid and often smiling. The greatest Gothic churches of thirteenth-century France—Bourges, Chartres, Amiens, Reims, Sainte-Chapelle—are superb syntheses of many separate arts. The pictures in the glass, the sculpture, and the architecture of the buildings themselves are all fused and directed to a single end: the expression and illumination of a deep, vital faith.

High Gothic sculpture: *Apostle's head, from Sens Cathedral (central France, c. 1190–1200). Head of the Virgin Mary, from the west facade of Reims Cathedral; first half of the thirteenth century.*

287

14

the world of intellect

The Rise of Universities

Like the Gothic cathedral, the university was a product of the medieval town. The urban revolution of the eleventh and twelfth centuries brought about the decline of the old monastic schools which had done so much to preserve culture over the previous centuries. They were superseded north of the Alps by cathedral schools locatd in the rising towns, and in Italy by semisecular municipal schools. Both the cathedral schools and the municipal schools had long existed, but it was only in the eleventh century that they rose to prominence. Many of these schools now became centers of higher learning of a sort that Europe had not known for centuries. Their enrollments increased steadily and their faculties grew until, in the twelfth century, some of them evolved into universities.

In the Middle Ages, *university* was a vague term. A university was simply a group of persons associated for any purpose. The word was commonly applied to the merchant guilds and craft guilds of the rising towns. A guild or university of students and scholars engaged in the pursuit of higher learning was given the more specific name, *studium generale*. When we speak of the medieval university, therefore, we are referring to an institution that would have been called a *studium generale* by a person of the thirteenth century. It differed from lesser schools in three significant respects: (1) the *studium generale* was open to students from many lands, not simply those from the surrounding districts; (2) the *studium generale* was a large school with a number of teachers rather than merely one omnicompetent master; (3) the *studium generale* offered both elementary and advanced curricula. It offered a basic program of instruction in the traditional "seven liberal arts": astronomy, geometry, arithmetic, music, grammar, rhetoric, and dialectic; and also instruction in one or more of the "higher" disciplines: theology, law, and medicine. Upon the successful completion of his liberal arts curriculum, the student could apply for a license to teach, but he might also wish to continue his studies by specializing in medicine, theology, or—most popular of all—civil or canon law. Legal training offered as its reward the promise of a lucrative administrative career in royal government or the Church.

Fundamentally, the medieval university was neither a campus nor a complex of buildings, but a guild—a privileged corporation of teachers, or sometimes of students. With its classes normally held in rented rooms, it was a highly mobile institution, and on more than one occasion, when a university was dissatisfied with local conditions it won important concessions from the townsmen simply by threatening to move elsewhere.

In the thirteenth century, flourishing universities were to be found at Paris, Bologna, Naples, Montpellier, Oxford, Cambridge, and elsewhere. Paris, Oxford, and a number of others were dominated by guilds of instructors in the liberal arts. Bologna, whose pattern was followed by other universities of southern Europe, was governed by a guild of students. The Bologna student guild managed to reduce the exorbitant local prices of food and lodgings by threatening to move collectively to another town, and established strict rules of conduct for the instructors. Professors, for example, were placed under the outrageous obligation to begin and end their classes on time and to cover the prescribed curriculum. Since Bologna specialized in legal studies, its pupils were older professional students for the most part—men who had completed their liberal arts curriculum and were determined to secure sufficient training for successful careers in law.

The students of the medieval universities were, on the whole, exuberant and riot-prone. Their underlying hostility toward the surrounding towns often exploded into town-gown violence. New students were hazed unmercifully; unpopular professors were hissed, shouted down, and even pelted with stones. Most of the students were of relatively humble origin—from the towns or the ranks of the lesser nobility—but they were willing to spend their student days in poverty if necessary in order to acquire the new knowledge and prepare themselves for the rich social and economic rewards that awaited many graduates.

The differences between medieval and modern university life are obviously enormous, yet the modern university is a direct outgrowth of the institution that came into being in high medieval Europe. We owe to the medieval university the concept of a formal teaching license, the custom—unknown to antiquity—of group instruction, the idea of academic degrees, the notion of a liberal arts curriculum, the tradition of professors and students dressing in clerical garb (caps and gowns) on commencement day, and numerous other customs of university life. Even the letters written by medieval students to their parents or guardians have a curiously modern ring:

This is to inform you that I am studying at Oxford with the greatest diligence, but the matter of money stands greatly in the way of my promotion, as it is now two months since I spent the last of what you sent me. The city is expensive and makes many demands; I have to rent lodgings, buy necessities, and provide for many other things which I cannot now specify. [A fuller elaboration here would have been illuminating.] Wherefore I respectfully beg your paternity that by the promptings of divine pity you may assist me, so that I can complete what I have well begun. For you must know that without Ceres and Bacchus, Apollo grows cold.

Medicine and Law

The chief medical school of medieval Europe was the University of Salerno in southern Italy. Here, in a land of vigorous cultural intermingling, scholars were able to draw from the medical heritage of Islam and Byzantium. In general, medieval medical scholarship was a bizarre medley of cautious observation, common sense, and gross superstition. In one instance we encounter the good advice that a person should eat and drink in moderation. But we are also instructed that onions will cure baldness, that the urine of a dog is an admirable cure for warts, and that all one must do to prevent a woman from conceiving is to bind her head with a red ribbon. Yet in the midst of all this, important progress was being made in medical science. The comprehensive medical writings of the second-century scientist Galen were studied and digested, along with the important works of Arab medical scholars. And to this invaluable body of knowledge Europeans were now making their own original contributions on such subjects as the curative properties of plants and the anatomy of the human body. It is probable that both animal and human dissections were performed by the scholars of twelfth-century Salerno. These doctors, crude and primitive though their methods were, laid the foundations on which western European medical science was to rise.

Medieval legal scholarship addressed itself to two distinct bodies of material: civil law and canon law. The legal structure of early medieval society was largely Germanic in inspiration and custom-based, particularly in northern Europe where Roman law had virtually disappeared. Customary law remained strong throughout the High Middle Ages: it governed the relationships among the feudal aristocracy and determined the manorial obligations of the medieval peasantry. It limited the feudal prerogatives of kings, and underlay Magna Carta. But from the late eleventh century on, Roman law was studied in Bologna and other European universities. Christendom was now exposed to a distinctly different legal tradition—coherent and logical—which began to compete with Germanic law, to rationalize it, and in some instances to replace it.

The foundation of medieval Roman law was the *Corpus Juris Civilis* of Justinian, which was all but unknown in the West throughout most of the Early Middle Ages but reappeared at Bologna in the last quarter of the eleventh century. Italy remained the center of Roman legal studies throughout the High Middle Ages. The traditions of Roman law had never entirely disappeared there, and the Italian peninsula therefore provided the most fertile soil for their revival. From Italy the study of Roman law spread northward. A great school of law emerged at Montpellier in southern France, and others flourished at Orleans, Paris, and Oxford. But Bologna remained the foremost center of Roman legal studies. There, scholars known as "glossators" wrote analytical commentaries on the *Corpus Juris,* elucidating difficult points and reconciling apparent contradictions. Later on they began to produce textbooks and important original treatises on the *Corpus* and to reorganize it into a coherent sequence of topics. Eventually such an extensive body of supplementary material existed that the glossators turned to the task of glossing the glosses—elucidating the elucidations. Around the mid-thirteenth century the work of the earlier glossators was brought to culmination with a comprehensive work by the Bolognese scholar Accursius—the *Glossa Ordinaria*—which was a composite synthesis of all previous commentaries on the *Corpus Juris*. Thereafter the *Glossa Ordinaria* became the authoritative supplement to the Corpus Juris in courts of Roman law.

The impact of the glossators was particularly strong in Italy and southern France where elements of Roman law had survived as local custom. By the thirteenth century Roman law was beginning to make a significant impact in the north as well, for by then civil lawyers trained in the Roman tradition were achieving an increasingly dominant role in the courts of France, Germany, and Spain. These men devoted themselves wholeheartedly to the royal service and used their legal training to exalt their monarchs. Although the Roman legal tradition had originally contained a strong element of constitutionalism, it inherited from Justinian's age an autocratic cast which the court lawyers of the rising monarchies put to effective use. Thus as Roman law gained an increasingly firm hold in the states of continental Europe it tended to make their governments at once more systematic and more absolute. In France, for example, civil lawyers played an important part in the gradual transformation of the early Capetian feudal monarchy into the royal autocracy of later times. And the development and durability of the parliamentary regime in England owed much to the fact that a strong monarchy, founded on the principles of Germanic law with its custom-based limitations on royal authority, was already well established before Europe felt the full impact of the Roman law revival.

Canon law developed alongside Roman law and derived a great deal from it. Methods of scholarship were similar in the two fields—commentaries and glosses were common to both—and the ecclesiastical courts borrowed much from the principles and procedures of Roman law. But whereas Roman law was based on the single authority of Justinian's *Corpus Juris*, canon law drew from many sources: the Bible, the writings of the ancient Church fathers, the canons of Church councils, and the decretals of popes. The *Corpus Juris*, although susceptible to endless commentary, was fundamentally complete in itself; popes and councils, on the other hand, continued to issue decrees, and canon law was therefore capable of unlimited development.

Canon law, like civil law, first became a serious scholarly discipline in eleventh-century Bologna and later spread to other major centers of learning. The study of canon law was strongly stimulated by the Investiture Controversy and subsequent church-state struggles, for the papacy looked to canon lawyers to support its claims with cogent, documented arguments and apt precedents. But the medieval scholars of canon law were far more than mere papal propagandists. They were grappling with the formidable problem of systematizing their sources, explaining what was unclear, reconciling what seemed contradictory—in other words, imposing order on the immense variety of dicta, opinions, and precedents upon which their discipline was based.

The essential goal of the canon lawyers was to assemble their diverse sources—their canons—into a single coherent work. It was up to them, in short, to accomplish the task that Justinian had performed for Roman law back in the sixth century. The civil lawyers had their *Corpus Juris Civilis*; it was up to the canon lawyers to create their own "Corpus Juris Canonici." The first attempts to produce comprehensive canonical collections data from the Early Middle Ages, but it was not until the eleventh-century revival at Bologna that serious scholarly standards were applied to the task. The definitive collection was completed around 1140 by the great Bolognese canon lawyer Gratian. Originally entitled *The Concordance of Discordant Canons*, Gratian's work is known to posterity as the *Decretum*.

Gratian not only brought together an immense body of canons from a bewildering variety of sources; he also framed them in a logical, topically organized scheme. Using scholarly methods that were just beginning to be employed by scholastic philosophers and logicians, he raised questions, quoted the relevant canons, endeavored to reconcile those that disagreed, and thereby arrived at firm conclusions. The result was an ordered body of general legal principles derived from particular passages from the Bible, the fathers, and papal and conciliar decrees. The *Decretum* became the authoritative text in ecclesiastical tribunals and the basis of all future study in canon law.

As time passed, and new decrees were issued, it became necessary to supplement Gratian's *Decretum* by collecting the canons issued subsequent to 1140. One such collection was made in 1234 under the direction of the lawyer-pope Gregory IX, another in the pontificate of Boniface VIII, and still others in later generations. Together, the

Decretum and the supplementary collections were given the title *Corpus Juris Canonici,* and became the ecclesiastical equivalent of Justinian's *Corpus.* These two great compilations, ecclesiastical and civil, symbolize the parallel growth of medieval Europe's two supreme sources of administrative and jurisdictional authority: church and monarchy.

The Background of
High Medieval Philosophy

It is only to be expected that an age which witnessed such sweeping economic and political changes and such vigorous creativity in religious and artistic expression would also achieve notable success in the realms of abstract thought. Medieval philosophy is marked by boundless curiosity and heated controversy. Although every important philosopher in the High Middle Ages was a churchman of one sort or another, ecclesiastical authority did not stifle speculation. Catholic orthodoxy, which hardened noticeably at the time of the Protestant Reformation, was still flexible in the twelfth and thirteenth centuries, and the philosophers of the age were far from being timid apologists for official dogmas. If some of them were impelled by conviction to provide the Catholic faith with a logical substructure, others asserted vigorously that reason does not lead to the truth of Christian revelation. And among those who sought to harmonize faith and reason there was sharp disagreement as to what form the logical substructure should take. All were believers—all were Catholics—but their doctrinal unanimity did not limit their diversity or curb their adventurous spirit.

The high medieval philosophers drew nourishment from five earlier sources: (1) From the Greeks they inherited the great philosophical systems of Plato and Aristotle. At first these two Greek masters were known in the West only through a handful of translations and commentaries dating from late Roman times. By the thirteenth century, however, new and far more complete translations were coming into Christendom from Spain and Sicily, and Aristotelian philosophy became a matter of intense interest and controversy in Europe's universities. (2) From the Islamic world came a flood of Greek scientific and philosophical works that had long before been translated into Arabic and were now translated from Arabic into Latin. These works came into Europe accompanied by extensive commentaries and original writings of Arab philosophers and scientists, for the Arabs had come to grips with Greek learning long before the advent of the High Middle Ages. Islamic thought made its own distinctive contribution to European science; in philosophy it was important chiefly as an agency for the transmission and interpretation of Greek thought. (3) The early Church fathers, particularly the Latin Doctors, had been a dominant influence on the thought of the Early Middle Ages and their authority remained strong in the twelfth and thirteenth centuries. St. Augustine retained his singular significance and was, indeed, the chief vessel of Platonic and Neoplatonic thought in the medieval universities. No philosopher of the High Middle Ages could ignore him, and some of the most distinguished of them were conscious and devoted Augustinians. (4) The early medieval scholars themselves contributed significantly to the high medieval intellectual revival. Gregory the Great, Isidore of Seville, Bede, Alcuin, Raban Maur, John the Scot, and Gerbert of Aurillac were all studied in the new universities. The original intellectual contributions of these men were less important, however, than the fact that they and their contemporaries had kept learning alive, fostered and perpetuated the classical tradition in Europe, and created an intellectual climate that made possible the reawakening of philosophical speculation in the eleventh century. Although stimulated by contacts with other civilizations, the intellectual surge of he High Middle Ages was fundamentally an internal phenomenon with roots in Ottonian, Carolingian, and pre-Carolingian Europe. (5) The high-medieval philosophers looked back beyond the scholars of the Early Middle Ages, beyond the fathers of the early Church, to the Hebrew and primitive Christian religious traditions as recorded in Scripture. Among medieval theologians the Bible, the chief written source of divine revelation, was the fundamental text and the ultimate authority.

Such were the chief elements—Greek, Islamic, Patristic, early medieval, and scriptural—that underlay the thought of the scholastic philosophers. Strictly defined, scholasticism is simply the philosophical movement associated with the high medieval schools—the cathedral and monastic schools, and later the universities. More basically it was a movement concerned above all with exploring the relationship between rationalism and theism—reason and revelation. All medieval scholastics were theists, all were committed, to some degree, to the life of reason. Many of them were immensely enthusiastic over the intellectual possibilities inherent in the careful application of Aristotelian logic to basic human and religious problems. Some believed that the syllogism was the master key to a thousand doors and that with sufficient methodological rigor, with sufficient exactness in the use of words, the potentialities of human reason were all but limitless.

The scholastics applied their logical method to a vast number of problems. They were concerned chiefly, however, with matters of basic significance to human existence: the nature of man, the purpose of human life, the existence and attributes of God, the fundamentals of human morality, the ethical imperatives of social and political life, the relationship between God and man. It would be hard to deny that these are the most profound sorts of questions that men can ask, although many philosophers of our own day are inclined to reject them as unanswerable. Perhaps they are, but the scholastics, standing near the beginning of Europe's long intellectual journey, and lacking the modern sense of disillusionment, were determined to make the attempt.

The Relationship of Faith and Reason

Among the diverse investigations and conflicting opinions of the medieval philosophers, three central issues deserve particular attention: (1) the degree of interrelationship between faith and reason; (2) the relative merits of the Platonic-Augustinian and the Aristotelian intellectual traditions; and (3) the reality of the Platonic-archetypes, or, as they were called in the Middle Ages, "universals."

The issue of faith vs. reason was perhaps the most far-reaching of the three. Ever since Tertullian in the third century, there had been Christian writers who insisted that God so transcended reason that any attempt to approach him intellectually was useless and, indeed, blasphemous. It was the mystic who knew God, not the theologian. Tertullian had posed the rhetorical questions,

What has Athens to do with Jerusalem? What concord is there between the Academy and the Church? . . . Let us have done with all attempts to produce a bastard Christianity of Stoic, Platonic, and dialectic composition! We desire no curious disputation after possessing Christ Jesus, no inquisition after enjoying the Gospel!

Tertullian had many followers in the Middle Ages. St. Peter Damiani, standing at the source of the new medieval piety, rejected the intellectual road to God in favor of the mystical. Damiani had insisted that God, whose power is limitless, cannot be bound or even approached by logic. He was followed in this view by such later mystics as St. Bernard, who denounced his brilliant rationalist contemporary Peter Abelard, and St. Francis, who regarded intellectual speculation as irrelevant and perhaps even dangerous to salvation. A later spiritual Franciscan, Jacopone da Todi, expressed the anti-intellectual position in verse:

> *Plato and Socrates may oft contend,*
> *And all the breath within their bodies spend,*
> *Engaged in disputations without end.*
> *What's that to me?*
> *For only with a pure and simple mind*
> *Can one the narrow path to heaven find,*
> *And greet the King; while lingers far behind,*
> *Philosophy.*

The contrary view was just as old. Third-century theologians such as Clement and Origen in the school of Alexandria had labored to provide Christianity with a sturdy philosophical foundation and did not hesitate to elucidate the faith by means of Greek—and particularly Platonic—thought. The fourth-century Latin Doctors, Ambrose, Jerome, and Augustine, had wrestled with the problem of whether a Christian might properly use elements from the pagan classical tradition in the service of the Faith, and all three ended with affirmative answers. As Augustine expressed it,

If those who are called philosophers, and especially the Platonists, have said anything that is true and in harmony with our faith, we must not only not shrink from it, but claim it for our own use from those who have unlawful possession of it.

Such is the viewpoint that underlies most of high medieval philosophy—that reason has a valuable role to play as a servant of revelation. St. Anselm, following Augustine, declared, "I believe so that I may know." Faith comes first, reason second; faith rules reason, but reason can perform the useful service of illuminating faith. Indeed, faith and reason are separate avenues to a single body of truth. By their very nature they cannot lead to contradictory conclusions, for truth is one. Should their conclusions ever *appear* to be contradictory, the philosopher can be assured that some flaw exists in his logic. Reason cannot err, but man's use of it can, and revelation must therefore be the criterion against which reason is measured.

This, in general, became the common position of later scholastic philosophers. The intellectual system of St. Thomas Aquinas was built on the conviction that reason and faith were harmonious. Even the arch-rationalist of the twelfth century, Peter Abelard, wrote: "I do not wish to be a philosopher if it means resisting St. Paul; I do not wish to be Aristotle if it must separate me from Christ." Abelard believed that he could at once be a philosopher and a Christian, but his faith took first priority.

Among some medieval philosophers the priorities were reversed. Averroës, a profound Aristotelian Muslim of twelfth-century Spain, boldly asserted the superiority of reason over faith. He affirmed the truth of several propositions which were logical byproducts of Aristotle's philosophy but were directly contrary to Islamic and Christian doctrine. Averroës taught, for example, that the world had always existed and was therefore uncreated—that all human actions were determined—that there was no personal salvation. In the thirteenth century a Christian philosophical school known as Latin Averroism became active at the University of Paris and elsewhere. Latin Averroists such as Siger of Brabant took the position that reason and revelation led to radically contrary conclusions. As Christians they accepted the teachings of the Church as ultimate truth, but as scholars they insisted that the conclusions of Aristotle and Averroes, being logically air-tight, were "philosophically necessary." This position came to be called the doctrine of the "two-fold truth."

The Latin Averroists shared with anti-intellectuals such as Damiani the belief that reason did not lead to the truth of revelation; they shared with Anselm and Aquinas the conviction that ultimate truth was revealed truth. Yet unlike most scholastics they abandoned altogether the effort to harmonize reason and revelation, and unlike the anti-intellectuals they did not reject philosophy but made it their profession. As believers they conceded the supremacy of dogma; as philosophers they insisted on the supremacy of reason. And although Siger of Brabant and most of his contemporaries appear to have held this awkward position in full sincerity, some of their successors became outright religious skeptics and only paid the necessary lip service to Christian doctrine. The fourteenth-century Latin Averroist John of Jaudun, for example, never lost an opportunity to poke subtle fun at any Christian dogma that seemed to him contrary to reason. On the subject of the Creation, John points out that according to reason the world has always existed. He concludes—with tongue in cheek—that as Christians we must nevertheless believe that God created the world; "Let it be added that creation very seldom happens; there has been only one, and that was a very long time ago."

Platonism-Augustinianism versus Aristotelianism

Thus, medieval thought produced a diversity of views on the proper relationship of reason and revelation. The same is true of the other two issues that we are to consider: the rivalry between Platonism and Aristotelianism, and the controversy over universals. The conflict between the intellectual systems of Plato-Augustine and Aristotle did not emerge clearly until the thirteenth century when the full body of Aristotle's writings came into the West in Latin translations from Greek and Arabic. Until then, most efforts at applying reason to faith were based on the Platonic tradition transmuted and transmitted by Augustine to medieval Europe. St. Anselm, for example, was a dedicated Augustinian, as were many of his twelfth-century successors. The tradition was carried on brilliantly in the thirteenth century by the great Franciscan, St. Bonaventure. Many thoughtful Christians of the thirteenth century were deeply suspicious of the newly recovered Aristotelian writings, and the rise of Latin Averroism served to deepen their apprehensions. They regarded Aristotle as pagan in viewpoint and dangerous to the Faith. Other thirteenth-century intellectuals, such as St. Thomas Aquinas, were much too devoted to the goal of reconciling faith and reason to reject the works of a man whom they regarded as antiquity's greatest philosopher. St. Thomas sought to Christianize Aristotle much as Augustine had Christianized Plato and the Neoplatonists. In the middle decades of the thirteenth century, as high medieval philosophy was reaching its crescendo, the Platonic and Aristotelian traditions flourished side by side, and in the works of certain English scientific thinkers of the age they achieved a singularly fruitful synthesis.

The Conflict over Universals

The contest between Platonism and Aristotelianism carried with it the seeds of yet another controversy: the argument over archetypes or universals. Plato had taught that terms such as "dog," "man," or "cat" not only described particular creatures but also had reality in themselves—that individual cats are imperfect reflections of a model cat, an archetypal or universal cat. Similarly, there are many examples of circles, squares, or triangles. Were we to measure these individual figures with sufficiently refined instruments we would discover that they were imperfect in one respect or another. No circle in this world is absolutely round. No square or triangle has perfectly straight sides. They are merely crude approximations of a perfect "idea." In "heaven," Plato would say, the perfect triangle exists. It is the source of the concept of triangularity that lurks in our minds and of all the imperfect triangles that we see in the physical world. The heavenly triangle is not only perfect but *real*. The earthly triangles are less real, less significant, and less worthy of our attention. To take still another example, we call certain acts "good" because they partake, imperfectly, of a universal good which exists in heaven. In short, these universals—cat, dog, circle, triangle, beauty, goodness, etc.—exist apart from the multitude of individual dogs, cats, circles, triangles, and beautiful and good things in this world. And the person who seeks knowledge ought to meditate on these universals rather than study the world of phenomena in which they are only imperfectly reflected.

St. Augustine accepted Plato's theory of universals but not without amendment. Augustine taught that the archetypes existed in the mind of God rather than in Plato's abstract "heaven." And whereas Plato had ascribed our knowledge of the universals to dim memories from a prenatal existence, Augustine maintained that God puts a knowledge of universals directly into our minds by a process of "divine illumination." Plato and Augustine agreed, however, that the universal existed apart from the particular and, indeed, was *more real* than the particular. In the High Middle Ages, those who followed the Platonic-Augustinian approach to universals were known as *realists*—they believed that universals were real.

The Aristotelian tradition brought with it another viewpoint on universals: they existed, to be sure, but only in the particular. Only by studying particular things in the world of phenomena could men gain a knowledge of universals. The human mind drew the universal from the particular by a process of abstraction. The universals were real, but in a sense less real—or at least less independently real—than Plato and Augustine believed. Accordingly, medieval philosophers who inclined toward the Aristotelian position have been called *moderate realists*.

Medieval philosophers were by no means confined to a choice between these two points of view. Several of them worked out subtle solutions of their own. As early as the eleventh century the philosopher Roscellinus declared that universals were not real at all. They were mere names that men gave to arbitrary classes of individual things. Reality was not to be found in universals but rather in the multiplicity and variety of objects which we can see, touch, and smell in the world around us. Those who followed Roscellinus in this view were known as *nominalists*: for them, the universals were *nomina*—"names." Nominalism remained in the intellectual background during the twelfth and thirteenth centuries but was revived in the fourteenth. Many churchmen regarded it as a dangerous doctrine, since its emphasis on the particular over the universal seemed to suggest that the Church was not, as Catholics believed, a single universal body but rather a vast accumulation of individual Christians.

St. Anselm

Having examined three central issues of high medieval philosophy—the relationship of reason to revelation, the relative validity of the Platonic-Augustinian and Aristotelian systems of thought, and the problem of universals—we shall now see how they developed in the minds of individual philosophers between the eleventh and fourteenth centuries.

The scholastic philosophers first made their appearance in the later eleventh century as an aspect of the general reawakening that Europe was just then beginning to experience. The earliest important figure in scholastic philosophy was St. Anselm (ca. 1034–1109), the Italian intellectual who became abbot of Bec in Normandy and later, as archbishop of Canterbury, brought the Investiture Controversy into England. During his eventful career he found time to write profoundly on a variety of philosophical and theological subjects.

As an Augustinian, Anselm took the realist position on the problem of universals. It was from Augustine, too, that he derived his attitude on the relationship of faith and reason. He taught that faith must precede reason, but that reason could serve to illuminate faith. His conviction that reason and faith were compatible made him a singularly important pioneer in the development of high medieval rationalism. He worked out several proofs of God, and in his important theological treatise, *Cur Deus Homo,* he subjected the doctrines of the incarnation and atonement to rigorous logical analysis.

Anselm's emphasis on reason, employed within the framework of a firm Christian conviction, set the stage for the significant philosophical developments of the following generations. With Anselm, Western Christendom regained at last the intellectual level of the fourth-century Latin Doctors.

Abelard

The twelfth-century philosophers, intoxicated by the seemingly limitless possibilities of reason and logic, advanced across new intellectual frontiers at the very time that their contemporaries were pushing forward the territorial frontiers of Europe. The most audacious of these twelfth-century Christian rationalists was Peter Abelard (1079–1142), an immensely popular teacher whose dazzling career ended in tragedy and defeat.

Abelard is perhaps best known for his love affair with the young Heloise, a relationship that ended with Abelard's castration at the hands of thugs hired by Heloise's enraged uncle. The lovers separated permanently, both taking monastic vows, and in later years Abelard wrote regretfully of the affair in his autobiographical *History of My Calamities.* There followed a touching correspondence between the two lovers in which Heloise, now an abbess, confessed her enduring love, and Abelard, writing almost as a father confessor, offered her spiritual consolation but nothing more. Abelard's autobiography and the correspondence with Heloise survive to this day, providing modern students with a tender, intimate picture of romance and pathos in a society far removed from our own.*

Abelard was the supreme logician of the twelfth century. Writing several decades before the great influx of Aristotelian thought in Latin translation, he anticipated Aristotle's position on the question of universals by advocating a theory rather similar to Aristotle's moderate realism. Universals, Abelard believed, had no separate existence, but were derived from particular things by a process of abstraction. In a famous work entitled *Sic et Non* ("Yes and No"), Abelard collected opinions from the Bible, the Latin fathers, the councils of the Church, and the decrees of the papacy on a great variety of theological issues, demonstrating that these hallowed authorities often disagreed on important religious matters. Others before him had collected authoritative opinions on various theological and legal issues, but never so thoroughly or systematically. Abelard, in his *Sic et Non,* employed a method of inquiry that was developed and perfected by canon lawyers and philosophers over the next several generations. We have already seen how the canonist Gratian, in his *Decretum,* used the device of lining up conflicting authorities and reconciling them. Similarly, Abelard's successors in theology sought to reconcile contradictions and arrive at conclusions, whereas Abelard had earned the enmity of his conservative contemporaries by leaving many of the issues unresolved. Abelard was a devoted Christian, if something of an intellectual show-off, but many regarded him as a dangerous skeptic. Thus he left himself open to attacks by men such as St. Bernard who were deeply hostile to the Christian rationalist movement which he so flamboyantly exemplified. The brilliant teacher was driven from one place to another. At length his opinions were condemned by an ecclesiastical council in 1141. He died at Cluny, on his way to Rome to appeal the condemnation, and the abbot of Cluny wrote a touching letter to Heloise describing his final days.

Peter Lombard
and Hugh of Saint-Victor

But twelfth-century rationalism was far more than a one-man affair, and the attacks on Abelard failed to halt its growth. His student Peter

* It has recently been argued that Heloise's letters are forgeries. Nothing is sacred to the modern revisionist historian.

Lombard (*c.* 1100–60) produced an important theological text, the *Book of Sentences,* which set off conflicting opinions on the pattern of the *Sic et Non,* but which, like Gratian's *Decretum,* took the further step of reconciling the contradictory authorities. Lombard's *Book of Sentences* remained for centuries a fundamental text in schools of theology.

The Augustinian tradition was best represented in Abelard's time at the school of Saint-Victor in Paris, and in particular by the distinguished scholar, Hugh of Saint-Victor (d. 1141). Hugh was a Christian rationalist, but he believed that reason was only the first step in man's approach to God. Beyond reason lay mysticism, and God could not be circumscribed by logic alone. Hugh and his school emphasized the subordination of the material to the spiritual, and—drawing on the ancient tradition of Biblical allegory—interpreted the entire natural world as a vast multitude of symbols pointing to spiritual truths.

John of Salisbury

The intellectual mood of the twelfth century was one of immense excitement at the possibilities of logic or dialectic. In this atmosphere, the remaining liberal arts—and especially the study of humanistic disciplines such as Latin literature—began to lose out in the competition. Cathedral schools of northern France such as Chartres, Paris, and Laon were important centers of literary studies in the eleventh century and remained so throughout much of the twelfth. But as the century progressed, as more and more Aristotelian texts became available, and as the vision of rational solutions to the great questions became ever more captivating, the interest of students and scholars shifted increasingly from literature to logic. The accomplished twelfth-century English scholar, John of Salisbury (*c.* 1115–80), was a student of Abelard's, a scholar of Greek, and a well-trained logician, but he was above all a humanist—a student of classical literature. He approved of dialectic but regretted that it was growing at the expense of other studies; he complained that the schools were tending to produce narrow logicians rather than broadly educated men.

In his *Policraticus* (1159), John of Salisbury made a major contribution to medieval political philosophy. Drawing on the thought of Classical Antiquity and the Early Middle Ages, he stressed the divine nature of kingship but emphasized equally its responsibilities and limitations. The king drew his authority from God but was commissioned to rule for the good of his subjects rather than himself. He was bound to give his subjects peace and justice and to protect the Church. If he abused his commission and neglected his responsibilities he lost his divine authority, ceased to be a king, and became a tyrant. As such he forfeited his subjects' allegiance and was no longer their lawful ruler. Under extreme circumstances, and if all else failed, John of Salisbury recommended tyrannicide. A good Christian subject, although obliged to obey his king, might kill a tyrant. Apart from the highly original doctrine of tyrannicide, the views expressed in the *Policraticus* mirror the general political attitudes of the twelfth century—responsible limited monarchy and government in behalf of the governed. These theories, in turn, were idealizd reflections of the actual feudal monarchies of the day which were deterred from autocracy by the power of the nobility, the authority of the Church, and ancient custom.

The New Translations

In the later twelfth and early thirteenth centuries the movement of Christian rationalism was powerfully reinforced by the arrival of vast quantities of Greek and Arabic writings in Latin translation. Significant portions of the philosophical and scientific legacy of ancient Greece became available to European scholars. Above all, the full Aristotelian corpus now came into the west through the labors of translators in Spain, Sicily, and the Latin Empire of Constantinople.

These translations did not just happen by chance. They came in answer to a deep hunger on the part of Western thinkers for a fuller knowledge of the classical heritage in philosophy and science. The introduction of certain new Aristotelian works provoked a crisis in Western Christendom, for they contained implications that seemed hostile to the Faith. And with them, as we have seen, came the skeptical and intellectually impressive works of the Islamic Spaniard Averroës which gave rise to the doctrine of the "two-fold truth." For a time it seemed as though reason and revelation were sundered, and the Church reacted in panic by condemning certain of Aristotle's writings. It was one of the major goals of thirteenth-century thought to refute the Latin Averroists—to rescue Aristotle and, indeed, reason itself for Western Christianity.

The Shape of Thirteenth-Century Thought

The thirteenth century differed sharply in spirit from the twelfth. The philosophers of the twelfth century were intellectual pioneers undertaking a great adventure. They were daring, original, and often radical; their mood was one of youthful exploration. The thirteenth century, although by no means lacking in originality, was preeminently an age of consolidation and synthesis. Its scholars digested the insights and conclusions of the past and cast them into comprehensive systems of thought. The characteristic products of the age were encyclopedias and summas. Vincent of Beauvais (d. 1264), attempted in his *Speculum Majus* to bring together all knowledge of all imaginable subjects into one immense compendium. At a much higher level, theologians such as Alexander of Hales (d. 1245), Albertus Magnus (1193–1280), and Thomas Aquinas (1225–74) produced great systematic treatises on theology, known as summas, in which they gave majestic structure and unity to the theological speculations of theirs and past ages.

St. Bonaventure

The thought of Aristotle loomed large in the thirteenth-century schools, but the Platonic-Augustinian tradition was well represented, too. There was a tendency for the Dominican scholars to espouse Aristotle, and the Franciscans to follow Plato and Augustine. Thus, the outstanding thirteenth-century exponent of Platonism-Augustinianism was the Franciscan St. Bonaventure (1221–74), an Italian of humble origin who rose to become a cardinal of the Church and minister-general of the Franciscan order.

Bonaventure was at once a philosopher and a mystic. Following in the Augustinian tradition, he was a realist on the matter of universals and a rationalist who stressed the subordination of reason to faith. He accepted the nature symbolism of Hugh of Saint-Victor, and visualized the whole physical universe as a multitude of symbols pointing to God and glorifying Him. For example, he regarded everything in the natural world that could possibly be divided into three parts as a reflection of the Holy Trinity. Bonaventure's universe was eternally reaching upward toward the Divine Presence.

Bonaventure, like many of his intellectual predecessors and contemporaries, saw the cosmos as an immense series of transparent concentric spheres. At its periphery, beyond the range of mortal eyes, were the nine spheres of angels. According to medieval theology, the angels were divided into nine ranks arrangd hierarchically into three major groups, each containing three subgroups. Characteristically, Bonaventure interpreted these three angelic triads as multiple symbols of the Trinity. Inside the spheres of angels was the sphere of stars which whirled daily round the earth. Within the stellar sphere were the spheres of the planets, sun, and moon. Such, in essence, had been Plato's conception of the universe, and Bonaventure remained faithful to it.

At the center of all the celestial spheres was the earth itself, and on the earth was man—the ultimate reason for the physical universe. Man was a creature of immense dignity and importance—the lord of the earth, the master of all lower creatures. The cosmos was created for man—to sustain him and, through its myriad symbols, to lead him to God. Indeed, it was for man that God himself had died on the cross.

Man was at the fulcrum of creation. His body gave him kinship with beasts; his soul gave him kinship with the angels. The human soul was created in the image of the Trinity, with three components: intellect, will, and memory. Man perceived the physical universe through his senses, but he knew the spiritual world—the world of universals—through the grace of divine illumination. The road to God and to truth, therefore, lay in introspection, mediation, and worship, not in observation and experiment.

Bonaventure's philosophy is not coldly intellectual but warm, emotional, and deeply spiritual. His discussion of God's attributes becomes a litany—an act of worship. His emphasis is less on knowledge than on love, and his entire system of thought was a kind of prayer in praise of God.

The New Aristotelianism;
St. Albertus Magnus

While Bonaventure was bringing new dimensions to traditional Platonism-Augustinianism, several of his contemporaries were coming to
grips with the great Aristotelian-Averroistic challenge to orthodox
Christian rationalism. The conflicting intellectual currents of the
age were brilliantly represented by philosophers and theologians on
the faculty of the mid-century University of Paris—the Augustinian
Bonaventure, the Latin Averroist Siger of Brabant, and the orthodox
Aristotelians Albertus Magnus and Thomas Aquinas.

Albertus and his student, Thomas Aquinas, were both Dominicans,
and both devoted themselves wholeheartedly to the reconciliation of
reason and faith through the fusion of Aristotelianism and Christianity. They sought to confound the Latin Averroists by demonstrating that reason and revelation pointed to one truth, not two. A
product of Germany, Albert Magnus was a scholar of widely ranging
interests who made important contributions to natural science—especially biology—as well as to philosophy and theology. He was a master
of Aristotelian thought and a summa writer, whose goal was to purge
Aristotle of the heretical taint of Averroism and transform his philosophy into a powerful intellectual foundation for Christian orthodoxy.
Albertus Magnus came near to realizing this goal, but its full achievement was left to his gifted student, Thomas Aquinas.

St. Thomas Aquinas

St. Thomas was born of a Norman-Italian noble family in 1225. His
parents intended him to become a Benedictine monk and to rise in
due course to a lucrative abbacy. But in 1244 he shocked them by
joining the radical new Dominican Order. He went to the University
of Paris in 1245 and spent the remainder of his life traveling, teaching, and writing. Unlike Augustine he had no youthful follies to
regret. Unlike Anselm, Bernard, and Bonaventure, he played no
great role in the political affairs of his day. His biography is agoniz-
ingly dull except for an incident late in his life in which he
abandoned his theological work, asserted that all his writings were
worthless, and devoted his remaining days to mysticism. At his death,

the priest who heard his final confession described it as being as innocent as that of a five-year-old child.

From the standpoint of intellectual history St. Thomas is a figure of singular interest and significance. In his copious writings—particularly his great comprehensive work, the *Summa Theologica*—he explored all the great questions of philosophy and theology, political theory and morality. He used Aristotle's logical method and Aristotle's categories of thought but arrived at conclusions that were in complete harmony with the Christian faith. Like Abelard, St. Thomas assembled every possible argument, pro and con, on every subject that he discussed, but unlike Abelard he drew conclusions and defended them with cogent arguments. Few philosophers before or since have been so generous in presenting and exploring opinions contrary to their own, and none has been so systematic and exhaustive.

St. Thomas created a vast, unified intellectual system, ranging from God to the natural world, logically supported at every step. His theological writings have none of the fiery passion of St. Augustine, none of the literary elegance of Plato; rather, they have an *intellectual* elegance, an elegance of system and organization akin to that of Euclid's geometry. His *Summa Theologica* is organized into an immense series of separate sections, each section dealing with a particular philosophical question. In Part I of the *Summa*, for example, Question 2 takes up the problem of God's existence. The *Question* is subdivided into three Articles: (1) "Whether God's existence is self-evident" (St. Thomas concludes that it is not); (2) "Whether it can be demonstrated that God exists" (St. Thomas concludes that it can be so demonstrated); and (3) "Whether God exists" (here St. Thomas propounds five separate proofs of God's existence).

In each article, St. Thomas takes up a specific problem and subjects it to rigorous formal analysis. First, he presents a series of *Objections* (*Objection 1, Objection 2,* etc.) in which he sets forth as effectively as he possibly can all the arguments *contrary* to his final conclusion. For example, *Question 2, Article 3,* "Whether God exists," begins with two *Objections* purporting to demonstrate that God does not exist. One of them runs as follows:

Objection 1. It seems that God does not exist, because if one of two contraries can be infinite, the other would be altogether destroyed. But the name "God" means that He is infinite goodness. Therefore, if God existed there would be no evil discoverable; but there is evil in the world. Therefore God does not exist.

After presenting the *Objections*, St. Thomas then turns to the second step in his analysis, the appeal to authority. This appeal is always introduced by the phrase, *On the contrary*, followed by a quotation from Scripture or from some authoritative patristic source that supports St. Thomas's own opinion on the subject. In the *Article* on God's existence the *Objections* are followed by the statement, "On the contrary, It is said in the person of God: 'I am Who I am' (Exodus, 3:14)." Having cited his authority, St. Thomas next appeals to reason and subjects the problem to his own logical scrutiny, beginning always with the formula, *I answer that...*, for example, "I answer that, The existence of God can be proved in five ways" (followed by a presentation of five proofs of the existence of God). Here is one:

The fifth way is taken from the governance of the world. We see that things which lack knowledge, such as natural bodies, act for an end, and this is evident from their acting always or nearly always in the same way, so as to obtain the best result. Hence it is clear that they achieve their end not only by chance but by design. Now whatever lacks knowledge cannot move toward an end unless it be directed by some being endowed with knowledge and intelligence, as the arrow is directed by the archer. Therefore some intelligent being exists by whom all natural things are directed to their end; and this being we call God.

The analysis concludes with refutations of the earlier *Objections*:

Reply to Objection 1. As Augustine says, 'Since God is the highest good, He would not allow any evil to exist in His works unless His omnipotence and goodness were such as to bring good even out of evil." This is part of the infinite goodness of God, that He should allow evil to exist, and out of it to produce good.

Having completed his analysis, St. Thomas then turns to the next *Article* or the next *Question* and subjects it to precisely the same process of inquiry: *Objections; On the contrary, I answer that; and Reply to Objections.* And as in Euclidian geometry so in Thomistic theology, once a problem is settled the conclusion can be used in solving subsequent problems. Thus the system grows, problem by problem, step by step, as St. Thomas's wide-ranging mind takes up such matters as the nature of God, the attributes of God, the nature and destiny of man, human morality, law, and political theory. The result is an imposing, comprehensive intellectual edifice embracing all major theological issues.

As the Gothic cathedral was the artistic embodiment of the high medieval world, so the philosophy of Aquinas was its supreme intellectual expression. Both were based on clear and obvious principles of structure. St. Thomas shared with the cathedral builders the impulse to display rather than disguise the structural framework of his edifice. Like the boldly executed Gothic flying buttress, the Thomistic *Questions, Articles, and Objections* allowed no doubt as to what the builder was doing, where he was going, or how he was achieving his effects. The scholastics were nothing if not systematic—they loved to exhibit the underlying principles of their organization—and none carried this tendency farther than St. Thomas. It is not without reason that the *Summa Theologica* has been called a cathedral of thought.

As a devoted Christian and Aristotelian, Aquinas contended against both the Augustinians, who would reject Aristotle altogether, and the Latin Averroists, who would make a heretic of him. St. Thomas distinguished carefully between revelation and reason but endeavored to prove that they could never contradict one another. Since human reason was a valid avenue to truth, since Christian revelation was undoubtedly authoritative, and since truth was one, then philosophy and Christian doctrine had to be compatible and complementary. "For faith rests upon infallible truth, and therefore its contrary cannot be demonstrated." This was the essence of St. Thomas's philosophical position. This was the conviction that separated him so radically from the Latin Averroists.

As against the Augustinianism of St. Anselm, Hugh of Saint-Victor, and St. Bonaventure, Aquinas emphasized the reality of the physical world as a world of things rather than symbols. Embracing the moderate realism of Aristotle, he declared that universals were to be found in the world of phenomena and nowhere else—that knowledge came from observation and analysis, not from divine illumination. Whereas Augustine, following Plato, had emphasized the *duality* of matter and spirit, earth and heaven, body and soul, Aquinas emphasized the oneness of God's creation. He asserted the unity of ideas and phenomena—the universal was not outside the particular but within it—and thus he shared with St. Francis and others the notion that the physical world was deeply significant in itself, that matter mattered. He affirmed the unity of intellectual knowledge and sensation, maintaining that knowledge is acquired by a gradual ascent from things to concepts, from the visible to the invisible world. He stressed the unity of man, declaring that a human being was not a soul-using a body or a spirit imprisoned in flesh, as the Platonists suggested, but an inseparable composite of body and soul. The human body, although a source of temptation, was good in itself and was an essential part of man.

Likewise, the state, which previous Christian thinkers had commonly regarded as a necessary evil—an unfortunate but indispensable consequence of the Fall of Adam—was accepted by Aquinas as a good and natural outgrowth of man's social impulse. He echoed Aristotle's dictum that "Man is a political creature" and regarded the justly governed state as a fitting part of the Divine Order. Like John of Salisbury, St. Thomas insisted that kings must govern in their subjects' behalf and that a willful, unrestrained ruler who ignored God's moral imperatives was no king but a tyrant. Just as the human body could be corrupted by sin, the body politics could be corrupted by tyranny. But although the Christian must reject both sin and tyranny, he should nevertheless revere the body, the state, and indeed all physical creation as worthy products of God's will, inseparable from the world of spirit, and essential ingredients in the unity of existence.

Such was the Thomistic vision. In binding together matter and spirit, the concrete and the abstract, body and soul, God and man, Aquinas was seeking to encompass the totality of being in a vast existential unity. At the center was God, the author of physical and spiritual creation, the maker of heaven and earth, who himself had assumed human form and redeemed mankind on the cross, who discloses portions of the truth to man through revelation, permits him to discover other portions through the operation of his intellect, and will lead him into all truth through salvation. Ultimately, truth is God Himself, and it is man's destiny, upon reaching heaven, to stand unshielded in the divine presence—to love and to know. Thus the roads of St. Thomas, St. Bonaventure, St. Bernard, and Dante, although passing over very different terrain, arrive finally at the same destination. It is not so surprising, after all, that in the end St. Thomas rejected the way of the philosopher for the way of the mystic.

Critics of St. Thomas

To this day there are men of keen intelligence who accept the philosophy of St. Thomas. On the other hand, many of his own thirteenth-century contemporaries rejected it in whole or in part, and it remained a source of intense controversy in the centuries that followed. Franciscan intellectuals such as Bonaventure were particularly suspicious of the intellectual *tour de force* of this gifted Dominican. Bonaventure was a rationalist, but in a far more limited sense than was Aquinas, and Bonaventure's Franciscan successors came increasingly to the opinion that reason was of little or no use in probing metaphysical problems. The Scottish Franciscan, Duns Scotus (d. 1308), undertook a rigorous and subtle critique of St. Thomas' theory of knowledge. And in the philosophy of the astute English Franciscan, William of Ockham (c. 1300–1349), reason and revelation were divorced altogether.* Christian doctrine, Ockham said, could not be approached by reason at all but had to be accepted on faith. The Thomist synthesis was a mirage. Reason's province was the natural world and that alone.

Science

The Ockhamist position, with its duality of mysticism and empiricism, blazed two paths into the future: pietism uninhibited by reason and science uninhibited by revelation. In Ockham's time Western science was already well evolved. As far back as the later decades of the tenth century, Gerbert of Aurillac had visited Moorish Spain, familiarized himself with Islamic thought, and made his own modest contributions to scientific knowledge.† Gerbert built a simple "planetarium" of balls, rods, and bands to illustrate the rotation of the stellar sphere and the motions of the planets. He introduced the abacus and Arabic numerals into the West and, following the Greeks and Arabs, he taught that the earth was round.

* see below, pp. 356–357.
† See p. 126.

Islamic science continued thereafter to inspire western scholars, particularly in the late-eleventh and twelfth centuries. Men such as Adelard of Bath (d. 1150) retraced Gerbert's pilgrimage into Islamic lands and returned with a new respect for scientific inquiry—as well as an abundance of astrological texts. Among the works that Adelard translated from Arabic into Latin were Euclid's *Elements* and an important Muslim work on arithmetic that used Arabic numerals. Through the labors of the twelfth-century translators, the great scientific works of Greece and Islam were made known in the West— Aristotle's *Physics*, Ptolemy's *Almagest*, Arabic books on algebra, astrology, and medicine, and many others. And now Western scholars began to write scientific books of their own, such as Adelard of Bath's *Natural Questions*. Such works, however, were mere summaries of Greek and Arabic knowledge. The purely assimilative phase of western science continued until the thirteenth century when, particularly among the Franciscans, the first serious original work began.

Thirteenth-century Franciscans, anticipating the later duality of Ockham, were inclined toward both pietism and the investigation of nature. The mysticism of St. Bonaventure represents one pole of Franciscan thought; at the other stands a group of scientific thinkers, who, inspired perhaps by St. Francis's love of nature, applied their logical tools to the task of investigating the physical world. Thirteenth-century Oxford became the leading center of scientific work, and it was there that western European science began to be creative.

The key figure in the development of medieval science was the English scholar, Robert Grosseteste (1168–1253), who, although not a Franciscan himself, was chief lecturer to the Franciscans at Oxford. Grosseteste was on intimate terms with Platonic and Neoplatonic philosophy, Aristotelian physics, and the rich scientific legacy of Islam. At bottom, he was a Platonist and an Augustinian, but he wrote important commentaries on the scientific works of Aristotle and was able to draw on both traditions. From Plato Grosseteste derived the notion that mathematics is a basic key to understanding the physical universe; the fundamental importance of numbers is very much in keeping with the Platonic realist interpretation of universals, and Plato himself had once asserted that "God is a mathematician." From Aristotle Grosseteste learned the importance of abstracting knowledge from the world of phenomena by means of observation and experiment. Thus, bridging the two traditions, Grosseteste brought together the mathematical and experimental components that together underlie the rise of modern science. More than that, drawing on the suggestive work of his Islamic predecessors he worked out a far more rigorous experimental procedure than is to be found in the pages of Aristotle. A pioneer in the development of scientific method, he outlined a system of observation, hypothesis, and experimental verification that was elaborated by his successors into the methodology that modern physical scientists still employ.

Like other pioneers, Grosseteste followed many false paths. He was better at formulating a scientific methodology than in applying it to specific problems, and his explanations of such phenomena as heat, light, color, comets, and rainbows were rejected in later centuries. But the experimental method which he formulated was to become in time a powerful intellectual tool. The problem of the rainbow, for example, was largely solved by the fourteenth-century scientist Theoderic of Freiburg, who employed a refined version of Grosseteste's experimental methodology. The great triumphs of European science lay far in the future, but with the work of Robert Grosseteste the basic instrument had been forged. Grosseteste's career illustrates not that science was born in the thirteenth century but rather that scientific thought evolved gradually from antiquity to modern times, and that the High Middle Ages contributed markedly to its development.

Grosseteste's work was carried further by his famous disciple, the Oxford Franciscan Roger Bacon (c. 1214–94). The author of a fascinating body of scientific sense and nonsense, Roger Bacon was more an advocate of experimental science than a consistent practitioner of it. He dabbled in the mysteries of alchemy and astrology, and his boundless curiosity carried him along many strange roads. He led a turbulent life, at times enjoying the friendship of the papacy, at other times imprisoned by his own Franciscan order, which suspected him of practicing magic. Roger Bacon was critical of the deductive logic and metaphysical speculations that so intrigued his scholastic contemporaries: "Reasoning," he wrote, "does not illuminate these matters; experiments are required, conducted on a large scale, performed with instruments and by various necessary means."

At his best, Roger Bacon was almost prophetic:

Experimental science controls the conclusions of all other sciences. It reveals truths which reasoning from general principles would never have discovered. Finally, it starts us on the way to marvelous inventions which will change the face of the world.

One such marvelous invention, the telescope, was not to be invented for another three centuries, yet Roger Bacon described it in astonishing detail:

We can give such figures to transparent bodies, and dispose them in such order with respect to the eye and the objects, that the rays will be refracted and bent toward any place we please, so that we will see the object near at hand or at a distance, under any angle we wish. And thus from an incredible distance we may read the smallest letters, and may number the smallest particles of dust and sand, by reason of the greatness of the angle under which we see them. . . . The sun, moon, and stars may be made to descend hither in appearance, and to be visible over the heads of our enemies, and many things of a like sort which persons unacquainted with such matters would refuse to believe.

The Medieval Intellectual Achievement

Thus the intense intellectual activity of the thirteenth century produced both the supreme synthesis of Christian rationalism in the philosophy of St. Thomas and the genesis of a new method of scientific inquiry in the thought of Robert Grosseteste and his successors. In the realm of the intellect, as in so many others, the thirteenth century was both synthetic and creative.

With the coming of the fourteenth century, the growth of scientific thought was accompanied by the gradual erosion of the Thomist synthesis. Universal systems such as that of St. Thomas have seldom been lasting, but for a few brief years Thomism represented, for many, the perfect fusion of intellect and belief. As such, it takes its place alongside the Gothic cathedral, the *Divine Comedy* of Dante, and the piety of St. Francis as a supreme and mature expression of high medieval culture.

Conclusion

The world of the High Middle Ages is described in some outworn books as stagnant, gloomy, and monolithic. At the other extreme, it has been portrayed as an ideally constituted society, free of modern fears and tensions, where men of all classes could live happily and creatively, finding fulfillment in their service to the common good. In reality, the medieval era was neither of these things. It was an age of vitality, of striking contrasts, of dark fears and high hopes, of poverty that was often brutal yet gradually diminishing. Above all, it was an age in which Europeans awoke to the rich variety of possibilities that lay before them. A thirteenth-century poet, in his celebration of springtime, captured perfectly the spirit of this awakening:

> *The earth's ablaze again*
> *With lustrous flowers.*
> *The fields are green again,*
> *The shadows, deep.*
> *Woods are in leaf again,*
> *And all the world*
> *Is filled with joy again.*
> *This long-dead land*
> *Now flames with life again.*
> *The passions surge,*
> *Love is reborn,*
> *And beauty wakes from sleep.*

Suggested Readings

The asterisk indicates a paperback edition.

GENERAL WORKS

*John W. Baldwin, *The Scholastic Culture of the Middle Ages: 1000–1300.* Lexington, Mass.: D. C. Heath, 1971. An interestingly organized treatment of high-medieval culture focusing on the universities, thought, and Gothic architecture in their urban setting.

*Christopher Brooke, *The Structure of Medieval Society.* New York: McGraw-Hill, 1971. Graceful, perceptive essays on medieval people and their ideas and customs, using St. Francis' meeting with Innocent III as the point of departure.

*Marshall Clagett, Gaines Post, and Robert Reynolds, eds., *Twelfth-Century Europe and the Foundations of Modern Society.* Madison: Univ. of Wisconsin Press, 1966. A collection of essays on twelfth-century intellectual and economic achievements and on the contributions of neighboring cultures to Europe's creative breakthrough.

*R. W. Southern, *The Making of the Middle Ages.* New Haven: Yale Univ. Press, 1953. A sympathetic, thought-provoking interpretation of the eleventh and twelfth centuries.

ECONOMIC HISTORY AND THE FRONTIERS

*Robert-Henri Bautier, *The Economic Development of Medieval Europe.* New York: Harcourt Brace Jovanovich, 1971. An important and original work, well-written and superbly illustrated.

*David Douglas, *The Norman Achievement.* Berkeley: Univ. of California Press, 1969. An expert and readable comparative study of Norman activities in Normandy, Syria, Italy, Sicily, and England during the heroic age of Norman international enterprise, c. 1050–1100.

*Robert S. Lopez, *The Commercial Revolution of the Middle Ages: 950–1350.* Englewood Cliffs, N.J.: Prentice-Hall, 1971. A lively, provocative book, advancing the thesis that the medieval commercial revolution was unique in world history and an essential prerequisite to later industrialization.

Fritz Rorig, *The Medieval Town.* Berkeley: Univ. of California Press,

1967. This study explores the relationships between commerce and town growth in central Europe.

*Steven Runciman, *A History of the Crusades*. 3 vols. New York: Harper & Row, 1964–1967. Comprehensive and authoritative.

CHRISTIANITY

Russell's *History of Medieval Christianity* (above, p. 138) remains useful throughout the medieval period.

Christopher Brooke, *Medieval Church and Society*. London: Sidgwick & Jackson, 1971. Perceptive essays on Gregory VII, medieval forgery, Becket, heresy, Francis and Dominic, and other topics.

Dom David Knowles, *From Pachomius to Ignatius*. Oxford: Clarendon Press, 1966. A brief, authoritative account of the organization of religious orders, emphasizing the period from the rise of Cluny through the death of Dominic. For a classic, comprehensive treatment of the Benedictines and later religious orders in England, see, by the same author, *The Monastic Order in England*, 2nd ed. New York: Cambridge Univ. Press, 1963, and *The Religious Orders in England*, 3 vols. New York: Cambridge Univ. Press, 1948–1959.

*Jean Leclerc, *The Love of Learning and the Desire for God*, translated by Catherine Misrahi. New York: Fordham Univ. Press, 1961. The best short study of monasticism in English.

Paul Sabatier, *St. Francis of Assisi*. New York: Scribner's, 1894. A warm and deeply sympathetic older work.

*R. W. Southern, *Western Society and the Church in the Middle Ages*. Baltimore: Penguin Books, 1970. A masterful survey and interpretation showing the interactions between the Church and the world from Carolingian times to the Reformation.

EMPIRE AND PAPACY

*Geoffrey Barraclough, *The Medieval Papacy*. New York: Harcourt Brace Jovanovich, 1968. A thoughtful interpretive survey, beautifully illustrated.

Friedrich Heer, *The Holy Roman Empire*. New York: Praeger Publishers, 1968. A brilliantly written study that defends the empire as a viable "federal" system.

Marcel Pacaut, *Frederick Barbarossa*, translated by A. J. Pomerans. London: William Collins' Sons, 1970 (French edition, 1967). An "unashamed work of popularization" by an able scholar who portrays Barbarossa as the person who, "better than anyone else, expressed the imperial ideal."

Gerd Tellenbach, *Church, State and Christian Society at the Time of the*

Investiture Contest, translated by R. F. Bennett. New York: Humanities Press, 1940. The finest analysis of the Investiture Controversy in English.

Walter Ullmann, *The Growth of Papal Government in the Middle Ages.* 2nd ed. New York: Barnes & Noble, 1962. An intellectual history of the medieval papal ideology.

Thomas C. Van Cleve, *The Emperor Frederick II of Hohenstaufen: Immutator Mundi.* New York: Oxford University Press, 1972. A comprehensive new study of Frederick's career and its socio-cultural setting.

ENGLAND AND FRANCE

For high-medieval England, the appropriate volumes of the monumental Oxford History of England are authoritative but rather heavy:

A. L. Poole, *From Domesday Book to Magna Carta: 1078–1216.* 2nd ed. New York: Oxford Univ. Press, 1955.

Sir Maurice Powicke, *The Thirteenth Century: 1216–1307.* New York: Oxford Univ. Press, 1953.

For a lighter treatment of the period see:

*Christopher Brooke, *From Alfred to Henry III.* New York: Thomas Nelson, 1966.

*C. Warren Hollister, *The Making of England.* 2nd ed. Lexington, Mass.: D. C. Heath, 1971.

*R. Allen Brown, *The Normans and the Norman Conquest.* New York: Thomas Y. Crowell, 1969. A well-written, slightly pro-Norman account of the Conquest and its background and aftermath.

*David Douglas, *William the Conqueror.* Berkeley: Univ. of California Press, 1964. This beautifully written work of scholarship is the best account of the Conqueror's career. Due attention is given to William's background and achievements in Normandy.

*Robert Fawtier, *The Capetian Kings of France*, translated by Lionel Butler and R. J. Adam. New York: St. Martin's Press, 1960. A short, masterful treatment, highly recommended.

*C. Warren Hollister, ed., *The Impact of the Norman Conquest.* New York: John Wiley, 1969. A collection of modern opinions and original sources relating to the question of the Norman Conquest's effect on history.

*James C. Holt, ed., *Magna Carta and the Idea of Liberty.* New York: John Wiley, 1972. An exploration of original sources and modern scholarly writings relating to Magna Carta and its influence on English history over subsequent centuries, with an illuminating section on similar charters of liberties issued elsewhere in medieval Europe.

*Amy Kelly, *Eleanor of Aquitaine and the Four Kings*. Cambridge, Mass.: Harvard Univ. Press, 1971 (originally published in 1950). Enertaining and sound. The kings are Eleanor's two husbands, Louis VII and Henry II, and her two sons, Richard and John.

Dom David Knowles, *Thomas Becket*. Stanford, Calif.: Stanford University Press, 1970. A short, well-balanced biography of this controversial churchman, which ultimately ascribes the controversy to Henry II's demand to treat the non-spiritual affairs of the Church as under his sole jurisdiction.

*Bertie Wilkinson, *The Creation of Medieval Parliaments*. New York: John Wiley, 1972. A stimulating, original essay illustrated by contemporary sources and excerpts from modern scholarly writings.

THOUGHT, LETTERS, AND THE ARTS

*Christopher Brooke, *The Twelfth-Century Renaissance*. New York: Harcourt Brace Jovanovich, 1969. A well-illustrated, sensitively-written essay on some of the key cultural figures of twelfth-century Europe.

*Edward Grant, *Physical Science in the Middle Ages*. New York: John Wiley, 1971. This brief, valuable work stresses the impact of Aristotelian physical science on the medieval mind after c. 1200.

*C. H. Haskins, *The Renaissance of the Twelfth Century*. Cambridge, Mass., Harvard Univ. Press, 1971, first published 1927. A pioneering book, particularly strong on Latin literature.

*C. H. Haskins, *The Rise of the Universities*. Ithaca, N.Y.: Cornell Univ. Press, 1957, first published 1923. Brief, informative, and a delight to read.

*George Henderson, *Gothic*. Baltimore: Penguin Books, 1967. A good, well-illustrated study of the Gothic style in its historical and cultural context.

*C. Warren Hollister, ed., *The Twelfth-Century Renaissance*. New York: John Wiley, 1969. Excerpts and commentaries on Haskins' *Renaissance of the Twelfth Century* followed by documents and pictures illustrating twelfth-century civilization.

*David Knowles, *The Evolution of Medieval Thought*. New York: Random House, 1964. A short, lucid survey of medieval intellectual history; sympathetic, judicious, and readable.

*C. S. Lewis, *The Allegory of Love: A Study in Medieval Tradition*. New York: Oxford Univ. Press, 1958, first published 1936. An illuminating, beautifully written study of courtly love and the medieval romance.

*John C. Moore, *Love in Twelfth-Century France*. Philadelphia: Univ. of Pennsylvania Press, 1972. Short, sensitive, learned, and graceful.

*R. W. Southern, *Medieval Humanism and Other Studies*. Oxford: Basil Blackwell & Mott, 1970. A series of important related essays on medieval thought and life containing a fundamental reinterpretation of medieval humanism and its relationship to scholasticism.

Whitney Stoddard, *Monastery and Cathedral in France*. Middletown, Conn.: Wesleyan Univ. Press, 1966. A superbly illustrated account of French Romanesque and Gothic art.

*Walter Ullman, *A History of Political Thought: The Middle Ages*. Baltimore: Penguin Books, 1965. A short, synthetic work that stresses the ideology of the papal monarchy and points to the medieval background of modern political thought.

SOURCES

*Dante Alighieri, *The Divine Comedy*, translated by Thomas Bergin. New York: Crofts Classics, 1955. One of many available translations.

Angel Flores, *An Anthology of Medieval Lyrics*. New York: Modern Library, 1962. English translations of medieval lyric poems from France, Italy, Germany, and Spain.

The Correspondence of Pope Gregory VII, edited and translated by Ephraim Emerton. New York: Columbia Univ. Press, 1969, first published 1932.

*Guibert of Nogent, *Self and Society in Medieval France*, translated by John F. Benton. New York: Harper & Row, 1970. The revealing autobiography of a twelfth-century abbot and scholar, to which Benton gives a Freudian twist in his provocative introduction.

*Bennett D. Hill, *Church and State in the Middle Ages*. New York: John Wiley, 1970. Sources and modern· interpretive essays on key church-state issues from New Testament times to Pope Boniface VIII, including the controversies surrounding Gregory VII, Becket, and Innocent III.

*Otto of Freising, *The Deeds of Frederick Barbarossa*, translated by C. C. Mierow and Richard Emery. New York: W. W. Norton, 1966, first published 1953. A good example of medieval historical writing.

Anton C. Pegis, ed. *Introduction to St. Thomas Aquinas*. New York: Modern Library, 1948. Intelligently-chosen selections with a stimulating introduction.

The Song of Roland, translated by D. L. Sayers. Baltimore: Penguin Books, 1957.

*Villehardouin and de Joinville, *Memoirs of the Crusades*, translated by Sir Frank Marzials. New York: E. P. Dutton, first published 1908. Contemporary accounts of the Fourth Crusade and the crusading exploits of St. Louis.

part III The Late Middle Ages: the ordeal of transition

15

church and state in the 14th and 15th centuries

The Decline of the High-Medieval Synthesis

Like most eras of transition, the fourteenth and fifteenth centuries were violent and unsettled, marked by a gradual ebbing of confidence in the values on which the high-medieval synthesis had rested. Prosperity gave way to sporadic depression, optimism to disillusionment, and the thirteenth-century dream of fusing the worlds of matter and spirit came to an end. Social behavior ran to extremes—to rebellion, sensualism, flagellation, cynicism, and witchcraft. Powerful creative forces were at work in these centuries, but they were less evident to most contemporary observers than the forces of disintegration and decay. The shrinking of Europe's economy, population, and territorial frontiers was accompanied by a mood of pessimism and claustrophobia, exploding periodically into frenzied enthusiasm or blind rage. The literature and art of the period are often preoccupied with fantasy, eccentricity, and death. England and France were torn by war, and both were ruled for a time by madmen. The Black Death struck Europe in the mid-fourteenth century and returned periodically to darken men's spirits and disrupt society.

These varied symptoms of social and psychological disorder were associated with a gradual shift in Western Europe's political orientation—from a Christian commonwealth to a constellation of territorial states. The Roman Catholic Church fared badly during the late middle ages. The western kingdoms were racked by civil and external war and, at times, by a near-breakdown of royal government. Yet during the final half-century of the period (*c.* 1450–1500) strong monarchies emerged in England, France, and Spain. These three states were destined to dominate Western European politics far into the future. By 1500 the monarchy was beginning to replace the Church as the object of men's highest allegiance. The pope had become mired in local Italian politics, and medieval Christian internationalism was breaking up into sovereign fragments.

The Church in the Late Middle Ages

The late-medieval evolution from Christendom toward nationhood was not so much a transformation as a shift in balance. Even during the high middle ages the ideal of a Christian commonwealth, guided by pope and clergy, had never been fulfilled. At best, popes could win momentary political victories over kings and could achieve an uneasy equilibrium between royal and clerical authority within the European kingdoms. And by the end of the thirteenth century the balance was already tipping in favor of monarchs such as Edward I of England and Philip the Fair of France. Two centuries later, in 1500, the papacy was far weaker as an international force and the monarchies stronger, but "nationhood," by any strict definition, had not yet come. Still, papal authority over the churches of various kingdoms, which had been a significant reality in the high middle ages, was becoming tenuous by 1500. The princely electors of Germany had long before denied the papacy any role in imperial elections or coronations, and papal influence in the appointment of French, English, and Spanish prelates had ebbed. More important still, the late middle ages witnessed a collapse of papal spiritual prestige and a widening chasm between Christian piety and the organized Church.

Mystics and Reformers

Christianity did not decline noticeably during this period; it merely became less ecclesiastical. The powerful movement of lay piety, which had been drifting away from papal leadership all through the high middle ages, now became increasingly hostile to ecclesiastical wealth and privilege, increasingly individualistic, and increasingly mystical. The wave of mysticism that swept across late-medieval Europe was not, for the most part, openly heretical. But by stressing the spiritual relationship between the individual and God the mystics tended to deemphasize the role of the ordained clergy and the sacraments as channels of divine grace. The mystic, although he believed in the efficacy of the Holy Eucharist, devoted himself chiefly to the direct mystical apprehension of God, for which no clerical hierarchy, no popes, and no sacraments were needed.

Mysticism had always been an element in Christian devotional life, and it was well known to the high middle ages. But with the growth of complacency and corruption within the Church, mysticism became, for the first time, a large-scale movement among the laity. Early in the fourteenth century, the great Dominican mystic, Meister Eckhart (*d.* 1327), taught that man's true goal is utter separation from the world of the senses and absorption into the Divine Unknown. Eckhart had many followers, and as the century progressed, several large mystical brotherhoods took form. The greatest of them, the Brethren of the Common Life, was founded about 1375 by the Flemish lay preacher Gerard Groot, a student of one of Eckhart's disciples.

The Brethren of the Common Life devoted themselves to simple lives of preaching, teaching, and charitable works. Their popularity in fifteenth-century Northern Europe approached that of the Franciscans two centuries before, but the Brethren, unlike the Franciscans, took no lifetime vows. Their schools were among the finest in Europe and produced some of the leading mystics, humanists, and reformers of the fifteenth and sixteenth centuries. Erasmus and Luther were both products of the Brethren's schools, as was Thomas à Kempis (*d.* 1471) whose *Imitation of Christ* stands as the supreme literary expression of late-medieval mysticism.* The *Imitation of Christ* typifies the mystical outlook in its emphasis on adoration over speculation, inner spiritual purity over external "good works," and direct experience of God over the sacramental avenues to divine grace. The *Imitation* remained well within the bounds of Catholic orthodoxy, yet

---

* Although most scholars attribute *The Imitation of Christ* to Thomas à Kempis, the attribution is not certain.

it contained ideas that had great appeal to the sixteenth-century Protestant reformers. The emphasis on individual piety, common to all the mystics, tended to erode the medieval Christian commonwealth by transforming the Catholic Church into a multitude of individual souls, each groping his way toward salvation alone.

The element of Christian individualism was carried at times to the point of outright heresy. John Wycliffe (d. 1384), a professor at Oxford, anticipated the later Protestants by placing the authority of Scriptures over the pronouncements of popes and councils. Extending the implications of contemporary mysticism to their limit, Wycliffe stressed the individual's inner spiritual journey toward God, questioned the real presence of Christ in the Holy Eucharist, deemphasized the entire sacramental system, and spoke out strongly against ecclesiastical wealth. This last protest had been implicit in the thirteenth-century Franciscan movement, although St. Francis had shown his devotion to apostolic poverty by living it rather than forcing it on others. The compromises of later Franciscanism on the matter of property had given rise to a zealous splinter group—the "Spiritual Franciscans"—whose insistence on universal ecclesiastical poverty had made them anticlerical and antipapal. John XXII (1316–1334), the shrewd Avignonese "financier-pope," had seen fit in 1323 to denounce the doctrine of apostolic poverty as heretical. And Wycliffe, more than a half century later, was stripped of his professorship and convicted of heresy. Owing to his powerful friends at court, and to the unpopularity of the papacy in fourteenth-century England, he was permitted to die peacefully, but his followers, the Lollards, were less fortunate. Their fate is suggested by the title of a parliamentary act of 1401: "The Statute on the Burning of Heretics." There were to be no Lollards in England to celebrate King Henry VIII's break with Rome in the 1530s.

English Lollardy represented an extreme expression of a growing discontent with the official Church. Wycliff's doctrines spread to faraway Bohemia where they were taken up by the reformer John Hus. The Hussites used Wycliffe's anticlericalism as a weapon in the struggle for Czech independence from German political and cultural influence. John Hus was burned at the stake at the Council of Constance in 1415, but his followers survived into the Reformation era as a dissident national group. Both Wycliffe and Hus represented, in their opposition to the organized international church, a reconciliation of personal religious faith with the idea of national sovereignty. If Christianity was to be an individual affair, then the political claims of popes and prelates were meritless, and secular rulers might govern without ecclesiastical interference. Thus the radical thrust of late-medieval Christianity, by its very anticlericalism, tended to support the growing concept of secular sovereignty. Ardent religious spirits such as John Hus—and Joan of Arc, burned as a heretic in 1431—could fuse Christian mysticism with the beginnings of patriotism.

Popes and Councils

The mystics and reformers, implicitly or explicitly, rejected the pope as the chief link connecting God and the Christian community. Actually, the late-medieval papacy did little to merit the awesome responsibility of mediating between heaven and earth. Under pressure from King Philip the Fair the papacy had moved to Avignon, on the Rhône River, officially outside the domains of France yet always in their shadow. There a series of French popes ruled from 1309 to 1376. The Avignon popes were subservient to the French crown only to a degree. They were capable of independent action particularly when France had weak rulers, but their very location suggested to non-Frenchmen that they were no longer an imperial international force. Until 1376 attempts to return the papacy to Rome were foiled by the insecurity and violent factionalism of the holy city. Meanwhile the Avignon popes carried the thirteenth-century trend toward administrative and fiscal efficiency to its ultimate degree. Englishmen and Germans resented paying high taxes to an apparent tool of the French crown. And the immense, bureaucracy of papal Avignon could hardly be expected to inspire mystics and reformers. As the material wealth of the papacy grew, its spiritual capital declined.

In 1376, Pope Gregory XI finally moved the Holy See from Avignon back to Rome. Chagrined by the turbulent conditions he encountered there, he made plans to return to France, but died in 1378 before he could carry them out. Urged on by a Roman mob, the cardinals—most of whom were homesick Frenchmen—grudingly elected an Italian to the papal throne. The new pope, Urban VI, had previously been a colorless functionary in the ecclesiastical establishment. Now, to everyone's surprise, he became a zealous reformer and began taking steps to reduce the cardinals' revenues and influence. The

French cardinals fled Rome, canceled their previous election on the grounds of mob intimidation, and elected a French pope who returned with them to Avignon. Back in Rome, Urban VI appointed new cardinals and for the next 37 years the Universal Church was torn by schism. When the rival popes died, their cardinals elected rival successors. Excommunications were hurled to-and-fro between Rome and Avignon, and the states of Europe chose their sides according to their interests. France and its allies supported Avignon, England and the Holy Roman Empire backed Rome, and the Italian states shifted from one side to the other as it suited their purposes. Papal prestige was falling in ruin, yet in the face of agelong papal claims to absolute spiritual authority, there seemed no power on earth that could purport to arbitrate between two rival popes. The Church was at an impasse.

As the schism dragged on, increasing numbers of Christians became convinced that the only solution was the convening of a general church council. Both popes argued that councils were inferior to them and could not judge them, and Christians were perplexed as to who, if not the popes, had the authority to summon a council. At length some of the cardinals themselves, in both camps, called a council to meet in Pisa. There, in 1409, a group of 500 prelates deposed both popes and elected a new one. Since neither pope recognized the conciliar depositions, the effect of the Council of Pisa was to transform a two-way schism into a three-way schism. The situation was not only scandalous but ludicrous. Finally the Holy Roman emperor, drawing on the ancient precedent of the Emperor Constantine, summoned the prelates of Europe to the Council of Constance (1415–1418). Here, at last, the depositions of all three popes were voted and enforced, and the schism was healed by the election of a conciliar pope, Martin V (1417–1431).

To many thoughtful Christians the healing of the schism was not enough. The papacy stood discredited, and it was argued that future popes should be guided by general councils meeting regularly and automatically. The role of councils and assemblies was familiar enough to contemporary secular governments. Why should not the Church, too, be governed "constitutionally"? Such views were being urged by political philosophers such as Marsilius of Padua in the fourteenth century and Nicolas of Cusa in the fifteenth, and they were widely accepted among the prelates at Constance. That these delegates were essentially conservative is suggested by their decision to burn John Hus, who came to Constance with an imperial promise of safe conduct. Yet the Council of Constance made a genuine effort to reform the constitution of the Church along conciliar lines. The delegates affirmed, against papal objection the ultimate authority of councils in matters of doctrine and reform, and they decreed that thenceforth general councils would convene at regular intervals.

These broad principles, together with a number of specific reforms voted by the Council of Constance, met with firm opposition from Pope Martin V and his successors, who insisted on absolute papal supremacy. The popes reluctantly summoned a council in 1423 and another in 1431, but worked to make them ineffective. The last of the important medieval councils, the Council of Basel (1431–1449), drifted gradually into open schism with the recalcitrant papacy and petered out ingloriously in 1449. By then Europe's enthusiasm for conciliarism was waning; the conciliar movement died, and a single pope ruled unopposed once more in Rome.

The men who sat on the papal throne between the dissolution of Basel (1449) and the beginning of the Protestant Reformation (1517) were radically different from their high-medieval predecessors. Abandoning much of their former jurisdiction over the international Church, they devoted themselves to the beguiling culture and bitter local politics of Renaissance Italy. By now the popes were mostly Italian, and so they would remain on into the future. Struggling to strengthen their hold on the Papal States, maneuvering through the shifting sands of Italian diplomacy, they conceded to northern monarchs an extensive degree of control over Church and clergy in return for a formal recognition of papal authority and an agreed division of Church revenues between pope and king.

The fifteenth century ended with the pontificate of the Borgia pope, Alexander VI (1492–1503), whose scandalous behavior was sufficient even to raise eyebrows in high-Renaissance Italy. Alexander's pontificate is a caricature of all that ailed the papacy at the end of the Middle Ages. He divided his time between ruthless political aggrandizement and sensual pleasures. Contemporary rumor had it that he numbered his own illegitimate daughter Lucretia among his mistresses. However this may be, he gave full support to the unprincipled military and diplomatic activities of his son, Caesar, who used assassination, treachery, and force to carve out a great Borgia state in central Italy.

As the Borgia pontificate vividly illustrates, the papacy, by 1500, had ceased to be an international spiritual power. Fourteen years after Alexander VI's death, the Protestant Reformation began, and the tremendous popular response to Luther's rebellion bespeaks the failure of the late-medieval popes. Europeans were not prepared to abandon Christianity, but they were willing, in large numbers, to desert tarnished Rome.

CHRONOLOGY OF THE LATE-MEDIEVAL CHURCH

1309–1376:	Avignon papacy prior to the Great Schism
1316–1334:	Pontificate of John XXII, the "financier pope"
1327:	Meister Eckhart dies
c. 1375:	Gerard Groot founds the Brethren of the Common Life
1378–1415:	Great Schism: Rome versus Avignon
1384:	John Wyclif dies
1409:	Council of Pisa: three-way schism
1415–1418:	Council of Constance: schism healed; beginning of Conciliarism
1415:	John Hus burned at the stake
1417–1431:	Pontificate of Martin V
1431–1449:	Council of Basel: waning of conciliarism
1492–1503:	Pontificate of Alexander VI, the Borgia pope
1517:	Outbreak of Lutheran Reformation

The Western Monarchies

The late-medieval trend from international Catholicism toward secular sovereignty found forceful expression in Marsilius of Padua's important treatise, the *Defensor Pacis* (1324). Here the dilemma of conflicting sovereign jurisdictions, secular and ecclesiastical, was resolved uncompromisingly in favor of the state. The Church, Marsilius argued, should be stripped of political authority, and the state should wield sovereign power over all its subjects, lay and clerical alike. Thus the Church, united in faith, would be divided politically into dozens of state churches obedient to their secular rulers and not to the pope. In its glorification of the sovereign state, the *Defensor Pacis* foreshadowed the evolution of late-medieval and early-modern politics.

It was only after 1450, however, that the western monarchies were able to assert their authority with any consistency over the particularistic nobility. During the period from the early-fourteenth to the mid-fifteenth century, the high-medieval trend toward royal centralization seemed to have reversed itself. The major Iberian powers—Aragon, Castile, and Portugal—were tormented by sporadic internal upheavals and made no progress toward reducing Granada, the remaining Islamic enclave in the peninsula. For most of the period, England and France, were involved in the Hundred Years' War (1337–1453), which drove England to the brink of bankruptcy and ravaged the French countryside and population.

England

Nevertheless, the unwritten English constitution developed significantly during these years. In the course of the fourteenth century, Parliament changed from a body that met occasionally to a permanent institution and split into Lords and Commons. The House of Commons, consisting of representative townsmen and shire knights, bargained with a monarchy hard pressed by the expenses of the Hundred Years' War. Commons traded its fiscal support for important political concessions, and by the century's end it had gained the privilege of approving or disapproving all taxation not sanctioned by custom. With control of the royal purse strings secured, Commons then won the power to legislate. Adopting the motto, "redress before supply," it refused to pass financial grants until the king had approved its petitions, and, in the end, Commons petitions acquired the force of law.

Notwithstanding these constitutional advances, the late-medieval Commons was by no means the independent voice of a rising middle class. By and large it was controlled by the force of manipulation of powerful aristocrats. Elections could be rigged; representatives could be bribed or overawed. And although Parliament deposed two English kings in the fourteenth century—Edward II in 1327 and Richard II in 1399—in both instances it was simply ratifying the results of aristocratic power struggles. It is significant that such parliamentary ratification should seem necessary to the nobility, but one must not conclude that Parliament had yet become a free agent. Symbolically, it represented the will of the English community; actually it remained sensitive to aristocratic force and tended to affirm decisions already made in castles or on battlefields.

The Hundred Years' War, which proved such a stimulus to the growth of parliamentary privileges, also constituted a serious drain on English wealth and lives. Beginning in 1337, the war dragged on fitfully for 116 years with periods of savage warfare alternating with prolonged periods of truce. Broadly speaking, the conflict was a continuation of the Anglo-French rivalry that dated from the Norman Conquest. Since 1066 England and France had battled on numerous occasions. In 1204 the Capetian crown had won the extensive northern French territories of the Angevin Empire, but the English kings retained a tenuous lordship over Gascony in the southwest. The English Gascon claim, cemented by a brisk commerce in Bordeaux wine and English cloth, gave rise to an expensive but inconclusive war (1294–1303) between Philip the Fair of France and Edward I of England. Competing English and French claims to jurisdiction in Gascony constituted one of several causes for the resumption of hostilities in 1337.

Another cause of the Hundred Years' War was the Anglo-French diplomatic struggle for control of Flanders, which France needed to round out its territories and which England needed to secure its profitable wool trade. Tension mounted in 1328 when, on the death of the last French Capetian, King Edward III of England (1327–1377) laid claim to the throne of France. Edward III's mother was a daughter of Philip the Fair, but the French nobility, refusing to be governed by an English monarch, revived the ancient custom that the succession could not pass through a female. Accordingly, they chose Philip VI (1328–1350), the first king of the long-lived Valois dynasty. Edward III accepted the decision at first, but in 1337, when other reasons prompted him to take up arms, he revived his claim and titled himself king of France and England.

None of these causes can be considered decisive, and war might yet have been avoided. But Edward III and Philip VI were chivalric, high-spirited romantics longing for heroic clashes of arms, and the same spirit infected the nobility on both sides. The French knights lost much of their ardor when English longbowmen won smashing victories at Crécy (1346) and Poitiers (1356). The English revered

Edward III so long as English arms were victorious, but they deposed his successor, Richard II (1377–1399), who showed no interest in fighting Frenchmen. Henry V (1413–1422) revived hostilities and gained the adulation of his subjects by winning a momentous victory over the French at Agincourt in 1415. But Henry V's early death, and the subsequent career of Joan of Arc* turned the tide of war against the English. By 1453, when the long struggle ended at last, England had lost all of France except the port of Calais. The centuries-long process of Anglo-French disentanglement was completed, and Joan of Arc's vision was realized: The Valois Charles VII ruled France unopposed.

The Hundred Years' War had been over for scarcely two years when England entered an era of civil strife between the rival houses of York and Lancaster. The Wars of the Roses, which raged off and on between 1455 and 1485, were the medieval English nobility's last orgy of violence. Most Englishmen were tired of endless bloodshed and longed for firm royal governance. They achieved it, to a degree, in the reign of the Yorkist Edward IV (1461–1483). And after a final burst of warfare, strong monarchy came permanently to England with the accession of the first Tudor king, Henry VII (1485–1509). Both

* See p. 338.

Edward IV and Henry VII sought peace, a full treasury, and effective government, and by the late fifteenth century these goals were coming within reach. The economy was reviving, many of the more troublesome nobles had perished in the Wars of the Roses, and the English were more than willing to exchange anarchy for obedience and peace. All that was needed now was strong royal leadership, and that was supplied in full measure by the willful, determined Tudors.

France

The Hundred Years' War was a far greater trial to France than to England. All the fighting took place on French soil, and mercenary companies continually pillaged the French countryside, even when they were not engaged in actual warfare. King John the Good (1350–1364)—a very bad king indeed—was powerless to cope with the English or bring order to a demoralized, plague-ridden land. In 1356, a decade after the French military debacle at Crecy and eight years after the onset of the Black Death, France was stunned by a crushing defeat at Poitiers. French nobles fell in great numbers, and King John himself was taken prisoner by the English.

The Estates General, meeting in Paris under the leadership of a dynamic Parisian cloth merchant, Etienne Marcel, momentarily assumed the reins of government. In 1357 they forced King John's son, the young Dauphin* Charles, to issue a radical constitutional statute known as the "Great Ordinance." This statute embodied the demands of the bourgeois-dominated Estates General to join with the monarchy in the governance of France. The Estates General were thenceforth to meet on regular occasions and to supervise the royal finances, courts, and administration through a small standing committee. The Dauphin Charles, deeply hostile to this infringement of royal authority, submitted for a time, then fled Paris to gather royalist support in the countryside.

By 1358 the horrors of plague, depression, and mercenary marauders had goaded the French peasantry into open revolt. The Jacquerie —as the rebellious peasants were called—lacked coherent goals and effective leaders, but they managed for a time to terrorize rural

* Crown prince.

France. On one occasion they are reported to have forced an aristocratic wife to eat her roasted husband, after which they raped and murdered her. But within a few months the aristocracy and urban elites succeeded in crushing the Jacquerie with a savagery worthy of the rebels themselves. The peasants' rebellion of 1358 evoked a widespread longing for law and order and a return to the ways of old. This conservative backlash resulted in a surge of royalism which doomed Etienne Marcel's constitutional movement in Paris. Marcel himself was murdered in midsummer, 1358, and the Dauphin Charles returned to the city in triumph.

The Great Ordinance of 1357 became a dead letter after Marcel's fall, and in later centuries the Estates General met less and less frequently. The Dauphin Charles, who became the able King Charles V (1364–1380), instituted new tax measures that largely freed the monarchy from its financial dependence on assemblies and made it potentially the richest in Europe. The Estates General, unlike the English Parliament, failed to become an integral part of the government, and French kings reverted more and more to their high-medieval practice of dealing with their subjects through local assemblies. There were "Parlements" in France—outgrowths of the central and regional courts—but their functions remained judicial; they did not deliberate on the granting of taxes, and they did not legislate. French national cohesion continued to lag behind that of England, because France was much larger, more populous, and more culturally diverse. During the late middle ages its great dukes still ruled whole provinces with little interference from Paris. In the absence of an articulate national parliament the only voice that could claim to speak for all the French people was the voice of their king.

Charles V succeeded in turning the tide of war by avoiding pitched battles. His armies harassed the English unceasingly and forced them, little by little, to draw back. By Charles's death the French monarchy was recovering. The English, reduced to small outposts around Bordeaux and Calais, virtually abandoned the war for a generation.

But Charles V was succeeded by the incompetent Charles VI (1380–1422)—"Charles the Mad"—who grew from a weak child into an unstable adult, periodically insane. His reign was marked by a bloody rivalry between the houses of Burgundy and Orleans. The Duke of Orleans was Charles the Mad's brother, the Duke of Burgundy his uncle. In Capetian times, such powerful fief-holding members of the royal family had usually cooperated with the king, but now, with a madman on the throne, Burgundy and Orleans struggled for control of the kingdom. In the course of the fifteenth century, the Orleanist faction became identified with the cause of the Valois monarchy, and Burgundy evolved into a powerful independent state between France and Germany. But at the time of Charles the Mad all was uncertain.

With France ravaged once again by murder and civil strife, King Henry V of England resumed the Hundred Years' War and, in 1415, won his overwhelming victory at Agincourt. At this the Burgundians joined forces with the English, and Charles the Mad was forced to make Henry V his heir. But both kings died in 1422, and while Charles the Mad's son, Charles VII (1422–1461), carried on a half-hearted resistance, the Burgundians and English divided northern France between them and prepared to crush the remaining power of the Valois monarchy.

At the nadir of his fortunes, Charles VII, as yet uncrowned, accepted in desperation the military services of the peasant visionary Joan of Arc. Joan's victory at Orleans, her insistence on Charles' coronation in Rheims, and her capture and death at the stake in 1431 have become legendary. The spirit that she kindled raised French hopes, and in the two decades following her death Charles VII's armies went from victory to victory. The conquest of France had always been beyond English resources, and English successes in the Hundred Years' War had been largely a product of wretched French leadership and paralyzing internal division. Now, as the war drew at last to a close, Charles VII could devote himself to the rebuilding of the royal government. He was supported in his task by secure tax revenues, a standing army, and the steady development of effective administrative institutions.

As with the English, the French in the later fifteenth century longed for strong monarchy and effective government. And Charles VII and his Valois successors, like the Tudors, were prepared to govern firmly. By 1500 the French monarchy was ruling through a central administration of middle-class professional bureaucrats. The nobility was pampered but apparently tamed, the towns were flourishing, and new royal armies were carrying the dynastic claims of the Valois kings into foreign lands.

CHRONOLOGY OF LATE-MEDIEVAL ENGLAND AND FRANCE

England	France
1307–1327: Reign of Edward II	1328–1589: Valois Dynasty
1327–1377: Reign of Edward III	1328–1350: Reign of Philip VI
1337–1453: Hundred Years' War	1337–1453: Hundred Years' War
1346:　　　Battle of Crécy	1345:　　　Battle of Crécy
1348–1349: Black Death	1348–1349: Black Death
	1350–1364: Reign of John "the Good"
1356:　　　Battle of Poitiers	1356:　　　Battle of Poitiers
	1357:　　　The Great Ordinance
	1358:　　　Jacquerie Rebellion
1377–1399: Reign of Richard II	1364–1380: Reign of Charles V
1381:　　　Peasants' Revolt	1380–1422: Reign of Charles VI, "Mad"
1413–1422: Reign of Henry V	
1415:　　　Battle of Agincourt	1415:　　　Battle of Agincourt
1455–1485: Wars of the Roses	1422–1461: Reign of Charles VII
1461–1483: Reign of Edward IV	1429–1431: Career of Joan of Arc
1485–1509: Reign of Henry VII. Beginning of Tudor Dynasty	1461–1483: Reign of Louis XI

Spain

The course of Spanish history in the late middle ages runs parallel to that of England and France, with generations of internal turmoil giving way in the later fifteenth century to political coherence and royal consolidation. As the high-medieval *Reconquista* rolled to a stop around 1270, the Iberian Peninsula contained two strong Christian kingdoms—Castile and Aragon—the weaker Christian Kingdom of Portugal along the western coast, and Muslim Granada in the extreme south. Of the two major kingdoms, Castile was the larger but Aragon was the more urbanized and imperialistic. During the thirteenth and fourteenth centuries Aragonese kings conquered the

Mediterranean islands of Majorca, Minorca, Sardinia, and Sicily, and Araganese merchants began to play a significant role in international commerce.

Aragon and Castile were both plagued by civil turbulence during the late Middle Ages. The Aragonese monarchy strove with only limited success to placate the nobility and townsmen by granting significant concessions to the Cortes, the regional representative assemblies. A prolonged revolt by the mercantile class in the Aragonese province of Catalonia was put down in 1472 only with the greatest difficulty. Castile, in the meantime, was torn by constant aristocratic uprisings and disputed royal successions. Peace and strong government came within reach at last when Ferdinand of Aragon married Isabella of Castile in 1469. Isabella inherited her throne in 1474; Ferdinand inherited his in 1479. And thereafter, despite the continuation of regional Cortes, tribunals, and customs, an efficient central administration governed the two realms and eventually transformed them into the Kingdom of Spain.

In 1492 the new kingdom completed the long-delayed *Reconquista* by conquering Muslim Granada. Working tirelessly to enforce obedience, unity, and orthodoxy, the Spanish monarchy presented its Muslim and Jewish subjects with the choice of conversion or banishment, and the consequent Jewish exodus drained the kingdom of valuable mercantile and intellectual talent. The Catholic Inquisition became a tool of the state and, as an instrument of both political and doctrinal conformity, it brought the crown not only religious unity but lucrative revenues as well. The nobility was persuaded that its best interests lay in supporting the monarchy rather than in opposing it, and regional separation was curbed. With unity established and with the immense wealth of the New World soon to be pouring in, Spain in 1500 was entering a period of rich cultural expression and international power.

The wealth of Spain and Portugal in the sixteenth century resulted from their strategic location at the extreme west of Europe, facing the Atlantic. Important advances in shipbuilding and navigation opened the way for long ocean voyages, and by 1500 European captains had traversed the Atlantic and Indian Oceans. The conquest of these seas brought Spain a New World empire and the wealth of the Incas and Aztecs. It brought Portugal a direct sea route to India and a vast commercial empire in the Far East. The first Atlantic ex-

SPAIN AT THE TIME OF FERDINAND AND ISABELLA

Scale of Miles
0   100   200

FRANCE

Minorca

Majorca

Iviza

Mediterranean Sea

NAVARRE (to 1512) Pyrenees Mts. ROUSSILLON

Pamplona

ARAGON

Ebro R.

CATALONIA

Barcelona

Saragossa

KINGDOM OF ARAGON

VALENCIA

Valencia

Bilboa

ASTURIAS

Burgos

LEON

OLD CASTILE

Vallodolid Duero R.

Segovia

KINGDOM OF CASTILE AND LEON

Madrid Alcalá

Salamanca

Toledo

Tagus R.

NEW CASTILE

MURCIA

Guadiana

JAEN

Cordova CORDOVA

Guadalquivir R.

GRANADA (to Castile 1492)

Granada

SEVILLE

Seville

Cadiz

GALICIA

KINGDOM OF PORTUGAL

Lisbon

Lagos

Atlantic Ocean

341

plorations, however, were pioneered by Italian seamen who could draw on their experience in Mediterranean commerce. In the early fourteenth century, Venetian galley fleets were making yearly expeditions through the Straits of Gibraltar to England and Flanders, and Genoese merchants were trading with the Canary Islands. By the mid-fifteenth century the Canaries, Madeiras, Azores, and Cape Verde Islands had all passed into Spanish or Portuguese hands, but the ships of the Iberian monarchies continued to depend often on the skill of Italian captains and crews. It was the Genoese captain, Columbus, who brought the Spanish monarchy its claim to the New World.

Missionary zeal, curiosity, and greed were the mixed motives of these explorations. In the long run, greed was the primary consideration of both the sponsoring monarchies and the captains and private merchants who stood to make their fortunes from successful voyages. But the great patron of Portuguese West-African exploration, Prince Henry the Navigator (1394–1460), seems to have been driven in large measure by the hope of Christian evangelism and the longing to discover unknown lands. From his court at Sagres, ships were sent westward to the Atlantic islands and southward down the African coast, and at Sagres itself Prince Henry collected an invaluable store of geographical and navigational data for the instruction of his captains. The Portuguese West-African voyages continued intermittently after Prince Henry's death and reached their climax in 1497–1499 when Vasco de Gama rounded the Cape of Good Hope and reached India. The 6000 percent profit realized by da Gama's voyage demonstrated emphatically the commercial potentialities of this new, direct route to the Orient. The old trade routes were short-circuited, and the Ottoman Empire and Renaissance Italy both underwent a gradual commercial decline. The future lay with the rising Atlantic monarchies.

Germany and Italy

Late medieval Germany and Italy suffered from much the same sort of regional particularism that afflicted England, France, and the Iberian Peninsula, but the late fifteenth century brought no corresponding trend toward centralization. Both lands passed into the modern era divided internally and incapable of competing with the western monarchies. The weak elective Holy Roman Empire that emerged in Germany from the papal-imperial struggles of the high Middle Ages was given formal sanction in the Golden Bull of 1356. The Bull made no mention of any papal role in the imperial appointment or coronation, but left the choice of succession to the majority vote of seven great German princes. These "electors" included the archbishops of Mainz, Trier, and Cologne, the Count Palatine of the Rhine, the Duke of Saxony, the Margrave of Brandenburg, and the King of Bohmia. The electoral states themselves remained relatively stable, as did other large German principalities such as the Hapsburg duchy of Austria, but the empire itself became powerless. Germany in 1500 was a Chinese puzzle of more than 100 principalities—fiefs, ecclesiastical city-states, free cities, counties, and duchies—their boundaries shifting periodically through war, marriage, and inheritance. Imperial authority in Italian politics was as dead as papal authority in imperial elections. Germany and Italy was disengaged at last, but both continued to suffer the prolonged consequences of their former entanglement.

Through the domination of small states by larger ones, the political crazy-quilt of late-medieval Italy had evolved by the fifteenth century into a delicate power balance between five strong political units: the Kingdom of Naples, the Papal States, and the three northern city-states of Florence, Milan, and Venice. Naples was ruled first by a French dynasty, and later by Aragon. Central Italy remained subject to a tenuous papal control, compromised by the particularism of local aristocrats and the political turbulence of Rome itself. Milan, and later Florence, ceased to be republics and fell under the rule of self-made despots. Throughout this period, Venice remained a republic dominated by a narrow commercial oligarchy.

The despots, ruling without the sanction of royal anointment or legitimate succession, governed by their wits and by the realities of power, uninhibited by traditions or customs. They have often been regarded as symbols of the "new Renaissance man," but in fact their opportunism was a quality well known to the northern monarchs, and their ruthlessness would have surprised neither William the Conqueror nor Philip the Fair. Yet the very insecurity of their positions and the fragile equilibrium of the five major Italian powers gave rise to a considerable refinement of traditional diplomatic practices. Ambassadors, skilled at compliments and espionage, were exchanged on a regular basis, and emerging from the tendency of two or three

ITALY
C.1490

SWISS CONFEDERATION

Tyrol   Carinthia

Trent

SAVOY   Milan   Carniola

Turin   Verona   Padua

MILAN   Venice

Genoa   MANTUA   VENETIAN REPUBLIC

GENOA   MODENA   FERRARA

Bologna   Dalmatia

Lucca   Florence

Pisa   FLORENCE   Urbino

Siena   The Marches

SIENA

Umbria

PAPAL

STATES

Rome

Adriatic Sea

Naples

KINGDOM

Otranto

OF THE

Palermo

TWO SICILIES

Scale of Miles
0   100   200

weaker states to combine against a stronger one came the shifting alliances known as the "balance of power" principle.

The Italian power balance was upset in 1494 when a powerful French army invaded the peninsula. For generations thereafter Italy was a battleground for French-Spanish rivalries, and the techniques and concepts of Italian Renaissance diplomacy passed across the Alps to affect the relations of the northern kingdoms. The modern tendency to ignore moral limitations and ecclesiastical mediation—to base diplomacy on a calculated balance of force—was growing throughout late-medieval Europe, but it reached fruition first in Renaissance Italy.

Eastern Europe

Eastern Europe, was, in general, no more successful than Germany and Italy in achieving political cohesion. Poland, Lithuania, and Hungary (as well as the Scandinavian states to the north) were all afflicted by aristocratic turbulence and dynastic quarrels. The Teutonic Knights were humbled by Slavic armies and internal rebellions, and most of the Balkan peninsula was overwhelmed by the Ottoman Turks. Only the Russians and Ottomans were able to build strong states, and both, by 1500, were uncompromisingly autocratic.

Poland had become a Catholic-Christian kingdom around A.D. 1000, but throughout the High Middle Ages it had been paralyzed by aristocratic factions and disputed successions. In 1386 it united for a time with rapidly expanding Lithuania, and the Polish-Lithuanian state became the largest political unit in Europe. It was also, very possibly, the worst governed. Under the Lithuanian warrior-prince Jagiello (1377–1434), who converted from heathenism to Catholicism when he accepted the Polish crown, the dual state humbled the Teutonic Knights at the decisive battle of Tannenberg (1410). But even under Jagiello, Poland-Lithuania had no real central government; its nobles would cooperate with their ruler only against the hated Germans, and even then only momentarily. Stretching all the way from the Black Sea to the Baltic, incorporating many of the former lands of the Teutonic Order and most of the old state of Kievan Russia, Poland-Lithuania lacked the skilled administrators and political institutions necessary to govern its vast territories. Its nobles were virtually all-powerful, and its peasantry was slipping toward serfdom. Its political impotence guaranteed that no strong state would emerge

THE EMPIRE
AND CENTRAL
EUROPE, C.1490

Black Sea

Moscow

MUSCOVY

Kiev

LITHUANIA

Baltic Sea

Copenhagen

Königsberg

Danzig

DENMARK

Lübeck

Bremen

Hamburg

Brunswick

Magdeburg

BRANDENBURG

Saxony

KINGDOM OF POLAND

Vistula R.

Warsaw

Nuremberg

Frankfort

Prague

BOHEMIA

MORAVIA

Vienna

AUSTRIA

Budapest

KINGDOM OF HUNGARY

Danube R.

OTTOMAN

EMPIRE

Adriatic Sea

REP. OF VENICE

Bavaria

Munich

Tyrol

Zürich

SWISS
CONFED.

Milan

Turin

GENOA

Worms

Strasbourg

Rhine R.

Paris

Antwerp

FRANCE

Avignon

Corsica
(to Genoa)

NAPLES

PAPAL
STATES

Rome

346

between Germany and Russia during Europe's early modern centuries.

Russia had acquired its religion from Constantinople rather than from the West, and Byzantine civilization was a potent factor in the development of Russian culture. This development was set back for a time by the Mongols, who had swept westward out of Asia between 1237 and 1242, crossing Russia and penetrating momentarily into the heart of Central Europe. The Mongols had quickly withdrawn from most of Europe, but they remained in Russia for about 240 years, allowing local autonomy to the Russian Christian princes but ruthlessly enforcing the collection of tribute.

During the centuries of Mongol domination, the Muscovite principality managed not only to survive but to expand and flourish. The Christian "Grand Princes" of Moscow extended their influence in northern Russia by collaborating with their Mongol Khans and winning the support of the Orthodox church. They were appointed sole collectors of the Mongol tribute, and on occasion they helped the Mongols crush the rebellions of other Russian princes. Moscow became the headquarters of Russian Orthodox Christianity, and when the Turks took Constantinople in 1453, Moscow, the "Third Rome," claimed spiritual sovereignty over the Orthodox Slavic world.

At first the Muscovite princes strengthened their position with the full backing of the Mongol Khans. But toward the end of the fourteenth century Moscow began taking the lead in anti-Mongal resistance. At last, in 1480, Ivan III, the Great, Grand Prince of Moscow and Czar of the Russians, repudiated Mongol authority altogether and abolished the tribute.

The Muscovite princes enjoyed a certain measure of popular support in their struggle against the Mongols and in their battles against the Roman Catholic Lithuanians, but their rule was autocratic to a degree worthy of Byzantine emperors and Mongol khans. Nascent republicanism in city-states such as Novgorod was crushed with the expansion of Muscovite authority. The Grand princes were despots, inspired politically by Central Asia rather than by the West. Their state had no local nor national assemblies and no articulate middle class. Russia was eventually to acquire the material and organizational attributes of a great power, but the centuries during which it had been isolated from the rest of Europe could not be made up overnight.

The Ottoman Empire

The great outside threat to Eastern Europe came from the southeast, where the Ottoman Turks pressed into the Balkans from Asia Minor. These Altaic tribesmen, driven from their Central Asia homeland by the Mongols, came into Asia Minor first as mercenaries, then as conquerors. Adopting the Islamic faith, the Ottomans subjected the greater part of Asia Minor to their rule and intermarried with the local population. In 1354, bypassing the diminutive Byzantine Empire, they invaded Europe. During the latter half of the fourteenth century they crushed Serbia and Bulgaria and extended their dominion over most of the Balkan Peninsula. And in 1444, at the decisive battle of Varna, they decimated an anti-Turkish crusading army and consolidated their hold on southeastern Europe. After the great Ottoman victory at Varna, the storming of Constantinople in 1453 was little more than a postscript. Yet all Europe recognized that the sultan Mohammed II, in conquering the unconquerable city, had ended an era.

The Ottoman Empire endured until the twentieth century; as the Republic of Turkey it endures still. Like the Muscovite princes, the Ottoman sultans were autocrats. Slaves served in their administration and fought in their armies alongside mounted noblemen of the Ottoman landed aristocracy. And while the sultans were living in splendor on the Golden Horn, overlooking the Bosporus, their government was insulating southeastern Europe from the civilization of the West.

CHRONOLOGY OF LATE-MEDIEVAL EASTERN EUROPE

1237–1242:	Mongols invade Eastern Europe
1354:	Ottoman Turks invade Balkans
1377–1434:	Jagiello rules Lithuania
1386:	Union of Poland and Lithuania under Jagiello
1410:	Poland-Lithuania defeats Teutonic Knights at Tannenberg
1444:	Ottomans defeat Christians at Varna
1453:	Ottomans conquer Constantinople
1480:	Czar Ivan III the Great discontinues Mongol tribute

THE
OTTOMAN
ADVANCE

16

economic and cultural change

Towns and Commerce

The shift from boom to depression came gradually and unevenly to Western Europe in the years around 1300. From the early fourteenth century through much of the fifteenth, a number of related trends —shrinking population, contracting markets, an end to the long process of land reclamation, and a creeping mood of pessimism and retrenchment—resulted in a general economic slump and a deepening of social antagonisms. These trends were far from universal. They were less marked in northen Italy than elsewhere, and various localities north of the Alps, profiting from favorable commercial situations or technological advances, became more prosperous than before. At a time when many English towns were declining, Coventry and certain others grew wealthy from the rise of woolen-cloth production. The Flemish town of Bruges remained throughout most of the late Middle Ages a bustling center of commerce on the northern seas. Florence, with its large textile industry and its international banking, was to become the focal point of Italian Renaissance culture. In Florence and elsewhere, enterprising individuals and families grew wealthy from the profits of international commerce and banking. The Bardi, Peruzzi, and Medici were the great Florentine banking families, and they had their counterparts north of the Alps in such figures as Jacques Coeur of Bourges—financier of the fifteenth-century French monarchy—and the Fuggers of Augsburg. But such great financiers as these were exceedingly insecure in the turbulent years of the late middle ages. The Bardi and Peruzzi houses collapsed in the mid-fourteenth century, and Jacques Coeur was ruined by his royal debtor, King Charles VII. Even though some fortunes continued to grow, the total assets of late-medieval bankers fell considerably below those of their thirteenth-century predecessors.

The depression began well before the coming of the Black Death (1348–1349). The fundamental trends of demographic and economic decline were not initiated by the plague, but they were enormously aggravated by it. Carried by fleas that infested black rats, the bubonic plague entered Europe along the trade routes from the East and spread with frightening speed. The death toll cannot be determined with any precision. The best estimate would probably be one-fourth to one-third of Europe's population. In many crowded towns the mortality rate may well have exceeded 50 percent, whereas isolated rural areas tended to be spared. Consequently, the most progressive, most enterprising, and best-trained Europeans were hit the hardest. Few urban families can have been spared altogether. Survivors of the terrible years 1348 to 1349 were subjected to period recurrences of the plague. Indeed, Europeans for the next three centuries experienced recurring bouts of the dread disease. Fourteenth-century medical science was at a loss to explain the process of infection, while lack of sanitation in the towns encouraged its spread. Some fled their cities, some gave way to religious frenzy or debauchery, and some remained faithfully at their posts, hoping for divine protection against the pestilence. But none emerged from the ordeal unaffected.

The towns of late-medieval Europe, confronted with shrinking markets and decreasing opportunities, lost their earlier social mobility and buoyancy. Privileged classes closed their ranks, guilds guarded their monopolies, and heredity became the chief avenue to the status of guild master. In their grim efforts to retain their share of declining markets, guilds struggled with one another, with the district nobility, and with the increasingly desperate urban proletariat, its class consciousness growing as its upward mobility was choked off.

Many of the Italian cities, as we have seen, evolved in the late Middle Ages from oligarchic republics to despotisms. Florence, for example, ravaged by the Black Death, terrorized by a workers' rebellion in 1378, and impoverished by decades of inconclusive warfare, passed in 1434 into the control of the Medici family. Over a century before, Milan had fallen under the domination of the ambitious Visconti family, which gave way in 1450 to still another dynasty of despots—the Sforzas. In general, the rich businessmen retained their privileged economic status in the face of lower-class pressure by sharing their political authority with great magnates or kings or, in Italy, by abdicating it to despots. The wealthy merchants and bankers were usually able, through political control or manipulation, to keep down wages despite the plague-induced labor shortage and to smash the resulting lower-class uprisings.

The Landed Nobility and Peasantry

The rural nobility of Western Europe, like the urban upper class, managed to survive the turbulent socio-economic changes of the late Middle Ages. Faced with a gradual shift from a barter to a money economy, the nobles were able, with some exceptions, to hold their extensive lands and preserve much of their wealth. They responded to the decline in grain prices by accelerating the high-medieval processes of leasing their own lands to peasants and commuting customary peasant services to fixed money payments. In this way, aristocratic incomes were protected against deflation so long as peasants could manage the agreed payments. The peasantry continued to rise in legal status from land-bound serfs to free tenant farmers until, by 1500 serfdom had almost disappeared from Western Europe. But the passing of serfdom was by no means accompanied by increased peasant prosperity. On the contrary, the declining population and the contracting grain market resulted in abandoned fields and a growing class of landless paupers. Some rural noblemen retained direct control of their land, hiring workers to farm it or converting it from grain crops to the more profitable wool growing.

In general, then, the peasant lost much of his earlier servile status by commuting his manorial obligations of payments in goods and labor services into cash; by 1500 he tended to be a rent-paying tenant or a landless wage earner. And the nobleman dealt in receipts and expenditures rather than in the exploitation of customary services. These changes had begun in the high middle ages and were largely completed by 1500. At times of drastic population decline, as in the decades following the Black Death, the resulting labor shortage tended to force up wages, and the nobility fought this tendency either through collective conspiracy or through legislation. In England, for example, the Statutes of Laborers of 1351 and thereafter were aimed at freezing wages in the wake of the plague. They succeeded only to a point, and they created among the peasantry a deep sense of grievance which contributed to the abortive English Peasants' Revolt of 1381. This confused and bloody uprising was merely one of a considerable number that terrorized late-medieval Europe. Like the Jacquerie rebellion in France, and like many similar peasant insurrections of the period, it bore witness to a society in which classes struggled bitterly for their share of a declining wealth.

In Eastern Europe the peasant's lot was worse than in the West, for the eastern nobility was reducing its peasantry to serfdom at the very time that western peasants were achieving legal freedom. The late-medieval landed nobility of both Eastern and Western Europe jealously guarded its privileges against peasantry and monarchy, and for a time, in both East and West, the high medieval trend toward stronger royal government seemed to have reversed itself. With the exception of Russia, eastern monarchies made no real progress against their nobles, but by the later fifteenth century, western monarchies were beginning to curb the fractious independence of the landed aristocracy. The new Tudor monarchy in England tended to favor the mercantile class, but in Spain and France the nobility was rewarded for its political submissiveness by economic favoritism and privileged position in the royal administration, the army, and the church.

Thus, the western nobles were evolving from war lords into silk-clad courtiers. The traditional role of mounted knight in the feudal host was a thing of the past, for monarchs were now manning their armies with mercenaries, and footsoldiers were winning most of the major battles. Moreover, the increasing use of gunpowder was making knightly armor and knightly castles highly vulnerable. But while the feudal knight was vanishing from European armies, he was, becoming ever more prominent in art, literature, and court ceremonial. The fifteenth century was an age of elaborate shining armor, fairy-tale castles, coats of arms, and extravagant tournaments. Knighthood, driven from the battlefield, took refuge in fantasy, and an age of ruthless political cynicism saw the full flowing of a romantic code of chivalric ethics. Behind this fanciful façade, the landed aristocracy retained its privileged position atop the social order.

Economic Recovery

The consolidation of royal authority in late-fifteenth-century Western Europe coincided with a general economic upturn following a long recession. Europe's population in 1500 may well have been lower than in 1300, but it was increasing again. Commerce was quickening and towns were growing. Technological progress had never ceased, and now water-driven fulling mills were increasing wool production, while water-driven pumps were draining mines. With advances in mining technology, Europe was increasing its supply of silver and the various metals essential to its rising industres: iron, copper, alum, and tin. The development of artillery and movable-type printing depended not merely on the inventive idea but also on many generations of progress in the metallurgical arts. And advances in ship design and navigation lay behind the Atlantic voyages that would soon bring a torrent of wealth into Western Europe. By 1500 the long economic crisis had passed. Europe had entered on an era of economic growth and world expansion that would far outstrip her earlier surge in the High Middle Ages.

Growth and Decay

Printing and gunpowder were the two most spectacular technological innovations of the late middle ages. Gunpowder came first, and by the fifteenth century it was being used with some effect in the Hundred Years' War, the Turkish conquests and, indeed, most of the military engagements of Europe. Printing from movable type was developed midway through the fifteenth century, and although its effect on European culture was immense, the full impact was not felt until after 1500. Even among the "new men" of the Italian Renaissance, printed books were regarded as vulgar imitations of handwritten originals. This fact should warn us against viewing late-medieval Europe—and even Renaissance Italy—exclusively in terms of new beginnings. There was, to be sure, a strong sense of the new and "modern" among many creative Europeans of the period, but there was also a perpetuation of medieval ways, styles, and habits of thought. Often one encounters a sense of loss over the fading of medieval ideals and institutions, a conviction that civilization was declining. The Renaissance humanist Aeneas Sylvius—later Pope Pius II (d. 1464)—could look at the Turish threat and the strife among Christian states and conclude that nothing good was in prospect. The generation living after 1500, aware of the voyages of exploration and of the growing prosperity and political consolidation, might well be hopeful of the future, but between 1300 and 1500 a gloom hung over much of Europe. The rise of modern civilization was less apparent than the decay of the middle ages.

Beneath the gloom one finds a sense of nervous unrest, a violent emotionalism that gives dramatic intensity to late-medieval works of art. The thirteenth-century ideal of balanced serenity lost its relevance in this new age of crisis and recession. The practice of self-flagellation acquired wide popularity, and the Dance of Death became a favorite artistic theme. In an era of depression, plague, and disorder, the high-medieval synthesis could no longer hold together. Unity was giving way to diversity.

The breakdown of hierachy and order expressed itself in a hundred ways—in the intensifying conflict between class and class, in the architectural shift from organic unity to flamboyant decoration, in the divorce between knightly function and chivalric fantasy, in the evolution from Christian commonwealth to territorial states, and in the disintegration of St. Thomas Aquinas's fusion of faith and reason. The medieval dream of a City of God on earth had achieved its supreme intellectual embodiment in Aquinas's hierarchical ordering and reconciliation of matter and spirit, body and soul, logic and revelation. The fading of that dream is nowhere more evident than in the attacks of fourteenth-century philosophers on the Thomist system.

Late-Medieval Thought

St. Thomas' *Summa Theologica*, like the cathedral of Chartres, unifies religious aspiration and logical order on the basis of an omnipotent God who is both loving and rational. The fourteenth-century attack on this reconciliation was founded on two related propositions. (1) To ascribe rationality to God is to limit his omnipotence by the finite rules of human logic. Thus, the Thomist God of reason gave way to a God of will, and the high-medieval notion of a logical divine order was eroded. (2) Human reason, therefore, can tell us nothing of God; logic and Christian belief inhabit two separate, sealed worlds.

The first steps toward this concept of a willful, incomprehensible God were taken by the Oxford Franciscan, Duns Scotus (*d.* 1308), who produced a detailed critique of St. Thomas's theory of knowledge. Duns Scotus did not reject the possibility of elucidating revealed truth through reason, but he was more cautious in his use of logic than Aquinas had been. Whereas St. Thomas is called "The Angelic Doctor," Duns Scotus is called "The Subtle Doctor," and the extreme complexity of his thought prompted men in subsequent generations to describe anyone who bothered to follow Duns' arguments as a "dunce." The sobriquet is unfair, for Duns Scotus is an important and original figure in the development of late scholasticism. Yet one is tempted to draw a parallel between the intricacies of his intellectual system and the decorative elaborations of late-Gothic churches. A Christian rationalist of the most thoroughgoing kind, he nevertheless made the first move toward dismantling the Thomist synthesis and withdrawing reason from the realm of theology.

Another Oxford Franciscan, William of Ockham (*d.* 1349), attacked the Thomist synthesis on all fronts. Ockham argued that God and Christian doctrine, utterly undemonstrable, must be accepted on faith alone, and that human reason must be limited to the realm of observable phenomena. In this unpredictable world of an unpredictable Creator, one can reason only about things that one can see or directly experience. Ockham's radical empiricism ruled out all metaphysical speculations, all rational arguments from an observable diversity of things to an underlying unity of things. And out of this great divorce of reason and faith came two characteristic expressions of late-medieval thought: the scientific manipulation of material facts, and pietistic mysticism untouched by logic. In Ockham and many of his followers, one finds empiricism and mysticism side by side. For since the two worlds never touched, they were in no way contradictory. An intelligent Christian could keep one foot in each of them.

The Ockhamist philosophy served as an appropriate foundation for both late-medieval mysticism and late-medieval science. Some mystics, indeed, regarded themselves as empiricists. For the empiricist is a person who accepts only those things that he experiences, and the mystic, abandoning the effort to *understand* God, strove to *experience* him. Science, on the other hand, was now freed of its theological underpinings and could proceed on its own. Nicholas Oresme, a teacher at the University of Paris in the fourteenth-century, attacked the Aristotelian theory of motion and proposed a rotating earth as a possible explanaiton for the apparent daily movement of the sun and stars across the sky. Oresme's theories probably owed more to thirteenth-century scientists such as Robert Grosseteste than to Ockham, but his willingness to tinker with traditional explanations of the physical structure of God's universe is characteristic of an age in which scientific speculation was being severed from revealed truth.

Many late-medieval philosophers rejected Ockham's criticism and remained Thomists. But owing to the very comprehensiveness of Aquinas' achievement, his successors were reduced to detailed elaboration or minor repair work. Faced with a choice between the tedious niggling of late Thomism and the drastic limitations imposed by Ockham on the scope of philosophical inquiry, many of Europe's finest minds shunned philosophy altogether for the more exciting fields of science, mathematics, and classical learning. When the philosopher John Gerson (*d*. 1429), chancellor of the University of Paris, spoke out in his lectures against "vain curiosity in the matter of faith," the collaspe of the faith-reason synthesis was all but complete.

The fifteenth century witnessed a revival of Platonism and Neoplatonism, in Renaissance Italy and in the north as well. The two leading philosophers of the Italian Renaissance, Marsilio Ficino (*d*. 1499) and Pico della Mirandola (*d*. 1494), were both Platonists. They were able to draw from an extensive body of Plato's writings that had been unknown to the high-medieval West, yet neither Ficino nor Pico was a first-echelon figure in the history of Western thought. Neither possessed the acumen of the best high-medieval philosophers, and neither approached the profoundity of their great contemporary north of the Alps, Nicholas of Cusa (*d*. 1464).

Educated by the mystical Brethren of the Common Life, Nicolas of Cusa became first a conciliarist and later an ardent papist. He agreed, up to a point, with Ockham's view that human reason is limited to the disconnected phenomena of the physical universe. But he insisted that the contradictions and diversity of the material world were reconciled and unified in an unknowable God. Nicolas of Cusa regarded God, as beyond rational apprehension—approachable only through a mystical process which he termed "learned ignorance." Like Aquinas, he believed in an underlying universal order, but like Ockham he denied that any such order could be grasped by human reason. Yet his concept of an unknowable God was derived from a tradition far older than Ockhamism. It was rooted in the late-Roman Neoplatonism of the pagan Plotinus* and his Christian followers, a tradition that had run as an undercurrent through the entire Middle

---

* See p. 6.

Ages. Like the older Neoplatonists, Nicholas of Cusa conceived of the universe as a ceaseless creative unfolding of the infinite God. But going far beyond his Neoplatonic predecessors, he reasoned that a universe emanating from an infinite deity cannot be limited by human concepts of space and time. In short, God's created universe was potentially infinite. And since a universe without bounds is a universe without a physical center, Nicholas of Cusa concluded that neither the earth nor the sun occupied any special position in it. The earth was not at the center, nor was it stationary, since in an infinite universe position and motion are entirely relative. God was at the center, Christ was at the center, but only in the sense of metaphysical priority, not in the sense of physical location.

In his emphasis on mysticism and the limitation of human reason, Nicholas of Cusa was in tune with his age. In his synthetic vision of an ordered cosmos he echoed the thirteenth century. And in his bold conception of an infinite universe he anticipated modern philosophy and astronomy.

Arts and Letters

The change from high-medieval synthesis to late-medieval diversity is clearly evident in the field of art. The high-Gothic balance between upward aspiration and harmonic proportion—between the vertical and horizontal—was shifting in the cathedrals of the later thirteenth century toward an ever-greater emphasis on verticality. Formerly, elaborate capitals and horizontal decorative lines had balanced the soaring piers and pointed arches of the Gothic cathedrals, creating a sense of tense equilibrium between heaven and earth. But during the late middle ages, capitals disappeared and horizontal lines became discontinuous, leaving little to relieve the dramatic upward thrust from floor to vaulting. Late medieval churches achieved a fluid, uncomprising verticality, a sense of heavenly aspiration that bordered on the mystical.

By about the mid-thirteenth century, the basic structural potentialities of the Gothic style had been fully exploited. Windows were as large as they could possibly be, vaultings could be raised no higher without structural disaster, and flying buttresses were used with maximum efficiency. The fundamental Gothic idea of a skeletal stone framework with walls of colored glass had been embodied in churches of incomparable nobility and beauty. During the late middle ages, buildings changed in appearance as tastes changed, but the originality of post-thirteenth-century Gothic architects was inhibited by their devotion to a style that had already achieved complete structural development. Accordingly, the innovations of late-Gothic architecture consisted chiefly of new and more elaborate decoration, with the result that a number of late-medieval churches are, to some modern tastes, overdecorated sculptural jungles.

Unrestrained verticality and unrestrained decorative elaboration were the architectural hallmarks of the age, and both reflected a shift away from rational unity and balance. Like Ockham's universe, the fourteenth- and fifteenth-century church became a fascinating miscellany of separate elements. Thus the "flamboyant Gothic" style emerged in late-medieval France, while English churches were evolving from the "decorated Gothic" of the fourteenth century to the "perpendicular Gothic" of the fifteenth and sixteenth, with its lacelike fan vaulting, its sculptural profusion, and its sweeping vertical lines. In the course of the sixteenth century, Gothic architecture, having reached its decorative as well as its structural limits, gave way throughout northern Europe to the classical Greco-Roman style which had been revived and developed in fifteenth-century Italy and flowed north with the spread of Renaissance humanism.

Sculpture and painting, like architecture and thought, evolved during the Late Middle Ages toward multiuniformity. The serene, idealized humanism of thirteenth-century sculpture gave way to heightened emotionalism and an emphasis on individual peculiarities. Painting north of the Alps reached its apogee in the mirrorlike realism of the Flemish school. Painters such as Jan van Eyck (*d.* 1440), pioneering in the use of oil paints, excelled in reproducing the natural world with a devotion to detail that was all but photographic. Critics of the style have observed that detail seems to compromise the unity of the total composition, but in a world viewed through Ockham's eyes, such is to be expected. It was Italy, again, that developed a new style of painting and sculpture, based on the classical canon of realism subordinated to a unifying idea. And the Italian Renaissance style of painting, like Renaissance architecture, streamed northward in the sixteenth century to bring a new vision to transalpine artists.

The decay of high-medieval forms of expression is vividly demonstrated in the late-medieval romance, which had once served as a

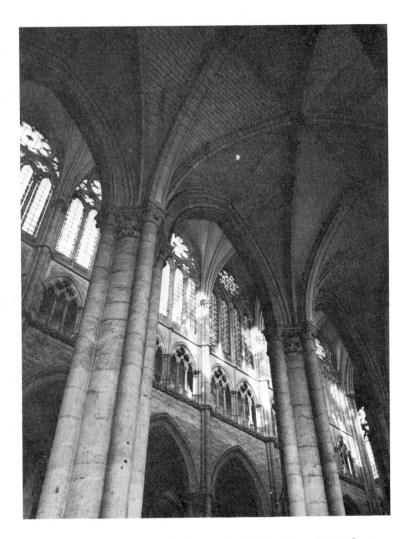

High Gothic interior: Nave of Amiens Cathedral, begun 1220, showing the capitals and decorated stringcourse.

Late Gothic interior: Choir of Saint-Étienne at Beauvais, 1506–c. 1550, showing the absence of capitals, inconspicuous and interrupted string-course, and elaborate vaulting.

Flamboyant Gothic exterior: Saint-Maclou, Rouen (1437–1517)

Perpendicular Gothic interior: Chapel of Henry VII, Westminster Abbey, London: early sixteenth century.

High Gothic sculpture: Le Beau Dieu, *west portal of Amiens Cathedral (thirteenth century).*

Late-medieval sculpture: Three Mourners *from the tomb of Philip the Bold of Burgundy, by Claus Sluter and Claus de Werve (early fifteenth century).*

The Madonna of the Chancellor Rolin, *by Jan van Eyck (Flemish School,* c. 1432).

vital literary form but now became sentimentalized, formalized, and drained of inspiration. Much of the popular literature of late-medieval Europe is beyond redemption, and writers could achieve vitality only by turning from warmed-over chivalry to graphic realism. Geoffrey Chaucer (*d*. 1400), in his *Canterbury Tales,* combines rare psychological insight with a descriptive skill worthy of the Flemish painters or the late-Gothic stone carvers. Chaucer describes one of his Canterbury pilgrims, a corrupt friar, in these words:

> *Highly beloved and intimate was he*
> *With country folk wherever he might be,*

And worthy city women with possessions;
For he was qualified to hear confessions,
Or so he said, with more than priestly scope;
He had a special license from the pope.
Sweetly he heard his penitents at shrift
With pleasant absolution, for a gift.

And François Villon (d. 1463), a brawling Parisian vagabond, expressed in his poems an anguished, sometimes brutal realism that captures the late-medieval mood of insecurity and plague:

Death makes one shudder and turn pale,
Pinches his nose, distends his veins,
Swells out his throat, his members fail,
Tendons and nerves grow hard with strains.

To Villon, writing in a society of sharp class distinctions, death was the great democrat:

I know this well, that rich and poor,
Fools, sages, laymen, friars in cowl,
Large-hearted lords and each mean boor,
Little and great and fair and foul,
Ladies in lace, who smile or scowl,
From whatsoever stock they stem,
Hatted or hooded, prone to prowl,
Death seizes every one of them.

Italian Renaissance Classicism

These northern moods and movements stood in sharp contrast to the growing, self-confident classicism of Renaissance Italy. Here the late-medieval economic depression was less severe and less prolonged, and although endemic interurban warfare made conditions just as insecure as in the North, the civic spirit of the independent north-Italian communes encouraged innovation and novel forms of expression. Italy had never been entirely at ease with Gothic architecture, and the triumphs of high-medieval culture were more characteristically French than Italian. England and France had enjoyed relative peace

Sistine Madonna, *by Raphael (High Renaissance: early sixteenth century).*

during much of the thirteenth century, whereas Italy had been battered by papal-imperial wars. Italy, in short, harbored no fond memories of the High Middle Ages, and the coming of the Renaissance was not so much the advent of a new epoch in European history as a reassertion of Italian culture over French. By the time Renaissance (left) The Golden Virgin, *from the south portal of Amiens Cathedral* (*thirteenth century*).

(right) David, *by Michelangelo (High Renaissance, Florence: completed 1504*).

Venus, *by Titian (Renaissance, Venetian School, sixteenth century*).

ideas were significantly affecting transalpine Europe, Renaissance Italy was already in sharp decline.

In an age of French arms and French culture, such as the thirteenth century had been, Italians could return in memory to the days when Rome ruled the world. Roman monuments and Roman sculpture were all around them, and when, in the fourteenth and fifteenth centuries, they abandoned the Gothic style and the intellectual habits of Paris theologians, it was to their indigenous classical heritage that they turned for inspiration. In sculpture, the calm spiritual nobility of stone saints gave way to a classical emphasis on the human body. The slender young Virgins of the High Middle Ages suddenly turned voluptuous. Architects, abandoning the Gothic spire and pointed arch, created buildings with domes and round arches and elegant classical façades. Scholars abandoned the logic of Aristotle and St. Thomas for the delights of Greco-Roman belles lettres. And painters, with few actual classical models to follow, pioneered in techniques of

Interior of S. Andrea at Matua, by Alberti (Renaissance: fiifteenth century).

linear and atmospheric perspective and imposed a classical unity upon their lifelike figures and landscapes.

The Italian Renaissance, while rebelling against the Middle Ages, retained much that was medieval. In 1492, while a worldly Borgia was acceding to the papacy and Columbus was discovering America, high-Renaissance Florence was passing under the influence of the austere Christian revivalist, Savonarola. Renaissance humanism was always an élitist phenomenon, restricted to urban nobilities and favored artists and leaving the Italian masses unchanged. Yet for all that, the Renaissance style represents a profound shift from the forms and assumptions of the Middle Ages. St. Thomas and his contemporaries had studied the Greek philosophers, but men of the Renaissance looked back on classical antiquity with a fresh perspective, seeing not a collection of ideas that might be used but a total culture that deserved to be revered and revived. It was this vision that underlay the new art and the new classical learning of early modern Europe.

The Genesis of Modern Europe

Historians of the past have probably overemphasized the impact of the Renaissance on the development of modern civilization. The Renaissance contributed much to art and classical studies, and to habits of intellectual precision which had been cultivated by Italian literary scholars. It contributed to the evolution of diplomatic techniques, but scarcely at all to constitutional development. Renaissance humanists were essentially scholars of the "humanities" and were no more interested in science than, say, a modern professor of English literature or Latin. Modern science grew out of the medieval universities. And modern legislatures—even if they meet in domed, round-arched buildings—are outgrowths of medieval representative assemblies.

In the Europe of 1500, Italian Renaissance ideas were beginning to move across the Alps. But the promise of the future did not depend on the Renaissance alone. All across Europe commerce was thriving again and the population was growing. New non-Renaissance inventions—gunpowder, the three-masted caravel, the windmill, the water pump, the printing press—were changing the ways people lived. The papacy had degenerated into a local principality, but England, France, and Spain had achieved stable, centralized governments, and were on the road toward nationhood. European ships had reached America and India, and the first cargo direct from the Orient had arrived in Portugal. The gloom was lifting and the world lay open.

Today, after half a millenium of European expansion, societies everywhere have been reshaped by traditions that extend back to the Middle Ages—to the parliamentary experiments of thirteenth-century England, the growth of rationalism and science in medieval universities, the evolution of governmental institutions in medieval royal households, the commercial revolution in medieval towns, the Gregorian dream of creating a justly-ordered society, the experience of an expanding technology that by 1500 had produced the cannon and the printing press. In our own time European political dominion is ebbing, but European ideas and institutions, for better or worse, have spread across the globe and transformed it.

Suggested Readings

The asterisk indicates a paperback edition.

GENERAL WORKS

Two good comprehensive accounts of the period are:

Wallace K. Ferguson, *Europe in Transition: 1300–1520.* Boston: Houghton Mifflin, 1962.

Denys Hay, *Europe in the Fourteenth and Fifteenth Centuries.* New York: Holt, Rinehart and Winston, 1966.

For somewhat shorter and lighter treatments see:

*Margaret Aston, *The Fifteenth Century.* New York: Harcourt Brace Jovanovich, 1968.

*Jerah Johnson and William Percy, *The Age of Recovery: The Fifteenth Century.* Ithaca, N.Y.: Cornell Univ. Press, 1970.

*Robert E. Lerner, *The Age of Adversity: The Fourteenth Century.* Ithaca, N.Y.: Cornell Univ. Press, 1968.

CHRISTIANITY AND THE CHURCH

J. M. Clark, *The Great German Mystics.* Oxford: Clarendon Press, 1949. A perceptive study of Meister Eckhart and two of his followers, John Tauler and Henry Suso.

*Norman Cohn, *The Pursuit of the Millennium.* New York: Harper & Row, 1957. A penetrating work on radical heresy.

E. F. Jacob, *Essays in the Conciliar Epoch.* Manchester, England: Manchester Univ. Press, 1953. A group of stimulating scholarly analyses.

*G. Mollat, *The Popes at Avignon: 1305–1378.* New York: Harper & Row, 1965. A reprint of an older account, still valuable.

Brian Tierney, *Foundations of the Conciliar Theory.* Cambridge, England: Cambridge Univ. Press, 1955. An illuminating work on the medieval canonists' contributions to conciliarism by a gifted American historian of the medieval Church.

*Russell's *History of Medieval Christianity*, cited earlier (p. 000). covers this period as well as earlier ones.

THE LATE-MEDIEVAL STATE

Several books noted in previous bibliographies includes this era:

Ostrogorsky, *History of the Byzantine State*; Hitti, *History of the Arabs*; Barraclough, *Origins of Modern Germany*; Lopez, *Birth of Europe*; and Hollister, *Making of England*.

The appropriate volumes in the Oxford History of England (New York: Oxford Univ. Press) are:

May McKisack, *The Fourteenth Century* (1959).

E. F. Jacob, *The Fifteenth Century* (1961).

Gene A. Brucker, *Florentine Politics and Society: 1343–1378*. Princeton, N.J.: Princeton Univ. Press, 1962. This scholarly study, based on a thorough investigation of Florentine archives, provides a valuable case history of political and social tensions in a major early-Renaissance city.

John Fennell, *The Emergence of Moscow: 1304–1359*. Berkeley: Univ. of California Press, 1968. An important, well-researched study; not light reading.

David Herlihy, *Pisa in the Early Renaissance*. New Haven: Yale Univ. Press, 1958. Another thoughtful, well-documented account of urban politics and society.

*George Holmes, *The Later Middle Ages: 1272–1485*. New York: W. W. Norton, 1966. A history of late-medieval England, less comprehensive and more readable than the Oxford History volumes.

P. S. Lewis, *Later Medieval France: The Polity*. New York: St. Martin's Press, 1968. Not a political narrative, but a highly original study of government and social structure.

J. H. Mariejol, *The Spain of Ferdinand and Isabella*. New Brunswick, N.J: Rutgers Univ. Press, 1961. Written originally in French in the nineteenth century, this valuable work has been edited and updated by B. Keen.

Garrett Mattingly, *Renaissance Diplomacy*. London: J. Cape, 1955. A thoughtful and original investigation of Italian diplomatic representation and dynastic policies.

*Edouard Perroy, *The Hundred Years' War*, translated by W. B. Wells. New York: Capricorn Books, 1965. A reprint of an older, comprehensive account, particularly illuminating on the history of late-medieval France.

*Ferdinand Schevill, *Siena: The History of a Medieval Commune*. New York: Harper & Row, 1964, first published 1909. A detailed, well-written classic with a new introduction by William M. Bowsky.

Richard Vaughan, *Philip the Bold: The Formation of the Burgundian*

State. Cambridge, Mass.: Harvard Univ. Press, 1962. Scholarly and readable.

*Daniel Waley, *The Italian City Republics.* New York: McGraw-Hill, 1969. A lucid, well-illustrated discussion of the social and political milieu of the city states.

ECONOMIC HISTORY

*Henri Pirenne, *Early Democracies in the Low Countries.* New York: Harper & Row, 1963. A reprint of a provocative older classic examining urban politics, institutions, and class struggles.

*Raymond de Roover, *The Rise and Decline of the Medici Bank: 1397–1494.* New York: W. W. Norton, 1963. An authoritative study which elucidates the policies and methods of this great financial institution in the context of both Florentine local politics and the fifteenth-century European economy.

*Sylvia L. Thrupp, *The Merchant Class of Medieval London.* Ann Arbor: Univ. of Michigan Press, 1962, first published 1948. An outstanding pioneering contribution to English social and economic history in the fourteenth and fifteenth centuries.

Three books noted in previous bibliographies and useful here are:

Bautier, *Economic Development of Medieval Europe*; Lopez, *The Commerical Revolution of the Middle Ages*; and White, *Medieval Technology and Social Change.*

INTELLECTUAL AND CULTURAL HISTORY

Again, several previously-cited books extend into the Late Middle Ages:

Grant, *Physical Science in the Middle Ages*; Henderson, *Gothic*; Knowles, *Evolution of Medieval Thought*; Stoddard, *Monastery and Cathedral in France*; and Ullmann, *A History of Political Thought: The Middle Ages.*

The important problem of changing historical interpretations of the Italian Renaissance can be approached through:

*Wallace K. Ferguson, *The Renaissance in Historical Thought.* New York: Harper & Row, 1948.

*Denys Hay, *The Renaissance Debate.* New York: Holt, Rinehart and Winston, 1965.

Joseph Calmette, *The Golden Age of Burgundy.* New York: W. W. Norton, 1963. A splendid exploration of Burgundian politics and culture.

*Johan Huizinga, *The Waning of the Middle Ages.* Garden City, N.Y.:

Doubleday Anchor, 1954, first published 1924. Concentrating on France and the Netherlands, this masterpiece of cultural history captures superbly the late-medieval mood.

*P. O. Kristeller, *Renaissance Thought*. New York: Harper & Row, 1955. A brief, lucid interpretation, particularly interesting on the meaning of Renaissance humanism.

*Gordon Leff, *Medieval Thought: St. Augustine to Ockham*. Baltimore: Penguin Books, 1958. A survey of metaphysical thought throughout the medieval period, particularly good on Ockham.

Erwin Panofsky, Early Netherlandish Paintings: Its Origins and Character. 2 vols. Cambridge, Mass.: Harvard Univ. Press, 1953. A brilliant work of original interpretation.

*J. H. Plumb, ed., *Renaissance Profiles*. New York: Harper & Row, 1965. Nine biographical sketches, each by a different scholar, on such Renaissance figures as Petrarch, Lorenzo de Medici, Leonardo da Vinci, and Pius II.

SOURCES

*Raymond B. Blakney, ed., *Meister Eckhart; A Modern Translation*. New York: Harper & Row, 1941.

*Jean Froissart, *Chronicles*. Several editions. A contemporary bourgeois writer (d. 1410) treats the Hundred Years War as a chivalric romance.

The Imitation of Christ, attributed to Thomas a Kempis. Many editions.

*William Langland, *Piers the Ploughman*, translated by J. F. Goodridge. Baltimore: Penguin Books, 1959. A profound allegorical poem of fourteenth-century England.

Two good anthologies of contemporary literature are:

*T. Morrison, ed., *The Portable Chaucer*. New York: Viking Press, 1949.

*J. B. Ross and M. M. McLaughlin, *The Portable Renaissance Reader*. New York: Viking Press, 1953.

Illustration Credits

Page 34: Marburg/ Art Reference Bureau. Page 35: Anderson/ Art Reference Bureau. Page 36: top, Alinari/ Art Reference Bureau; bottom, Alinari/ Art Reference Bureau. Page 37: Art Reference Bureau. Page 57: British Museum. Page 72: Marburg/ Art Reference Bureau. Page 78: Left, The Pierpont Morgan Library-M. 399 f. 8v; right, The Pierpont Morgan Library-M. 399 f. 10v. Page 85: Bibliotheque Nationale, Paris. Page 93: Marburg/ Art Reference Bureau. Page 125: Bayer. Staatsbibliothek, Munich-Clm 4452 fol. 24r. Page 134: Model after drawings by Professor K. J. Conant; photograph courtesy of J. Combier. Page 158: Alinari/ Art Reference Bureau. Page 159: Alinari/ Art Reference Bureau. Page 189: Alinari/ Art Reference Bureau. Page 267: Historical Pictures Service-Chicago. Page 274: Marburg/ Art Reference Bureau. Page 275: Marburg/ Art Reference Bureau. Page 277: Marburg/ Art Reference Bureau. Page 278: top, Marburg/ Art Reference Bureau; bottom, Marburg/ Art Reference Bureau. Page 279: top, Marburg/ Art Reference Bureau; bottom, Marburg/ Art Reference Bureau. Page 281: Marburg/ Art Reference Bureau. Page 282: French Embassy Press and Information Division. Page 283: Marburg/ Art Reference Bureau. Page 284: Bibliotheque Nationale, Paris. Page 286: Palais Synodale, Sens, France. Page 287: New York Public Library. Page 360: Courtesy of Professor Whitney S. Stoddard -Sandak, Inc. Page 361: Courtesy of Professor Whitney S. Stoddard -Sandak, Inc. Page 362: Marburg/ Art Reference Bureau. Page 363: Marburg/ Art Reference Bureau. Page 364: Marburg/ Art Reference Bureau. Page 365: 40.128 Purchase from the J. H. Wade Fund, 58.66-67 Bequest of Leonard C. Hanna, Jr., The Cleveland Museum of Art. Page 366: Cliche des Musees Nationaux, Louvre. Page 367: The Dresden Museum. Page 368: Top Left, Marburg/ Art Reference Bureau; Top Right, Alinari/ Art Reference Bureau (Accademia, Florence); bottom, Alinari/ Art Reference Bureau (Uffizi). Page 369: Alinari/ Art Reference Bureau.

index

Aachen, 91, 93, 104, 108
Abacus, 313
Abbasids, 67-70, 162
Abelard, Peter, 180, 297, 298, 302-303, 304, 309
Absolutism, 7, 21, 29, 30, 38, 43, 225, 241, 242, 347, 348
Accursius, 292
Acre, 167, 170
Acts of the Apostles, 98
Adelard of Bath, 314
Adrianople, battle of, 21
Aeneas Sylvius (Pope Pius II), 354
Agincourt, battle of, 335, 338
Agriculture, 15, 53, 75-77, 107, 129-133, 146, 148, 152-153, 181
Alaric, 22
Albertus Magnus, St., 187, 256, 306, 308
Albi, 183
Albigensian Crusade, 169, 183, 184, 187, 188, 209, 214, 213, 269
Albigensians, 182, 185
Alcuin of York, 57, 58, 95, 96, 100, 113, 295
Alexander III, Pope, 210, 212, 213, 237
Alexander VI (Borgia), Pope, 332
Alexander of Hales, 306
Alexandria, 63
Alfred the Great, King, 108, 113, 115, 116, 117
Ali, 64
Allah, 61-62
Allegory, 273, 304

Almagest, 314
Alps, 94, 124, 125, 150, 204
Alsace, 102
Alverno, Mount, 192
Amalfi, 148, 156, 159
Ambrose, St., 9, 10, 11, 25, 297
Amiens, Cathedral of, 260, 282, 284, 285, 360
Anagni, 222
Angles, 18, 25
Anglo-Saxon Church, 79, 80
Anglo-Saxons, 49, 108, 112
Anjou, 112, 136, 231, 239, 249
Anselm, St., 230, 297, 298, 299, 301-302
Anthony, St., 51
Anticlericalism, 176, 181, 182, 183, 328, 329
Antioch, city of, 164
  principality of, 165
Antwerp, 108
Apostles' Creed, 262
Apanages, 253
Apulia, 157, 159
Aquinas, St. Thomas, 11, 187, 298, 299, 306, 308-313, 316, 355, 356, 357, 369, 370
Aquitaine, 84, 97, 133, 231, 239, 256
Arabia, 60
Arabic language, 62, 63, 73, 295
Aragon, 155, 220, 254, 333, 339, 340
Arch, 277, 280
Archetype, 12

Architecture, Byzantine, 32-33, 37, 91, 93
   Carolingian, 91, 93
   Gothic, 176, 277, 280, 311, 356, 358, 359, 360, 364, 365
   Islamic, 71
   Romanesque, 176, 273-280
   Sicilian, 161
Arianism, 7, 8, 18, 21, 25
Aristocracy, 134, 150, 154, 156, 163, 228, 352, 353
   Arabian, 63-64, 68
   Carolingian, 74, 77, 78, 197
   English, 225, 226, 228, 231, 241, 243, 333-334
   French, 249, 251, 253, 264, 334, 336
   German, 197, 198, 201, 204
   Norman, 156, 157, 159
   Roman, 16
   city, 199
Aristotle, 71, 294, 298, 306, 309, 314, 315, 356, 369
Army, Byzantine, 28, 30
   Carolingian, 78, 87-90, 118
   Crusader, 155, 163
   English, 226
   feudal, 117-122, 152
   French, 334, 335
   Islamic, 63, 65
   Roman, 15, 16, 21
   Sicilian, 159
   Viking, 107
Arnold of Brescia, 209, 210
Arnulf, King of East Franks, 108
Art, Byzantine, 32, 33, 35, 43
   Celtic-Christian, 49, 51
   High Medieval, 273-285
   Late Medieval, 358, 359, 365
   Sicilian, 161
Arthur, King, 269
Asia Minor, 162, 164, 168
"Assassins," 64
Assisi, 187, 188
Assizes, 235
Astronomy, 72, 73
Athelney, Isle, 113

Athens, 32, 33, 74, 98, 100, 260
Attila, 23
Aucassin et Nicolette, 270
Augustine of Canterbury, St., 55, 80
Augustine of Hippo, St., 9, 10, 12, 96, 99, 100, 230, 295, 297, 300, 309, 311, 314
Augustinian Canons, 181, 185, 186
Augustus, Emperor, 20, 90, 91, 100
Austrasia, 77, 90, 91
Austria, 88
Avars, 40, 88
Averoës, 298
Averoism, Latin, 298, 306, 311
Avignon, 224, 249, 329, 330
Azores, 342

Babylon, 67
Bacon, Roger, 193, 315-316
Baghdad, 67-70, 74, 110, 162
Baillis, 252, 255
Baldwin IX, 167, 168
Bangeladesh, 63
Banking, 67, 151, 350
Barbarians, 8, 16, 17, 18, 19, 20-25, 42
Barcelona, 88, 154, 155
Bardi, house of, 350
Basel, Council of, 214, 331
Basques, 88
Battle of the Masts, 64
Beatrice, 272, 273
Beatritz de Dia, 266
Bec, monastery of, 230, 302
Becket, Thomas, St., 236-237
Benedict IX, Pope, 198, 199
Benedictine monasticism, development of, 52-54, 79, 80, 81, 97, 133-135
   High Medieval, 177, 185, 193
   rule of, 52, 80, 97, 197
Benedict of Aniane, St., 97
Benedict of Nursia, St., 52, 177, 178
Benefice, 117
Beowolf, 263

Bernard of Clairvaux St., 166, 179, 180, 181, 182, 195, 200, 273, 297, 303
Bethleham, 10
Bible, in Carolingian era, 75, 96
  in High Middle Ages, 292, 295, 303
  St. Jerome, *Vulgate,* 11
Black Death, 325, 336, 351, 352
Blanche of Castile, Queen, 254
Boethius, 24, 113
Bohemia, King of, 328
Bologna, School of, 210
  University of, 289, 291, 293
Bonaventure, St., 193, 256, 299, 306-307, 308, 314
Boniface, St., 56, 80-84, 95, 96, 113
Boniface VIII, Pope, 222, 224, 256, 257, 293
Book of Roger (Idrisi), 161
Book of Sentences (Peter Lombard), 304
Bordeaux, 337
Borgia, Caesar, 331, 370
Borgia, Lucretia, 331
Bourges, Cathedral of, 285
  town of, 350
Bouvines, battle of, 216, 239
Brandenburg, Margrave of, 343
Brethren of the Common Life, 327, 357
Breton March, 88
Bruce, Robert, 248
Bruges, 350
Brunswick, 214
Buddhism, 51
Bureaucracy, 68, 174, 340
  Byzantine, 30, 160, 161
  Carolingian, 77, 99, 118
  ecclesiastical, Roman Catholic, 200, 208, 329
  English, 226, 227, 233-237, 242-244
  French, 250, 252, 257
  German, 122, 125, 127
  Roman, 15, 16
  Sicilian, 218

Burgh, 148
Burghers, 148
Burgundy, 77, 102, 123, 133, 337
Buttress, flying, 283
Byzantine culture, 32-41, 111

Caesaropapism, 8, 9, 25, 29, 30, 32, 58
Cairo, 64, 69
Calabria, 157, 159
Calais, 335, 337
Calendar, Moslem, 61, 72
Cambridge, University of, 289
Camelot, 269
Canary Islands, 342
Canossa, 204, 205, 207, 222
Canterbury, 55, 213, 237, 239, 240
Canterbury Tales (Chaucer), 365
Canute, King, 116
Capella Palatina, Palermo, 161
Capetians, 117, 184, 228
Capitalism, 149, 150
Capitularies, 94, 95, 100
Carloman, son of Charles Martel, 79, 81
Carolingian Culture, 75, 94-99
Carthage, 40, 65
Carthusians, 178, 198
Cassiodorus, 24
Castile, 155, 333, 339, 340
Catalonia, 155
Cathari, 182
Cathedral Churches, 146, 147, 214, 311
Cavalry, 87, 118
Celibacy, 53
Celtic-Christian culture, 49, 50, 56, 79-81
Chambre des Comtes, 257
Champagne, 136, 249, 269
Chancery, 246
Chansons de geste, 262
Charlemagne, 74-76, 79, 84-100, 101, 106, 108, 113, 118, 124
Charles V, King of France, 337
Charles VI, "the Mad," King, 337
Charles VII, King, 335, 338, 351

Charles of Anjou, 220
Charles the Bald, King, 98, 102
Charles the Fat, King, 104
Charles the Simple, King, 104, 108, 110
Chartres, 285, 304, 355
Chaucer, Geoffrey, 365
China, 67, 70, 187
Chivalry, 120, 272
Chretien de Troyes, 269, 270
Christianity, development of, in Eastern Empire, 30, 31
  in High Middle Ages, 174-195
Cicero, 10
Cistercians, 178, 179, 181, 185, 193, 198
Citeaux, 179, 197
City of God (St. Augustine of Hippo), 12-13, 86, 100
Civitate, battle of, 199
Clare, St., 192
Clairvaux, abbey of, 179, 180
Classical culture, in Anglo-Saxon England, 113-115
  in Bethleham, 10
  in Byzantium, 32, 33, 43
  in Carolingian Empire, 96
  in Islam, 71-73
  in Italian Renaissance, 366-370
  among the Latin Doctor, 9-13, 16
  in Sicily, 160, 161
Clement V, Pope, 224, 256
Clement of Alexandria, 297
Clergy, 12, 13, 79-81, 94, 133, 175, 197, 201, 214
Clericos Laicos, 222
Clermont, Council of, 163
Clovis, King, 24, 25, 48, 49, 77
Cluny, monastery of, 133-135, 177, 196, 199, 205, 303
Coeur, Jacques, 350
Cologne, archbishop of, 343
Columbus, 110, 342
Comenus, Alexius, Emperor, 162, 163, 164
Comitatus, 19, 20, 77, 117
Commerce, in Anglo-Saxon

England, 115
  in Carolingian Empire, 120
  in High Middle Ages, 146-148, 151-156
  in Islam, 67, 69, 70
  in Late Middle Ages, 350
  in Roman Empire, 23, 28, 29
Committee of Fifteen, 243
Commons, House of, 258, 333
Conciliar Movement, 329
Concordance of Discordant Canons, (Gratian), 293
Concordat of Worms, 206, 207, 231
Confessions, (St. Augustine of Hippo), 11
Conrad III, Emperor, 166
Consolation of Philosophy, (Boethius), 24, 115
Constance, Council of, 330, 331
Constantine, 7, 8, 15, 29
Constantinople, 7, 22, 29, 30, 40, 42, 65, 68, 73, 74, 82, 83, 91, 110, 148, 159, 163, 164, 165, 168, 194, 199, 200, 347, 348
Constantinople, Council of, 31
Constitutionalism, 20, 219, 240, 249, 333
Constitutions of Claredon, 236
Conversion, 7, 8, 9, 40, 42, 53-56, 79-82, 106, 111, 113, 156, 171, 198
Copernicus, 73
"Corpus Juris Canonici," 293
Corpus Juris Civilis, 37, 38, 39, 160, 291, 292, 293
Corsica, 71
Cortes, 340
Councils, 246, 329
Courts of Law, 184
Coventry, 350
Crécy, battle of, 334, 336
Crete, 71
Crusades, 156, 162-171, 238, 254
Ctesiphon, 63
Cur Deus Homo (St. Anselm), 302
Curia Regis, 161, 242
Cyprus, 63

Da Gama, Vasco, 342
Damascus, 63, 64, 66, 67, 166
Damiani, St. Peter, 200, 202, 297, 298
Damietta, 169, 170
Dance of Death, 355
Danegeld, 133
Danelaw, 113, 155, 227
Danes, 106, 108, 110, 112, 113, 115, 116
Dante, 272, 312
Danube River, 18, 21
Dead Sea Scrolls, 51
De Clericorum Institutione (Raban Maur), 98
Decretum (Gratian), 293, 303, 304
Defensor Pacis (Marsilius of Padua), 330, 332
Democracy, 20, 245
Denmark, 166
De Universo (Raban Maur), 97
De Vulgari Eloquentia (Dante), 272
Dialectic, 304
Dialogue of the Exchequer, 232
Diocletion, 7, 15, 29
Dionysius the Areopagite, 98
Divine Comedy, 273, 316
Doctorine of the Two-Fold Truth, 305
Doctors, Latin, 9, 10, 13, 16, 47, 74, 295, 302
Domesday Book, 229
Dominic, St., 185, 186, 195
Dominicans, Order of the Friars Preachers, 185, 186, 193, 306, 308, 313
Donation of Constantine, 92
Donation of Pepin, 84
Dorset, 108
Drogo d' Hauteville, 157
Duns Scotus, 313, 355-356
Dyle, battle of, 108

Eastern Church, 30, 31, 32, 82-83, 199, 200
Eastern Europe, in the Late Middle Ages, 345-347

East March, *Ostmark,* 88
Ecclesiastical History of England (Bede), 56, 194
Eckhart, Meister, 327
Economic conditions, of barbarian West, 24, 45, 74-76, 88
    of Byzantium, 28, 38
    of High Middle Ages, 146-148, 150, 151-153, 171, 181, 195, 233, 290
    of Late Middle Ages, 325, 336, 342, 350, 351, 352, 353-354, 371
    of Roman Empire, 15, 18
Edessa, County of, 165, 166
Edington, battle of, 113
Education, Benedictine, 52, 94-97
    in High Middle Ages, 288, 295
    in Islam, 62, 71-73
Edward I, King, 245, 246-248, 256, 326, 334
Edward II, King, 333
Edward III, King, 334
Edward IV, King, 335, 336
Edward the Confessor, King, 166, 129, 135, 227
Egypt, 9, 31, 276
Einhard, 90, 91, 96, 84, 85, 95
Elbe River, 171
Eleanor of Aguitaine, Queen, 231, 237
Empire, Angevin, 232, 237, 239, 251, 252, 334
    Byzantine, development of, 7, 8, 28-44, 74
        inconoclastic controversy in, 82-83
    Carolingian, 74-100, 101
    Holy Roman, 17, 124, 196, 202, 219, 330, 342
    Latin, 305
Empiricism, 313
England, Anglo-Saxon, 48, 49, 113
    Celtic-Christian Culture in, 51, 79-80
    High Medieval, 231, 241, 269, 270, 333, 325-349

invasions of, 108, 113
Norman monarchy of, 225-231
Enquêteurs, 255
Epic, 262
Essenes, 51
Estates-General, 257, 336-337
Estonia, 171
Ethelred the Unready, King, 115, 116
Etymologies (St. Isidore of Seville),
47, 97
Euclid, 309, 314
Evesham, battle of, 244
Exchequer, 230, 246, 247
Excommunication, 199, 204, 205,
214, 218, 221, 330

Fable, 271
Fabliaux, 271
Fairs, 151
Famine, 77
Farming, *see* Agriculture
Fatima, 64
Fatimids, 64, 69
Fealty, 119, 120
Ferdinand, King, 340
Feudalism, decline of, 151, 152, 259,
353
development of, 87, 117-122, 128,
136
English, 228, 229, 234, 241, 259
French, 119-121, 249
German, 125, 207, 208, 218
Feudal Law, 228
Feudal obligations, 119-120
Ficino, Marsilio, 357
Fief, 119, 228, 253
Finance, *see* Economic conditions,
banking
Flanders, 122, 130, 136, 148, 249,
256, 334, 342
Fleury, Abbey of, 95
Florence, 146, 343, 351, 370
Fourth Lateran Council, 214
France, Capetians, 249-259
Carolingians, 74-100, 101-105, 117
Frankland, 24, 49
High Middle Ages, culture,

260, 269, 358
politics, 334, 336-339
relations with the Roman Catholic
Church, 183-184, 213, 214,
329-331
Francis, St., 186, 187, 188, 190, 192,
193, 195, 198, 297, 314, 316
Franciscans, Order of Friars Minor,
146, 185, 190, 193, 194, 209,
306, 313, 314, 315, 328
Franconia, 123, 128
Frankish Church, 79-84, 94, 95
Franks, 18, 49, 65, 68
Frederick II, Emperor, 170, 213,
217-218, 259
Frederick Barbarossa, Emperor, 166,
207-212, 219, 237
Friars, 186
Friars Minor, 191, 192
Friars Preachers, 186
Frisians, 79, 80, 84
Frontiers, Byzantine, 39, 40
Carolingian, 88
crusades, 154
Eastern, 122, 124
internal, 153, 171
pressure on, 16, 18, 21
Fuggers (Augsburg), 350
Fulda, Monastery of, 86, 95, 97
Fyrd, 227

Galahad, 270
Galen, 71, 291
Gascony, 248, 334
Genoa, 148
Gerbert of Aurillac (Pope Sylvester
II), 127, 295, 313
German Church, 81
Germania (Tacitus), 18
Germanic culture, 17, 18, 19, 74,
124
German law, 18, 19, 38, 247, 291
Germans, 8, 16, 18-25, 56
Germany, 74, 75, 250-255, 342
East Franland, 102, 108
expansion of, 171-173, 345
Late Medieval, 342

monarchy, 123-124, 127, 128
relations with Roman Catholic
  Church, 81
Gerson, John, 357
Glossa Ordinaria (Accursius), 292
Glossators, 292
Golden Bull, 343
Gothic architecture, *see* Architecture
Gothic Wars, 38
Granada, 155, 333, 339, 340
Grand Princes of Moscow, 347
Gratian, 293, 303
Great Mother Cult, 5
Great Ordinance, 336, 337
Greco-Roman culture, *see* Classical
  culture
"Greek Fire," 65
Greek Language, 32, 33, 86, 98, 161,
  304
Greenland, 110
Gregory I the Great, Pope, 47, 54,
  55, 295
Gregory VII, Pope, 200, 201, 203-
  205, 206, 210
Gregory IX, Pope, 192, 219, 221, 293
Gregory XI, Pope, 329
Gregory of Tous, St., 47
Groot, Gerard, 327
Grosseteste, Robert, 314, 315, 316,
  356
Guilds, 150
Gunpowder, 354

Hadrian IV, Pope, 208, 209, 210
Hamburg, 108
Hapsburgs, 219, 342
Harness, tandem, 146
Harold Godwinson, King, 227
Harun-al-Rashid, Caliph, 67, 68
Hastings, battle of, 225
Hegira, 61
Heloise, 302-303
Henry I, King of England, 229, 231,
  232
Henry II, King of England, 206, 231-
  238, 251, 252
Henry III, Emperor, 128, 135, 199,
  200, 201, 203, 204
Henry III, King of England, 242-245,
  254
Henry IV, Emperor, 201-205
Henry V, Emperor, 205, 207
Henry, V, King of England, 335, 338
Henry VI, Emperor, 167, 212, 213
Henry VII, King of England, 328,
  335-336
Henry the Lion, Duke of Saxony,
  208, 212
Henry the Navigator, Prince, 342
Heraclius, Emperor, 40, 63
Heresy, 6, 8, 11, 30, 31, 98, 174,
  182, 185, 327
Hesse, 81
High Middle Ages, culture of, 146,
  260-283, 366, 368
Hindus, 68, 73
Hippo, 11, 23
History of My Calamities (Peter
  Abelard), 302
History of the Franks (Gregory of
  Tours), 47
History of the Lombards (Paul the
  Deacon), 95
Hohenstaufens, 180, 207, 215, 216,
  220
Holy Grail, 270
Holy Land, 151, 156, 162, 163, 165,
  166
"Holy War," 61-62, 63
Homage, 119
Honorius, Emperor, 22
Horse collar, 76, 146
Horse-shoe, 76, 146
House of Wisdom, 68
Hugh Faloandus, 161
Hugh of St. Victor, 302-304
Hugolino, Cardinal (Pope Gregory
  IX), 192
Humanism, 6, 359, 370
Humbert, Cardinal, 200, 201
Humiliati, 182, 190
Humphrey d'Hauteville, 157
Hundred Years' War, 258, 333, 334,
  336, 338

Hungarians, 101, 104, 106, 122, 123, 124, 136
Hungary, 136, 145, 154
Huns, 21, 22, 25, 106
Hus, John, 328, 331

Iceland, 110
Iconoclasm, 82-83
Icons, 82
Idrisi, 161
Île de France, 249-251
Imitation of Christ, (Thomas à Kempis), 327
India, 63, 67, 70, 72, 371
Indian Ocean, 340
Industry, 15, 28
Inflation, 153
Innocent III, Pope, 167, 168, 183, 185, 188, 190, 213, 214, 215, 216, 217, 221, 222, 239, 240
Innocent IV, Pope, 219, 221
Inquest jury, 235
Inquisition, 182, 184, 185, 209
Interdict, 213, 214
Interregnum, 219
Invasions, barbarian, 21-25, 29
Islamic, 63-68
Viking, 104-111, 115, 121-124
Investiture controversy, 202-207, 293
Ireland, 98, 110
Irene, Empress, 91
Isabella, Queen, 340
Isidore of Seville, St., 47, 48, 50, 60, 295
Isis, cult of, 5
Islam, 61
Islamic Civilization, 60-73, 127, 136
Ismaili Sect, 64, 70
Italy, 88, 259, 342, 350
Byzantine influence on, 39, 40
French influence on, 83, 84, 88
German influence on, 123-124
heresy in, 187
High Medieval culture of, 272-273

invasions of, 22-23, 45
Investiture Controversy in, 203-205
Late Medieval, 350, 366-370
Itinerant justices, 234
Ivan III, Czar, 347

Jacopone da Todi, 297
Jacquerie (Rebellion of 1358), 337
Jagiello, 345
Jarrow, Monastery of, 56, 108
Jean de Meun, 271
Jerome, St., 9, 10, 11, 47, 297
Jerusalem, 63, 74, 162, 163, 164, 166, 170, 218
Kingdom of, 165
"Jerusalem the Golden," 261
Joan of Arc, 329, 335, 338
John XXII, Pope, 328
John, King of England, 213, 215, 216, 238, 239, 240
John of Jaudun, 299
John of Salisbury, 304-305, 312
John the Good, King of France, 336
John Scotus Erigena, 98-99, 295
Judaism, 5, 51, 340
Jupiter, 6
Justice, *see* Law
Justinian, Emperor, 33, 60

Kaaba, 61
Kent, 55, 80, 113
Khayyam, Omar, 72-73
Kiev, 42, 111
Knights Hospitallers, 170-181
Knights of Santiago de Compostella, 171
Knights Templars, 170, 181, 256, 257
Koran, 62, 63, 73

Lancaster, house of, 335
Lancelot, 270
Lanfranc, 230
Langton, Stephen, 240
Language, 17, 73, 62, 96, 98, 115
Las Navas de Tolosa, Battle of, 155
Latin Language, 17, 33, 47, 50, 86,

98, 113, 154, 161, 295, 305
Latin literature, 11, 47, 261
  in Anglo-Saxon era, 115, 127
  in Carolingian era, 74, 95-96
  in High Middle Ages, 261
  in Holy Roman Empire, 127-128
Latvia, 171
Law, canon, 210, 291, 292, 293
  Carolingian, 94
  civil, 290, 291
  English, 113, 235, 236, 247
  Roman, 17, 19, 32, 37-38
Lay investiture, 202, 219
Lay piety, 151, 174, 195, 217, 221,
    328
Lechfield, Battle of, 106, 124
Legnano, Battle of, 210
Leo I, Pope, 22, 25, 197
Leo III, Pope, 90
Leo IX, Pope, 199, 200, 201
Leonardo da Vinci, 94, 199, 200, 201
Leo the Isaurian, Emperor, 82
Lewes, Battle of, 244
Liberal arts, seven, 288
Life of Charlemagne (Einhard), 84
Literature, in barbarian West, 46-48
  in High Middle Ages, 261, 276, 304
  in Islam, 72-73
  Norse, 110, 111
  Renaissance, 366
  see also Latin literature; Vernacular
Lithuania, 171, 345
Lives of the Twelve Caesars
    (Suetonius), 84, 86
Lollards, 328
Lombard, Peter, 303-304
Lombard League, 210, 212
Lombards, 39, 82, 83, 84, 88, 124,
    157, 160
Lombardy, 202, 207, 208, 210, 220
London, 108, 113, 147
Lords, House of, 333
Lorraine, 102, 123, 200
Lorris, 149, 170
Lothar I, Emperor, 102, 104, 123
Louis VI, King of France, 250
Louis VII, King of France, 166, 250

Louis VIII, King of France, 253
Louis IX, St., King of France, 151,
    220, 254
Louis the Blind, King, 104
Louis the Child, King, 104, 123
Louis the German, King, 102, 123
Louis the Pious, Emperor, 97, 101,
    102
Love, courtly, 269
Luther, Martin, 332
Lyons, Council of, 218
Lyric poetry, 264-268

Madeiras, 340
Magna Carta, 240-243, 248, 291
Magyars, 105, 106
Mainz, 80
  Archbishop of, 343
Majorca, 340
Manfred, 220
Manichaeism, 11
Manor, 129, 131, 132
Manzikurt, Battle of, 42-43, 162
Marcel, Etienne, 337
Marsilius of Padua, 330, 332
Martel, Charles, 65, 78-79, 81, 87,
    102, 117, 154
Martin V, Pope, 330, 331
Martin of Tours, St., 45, 95, 96
Mary, St., 176
"Mary Church," 91, 93
Mathematics, 71-72, 127
Matilda, Queen (wife of Geoffrey
    Plantagenet), 231
"Mayor of the Palace," 77
Mecca, 58-60
Medici, house of, 350-351
Medicine, 71, 290, 291
Medina, 58-60
Mediterranean Sea, 63, 75, 105, 148,
    156, 160, 164, 340
Mendicantism, 185, 196
Mercia, 112, 113
Merovingians, 49, 77, 79, 81, 82, 83,
    84
Mesopotamia, 60
Middle classes, 16, 148, 257,

271, 333, 338, 340
Middle Kingdom, 104, 123
Milan, 10, 148, 202, 207, 209, 343,
    351
Military, *see* Army
Milvian Bridge, Battle of, 7
Mining, 354
Minnesingers, 270
Minuscule, Carolingian, 96
Mirandola, Pico della, 357
Missi dominici, 100
Missionaries, Arian, 8
  Benedictine, 49-56
  Byzantine, 40, 41
  Carolingian, 79, 80, 81, 90
  Celtic-Christian, 52-56
  Dominican, 186, 187
  Franciscan, 188
  Spanish, 342
Mithras, 5
Moderate realism, Aristotle, 301
Mohammed, 60-63
Monarchy, 320
  Carolingian, 77-100, 101-105
  English, 112, 115, 117, 135, 225-
    244, 326, 333
  French, 117, 122, 135, 136, 208,
    249-252, 326, 336
  German, 123-124, 127, 128, 196,
    204, 208, 219
  Papal, 213
  Scandinavian, 110, 111, 115, 116
  Spanish, 326
Monasticism, 51
  Benedictine, 49-56, 79-82, 97; *see*
    also Benedictine monasticism
  Carolingian, 95
  Celtic, 51
  High Medieval, 171-181, 196, 197,
    200, 208
  of St. Jerome in Bethlehem, 10
Mongols, 70, 347, 348
Monophysitism, 31, 38, 63
Monotheism, 60-62
Monreale, Cathedral of, 159
Monte Cassino, 52, 95
Montfort, Simon de, 244

Montpellier, University of, 289, 291
Morocco, 69
Mosaics, 277
Moscow, 42
Moses, 62
Moslem expansion, 9, 49, 60-68, 78,
    84, 88, 148, 238, 254
Mysticism, 5, 6-7, 16, 32, 96, 98,
    192, 307, 313, 326, 327, 328,
    329

Naples, city of, 156, 220
  kingdom of, 343
  university of, 289
Navy, 65, 105, 107, 113
Neoplatonism, 6, 11-98
Netherlands, 79, 102
Neustria, 77, 79
Newcastle-on-Tyne, 149
Nicaea, Ecumenical Council of, 8
Nicholas of Cusa, 330, 357, 358
Nominalism, 301
Norman Conquest, 116, 156, 163,
    334
Normandy, 110, 117, 122, 228, 239,
    247, 252
Normans, 156, 160, 199, 265
North Africa, 11, 23, 38-39, 63, 69, 73
North America, 110
Northumbria, 55, 79, 80, 95, 108,
    112
Norway, 111
Norwegians, 106, 107
Notre-Dame de Paris, 260, 280
Novgorod, 110, 111

Oder River, 171
Odovacar, 23
Omar Khayyam, 72, 73
Omayyads, 63-66
On Monarchy (Dante), 273
On the Celestial Hierarchy (Pseudo-
    Dionysius), 98
On the Divisions of Nature (John
    Scotus Erigena), 99
Open fields, 130
Oresme, Nicholas, 356

Origen, 9, 297
Original sin, 12
Orleans, 95, 249, 291, 337
  house of, 337
Ostrogoths, 18, 21, 23, 38
Oswy, King, 55
Otto I the Great, Emperor, 106, 123-125, 127
Otto II, Emperor, 127
Otto III, Emperor, 127
Ottoman Turks, 342, 345, 348
Otto of Brunswick, 215, 216, 217
Oxford, University of, 289, 291, 314, 315

Paganism, 5, 6, 8, 11, 18, 79, 80, 90
Painting, *see* Art
Pakistan, 59, 63
Palermo, 160, 161, 220
Palestine, 60
Pantheism, 99
Papacy, Crusades and, 162-163
  development of, 25, 54, 56
  in High Middle Ages, 175, 196-222, 326
  in Late Middle Ages, 329, 330, 331, 370
  relations with France, 80, 81, 82, 83, 90-91, 92, 93, 94
  relations with Sicily, 157
Papal Election Decree, 201
Papal States, 84, 153, 209, 212, 219, 220, 331, 343
Paris, 108, 249, 260, 280
  University of, 289, 291, 298, 304, 308, 356, 357
Parlement of Paris, 257, 337
Parliament, 225, 242-245, 248, 249, 333, 334, 337
Parthenon, 260
Particularism, in England, 229
  in France, 112, 122
  in Germany, 112, 123-127, 204, 206, 207, 212, 219, 342
  in Islam, 65-68
  in Italy, 342
Pastoral Care (Pope Gregory I), 54, 115

Patarenes, 202
Patrick, St., 50
Paul, St., 98
Paul the Deacon, 95, 96
Peasant life, 47, 68, 75, 77, 81, 121, 129, 130-133, 152-153, 154, 156, 336, 337, 352, 353
Peasants' Revolt, England (1381), 353
Pepin of Heristal, 77-78
Pepin the Short, 79, 80, 81, 82, 83, 84, 91, 93, 102
Perceval, 270
Perfecti, 183
Perruzi, house of, 350
Persecution, 7, 8, 71
Persia, 39, 40, 63, 64, 65, 66, 67, 68, 71, 183
Peter III, King of Aragon, 220
Peter, St., 197
Philip I, King of France, 250
Philip II Augustus, King of France, 166, 213, 215, 216, 238, 239, 252
Philip III, King of France, 256
Philip IV the Fair, King of France, 222, 248, 256-257, 326, 329, 334
Philip VI, King of France, 334
Philip of Swabia, 215
Philosophy, Byzantine, 43
  Carolingian, 98
  early Christian, 11
  High Medieval, 294-304, 306-313
  Islamic, 71, 73
  Late Medieval, 355-358
  Roman, 13
  Spanish, 154
Piety, *see* Lay piety
Pilgrimages, 61, 62, 106, 162, 167
Pipe Rolls, 232
Piracy, 23, 101, 105, 108, 111
Pisa, 148, 330
  Council of, 330
Pius II, Pope, 354
Plague, 325, 351, 355
Plantagenet, Geoffrey, 231

Platonism, 9-13, 24, 70, 71, 294, 299, 300, 306, 312, 314, 357
Plotinus, 6
Plow, 75, 76, 78, 146
Poetry, 73, 88, 95, 261
Poitiers, Battle of, 334, 336
Poland, 53, 171, 345
Policraticus (John of Salisbury), 304, 305
Political theory, 61, 62, 94, 305, 329, 332
Polytheism, 60
"Poor Catholics," 190
Poor Clares, 192
Population, 15, 16, 28, 107, 146, 148, 154, 326, 350, 351
Portiuncula, 188, 190
Portugal, 333, 339, 340, 371
Predestination, 12-13
Prince of Wales, 248
Printing, 354
Protestant Reformation, 332
Provence, 264
Provisions of Oxford, 243
Pseudo-Dionysius, 98, 99
Ptolemy, 72, 314
"Putting-out System," 149
Pyrenees, 65, 88

Quo warranto, 247

Raban Maur, 97, 295
Rationalism, 73, 180, 296
Ravenna, 22, 39, 83, 91
Realism, philosophical, 301
Reconquista, 339, 340
Reichenau, 94
Reims, Cathedral of, 260, 282, 285, 338
Renaissance, Anglo-Saxon (King Alfred), 113, 115
    Carolingian, 95-99
    German (Ottonian), 127
    Islamic (Baghdad), 68
    Italian, 220, 345, 350, 354, 357, 366, 367, 369, 370
    Northumbrian, 56

Ostrogothic, 23-24
Renard the Fox, 271
Rhine, 18, 21, 79
    Count Palatine of the, 343
Rhodes, 64
Rhône River, 329
Richard I the Lion-Hearted, King, 166, 238, 239
Richard II, King, 333
Robert Guiscard, 157, 159, 160, 199, 205
Roger I d'Hauteville, 159, 160
Roger II the Great, 160-162, 209
Roland, 88
Rolf, 108
Roman Catholic Church, in Carolingian era, 74, 75, 79, 80, 81, 92
    in High Middle Ages, 174-195, 196-224
    in Late Middle Ages, 326, 328
    its early development, 24, 25, 30
Roman culture, 5-9, 13, 16, 17, 24
Roman Empire, *see* Empire, Roman
Roman law, 17, 19, 20, 32, 33, 35, 41, 291, 292
Roman religion, 5-13
Roman synod, 199
Romance, 269
Romance of Renard, 272
Romance of the Rose (William of Lorris and Jean de Meun), 271
Romanesque Architecture, *see* Architecture
Romanticism, 265, 269
Rome, 10, 12, 74, 80, 104, 106, 199, 209, 329
Roscellinus, 301
Rouen, 108
Rubaiyat (Omar Khayyam), 73
Rudel, Jaufré, 265
Rudolph of Hapsburg, Emperor, 219
Russia, 41-42, 107, 110, 111, 171, 345, 347, 353

Sacraments, 175, 176, 214
Saga Norse, 110, 111

Sagres, 342
Sainte-Chapelle, Church of, Paris, 285
Saint-Denis, Monastery of, 84, 251, 280
St. Marks, Venice, 33, 36
Saladin, 166, 167
Salerno, 159, 205
  University of, 290
Salians, 128, 199, 204, 207
Sancta Sophia, Cathedral of, 32, 35, 37, 91, 199, 200
Saracens, 101, 104, 105, 106, 149
Sardinia, 71, 340
Savonarola, 370
Saxons, 18, 22, 25, 90, 122, 123, 128
Saxony, 88, 107, 207, 208, 212
  Duke of, 343
Scandinavia, 18, 53, 67, 107, 108, 111, 116, 133, 136, 154
Schism, 198, 209, 330
Scholasticism, 295, 296, 356
Schools, Monastic, 81, 95; *see also* Education
Science, 68, 71-73, 127, 154, 193, 294, 313-316, 356
Scientific Method, 315
Scotland, 55, 248
Sculpture, 284, 359
Scutage, 151
Seine, 110
Serbia, 348
Serfs, 122, 132, 133; *see also* Peasant life
Sforza, house of, 351
Sheriff, 226
Shi'ism, 64
Siberia, 76
Sic et Non (Peter Abelard), 303
Sicilian Vespers, War of the, 220
Sicily, 71, 154, 156, 157, 160, 163, 212, 214, 218, 220, 294, 305, 340
Siena, 220
Siger of Brabant, 298, 299
Simony, 197, 199, 200, 202
Slaves, 15, 133, 152
Slavs, 38, 40, 41, 75, 88, 110, 111, 154, 170, 345
Social conditions, barbarian, 18-19
  Carolingian, 100
  German, 130-133
  High Medieval, 146-154
  Late Medieval, 325, 351-355
  Roman, 15-16
  Scandinavian, 111
Soissons, 83
"Song of Brother Sun" (St. Francis), 191, 272
Song of Roland, 88, 263
Southern Italy, 157-160, 212, 215
Spain, 23, 25, 38, 39, 47, 59, 65, 69, 71, 88, 105, 127, 154, 155, 259, 294, 298, 305, 339
Spanish March, 88, 155
Speculum Majus (Vincent of Beauvais), 306
Spiritual Franciscans, 193, 328
Stained glass, 283
"Statute on the Burning of Heretics," 328
Statutes of Laborers, 352
Stephen of Blois, King, 231
Stigmata, 192
Stirrup, 87
Stoicism, 24
Studium Generale, 288, 289
Stupor Mundi, see Frederick II, Emperor, 217
Stylites, St. Simeon, 51
Succession, 20
  Carolingian, 77, 101-102
  English, 116, 227, 229, 231, 238, 333
  French, 249, 250, 334
  Germany, 215-219
  Islamic, 64, 67
  Merovingian, 49
  Papal, 201
Suetonius, 84, 86
Suger, Abbot, 251, 280
Summa Theologica (St. Thomas Aquinas), 309, 355
Summas, 306
Sufi, 70

Sutri, Synod of, 199
Swabia, 122, 123, 204, 208, 215
Swedes, 106, 107, 110, 111
Syllogism, 296
Sylvester II, Pope, 127
Syria, 8, 31, 40, 41, 60, 63, 69, 71,
    154, 164, 166

Tacitus, 18
Tallage, 132
Tancred d'Hauteville, 157
Tannenberg, Battle of, 345
Tartary, 187
Taxation, 148, 151
  Byzantine, 28, 29, 30
  Carolingian, 118
  Ecclesiastical, Roman Catholic,
      213, 221, 222, 224, 329, 331
  English, 115, 229, 241, 243, 245,
      333
  French, 257-258, 337
  Germany, 132
  High Medieval, 148, 149
  Islamic, 68, 71
  Roman Imperial, 15, 16, 46
Technology, Carolingian, 75-77, 87
  High Medieval, 146, 181
  Islamic, 68
  Late Medieval, 342, 354, 370
  monastic role in, 53, 54
  Roman, 15, 16
Tertiaries, 192
Tertry, Battle of, 77
Tertullian, 296
Teutonic Knights, 170, 171, 181, 345
Theism, 296
Thodore of Tarsus, 55
Theodoric, King of the Ostrogoths,
    23, 25, 34
Theodoric of Freiburg, 315
Theodosius I, Emperor, 7, 8, 10, 21,
    29
Theodulf of Orleans, 95-96
Thessalonica, 10
Thomas à Kempis, 327
Three Books Against Simoniacs, 200
Three-field system, 76, 130, 133, 146

Thuringia, 80
Tiber River, 209
Tibet, 187
Tigris River, 67
Toledo, 154, 155
Toulouse, 264
Tours, battle of, 65, 78
  cathedral of, 45
  monastery of, 94
Towns, 15, 16, 28, 45, 101, 146-149,
    151, 182, 190, 205, 207, 208,
    245, 272, 276, 288, 289, 350,
    351
Trade, *see* Commerce
Transcendentalism, *see* Mysticism
Trappists, 181
Trent, Council of, 214
Tribal duchies, 123
Tribute, 68, 88
Trier, Archbishop of, 343
Trinity, 12, 307
Tripolis, county of, 165
Tristan and Iseult, 269
Troubadours, 264
Tudors, 335, 338
Tunisia, 69, 170, 353
Turkey, 348
Turks, Ottoman, 67
  Seljuk, 42, 67, 69, 162
Turpin of Rheims, 263
Tuscany, 204, 212, 220
Two Sicilies, Kingdom of the, 160
Tyrannicide, 305

Unam Sanctam, 222, 224
Universals, 296, 300-301
Universities, 68, 146, 256, 288, 289,
    290, 295
Urban II, Pope, 163, 164, 205
Urban VI, Pope, 329-330
Urban Charters, 146-149
Urban Society, *see* Towns

Valens, Emperor, 21
Valois dynasty, 338
Vandals, 18, 21, 22, 23, 25, 38, 66
Van Eyck, Jan, 359

Varna, Battle of, 348
Vassals, 117-122, 125, 153, 157, 212, 225, 241, 249; *see also* Feudalism
Vault rib, 280
Vaults (barrel, cross), 277
Venice, 48, 167, 220, 343
Verdun, Treaty of, 102, 104, 123
Vernacular literature, 262-273
Vienna, 73
Vikings, 101, 104, 105, 106, 107, 108, 110, 113, 116, 117, 120, 121, 122
Village, 129-131, 145
Villon, Francois, 366
Vincent of Beauvais, 306
Virgil, 10, 273
Visconti, house of, 351
Visigoths, 12, 18, 21, 38
Vistula, 171
Vita Nuova (Dante), 272
Vladimir of Kiev, 111
Vulgate Bible, 11

Waldensians, 182, 184, 188, 209
Waldo, Peter, 182
Wales, 49, 113, 248
Wars of the Roses, 335-336

Water mill, 76, 146
Water pump, 354
Welfs, 180, 207, 208, 212, 215, 216
Wergeld, 19
Wessex, 80, 108, 112, 113, 115, 116, 226
Whitby, Synod of, 55
Wilfrid of Ripon, St., 78, 80, 95
William I the Conqueror, 116, 225, 227, 228, 230, 249
William II Rufus, King, 229-231
William IX of Aquitaine, Duke, 180, 264, 266
William Iron-Hand (d'Hauteville), 157
William of Lorris, 271
William of Ockham, 313, 314, 356, 357
Willibrord, 78, 80, 95
Windmill, 76, 78, 146
Witenagemot, 226
Wool, 130, 148, 181, 350, 354
Wyclif, John, 328

York, house of, 335

Zara, 168, 169
Zero, 72
Zoroastrianism, 60, 61, 63